SUBSIDIES IN INTERNATIONAL TRADE

Subsidies

GARY CLYDE HUFBAUER and

JOANNA SHELTON ERB

in International Trade

INSTITUTE FOR INTERNATIONAL ECONOMICS
Washington, DC 1984

Distributed by MIT Press
Cambridge, Massachusetts, and London, England

Gary Clyde Hufbauer is a Senior Fellow with the Institute for International Economics; Joanna Shelton Erb, formerly an international economist with the US Department of the Treasury, recently joined the Subcommittee on Trade of the House Ways and Means Committee.

The authors wish to thank the numerous people who have commented on this manuscript, in particular, C. Fred Bergsten, Richard Bird, William R. Cline, John D. Greenwald, John H. Jackson, Jeffrey J. Schott, and Alan Wm. Wolff.

INSTITUTE FOR INTERNATIONAL ECONOMICS

C. Fred Bergsten, *Director*

Kathleen A. Lynch, *Director of Publications*
Rosanne Gleason, *Editorial Assistant*
Stephen Kraft, *Designer*

The Institute for International Economics was created, and is principally funded, by the German Marshall Fund of the United States.

The views expressed in this publication are those of the authors. This publication is part of the overall program of the Institute, as endorsed by its Board of Directors, but does not necessarily reflect the views of individual members of the Board or the Advisory Committee. Neither does this publication necessarily reflect the views of the US Treasury Department or the Subcommittee on Trade of the House Ways and Means Committee.

First Printing, July 1984
Second Printing, October 1984

Library of Congress Cataloging in Publication Data

Hufbauer, Gary Clyde.
  Subsidies in international trade.

  Bibliography: p. 275
  1. Subsidies. I. Shelton Erb, Joanna. II. Title.
HF1430.5.H83 1984   382'.63   83-12825
ISBN 0-88132-004-8
ISBN 0-262-08138-5 (MIT Press)

To Friedrich Klein
Architect of International Discipline:

☐ *Antidumping Code—1967*

☐ *Arrangement on Guidelines for Officially*
   Supported Export Credits—1978

☐ *Code on Subsidies and Countervailing Duties—1979*

Contents

Preface

This volume addresses one of the most important and complex set of problems now facing the world trading system: subsidies and appropriate responses to them. The issue was considered at great length during the Multilateral Trade Negotiations (MTN or "Tokyo Round") during the late 1970s, from which emerged an agreed code to provide international governance of such sensitive "domestic" policy measures for the first time. Nevertheless, there remains widespread and growing dissatisfaction with the ways in which the trading system responds to the bewildering array of subsidy practices which countries use to support their industries. The purpose of this book is to analyze the nature and effect of such practices, assess the current state of national and international regulations which cover them, and suggest changes in those regimes which could do the job better.

This study of subsidies is part of a wide-ranging program of research on trade problems and policy being carried out by the Institute for International Economics, along with its work on international monetary issues (which frequently relate directly to the trade questions) and other global economic matters. In late 1982, the Institute published two of its POLICY ANALYSES IN INTERNATIONAL ECONOMICS on trade issues: *"Reciprocity": A New Approach to World Trade Policy?* by William R. Cline and *Trade Policy in the 1980s* by C. Fred Bergsten and William R. Cline, a comprehensive review of trade problems and proposals for dealing with them. In 1983, the Institute published the conference volume on which the latter analysis was based; also entitled *Trade Policy in the 1980s*, it includes twenty-two papers and thirteen commentaries on a wider range of current and prospective trade issues.

During the coming year, the Institute will conduct research on several additional trade topics. Sectoral studies on steel, automobiles, and textiles and apparel will be carried out by William R. Cline. An extensive analysis of adjustment to worker and industry dislocation is underway by Gary Clyde Hufbauer and Howard F. Rosen. I.M. Destler is studying the politics and institutional framework underlying US trade policy, under a contract from the Twentieth Century Fund. One aspect of trade policy, its control via national governments in their pursuit of broader objectives, has been addressed by Gary Clyde Hufbauer and Jeffrey J. Schott in their monograph, *Economic Sanctions in Support of Foreign Policy Goals*, and its backup volume, *Economic Sanctions Reconsidered: History and Current Policy*.

The Institute for International Economics is a private, nonprofit research institution for the study and discussion of international economic policy. Its purpose is to analyze important issues in that area, and to develop and communicate practical new approaches for dealing with them.

The Institute was created in November 1981 through a generous commitment of funds from the German Marshall Fund of the United States. Financial support is being received from other private foundations and corporations. The Institute is completely nonpartisan.

The Board of Directors bears overall responsibility for the Institute and gives general guidance and approach to its research program—including identification of topics which are likely to become important to international economic policymakers over the medium run (generally, one to three years) and which thus should be addressed by the Institute. The Director of the Institute, working closely with the staff and outside Advisory Committee, is responsible for the development of particular projects. The Director makes the final decision to publish an individual study, taking into account the views of a number of expert readers on each manuscript.

The Institute hopes that its studies and other activities will contribute to building a stronger foundation for international economic policy around the world. Comments as to how it can best do so are invited from readers of these publications.

C. FRED BERGSTEN
Director

Glossary

Organizations and Institutions

Big Seven

The major industrial countries: United States, Germany, Japan, United Kingdom, France, Italy, and Canada

EC

European Community. The short-form designation of adherents to the treaties forming the European Coal and Steel Community (ECSC), the European Economic Community (EEC), the European Atomic Energy Community (Euratom), and the treaties amending those treaties. Members are Belgium, Denmark, France, Germany, Greece, Ireland, Italy, Luxembourg, Netherlands, and United Kingdom. The "Ten."

FSC

Foreign Sales Corporation

GATT

General Agreement on Tariffs and Trade

IDA

International Development Association, the "soft loan" window of the World Bank

IMF

International Monetary Fund

ITA

International Trade Administration of the US Department of Commerce

MNE

Multinational enterprise

OECD

Organization for Economic Cooperation and Development. Members are Australia, Austria, Belgium, Canada, Denmark, Finland, France, Germany, Greece, Iceland, Ireland, Italy, Japan, Luxembourg, Netherlands, New Zealand, Norway, Portugal,

Spain, Sweden, Switzerland, Turkey, United Kingdom, and United States.

Subsidies Committee	The members of the GATT Code on Subsidies and Countervailing Duties
USITC	US International Trade Commission
USTR	US Trade Representative

Statutes and Legal Sources

DISC	US Domestic International Sales Corporation
FIRA	Canadian Foreign Investment Review Act
Fed. Reg.	US Federal Register
Section 301	An omnibus provision for relief against unfair trade practices, set forth in the US Trade Act of 1974

Terms of Art

Adverse effects	A standard of trade impact set forth in the GATT Subsidies Code, Article 8
Affirmative defense	A defense as to which the accused party must carry the burden of proof
Countermeasures	Remedies taken by one country in response to another country's subsidies, including countervailing duties
Countervailing duties (CVDs)	Duties imposed by one country on imports from another country to offset the other country's subsidies

xiv

Countervailing subsidies	Subsidies granted by one country on its exports to offset the subsidies previously granted by another country
Dumping	Sale of a commodity in a foreign market at "less than fair value." See GATT, Article VI.
FTI	Foreign trading income, a concept of income earned outside the United States
GATT Ministerial	Meeting of the trade ministers of the GATT member countries
GDP	Gross domestic product
Infant-industry argument	The argument that an industry that is not competitive in world markets today could, with appropriate government support, become competitive within a reasonable period of time
Material injury	A standard of trade impact set forth in GATT Article VI and in the national laws of most GATT members
MFN	Most-favored-nation. See GATT, Article I.
Nullification or impairment	A standard of loss of benefits legitimately expected under the GATT, set forth in GATT Article XXIII
Potentially troublesome subsidies	A class of subsidies, smaller than the class of all subsidies, which are thought to be fit objects for offsetting measures
Second-best analysis	The argument that if a particular economic distortion cannot be attacked directly, it may be attacked indirectly (though less efficiently) by government imposition of a counterdistortion

Serious prejudice	A standard of trade impact, set forth in GATT Article XVI
Tokyo Round	The seventh round of trade negotiations under the GATT
Track I	The national imposition of countervailing duties against imports from another nation, upon a finding of material injury consistent with the Code on Subsidies and Countervailing Duties
Track II	The imposition of multilaterally authorized countervailing measures against the trade of a subsidizing country, consistent with the Code on Subsidies and Countervailing Duties
VAT	Value-added tax

Introduction

First of all, there won't be a trade war. I don't think we should talk about it.[1]   John H. Block
US Secretary of
Agriculture
December 10, 1982

The newspaper headlines in recent years amply illustrate the growing importance of subsidies in international economic and political life.

The Setting

Subsidies are no longer an arcane issue discussed only by trade technicians in periodic bargaining sessions at mountaintop resorts. To the contrary, subsidies have captured the attention of senior government officials in virtually all important trading powers, including the United States, Canada, the European Community (EC), Japan, and key developing countries. The reason is simple: most countries have a stake in world markets and therefore, a stake in the increasingly acrimonious skirmishes over what governments may and may not do to help their industries and farmers in good times and bad. Secretary Block notwithstanding, these skirmishes have on occasion threatened to erupt into all-out economic warfare.

Is today's focus on subsidies merely passing rhetoric occasioned by sagging economic performance and high unemployment, or will this focus on subsidies

---

1. *Wall Street Journal*, 13 December 1982, p. 4. With these words, Block attempted to diffuse tension over earlier Reagan administration threats to dump surplus US dairy and agricultural products on the world market, if the European Community persisted in subsidizing the export of its own surplus agricultural stocks. A few weeks later, in January 1983, the United States decided to subsidize the sale of one million metric tons of wheat flour to Egypt. For an interesting colloquy on European agricultural policy, see Sir Roy Denman, "Farm Crisis: Don't Blame Europe," *Washington Post*, 17 March 1983, p. A19, and Senator Mack Mattingly, "No One Would Blame Europe—If Europe Played Fair," *Washington Post*, 29 March 1983, p. A15.

outlast the recent recession? Two reasons might explain why subsidies will remain a topic of concern after the return to economic prosperity. One reason may be called the "falling water level" hypothesis; the other, the "rising reef" hypothesis.

According to the falling water level hypothesis, as tariffs and other forms of protection decline, the remaining trade distortions have a more visible effect. Subsidies are a prominent distortion, and national differences in subsidy practices have perhaps become more apparent as the general level of protection has declined.

According to the rising reef hypothesis, subsidies and surrogate practices have escalated rapidly as industrial nations have responded to rising energy prices, slow growth, and antiquated factories. This hypothesis suggests that government subsidies have taken a sharp upward tilt. Senator Mack Mattingly (R-Ga.) reflected this hypothesis when he pronounced:[2] "The United States has been a patsy for what our trading partners have been doing for too long."

In a simple attempt to assess the strengths of the falling water level and rising reef hypotheses, we have compiled a range of data. These data roughly indicate the relative size of total subsidies and export subsidies (tables 1.1 to 1.3).

In table 1.1, current subsidies of all descriptions, however they may be measured for national accounting purposes, are compared with gross domestic product (GDP) for the "Big Seven" countries. Three points are clear from this table. First, the general upward drift in the importance of subsidies from the early 1950s to the late 1960s affected every country except the United Kingdom and possibly France, two nations that had already developed extensive systems of subventions by the end of World War II. Second, between 1968 and 1980, only two countries, Canada and Italy, noticeably increased the relative degree of subsidization. Third, and perhaps most important, the United States has persistently exhibited the lowest ratio of subsidies to GDP and, unlike other countries, the US ratio has declined since the late 1960s. This discrepancy in absolute level, together with the contrary US trend, may explain in large part the grievances expressed by US firms against the practices of other countries. Of course a high degree of subsidization is no proof of industrial success, as the examples of the United Kingdom and France indicate. Neither does a relatively low level of subsidization necessarily prevent a country's firms from being competitive, as the example of Japan suggests. But US business firms are not interested in generalities. They are concerned—justifiably or not—that foreign subsidies might give their own particular competitors an advantage.

In table 1.2, government finance of capital formation is related to total gross capital formation for the period 1964 to 1979, again for the Big Seven countries.

---

2. Alan Murray, "Special Report: Export Subsidies," *Congressional Quarterly,* 19 February 1983, p. 375.

Table 1.1   Subsidies as shown in national account statistics as a percentage of GDP[a]

Country	1952	1956	1960	1964	1968	1972	1976	1980
Italy	0.89	1.30	1.51	1.23	1.67	2.29	2.60	3.01
France	1.71	2.71	1.62	2.03	2.62	1.99	2.68	2.51
Canada	0.41	0.39	0.81	0.85	0.87	0.83	1.73	2.34
United Kingdom	2.68	1.76	1.93	1.56	2.06	1.82	2.78	2.32
Germany	0.65	0.20	0.79	0.99	1.44	1.48	1.49	1.59
Japan	0.79	0.26	0.34	0.65	1.11	1.12	1.32	1.32
United States	0.11	0.20	0.25	0.44	0.50	0.59	0.34	0.43

Source: OECD, *National Accounts 1951–1980,* vol. 1, Main Aggregates, 1982.
a. Countries listed in order of amount of subsidies as a percentage of GDP in 1980.

Table 1.2   Government finance of capital formation as a percentage of total gross capital formation[a]

Country	1964	1968	1972	1976	1979
Japan	13.9[b]	11.7	15.4	16.2	19.3
Italy	n.a.	n.a.	14.0	14.5	14.5
United Kingdom	20.9	25.4	23.8	22.2	14.1
Germany	17.0	15.0	14.8	15.5	14.1
France	15.6	17.4	14.3	13.5	12.9
Canada	16.7	18.3	16.9	13.7	12.2
United States	15.6	14.9	11.9	11.2	8.6[b]

n.a. Not available.
Source: OECD, *National Accounts of OECD Countries,* vol. 2, Detailed Tables, 1981 (in particular, table 7).
a. Countries listed in order of amount of government finance as a percentage of total gross capital formation in 1979.
b. Estimated.

Government finance of capital formation generally contains some element of future subsidization, since governments seldom earn market rates of interest on their fixed assets. The figures in table 1.2 do not reveal the subsidy; they do, however, indicate that the role of government finance has generally declined since the late 1960s. But market interest rates rose sharply between 1968 and 1979, and thus the implicit subsidy inherent in a given share of government capital formation may have increased dramatically, brought about *sub silentio* by the great inflation of the 1970s.

Noteworthy is the relatively low share of government capital formation in the United States. Again, this discrepancy with foreign practice probably contributes to the grievances expressed by US business firms.[3]

Table 1.3 illustrates one conspicuous form of export subsidy, namely official export credits. In table 1.3, official export credit authorizations of several large countries are compared with exports of manufactures for the period 1973 to 1979.

Several conclusions may be drawn from the level of export promotion revealed in table 1.3. First, most countries exhibit a jagged profile of ups and downs in the ratio between export credit activity and manufactured exports. Only Italy and the United Kingdom seem to show a long-term increase in the relative magnitude of official credits. Second, during the early 1970s, US export credit activity declined from a low base. Third, the United States, Canada, and Germany operate much smaller programs than their industrial competitors.

To be sure, export credit authorization levels reflect overt government export promotion more accurately than they reflect export credit subsidies. A better measure of export credit subsidy is the difference between interest rates actually charged for export credits and the market cost of money to governments. Throughout the 1970s and into the early 1980s, rising market interest rates, compared with rigidly low rates for officially supported export credits, implied rapidly rising subsidies per million dollars of official export credit authorization. By 1980, the annual level of interest rate subsidization provided by all Organization for Economic Cooperation and Development (OECD) nations through their official export credit programs had risen to about $4.0 billion to $5.5 billion (Axel Wallen and John M. Duff 1981, p. 475), compared to an amount probably under $1.0 billion in 1973. However, by 1983, with the negotiated rise in interest rates charged on officially supported credits and the decline in market interest rates, the annual level of subsidization certainly had declined from its 1980 peak.

Some of the fiercest competitive battles in international trade are fought in the realm of agriculture. In addition to protection resulting from import barriers, all industrial countries provide direct subsidies to their farmers. Total agricultural expenditures are running about $30 billion in the European Community—about $14 billion spent by the Common Market in Brussels and another $16 billion spent by member countries. In Japan, agricultural expenditures run at about $25

---

3. A key theme running through the US Treasury's annual reports on *The Operation and Effect of the Domestic International Sales Corporation Legislation*, the US Export-Import Bank's annual *Report to the Congress on Export Credit Competition and the Export-Import Bank*, and commentary by academic scholars such as John Mutti (1982), is that while the United States engages in subsidy practices, it does so to a much smaller degree than other countries.

billion; in the United States, they vary between $20 billion and $30 billion annually (Japan Economic Institute 1983). By contrast with the battle for export markets in manufactured goods, the battle for agricultural markets is fought with few ground rules, despite bitter competition and a growing level of subsidization.

All in all, the evidence in tables 1.1 through 1.3 suggests that conscious government policy decisions in the past decade have significantly elevated the readily observable subsidy programs only in a minority of cases involving manufactured goods: Canada and Italy with respect to current subsidies as a percentage of GDP; Japan with respect to government capital formation; Italy and the United Kingdom with respect to export credits. Other data suggest, however, that agricultural subsidy programs are very large and, stimulated by pre-1983 agricultural surpluses, grew quite fast. (For a cross-sectional analysis of types of subsidies within selected European countries, see Bo Carlsson 1982.)

Thus, with the notable exception of agriculture, continuing concern over the role of subsidies in international commerce cannot be explained by a rapid expansion of identifiable on-budget programs. Other forces are at work. Governments may be getting better at hiding their subsidies through a variety of off-budget techniques. The specter of "industrial targeting" is causing widespread anxiety. Subsidies have become more important because, in a generally more competitive and export-oriented environment, it is natural to point to the seemingly unfair advantages enjoyed by one's neighbors.

The Rationale for Disciplining Subsidies

Sovereign governments are free to adopt whatever macroeconomic, industrial, or social policies, including the use of subsidies, that they deem necessary to achieve their overall goals. Politicians, producers, and taxpayers may debate the relative merits of supporting one industry versus another, and whether the cost of government financial support is worth the drain on public resources. But in a representative government, the costs and benefits of public policies presumably are settled more or less to the satisfaction of the key interested parties.

An economist might, therefore, ask why the international community should concern itself with the subsidy practices of its member nations. After all, if one nation wishes to subsidize production or exports in the name of infant-industry arguments, second-best policies, or simply to assuage particular industries, isn't the resulting economic distortion principally the misfortune of the subsidizing nation? This question becomes especially pointed when an importing country can enjoy the advantage of cheaper goods made possible by another country's subsidy practices. To be sure, the producers in one country might, with the assistance of public subsidies, drive out foreign producers, capture their markets, and later make good any losses through monopolistic pricing (for a rigorous exposition of these themes, see Avinash Dixit 1983). But shouldn't the inter-

Table 1.3 Official export credit authorizations related to exports of manufactured goods[a]

	1973	1974	1975	1976	1977	1978	1979
Official export credit authorizations (million dollars)[b]							
United Kingdom	5,242	14,276	9,645	10,519	11,011	35,115	33,430
France	8,268	11,804	19,626	21,920	19,145	30,660	32,155
Japan	18,515	22,600	22,968	32,034	33,641	31,810	39,355
Italy	819	1,020	4,596	3,306	3,053	8,705	8,020
Canada	n.a.	n.a.	2,048	2,171	2,471	4,030	3,535
Germany	3,553	7,330	7,950	10,387	14,515	14,960	14,505
United States	8,798	8,458	7,949	6,584	5,545	7,375	9,490
Exports of manufactured goods (million dollars)[c]							
United Kingdom	25,638	32,046	36,546	38,315	46,795	57,643	70,381
France	26,087	33,600	40,120	43,006	49,709	59,279	75,736
Japan	34,741	52,499	53,167	64,576	77,695	94,181	99,041
Italy	18,614	24,884	29,143	31,177	38,014	47,818	61,062
Canada	13,689	16,521	16,682	20,648	23,083	27,137	30,282
Germany	60,302	78,953	79,619	90,729	104,344	125,462	150,577
United States	44,740	63,544	71,023	77,297	80,515	94,897	117,097

Official export credit
authorization related to
exports of manufactured goods (percentage)

United Kingdom	20.4	44.5	26.5	27.4	23.5	60.9	47.5
France	31.7	35.1	48.9	51.0	38.5	51.7	42.5
Japan	53.3	43.0	43.2	49.6	43.3	33.8	39.7
Italy	4.4	4.1	15.8	10.6	8.0	18.2	13.1
Canada	n.a.	n.a.	12.3	10.5	10.7	14.9	11.7
Germany	5.9	9.3	10.0	11.4	13.9	11.9	9.6
United States	19.7	13.3	11.2	8.5	6.9	7.8	8.1

n.a. Not available.

Sources: US Export-Import Bank, Report to the U.S. Congress on Export Credit Competition and the Export-Import Bank of the United States, biannual reports from July 1, 1974, through December 31, 1975; annual reports dated July 1977, July 1978, and October 1980. Official export credit authorization data are derived from information originally collected by the Berne Union. OECD, Trade Series C.

a. Countries ranked according to amount of official export credit authorizations as a percentage of manufactured goods in 1979.

b. In the case of Canada and the United States, authorizations represent the sum of direct and discounted loans plus insurance and guarantees. In the case of other countries, authorizations represent insurance and guarantees only, since all direct financing by those countries is covered by insurance or guarantees. For the most part the years refer to calendar years, but in some instances the export credit authorizations are fiscal year data.

c. Manufactured goods are defined as SITC 5, 6, 7, and 8.

national community require evidence of monopolistic intent or result before authorizing countermeasures? Put simply, apart from clear instances of grasping monopoly, why should the international community be the keeper of national export morals?

The answer is also simple: unbridled and competing national subsidies can undermine world prosperity. Whatever the analytic merits of a purist free trade, turn-the-other-cheek approach, the Great Depression taught the world that protective policies can quickly and destructively spread from nation to nation. Because the concentrated interests of producers command greater political support than the diffuse interests of consumers, national governments find it much easier to emulate the vices of protection than the virtues of free trade. This lesson has prompted the international community to fashion guidelines that distinguish between acceptable and unacceptable national subsidy measures and to codify those guidelines both in bilateral treaties and in multilateral agreements. In fact, a major purpose of the General Agreement on Tariffs and Trade (GATT) is to discipline protective import policies. Robert E. Baldwin has ably summarized negotiating history since the 1930s (1980, p. 86):

> The 1930s experience with export subsidies as well as with competitive devaluation, which has the effect of a general export subsidy and import surcharge, apparently convinced the GATT founders that export subsidies exacerbate international political tensions and should be eliminated. Though consumers in the importing country gain from export subsidization by other nations, domestic-producer groups in the importing countries are forced to curtail output and incur a producer-surplus loss . . . . The view that domestic producers are somehow more entitled to domestic compared to foreign markets is still widely held by the general public. Thus, in the case of export subsidies, it was not necessary for the founders of GATT to implement their international political objective with regard to this distortion only gradually (as with tariffs) and export subsidies were banned outright.

Firms do not like to surrender markets for any reason, and certainly not to another firm that is aided by its home government. If the international community cannot discipline subsidy practices, nations may be caught up in a wasteful spiral of escalating emulation. As Congressman David R. Obey (D-Wis.) put it:[4]

> As much as I detest the idea of export subsidies, I guess we have no choice but to participate in the stupidity. Given the general economic collapse, we have to grab at whatever life preservers are around when the ship is going down.

---

4. Murray, "Export Subsidies," p. 375.

The shipping industry dramatically illustrates the dangers of mixing free trade with undisciplined export subsidies. The great majority of ports are open to vessels of all flags; pure free trade thus nominally prevails in the world market for shipping services. However, in order to protect and enlarge their merchant fleets and shipyards, all major nations subsidize shipbuilding. They also subsidize up to 75 percent of their maritime operations. Overtonnage is a chronic problem, and excess capacity serves as a constant justification for government cargo-sharing arrangements and for liner conferences, a species of private cartel.

Guidelines on Subsidies

Many definitions of the term "subsidy" have been offered by academics, accountants, and trade practitioners, but virtually all definitions have failed to meet the practical needs of policymakers. To give but one example, the United Nations has set forth a definition of subsidies to be used for national accounting purposes:[5]

> Subsidies include all grants on current account which private industries receive from government. These are transfers which, in view of the basis on which they are made, represent additions to the income of the producers from current production. The grants may, for example, be based on the amount or value of the commodities produced, exported or consumed, the labour or land employed in production, or the manner in which production is organized and carried on. Transfers by public authorities to private industries for investment purposes or to cover destruction, damage and other losses in capital and working assets are classed as capital transfers rather than as subsidies . . . . Subsidies also include all grants on current account which government makes to public corporations, for example, in compensation for operating losses (negative operating surplus). In the case of government enterprises, transfers on current account should be treated as subsidies when it is clear that the transfers are the consequences of the policy of the government to maintain prices at a level at which the proceeds of the enterprise will not cover the current costs of production . . . .

---

5. United Nations, *A System of National Accounts*, New York, 1982, p. 124; cited by Malmgren, Golt, Kingston & Co. (1983). Another broad definition, offered by the US Joint Economic Committee (1965), reads as follows (cited by E. Bruce Butler 1969, pp. 82–83):

[A]n act by a governmental unit involving either (1) a payment, (2) a remission of charges, or (3) supplying commodities or services at less than cost or market price, with the intent of achieving a particular economic objective, most usually the supplying to a general market a product or service which would be supplied in as great quantity only at a higher price in the absence of the payment or remission of charges.

Malmgren, Golt, Kingston & Co. (1983, p. 3) raises three objections to the use of this definition in the context of setting international policy on permissible subsidies:

The first is that it disregards the principle of public finance theory that the effect rather than the form of a transfer is what is important. On this definition, for example, a payment to the producers of a particular commodity—say house-building firms—ranks as a subsidy; but a payment to individuals earmarked for expenditure on house-building would not, even if the resource allocation and other economic effects were identical. Similarly, moneys spent by a firm, out of a grant made to it, on retraining workers would be included in the "subsidy" made to the firm; but a government operated retraining scheme, with precisely the same results, would not.

The second criticism made by economists is on the vagueness of much of the terminology used: for example, the phrase "cover current costs of production" has a whole range of possible meanings, so that there is very unlikely to be consistency in interpretation over time in any one country, much more between countries.

Finally, the economists see the distinction between payment on current and capital account as highly artificial. This is a topic on which there is in any case much room for difference of view from both a theoretical and practical point of view.

To meet these objections, virtually any sort of government assistance to industry could be folded into a general definition of subsidies, whether the assistance takes the form of an outright grant, interest-free loan, protection from imports, or is bestowed less visibly through tax exemptions (for example, for export earnings) or relaxed health and safety or environmental regulations. But an all-encompassing definition would prove too sweeping for policy guidance. In the last quarter of the twentieth century, there are few purists who would condemn all forms of government intervention.

In view of the difficulty in arriving at a general but still workable definition of a subsidy, policymakers have turned to the question of degree. Under what circumstances can part of the cost of production permissibly be absorbed by government? And when can one country rightly retaliate against the subsidies of another country?

Four broad concepts underlie the international rules that discipline subsidies and countervailing measures. These concepts do not flow from a structured analytic framework designed by the authors or anyone else. Rather, these concepts reflect collective judgment that has evolved over time as to what practices are fair and what practices are unfair.

First, producers in each nation should have access to internationally traded inputs at "world" prices for use in export production and should be able to sell their own output on world markets at "world" prices. Broadly speaking, national policies that enable such access are accepted by the international community.

Second, governments should not subsidize exports, in the sense of offering incentives that encourage the sale of goods abroad at cheaper prices than their sale at home. Neither should governments operate preferential schemes for exempting wages, profits, and other types of income earned in the production of exported goods from direct taxation. Nor should governments introduce second-best schemes to compensate particular export sectors from the adverse impact of overvalued exchange rates, the distortions created by excessive protection for domestic industry, or labor market distortions.

Third, governments should be free to offer general incentives to industry or agriculture—for example, by way of tax relief, roads, ports, or schools—but governments should not offer sector-specific incentives that injuriously affect the commerce of another nation.

Fourth and finally, a nation should be able to take offsetting remedial action in cases where foreign governments violate the second or third principles *and* the resulting trade harms the nation's economic interests.

Flowing from these four broad concepts are guidelines governing the use of subsidies and countermeasures. In this section we briefly discuss subsidies. In the following section, we address guidelines on the use of countermeasures.

As to the use of subsidies, the international community has sanctioned certain measures designed to strip away selected "social charges" from goods entering export markets. The social charges that may be stripped away include, among others, final stage indirect taxes borne by the product, certain indirect taxes levied on purchased inputs prior to the final stage, and duties on imported inputs that are incorporated in the final product. These adjustments permit the producer to realize approximately the "world" price for its exports and to acquire traded inputs at their "world" prices for use in export production.

In addition, the guidelines attempt to distinguish between acceptable and unacceptable subsidies. Nearly every government subsidizes at least some productive activities, but a great many subsidies either have so little impact on trade flows or are so widely used that retaliation is generally thought to be inappropriate. For example, two of the most important industrial subsidies are protective measures (tariffs and nontariff barriers) that guarantee the domestic producer a larger share of the home market, which in turn can serve as an export platform; and government procurement that favors domestic firms, with the same potential export consequences.

The present framework of rules imposes some constraints on government procurement practices and other forms of nontariff barriers, but governments have retained a great deal of freedom to use these measures for their own commercial advantage. If other governments were to take countermeasures against all such subsidies, the incidence and level of trade protection could increase dramatically. In short, the international community has weighed the sheer impracticality of trying to prohibit *all* types of government intervention that might have trade distortive effects.

As a result, the international community has attempted to define a subset of subsidies, a subset that we have labeled "potentially troublesome subsidies," which is considerably smaller than the class of all subsidies. A potentially troublesome subsidy, when coupled with the requisite degree of trade impact, becomes an "actually troublesome" subsidy, liable to countermeasures. Agreed boundaries of the potentially troublesome subset have proved elusive. Therefore, until very recently, international negotiators looked to another standard for distinguishing between acceptable and unacceptable subsidies, namely, the trade impact of government intervention in private activities. If a subsidy has a harmful trade impact—that is, causes some degree of "injury" as seen through the eyes of a competing firm and, ultimately, as viewed by its national government—then the subsidy historically has been considered a fit candidate for offsetting countermeasures. Because international rules have grown up with a heavy emphasis on trade-impact, chapter 2 begins with a discussion of trade-impact standards.

The "trade-impact" approach to international guidelines has relegated to second place the precise definition and measurement of subsidies. Nevertheless, as a result of extensive international work, certain practices that clearly differentiate between products sold at home and abroad, and that are regarded as troublesome per se, are now explicitly defined as *export* subsidies. (These definitional questions are discussed in chapter 3.) The GATT, as originally drafted, and the Code on Subsidies and Countervailing Duties, agreed during the Tokyo Round of Multilateral Trade Negotiations (1974–79),[6] form the core of internationally accepted guidelines and definitions in the export incentive field. (The key articles of the GATT and the entire code are reproduced in appendix A.)

GATT Article XVI:1 calls for each member nation to notify and consult on (with an implied duty to consider limiting) those of its export subsidies that cause "serious prejudice" to the trading interests of another nation, while Article XVI:4 proscribes export subsidies on industrial products that lead to the sale of exported products at lower prices than like products sold domestically.[7] However,

---

6. Known formally as the Agreement on Interpretation and Application of Articles VI, XVI, and XXIII of the General Agreement on Tariffs and Trade. The code has been signed by 30 countries: Australia, Austria, Brazil, Canada, Chile, the "Ten," Egypt, Finland, Hong Kong, India, Japan, South Korea, New Zealand, Norway, Pakistan, Spain, Sweden, Switzerland, United States, Uruguay, and Yugoslavia. Colombia is considering accession to the code. Neither Egypt nor Yugoslavia has ratified; accordingly for the purposes of US law, neither country is entitled to the so-called "injury test."

7. Article XVI:4 specifically calls on Contracting Parties to cease to grant "any form of subsidy on the export of any product . . . which subsidy results in the sale of such product for export at a price lower than the comparable price charged for the like product to buyers in the domestic market." Article XVI:4 has been accepted by 17 nations, principally

Article XVI:4 does not apply to primary products, including agricultural goods, and this deliberate omission leaves a very large and troublesome gap in the application of agreed rules on international trade. The Subsidies Code took a modest step toward narrowing that gap by eliminating minerals from its definition of primary products and thereby bringing trade in minerals under tighter international discipline (see code Article 9, footnote 29). As the ongoing US–EC dispute over agricultural trade attests, however, the present loosely defined rules on trade in agricultural goods cannot cope with an increasingly abrasive situation.

Much less negotiation and scholarship has been addressed to the definition of potentially troublesome *domestic* subsidies, namely practices that assist the firm but make no overt distinction between goods sold at home and goods sold abroad. A vast range of government intervention practices affect a firm's ability to compete abroad as well as at home. For example, investment incentives are a commonplace feature of twentieth-century social policy and, like direct export subsidies, can easily influence the flow of traded goods. However, GATT Article III specifically permits "the payment of subsidies exclusively to domestic producers." As a result, international guidelines are just beginning to distinguish between domestic subsidies that are, or are not, potentially troublesome to a nation's trading partners.

As discussed in chapter 4, the definition of potentially troublesome domestic subsidies is now left largely to the case decisions of national authorities. However, international efforts in this area should gradually become more prominent. The Subsidies Code established a Committee of Signatories to oversee the workings of the code and to address emerging problems. With proper encouragement, the Subsidies Committee may come to play a constructive role in the eventual adoption of uniform national definitions concerning potentially troublesome subsidies.

Guidelines on Countermeasures

International guidelines on trade matters, even when sanctioned by treaty, cannot be enforced against an unwilling sovereign nation. For the most part, "enforcement" takes the form of self-discipline or retaliation. Self-discipline can be quite important, especially when domestic interest groups can be mobilized to support the international rules. In addition, the mere possibility of retaliation against an offending country can be an effective weapon against the proliferation of export

---

industrial countries, but not by other GATT contracting parties. A 1960 GATT Working Party drew up a list of measures which participants regarded as proscribed subsidies under Article XVI:4 (see appendix D). While the list was never officially adopted by GATT signatories, it acquired over the years an aura of authority and formed the basis of the Illustrative List of Export Subsidies in the 1979 code (see appendix A).

subsidies. But actual retaliation carries with it the danger of an unwitting escalation of trade-destroying practices. Recent flare-ups in the subsidies realm have been fueled not only by disagreement over the definition of potentially troublesome subsidies but also by the use of, and the threat to use, familiar remedies, such as countervailing duties and countervailing subsidies (i.e., subsidies that match the initiating country's bounties with respect to goods sold in third markets). In order to reduce this danger, the international community has attempted to codify acceptable procedures and means of retaliation—"countermeasures"—against unfair trade practices.

As a companion to the guidelines adopted to govern the use of subsidies, discussed in the previous section, the international community has sanctioned certain countermeasures that are designed to provide self-help in the quest for "fair trade." Broadly speaking, three fundamental concepts underlie the international acceptability of a country's use of countermeasures:

☐ The complaining country should be experiencing some economic discomfort.

☐ A causal link should be established between the subsidized trade and the economic discomfort.

☐ The countermeasure should simply offset the subsidy itself and not penalize the exporter for more than the benefit actually received.

GATT Article VI permits aggrieved countries to levy compensatory tariffs, namely countervailing duties, to offset harmful foreign subsidies, provided that the subsidized imports cause "material injury" to the domestic industry. Countervailing duties can be levied against the products of a specific country without regard to the unconditional most-favored-nation (MFN) obligations of Article I and without regard to whether the normal tariff has been the subject of an international binding under Article II. (Remedies in relation to MFN obligations are discussed in chapter 5.) GATT Article XVI, as mentioned earlier, entails a measure of self-restraint on the use of subsidies. GATT Article XXIII enables the Contracting Parties to authorize other unspecified countermeasures when actions by one government—for example, harmful subsidies—"nullify or impair" the benefits that another government can rightly expect from the GATT and from trade negotiations concluded under GATT auspices. However, the Contracting Parties have only authorized retaliatory measures in one case, and in that case the target country (the United States) essentially gave consent to the punishment meted out.

These basic GATT Articles—Articles VI, XVI, and XXIII—were the subject of very considerable elaboration and expansion in the Subsidies Code. Companion international understandings on export credit norms have been reached under OECD auspices.

The negotiating background of the Subsidies Code deserves brief mention. In broad terms, the Tokyo Round negotiation involved a bargain in which the United States agreed to change its countervailing duty statute to accept the principle of an "injury test," while the European Community accepted both a tighter definition of prohibited export subsidies and the principle that injurious domestic subsidies could be subject to countervailing action (Richard R. Rivers and John D. Greenwald 1979).

The US countervailing duty statute, first enacted in 1897, originally applied only to *dutiable* imports: evidence of a "bounty or grant" paid on the "manufacture, production or sale" of goods subject to the US tariff was sufficient for the imposition of countervailing duties, without demonstration of injury to domestic producers. The absence of an injury requirement for dutiable imports predates the GATT. Hence, the United States long relied on its "grandfather rights," preserved when it originally joined the GATT, to save it from violation of the standard of material injury, later set forth in GATT Article VI. *Nondutiable* imports were first covered under the US countervailing duty law as a result of a 1974 amendment. For these imports, the US law required proof of injury, consistent with GATT Article VI.

The absence of an injury requirement in the US countervailing duty statute, although legally protected by grandfather rights, was widely perceived by US trading partners as a departure from international norms. For much of the post–World War II period, this departure was principally of academic interest, since the US Treasury (the agency charged with enforcing the US countervailing duty law) rarely imposed countervailing duties. In fact, prior to the Tariff Act of 1930, the US Treasury imposed countervailing duties only 12 times, and between the 1930 Act and 1969, only 34 times (E. Bruce Butler 1969, pp. 85–86). There were only three outstanding US countervailing duty actions in 1973 (Wilfred J. Ethier 1982, p. 488).

In the Trade Act of 1974, however, private petitioners were given the right to mount court challenges to the US Treasury's actions or inactions, and equally important (some might say *more* important), time limits were imposed on the various steps in the decision-making process in countervailing duty cases. The right of court review, reinforced by the strict time limits, led to a surge of petitions, and, in many instances, countervailing duty relief was awarded. Thus there were 37 outstanding countervailing duty actions by 1979 (Ethier 1982, p. 487).

In order to avoid trade abrasion that might undermine the US negotiating position in the Tokyo Round, the Trade Act of 1974 also gave the secretary of the treasury authority (until January 3, 1979) to waive the imposition of a countervailing duty—provided that adequate steps were taken to reduce substantially the adverse effect of the subsidy, and provided that failure to waive the duty would jeopardize negotiations to develop an international code disciplining the use of subsidies. The waiver authority was liberally used, negotiations proceeded, and the 1979 Code on Subsidies and Countervailing Duties was the result.

But the code has not ushered in an era of harmony. The US General Accounting Office (1983), for example, recently released a critical appraisal of the code, declaring on the report's cover:

GAO reviewed three strategies used by the US Government between January 1980–83 to reduce the use of trade-related subsidies under the 1979 international agreement on subsidies.

1. Persuading developing countries to assume increased discipline over the use of subsidies.

2. Persuading Agreement signatories to report the subsidies they use.

3. Using the Agreement's dispute settlement procedure to help eliminate the effects of subsidies.

GAO concluded that to date, these strategies have met with little success.

An American Perspective

Before turning to the next chapters a fact that is already evident should be underscored: this book is written from an American perspective, not only because the authors are Americans but also because the whole question of subsidies and countervailing measures has been pioneered in the US Congress, in the administrative decisions of the US Treasury and US Commerce departments, and in the diplomatic initiatives mounted by the United States during the Tokyo Round. The European Community has only recently taken an active role in issuing countervailing duty orders (the Community adopted the Subsidies and Countervailing Duties Code as an internal regulation effective January 1980 and some six cases have since been initiated), while Japan has only initiated one countervailing duty action. Canada and Australia have each initiated eight actions since 1980. By contrast, the US countervailing duty statute, which differs in some respects from the Subsidies Code and the GATT, is an important and frequently used trade remedy, and the United States has initiated 123 actions since 1980 (see generally John H. Jackson, Jean-Victor Louis, and Mitsuo Matsushita 1982).

In the 1960s and 1970s, the European Community viewed the use of antidumping statutes from the perspective of an exporter. In the early 1980s, increasingly troubled by "cheap" imports from Eastern Europe and the Far East, the Community began to see the antidumping law more from the vantage point of an importer. A similar metamorphosis in EC perspectives toward the countervailing duty statute may take place in the late 1980s and early 1990s. Conversely, Americans may become more sympathetic to present-day EC views as the United States increasingly confronts foreign countervailing duties on its own exports. Under these circumstances, US and EC views and practices could converge in future years. However, at this writing, the subject of subsidies is very much a study in the law of the GATT and the law of the United States.

Many observers regard the present US system of countervailing duties (together with the companion antidumping duty statute and other more exotic remedies against "unfair" trade) as a vast and complicated system of contingent protection, largely erected for the benefit of US business. According to this view, the basic system is biased against small nations for two reasons: first, because producers in small countries are typically more dependent on world markets if their plants are constructed on a scale to produce at optimum efficiency levels;[8] second, because small countries are less able to wield the complicated machinery of a countervailing duty statute to protect their own markets. These criticisms have been voiced with eloquence by Rodney de C. Grey (1983).

These criticisms may strike a responsive chord among many readers. Nevertheless, in the main body of this volume, we accept the discipline inherent in the present US system of countervailing measures. While the system is far from perfect, the absence of meaningful discipline would stimulate a competitive race-to-the bottom in the realm of subsidies; country-by-country exceptions would prove unmanageable; and a less refined approach to "unfair" trade problems would, in the end, prove more protective than the present cumbersome mechanisms.[9]

---

8. Perhaps the best illustration of potential difficulties faced by producers in smaller economies arose in the *Michelin* tire case (*X-Radial Belted Tires from Canada*, 38 Fed. Reg. 1018, 8 January 1973). In that case, a plant was constructed in Canada with the intention of exporting most of its product to the sizable US market. Michelin benefited from various regional development assistance programs offered by the Canadian federal government, Nova Scotia, and the local municipality. Because such a large portion of Michelin's tire products was to be exported—and thus the assistance was highly focused on exports—the US Treasury Department considered the incentives an export subsidy. (For an early critical review of the treasury decision, see Robert V. Guido and Michael F. Morrone 1974.) In 1978, after several years of litigation, and acting on the basis of domestic statutory authority, the United States levied countervailing duties on Michelin tires entering the United States from Canada. This action drew a vigorous protest from the Canadian government and the case is still in litigation. The Michelin case inspired the negotiations that eventually led to the OECD Declaration on International Investment and Multinational Enterprises (see appendix F).

9. See Douglas R. Nelson (1981) and J. M. Finger (1982) for thoughtful analyses of the role that countervailing duty and antidumping laws play in the larger system of administered protection.

Trade-Impact Standards

International negotiators, attempting to define potentially troublesome subsidies and fashion surgical remedies directed against them, have encountered many difficulties. By comparison, it has proved somewhat easier for international negotiators to articulate the requisite trade-impact standard.

Standards for trade impact are central to multilateral or bilateral retaliation against national subsidies. After all, if there is no impact on trade, what foreigner is harmed by the subsidy? And if no foreigner is harmed, why should any foreigner retaliate?

There are two schools of thought on the role that trade impact should play in the scheme for disciplining subsidies. The "injury-only" school is principally concerned with redressing the harm that comes from subsidized trade. The "antidistortion" school focuses on the inefficient consequences of government intervention.

Briefly, the injury-only school believes that a country should retaliate against foreign subsidies only when those subsidies exert a significant impact on trade, and further, the remedy should be designed to redress that *impact*. By contrast, the antidistortion school believes that subsidies are a fit subject for retaliation even if they exert only a slight impact on trade, and that retaliation should be precisely designed to offset the *subsidy*.

The Injury-Only School

The injury-only school takes the view that subsidies and other forms of government intervention in private economic activity are a fact of modern life. Subsidies, according to this school, are often used to correct preexisting market imperfections and are almost impossible to apportion over units of output. Exchange rate movements will offset gross differences in subsidization between countries, leaving only micro problems for specific trade remedies. This school holds that the principal discipline against subsidization must come from domestic political processes, not international rules.[1]

If one country chooses to subsidize and goes about its work in a regular and predictable way, and there is no significant harm to the other countries, why should its trading partners be concerned? If the subsidy distorts the economy, the subsidizing country will suffer, while its trading partners will enjoy whatever benefits flow from cheap prices on subsidized goods.

Richard N. Cooper delivered a sophisticated expression of this view (1978, p. 120):

. . . perhaps we should not worry so much about government subsidies to economic activity—or rather government intervention of all types—as far as their effects on foreign trade are concerned, provided the interventions are introduced sufficiently gradually so that they do not impose acute adjustment costs on economic activities outside the country in question.

In a similar vein, before completion of the Tokyo Round, John J. Barcelo (1977) called for an injury-only approach to domestic subsidies and a strict prohibition of export subsidies. After the Tokyo Round, Barcelo (1980) called for an injury-only approach to *all* subsidies on exports to the complaining country's markets. Robert H. Mundheim and Peter D. Ehrenhaft (forthcoming 1984) also toyed with the injury-only approach.

A purist version of the injury-only approach would harmonize the level of trade impact required for an industry to receive relief somewhere between the trade-impact standards established in two US laws. The first standard, the "escape clause" standard set out in section 201 of the Trade Act of 1974, applies to relief from injurious but *fair* trade. Under this standard, a foreign trade practice must constitute a "substantial cause of serious injury" to domestic producers before relief is granted. The second standard is set out in the Trade Agreements Act of 1979 with reference to countervailing duties. This standard provides for relief from *unfair* trade when a foreign trade practice constitutes "a cause or threat of material injury" to an established industry or causes the "material retardation" of a new industry.

According to the injury-only school, these two trade-impact standards should be harmonized at the looser "fair trade" level, or at the stricter "unfair trade" level, or somewhere in between. Once the standards were harmonized, the injury-only school would dispense with the need to show subsidization. Relief would be designed to cure the injury, not to offset exactly the value of whatever

---

1. Early exponents of some of these ideas in the context of international policy toward subsidies were Warren F. Schwartz and Eugene W. Harper, Jr. (1972).

trade practice might exist. Barcelo, in his second article (1980), comes close to advocating this view.[2]

The Antidistortion School

The antidistortion school is guided by the belief that subsidies are bad for three reasons:

First, as used in practice (if not in economic theory), subsidies generally reduce world economic efficiency and thereby diminish the gains of international exchange to all nations.

Second and worse, a subsidy program may enable a country to gain an early lead in establishing a promising new industry (for example, fiber optics), or to avoid or delay painful adjustment in an old industry (for example, steel).

Third and finally, because other countries envy the early lead or adjustment avoided, subsidies may provoke emulation. Emulation will bring a spiral of wasteful distortion (as in shipbuilding) or overinvestment in seemingly promising technologies (as in supersonic aircraft).

The antidistortion school concedes that some subsidies may be used to offset preexisting market imperfections, but the school believes that this justification is vastly exaggerated; that any serious effort to distinguish corrective from distorting subsidies would quickly lead to an impenetrable and ultimately self-serving thicket of calculations; and that the market imperfection argument is merely a cover for applying the cynical doctrine, on a national and international scale, that one bad distortion deserves another.

Most members of the antidistortion school believe that even a very low threshold of trade impact warrants the imposition of penalties, and that the penalty should offset, as nearly as possible, the initial distortion. In this view, the magnitude of trade impact is nearly irrelevant to the imposition or the calculation of penalties against subsidization. In particular, subsidies that differentially favor export sales should be condemned outright. As Assistant Secretary of the Treasury (and later Deputy US Trade Representative) David R. Macdonald put the matter (1976):

It is our position that the GATT should be revised to eliminate the injury test in cases of an export-tilted subsidy. We analyze the export-tilted subsidy as nothing more than a unilateral [renegotiation] by one country of the legitimate tariff rate of the country to which the goods are shipped.

---

2. Prior to the Trade Act of 1974, the US escape clause required a connection between injurious imports and a previous trade concession. Dispensing with a showing of subsidization as an antecedent to relief would be analogous to dispensing with the trade concession test—a step that was taken by the United States in 1974.

The Subsidies Code

Largely influenced by the antidistortion school, but mindful of the use of subsidies by the United States, the US Congress directed the administration to seek discipline on foreign subsidies as a central element of the Tokyo Round. This directive was reinforced by legislation that threatened to unleash the countervailing duty statute (Matthew J. Marks and Harald B. Malmgren 1975). In response, the Ford administration advanced a "traffic light" concept in international negotiations:[3]

☐ Export subsidies, as defined in an international understanding, would automatically and unilaterally be subject to countervailing duties, or CVDs (the "red" category).

☐ Other subsidies, applied equally to domestic and export goods and having a significant trade impact, would be subject to CVDs, if they caused or threatened to cause material injury (the "amber" category).

☐ Domestic subsidies with a minor or indirect trade effect would not be subject to CVDs (the "green" category).

The "traffic light" approach clearly mixes the precepts of the injury-only school and the antidistortion school. While the light symbolism was rejected by the European Community (EC) much of the substance was reflected in the final text of the Subsidies Code.[4] The code envisaged two "tracks." Broadly speaking, domestic and export subsidies that cause measurable harm were assigned to the first track: a high threshold of trade impact (material injury) allows the *national* authorization of countervailing duties. The CVDs cannot exceed the amount of subsidy per unit of exported product. Moreover, CVDs preferably will be set at a level just sufficient to offset the trade injury, if that were a lesser amount.

In addition, developed country signatories to the code agreed not to grant export subsidies. Since most countries nevertheless do subsidize their exports to some extent, the code also provides remedies for use by aggrieved trading partners. Export subsidies can be attacked along a second track: a low threshold of trade impact (either a *presumption* of "adverse effects" or, in the case of developing countries, an actual *showing* of adverse effects) allows the *multilateral* authorization of compensatory measures. The compensatory measures can in principle take various forms—for example, countervailing duties or the withdrawal of a

---

3. The basic themes of the "traffic light" approach were announced by Assistant Secretary of the Treasury David R. Macdonald (1976). The approach was tabled in explicit form at the Geneva talks by both the Ford and Carter administrations.

4. For excellent histories of the code and its antecedents, see Richard R. Rivers and John D. Greenwald (1979), and Daniel K. Tarullo (forthcoming 1984).

"bound" tariff (that is, the injured country could unilaterally raise a tariff whose original level had been agreed to internationally).[5]

The two tracks conceived in the code are not separated by an impenetrable divider. A country may impose countervailing duties under its national procedures against export subsidies that cause material injury. In principle, the material injury standard is intended to be higher than the adverse effects standard, but the complaining industry may find it much easier to surmount national procedures than international procedures. As another example of overlap, a signatory may complain to the Subsidies Committee not only about another signatory's export subsidies but also about its domestic subsidies.

The distinction between "Track I" and "Track II" in the code just scratches the surface of the many gradations of trade-impact standards found in the code and the General Agreement on Tariffs and Trade (GATT). The standards also vary according to such collateral factors as: whether the subsidizing country is a developed or developing country; whether the subsidizing country is a code signatory (a distinction that seems to matter only under US law, as we will discuss in chapter 5); whether the product is a primary commodity; whether the complaint is brought by an industry under its national law or by a government in the GATT; and whether the harmful trade impact is located in the home market of the complaining country, in the home market of the subsidizing country, or in third-country markets.

There is no single, all-embracing rationale underlying the creation of different trade-impact standards, which vary among countries, products, and types of action, as laid out in the GATT and the code. Instead, a series of ad hoc arguments have been used to justify the variegated array of standards.

Differentiation of the trade-impact standard for domestic subsidies and export subsidies is based on the argument that domestic subsidies are more likely to serve a corrective function than export subsidies.

Differentiation for developing countries is based on the presumption that their subsidies are more likely to serve an infant-industry purpose than subsidies used by developed countries.

Differentiation in US law that favors code signatories over nonsignatories reflects the higher level of obligation accepted by signatories vis-à-vis other signatories and is meant to act as a spur toward code membership.

Differentiation for primary products is justified by political expediency: when GATT Article XVI:3 was drafted in 1955, US farm interests were too powerful to be disciplined; when code Article 10 was drafted in 1979, European farm interests were too powerful (Daniel K. Tarullo forthcoming 1984).

---

5. In practice, as Jeffrey J. Schott (1982) has emphasized, the GATT has historically failed to authorize retaliation against trade offenses, partly because major powers (United States, European Community, and Japan) can block effective measures.

Differentiation according to whether the petitioner is a government or a firm—only governments are allowed to bring cases before the GATT—is justified by the supposition that governments will balance other considerations against the single-minded pursuit of redress.

Differentiation by the location of impact reflects the pragmatic realities of designing effective remedies. The injured country can more easily retaliate in its home market than in the subsidizing country's home market or in third-country markets.

Table 2.1 attempts to summarize the possible actions against subsidized trade now available to the US government or a US company and the corresponding array of trade-impact standards for each action. Some of these standards deserve further comment.

Material Injury

Most celebrated, of course, is the standard of material injury (including the *threat* of material injury and material retardation of a new industry). In principle, the material injury standard applies to nearly all domestic countermeasures applied by GATT members against subsidized imports. (The only important exceptions are: (a) instances in which a developed country offers prohibited export subsidies, and those subsidies are condemned by a GATT panel; and (b) instances in which a nonsignatory to the code subsidizes exports to the United States. In both cases, countermeasures may be applied without the need to show material injury.)

The meaning of material injury has been the subject of much learned writing revolving around the 1967 Antidumping Code, the repudiation of that code by the US Congress, the evolving standards followed by the US International Trade Commission (USITC), the 1979 Antidumping Code, the 1979 Code on Subsidies and Countervailing Duties, and the US Trade Agreements Act of 1979 (Peter D. Staple 1980; Bruce A. Ortwine 1981; John D. Greenwald 1982).

Rather than define material injury, Article 6:3 of the Subsidies Code simply lists a number of factors that may be taken into account in making a determination of material injury. These factors include an actual or potential decline in output, sales, market share, profits, prices, or employment and, in the case of agriculture, whether there has been an increased burden on government support programs. Further, to give each national authority wide latitude in weighing the various factors, Article 6:3 concludes with a formula borrowed from the 1967 Antidumping Code: "This list is not exhaustive, nor can one or several of these factors necessarily give decisive guidance."

Material injury is defined in the US Trade Agreements Act of 1979 as "harm which is not inconsequential, immaterial or unimportant." This legislative doublespeak was carefully crafted both to erect a barrier against *de minimis* cases and

Table 2.1 Summary of possible actions by US firms or the US government against subsidized trade

Case 1

Petitioner: US firm

Respondent: A firm or industry in a country that is not entitled to MFN treatment, either as a code signatory or under a bilateral agreement

Practice subject to complaint	Location of trade impact	Elements of petitioner's case	Respondent's affirmative defenses	Remedy	Legal base (forum)
Any subsidy	US market	To show the existence of a subsidy within the meaning of US law	To show a narrow range of permitted offsets	CVD or price or quantity "undertakings" to offset injury	US CVD law (ITA)
Export subsidy or incentive with equivalent effect	US market or third-country market	(1) To show the existence of an export subsidy or other incentive having the equivalent effect (2) That substantially reduces petitioner's sales of a competitive product		Ad hoc	Section 301 (USTR)
Domestic subsidy	Subsidizing country market	(1) To show that the subsidy is an unjustifiable or unreasonable import restriction (2) That impairs the value of a trade commitment or (3) That burdens, restricts, or discriminates against US commerce		Ad hoc	Section 301 (USTR)

Table 2.1 Continued

Case 2

Petitioner: US firm

Respondent: A firm or industry in a country that is entitled to MFN treatment, either as a code signatory or under a bilateral agreement

Practice subject to complaint	Location of trade impact	Elements of petitioner's case	Respondent's affirmative defenses	Remedy	Legal base (forum)
Any subsidy	US market	(1) To show the existence of a subsidy (2) That causes material injury or threat thereof	To show a narrow range of permitted offsets	CVD or price or quantity "undertakings" to offset injury	US CVD law (ITA and USITC)
Export subsidy or an incentive with equivalent effect	US market or third-country market	(1) To show the existence of an export subsidy or other incentive having the equivalent effect (2) That substantially reduces petitioner's sales of a competitive product	To show that the subsidy is consistent with GATT and code commitments	Ad hoc	Section 301 (USTR)
Domestic subsidy	Subsidizing country market	(1) To show the existence of a subsidy (2) That causes material injury or the threat thereof	To show that the subsidy is consistent with GATT and code commitments	Ad hoc	Section 301 (USTR)

Case 3

Petitioner: US government

Respondent: A GATT country that is not a code signatory, is not otherwise entitled to MFN treatment, and has only subscribed to Article XVI:A

Practice subject to complaint	Location of trade impact	Elements of petitioner's case	Respondent's affirmative defenses	Remedy	Legal base (forum)
Any subsidy	Any market	(1) To show the existence of a subsidy (2) That increases respondent's exports or decreases its imports		Respondent must notify the subsidy	GATT Art. XVI:A (GATT)
Any subsidy—nullification or impairment	Subsidizing country market	(1) To show the existence of a subsidy (2) That nullifies or impairs benefits bargained for, for example, a bound tariff		Authorization of withdrawal of concessions	GATT Art. XXIII (GATT)
Any subsidy—serious prejudice	Any market	(1) To show the existence of a subsidy (2) That seriously harms the United States		Consultation as to limiting the subsidy	GATT Art. XVI:A (GATT)
Buy-national performance requirement	Subsidizing country market	(1) To show the existence of a subsidy (2) That amounts to a mixing requirement or a quantitative restraint		Authorization of withdrawal of concession	GATT Arts. III and XXIII (GATT)

Table 2.1 Continued

Case 4

Petitioner: US government

Respondent: A GATT country that is not a code signatory but has subscribed to both Article XVI:A and Article XVI:B

Practice subject to complaint	Location of trade impact	Elements of petitioner's case	Respondent's affirmative defenses	Remedy	Legal base (forum)
An export subsidy, other than on primary products	US market or third-country market	(1) To show the existence of an export subsidy (2) That results in dual pricing	To show that the subsidy has no adverse trade effect	Authorization of withdrawal of concessions	GATT Arts. XVI and XXIII (GATT)
An export subsidy on a primary product	US market or third-country market	(1) To show the existence of a subsidy (2) That increases the respondent's exports (3) In a way that captures "more than an equitable share" of world markets by comparison with a "previous representative period"		Authorization of withdrawal of concessions	GATT Arts. XVI and XXIII (GATT)

Note: These actions are cumulative with those in case 3.

Case 5

Petitioner: US government

Respondent: A country that is a signatory to the GATT Subsidies Code

Practice subject to complaint	Location of trade impact	Elements of petitioner's case	Respondent's affirmative defenses	Remedy	Legal base (forum)
Export subsidies given by a developed country signatory on nonprimary products	US market or third-country market	(1) To show existence of a subsidy (2) In the case of an export subsidy, other than those enumerated in items (a) to (k), to show dual pricing[a]	Rebut the presumption of adverse effects	Consultations and authorization of ad hoc countermeasures	Code Arts. 9 and 18 (GATT Subsidies Committee)
Export subsidy given by a developing country signatory on nonprimary products	US market or third-country market	(1) To show existence of a subsidy (2) That causes adverse trade or production effects and (3) In the case of an export subsidy, other than those enumerated in items (a) to (k), to show dual pricing[a]		Consultations and authorization of ad hoc countermeasures	Code Arts. 9 and 18 (GATT Subsidies Committee)
Export subsidy on certain primary products	US market or third-country market	(1) To demonstrate that the respondent is acquiring "more than an equitable share" of world export trade by		Consultations and authorization of ad hoc countermeasures	Code Arts. 10 and 18 (GATT Subsidies Committee)

Table 2.1 Continued

Practice subject to complaint	Location of trade impact	Elements of petitioner's case	Respondent's affirmative defenses	Remedy	Legal base (forum)
		comparison with a "previous representative period" or			
		(2) To show that the respondent is pricing below the prices offered by other countries			
Domestic subsidy—nullification or impairment	Any market	(1) To show that the subsidy "adversely affect[s] the conditions of normal competition" and exerts "possible adverse effects on trade" and		Consultations and authorization of ad hoc countermeasures	Code Arts. 11 and 18 (GATT Subsidies Committee)
		(2) To show a loss of expected GATT or code benefits			
Domestic subsidy—serious prejudice	Any market	To show that the trade impact of the subsidy seriously harms the United States		Consultations and authorization of ad hoc countermeasures	Code Arts. 11 and 18 (GATT Subsidies Committee)
Domestic subsidy—	Any market	(1) To show actual or potential harm to the		Consultations and authorization of ad hoc	Code Arts. 11 and 18 (GATT

material injury or threat thereof | (2) complaining industry That results from subsidized imports | countermeasures | Subsidies Committee)

Note: These actions are cumulative with those in cases 3 and 4.

a. It is arguable whether a showing of dual pricing is required.

Case 6

Petitioner: US government or US firm

Respondent: A participant country in the OECD Arrangements on Guidelines for Official Export Credits

Practice subject to complaint	Location of trade impact	Elements of petitioner's case	Respondent's affirmative defenses	Remedy	Legal base (forum)
An official export credit	Third-country market	A derogation (notified by respondent country) from the interest rate, term, or other guidelines of the Arrangement		US Export-Import Bank may match the derogating credit	US Export-Import Bank Act and OECD Arrangement (US Export-Import Bank)
An official export credit	US market	A derogation from the Arrangement		On authorization of US Treasury, US Export-Import Bank may match the derogating credit	US Export-Import Bank Act (US Treasury and Export-Import Bank)

Note: These actions are cumulative with the export subsidy actions in case 5.

Also see glossary for agency acronyms and explanation of terminology (for example, "affirmative defenses").

to avoid placing an undue burden of proof on an injured industry. This language reflected legislative efforts both to comport with the code and to ensure that the newly legislated material injury test did not significantly increase the US trade-impact standard. As a result, the language leaves large gray areas for case-by-case interpretation. This latitude gave rise to widespread European fears that the United States was attempting to recapture, through its domestic statute, concessions made during international negotiations.

However, the US Trade Agreements Act does spell out factors, not unlike those in code Article 6:3, that the USITC should consider in making an injury determination. The impact of import volume and price on a US industry must be "significant" and "all relevant factors which have a bearing on the state of the industry" must be taken into account prior to any finding of injury. Thus, the statutory draftsmen laid a foundation for the slow evolution of parallel treatment of material injury determinations under US practice and the practice of other code signatories.

Two clusters of factors seem to enter a USITC determination that imports are a cause or threat of material injury to an existing industry. First, the existence of material injury is predicated on some combination of declining sales, falling profits, low capacity utilization, or falling employment. Second, a finding that imports are a cause of material injury usually requires an absolute increase in imports, a rising market share of imports, or price undercutting or price depression by imports (Ortwine 1981).

The code is flexible enough to allow national authorities to distinguish, in their deliberations over material injury, between a 20 percent subsidy that violates the prohibition on export subsidies and a 20 percent subsidy that arises from a domestic program with no overt export bias (see code Article 6:1, footnote 1). The US Trade Agreements Act of 1979, section 771(7)(E)(i), enables the USITC, on the suggestion of the Department of Commerce, to make just that distinction: a finding of material injury can be made more readily if the foreign country offers a prohibited export subsidy.

Common sense would seem to suggest that a subsidy of 25 percent is more likely to attract a finding that imports are a cause of material injury than a subsidy of 5 percent. In a recent decision (*Carbon Steel Wire from Brazil and Trinidad and Tobago*, 47 Fed. Reg. 47452, 26 October 1982), the US International Trade Commission surprised common sense by declaring that the amount of subsidy was irrelevant to a finding of material injury. This decision will probably not be regarded as a model by authorities elsewhere.

An important issue, now attracting attention in the United States, is whether the impact of subsidized trade from two or more countries can be cumulated for purposes of meeting the material-injury test. In other words, should subsidized imports from each country be examined individually to determine whether they cause material injury? Or should subsidized imports from all countries be lumped together? Generally speaking, the USITC has allowed cumulation, except when one country has supplied a very small share of the market.[6] A common international approach to the problem of cumulation remains to be negotiated.

Nullification or Impairment

The GATT Article XXIII concept of "nullification or impairment" is based on the notion that, through mutually bargained tariff concessions or through other reciprocal GATT obligations, each Contracting Party has acquired certain trading benefits vis-à-vis other Contracting Parties. A party's benefits may be impaired or nullified by subsequent measures taken by another Contracting Party. Whether or not the subsequent measures are per se offensive is a secondary matter. The primary question in a nullification or impairment case is whether the subsequent measures have a harmful trade effect that defeats the legitimate expectations of the impacted country. Thus, a nullification or impairment case need not entail any breach of explicit GATT obligations. Conversely, a breach of GATT obligations must be more than technical to sustain a case.

The unanticipated grant of a new subsidy on a domestic product that competes with imports that are subject to a bound tariff, coupled with a slight but noticeable trade impact, would represent a classic case of nullification or impairment.[7] A more contemporary illustration might arise if a code signatory instituted a new subsidy program on its agricultural exports and made no effort, through internal deliberations or external consultations, to follow the injunction of code Article 8:3 "to seek to avoid causing . . . serious prejudice to the interests of another signatory."

Retaliation in an Article XXIII nullification or impairment case theoretically could take the form of a withdrawn tariff concession, the imposition of a quota, or some other merchandise trade action. In practice, however, there is very little case experience on the use of Article XXIII. Article XXIII action requires prior approval of the Contracting Parties, and the Contracting Parties seldom give their approval without the grudging consent of the offending country. Only once in GATT history has a dispute under Article XXIII led to the suspension of conces-

---

6. For a review of the cumulation issue, see the brief filed by Cravath, Swaine, and Moore, "Plaintiffs' Memorandum in Support of Their Motion for Review of Agency Determination upon the Agency Record (Cumulation Issue)," June 30, 1983, in *Republic Steel Co. v. United States*, No. 82-3-00372 (Court of International Trade).

7. This proposition is derived by extension from *The Australian Subsidy on Ammonium Sulphates*, 3 April 1950, reprinted in GATT, 2d Supp. *Basic Instruments and Selected Documents* 188–96 (1952). See also Robert E. Hudec (forthcoming 1984).

sions. That occurred in a 1951 case where the United States quietly agreed to retaliation by the Netherlands against US quota restrictions on dairy imports (Kenneth W. Dam 1970, p. 260).

Serious Prejudice

International jurisprudence is also rather slender as to the meaning of "serious prejudice." Article XVI imposes no penalty when serious prejudice is found to exist. Instead, each Contracting Party is free to request consultations with any other party, if it believes its trading interests are seriously prejudiced. In turn, the party granting the subsidy is merely required to discuss, bilaterally or multilaterally, "the possibility of limiting the subsidization."

Since the GATT holds out no remedy for serious prejudice, countries have little incentive to pursue complaints under this heading. Nevertheless, in two recent cases, brought by Australia (decided in 1979) and Brazil (decided in 1980), serious prejudice was found by a GATT panel to arise from the sugar export subsidies of the European Community.

In the Australian case, the GATT panel summarized the charge in the following manner:[8]

(c) The question of "Serious prejudice to Australian interests"

> 2.26 The Australian representative argued that the Community measures, applied to exports of sugar, had caused or threatened to cause, serious prejudice to Australian interests and had adversely affected the world sugar market to the detriment of the other members of the General Agreement. He said that this price response was due to the low elasticity of demand for sugar which meant that an increase in supply results in a disproportionate decline in price. He, therefore, argued that the Community export subsidies had been excessive, that Community sugar exports had increased, while at the same time, there had been a sharp fall in world sugar prices. He also argued that the Community measures had caused considerable instability in world sugar trade and the growing availability of subsidized Community sugar on the world market had displaced traditional suppliers who were thus forced to accept greatly diminished returns in order to sell their products. He further argued that Australia's right to increase its own market share and the foreign exchange earnings of the Australian sugar industry had been adversely affected, and that this had resulted

---

8. Report of the Panel, adopted on 6 November 1979, L/4833.

in diminished returns to Australian producers, which had fallen from $A 308.60/ton in 1975/1976 to $A 231.34/ton in 1977/1978. This 25 per cent reduction reflected an even steeper decline of 40 per cent in the world free market price over the same period.

As this statement of facts indicates, Australia equated serious prejudice with price depression and price uncertainty, brought on in part by subsidized exports. The GATT Panel accepted both contentions:[9]

V. Conclusion . . .

(g) The Panel noted however that the Community system for granting refunds on sugar exports and its application had contributed to depress world sugar prices in recent years and that thereby serious prejudice had been caused indirectly to Australia, although it was not feasible to quantify the prejudice in exact terms.

(h) The Panel found that the Community system of export refunds for sugar did not comprise any pre-established effective limitations in respect of either production, price or the amounts of export refunds and constituted a permanent source of uncertainty in world sugar markets. It therefore concluded that the Community system and its application constitutes a threat of prejudice in terms of Article XVI:1.

Similar findings were reached by the Panel in the sugar case brought by Brazil:[10]

V. Conclusion . . .

(f) The Panel concluded that in view of the quantity of Community sugar made available for export with maximum refunds and the non-limited funds available to finance export refunds, the Community system of granting export refunds on sugar had been applied in a manner which in the particular market situation prevailing in 1978 and 1979, contributed to depress sugar prices in the world market, and that this constituted a serious prejudice to Brazilian interests, in terms of Article XVI:1.

---

9. Ibid.
10. Report of the Panel, adopted on 7 October 1980, L/5011.

(g) The Panel found that the Community system of export refunds for sugar did not comprise any pre-established effective limitations in respect of either production, price or the amounts of export refunds and that the Community system had not been applied in a manner so as to limit effectively neither exportable surpluses nor the amount of refunds granted. Neither the system nor its application would prevent the European Communities from having more than an equitable share of world export trade in sugar. The Panel, therefore, concluded that the Community system and its application constituted a permanent source of uncertainty in world sugar markets and therefore constituted a threat of serious prejudice in terms of Article XVI:1.

Despite these two findings of serious prejudice, the European Community continued its system of subsidizing sugar exports. From fall 1981 to late 1982 and early 1983, the world sugar price dropped from between $0.12 and $0.14 per pound to under $0.07 per pound, partly because of the scale of subsidized European exports.

Adverse Effects

Code Articles 8:4 and 11:2 introduced a new term of art, "adverse effects," to encompass occasions of injury (in the sense of Part I of the code), nullification or impairment (in the sense of GATT Article XXIII), and serious prejudice (in the sense of GATT Article XVI:1). The language of code Article 8:4 requires that the complaining party demonstrate a causal connection between the subsidy and the adverse trade effect.

The code takes the position, however, that a departure from a code obligation—specifically, the provision of a prohibited export subsidy—gives rise to a rebuttable presumption of adverse effects. This presumption follows the burden of proof assignment in the Domestic International Sales Corporation (DISC) and related cases, discussed in chapter 3. In other words, adverse effects are presumed to exist when a signatory violates its code or GATT obligations with respect to export subsidies. The country that gives a prohibited export subsidy must attempt to show that its subsidies have no adverse effects on the trade of the complaining country. There is an exception to this general rule, however: in the case of a developing country, adverse effects must be shown to exist by positive evidence brought forth by the complaining country (code Article 14:4).

The code does more than devise a new label, adverse effects, to describe preexisting grounds for retaliation by GATT members. In instances where adverse effects cause nullification or impairment, or serious prejudice, code Article 8:4 states that:

The adverse effects to the interests of another signatory required to demonstrate nullification or impairment[26] or serious prejudice may arise through:

(a) the effects of the subsidized imports in the domestic market of the importing signatory;

(b) the effects of the subsidy in displacing or impeding the imports of like products into the market of the subsidizing country; or

(c) the effects of the subsidized exports in displacing[27] the exports of like products of another signatory from a third-country market.[28]

---

26. Signatories recognize that nullification or impairment of benefits may also arise through the failure of a signatory to carry out its obligations under the General Agreement or this Agreement. Where such failure concerning export subsidies is determined by the Committee to exist, adverse effects may, without prejudice to paragraph 9 of Article 18 below, be presumed to exist. The other signatory will be accorded a reasonable opportunity to rebut this presumption.
27. The term "displacing" shall be interpreted in a manner which takes into account the trade and development needs of developing countries and in this connection is not intended to fix traditional market shares.
28. The problem of third-country markets so far as certain primary products are concerned are dealt with exclusively under Article 10 below.

The concrete meaning of this language remains to be elucidated in future cases brought before the Subsidies Committee. It seems fair to speculate that the concept of adverse effects will ultimately be defined by the committee at least to include the case of lost sales traceable to subsidized competition, whether or not firms in the complaining country are experiencing an absolute or relative decline in sales, employment, or profits.

It should be pointed out that footnote 28 to code Article 8 relegates agricultural subsidies that affect third-country markets to the relaxed trade-impact standard of code Article 10. However, agricultural subsidies that affect conditions in the complaining country's market, or in the subsidizing country's market, are properly addressed by the adverse effects standard of Article 8.

Equitable Share and Price Undercutting

The most relaxed trade-impact standard in the code—relaxed in the sense of tolerating a high level of trade impact—was inherited from GATT Article XVI:3, which in turn traces its ancestry to the unratified Havana Charter (Butler 1969, p. 92). Article XVI:3 provides that subsidized agricultural exports are tolerable as long as they do not afford the subsidizing country "more than an equitable share of world trade" by comparison with a "previous representative period." Following this precedent, Article 10:1 of the 1979 Subsidies Code accepted the notion that, so long as an agricultural subsidy gave the exporting country no "more than an equitable share of world export trade," it was tolerable by GATT standards.

The question whether "equitable share" should be interpreted with reference to discrete national markets or the overall world market for a product has been debated since the inception of the GATT (John H. Jackson 1969, pp. 393–95). In 1955, the United States opposed strict rules—namely a reference to individual markets—while the French favored more discipline on agricultural subsidies. "During the 1955 drafting session, the French delegation felt that the regulations relating to agricultural export subsidies, weak as they were, would lose all value if they did not prevent such subsidies from destroying the position of another exporter in individual markets."[11] By 1979, the US and French positions were reversed: the United States enthusiastically advocated an individual market standard, while France supported the world-market-share standard in the context of the 1979 code.

Since subsidies are seldom so massive that they visibly change world-market shares, and since the baseline concept of an equitable share is defined in sketchy fashion, a country that brings a complaint under GATT Article XV1:3 faces an uphill battle in establishing the requisite level of trade impact. In the Australian case against the EC sugar subsidies, brought in 1979 under GATT Article XVI:3, the panel could not establish a connection between the EC subsidy program and the discomfort felt by Australia, despite a wealth of evidence brought by Australia:[12]

(f) In the light of all the circumstances related to the present complaint, and especially taking into account the difficulties in establishing clearly the causal relationships between the increase in Community exports, the developments of Australian sugar exports and other developments in the world sugar market, the Panel found that it was not in a position to reach a definite conclusion that the increased share had resulted in the European Communities "having more than an equitable share of world export trade in that product", in terms of Article XVI:3.

This panel decision, among others, contributed to Australian and US enthusiasm for an individual market standard. The 1979 code did not adopt the individual market standard, but it somewhat narrowed the definition of equitable share of world export trade. Thus code Article 10:2(a) introduced a "displacement" concept:

---

11. GATT Doc. SR9/41 (1955), p. 6.

12. Report of the Panel, adopted on 6 November 1979, L/4833.

(a) "more than an equitable share of world export trade" shall include any case in which the effect of an export subsidy granted by a signatory is to displace the exports of another signatory bearing in mind the developments on world markets;

Moreover, the code added a new impact standard. Article 10:3 provides that subsidies should not result in the sale of primary products at prices materially below prevailing prices:

Signatories further agree not to grant export subsidies on exports of certain primary products to a particular market in a manner which results in prices materially below those of other suppliers to the same market.

The displacement language of code Article 10:2(a) and the price-undercutting standard of code Article 10:3 were put to the test in the 1983 panel decision in the case of Wheat Flour from the European Economic Community. The United States presented extensive evidence on the impact of European sales on the US market share in several individual markets, including a number of instances where the US market share dwindled remarkably while the EC share rose sharply. The United States further argued that its loss of market share reflected price undercutting and adduced a handful of specific tenders to support this assertion. The GATT panel was not persuaded:[13]

1. EEC export refunds for wheat flour must be considered as a form of subsidy which was subject to the provisions of Article XVI of the General Agreement as interpreted and applied by the Code.

2. It was evident to the Panel that the EC share of world exports of wheat flour has increased considerably over the period under consideration when application of EC export subsidies was the general practice, while the share of the US and other suppliers has decreased.

3. The Panel found, however, that it was unable to conclude as to whether the increased share has resulted in the EC "having more than an equitable share" in terms of [code] Article X, in light of the highly artificial levels and conditions of trade in wheat flour, the complexity of developments in the markets, including the interplay of a number of special factors, the relative importance of which it is impossible to assess, and, most importantly, the difficulties inherent in the concept of "more than equitable share."

4. The Panel concluded that, despite the considerable increase in EC exports, market displacement in the sense of [code] Article X:2(A) was not evident in the 17 markets examined by the Panel.

---

13. Bureau of National Affairs, *US Export Weekly*, 29 March 1983, pp. 1049–55.

5. With regard to price undercutting in the sense of [code] article X:3, the Panel found that, on the basis of available information there was not sufficient ground to reach a definite conclusion as to whether the EC had granted export subsidies on export of wheat flour in a manner which resulted in prices materially below those of other suppliers to the same markets.

The panel went on to note that solutions to disputes in the area of agricultural export subsidies could be achieved only by strengthening pertinent provisions of the code, particularly the definition of the concept more than an equitable share.[14] But the European Community is quite satisfied with the present equitable share standard and its loose interpretation. For example, in 1982, Sir Roy Denman, head of the EC Commission's Delegation to the United States, had this to say:[15]

A statement of US views on the Common Agricultural Policy handed to us and widely distributed to Congress in February this year said, "the US cannot tolerate the evolution of the CAP to a common export policy . . . . EEC export subsidies are the single most harmful of EC policies. The US must seek an acceptable plan and timetable for their elimination." All this goes a million miles beyond what was negotiated in the Tokyo Round when not only the United States and the Community as two countries which subsidize their agriculture to a comparable degree agreed together with nearly 80 other Contracting Parties on the "equitable share of the world market" as the limiting factor.

Even before the Wheat Flour panel made its decision, the United States, in January 1983, contracted to sell Egypt one million metric tons of stockpiled wheat flour at subsidized prices well below world market prices. This move struck hard at EC agricultural policies. Egypt is among the fastest growing markets for wheat flour and reportedly buys nearly 25 percent of total world exports of the commodity.[16] The US contract could cut France out of the Egyptian market for over one year. US Secretary of State George P. Shultz expressed US sentiments by saying that "when all the world is mad, 'tis folly to be sane."[17]

---

14. The panel's decision is reminiscent of the report in the case brought by Brazil against EC subsidies on sugar exports. See GATT Report L/5011, adopted 7 October 1980, especially paragraph (f) of the conclusion.

15. Denman (May 1982, pp. 6–7); also see Denman (September 1982, pp. 9–12).

16. *Washington Post*, 3 March 1983, p. C1; *Journal of Commerce*, 16 March 1983, p. 1; Bureau of National Affairs, *US Export Weekly*, 29 March 1983, pp. 1028–30.

17. Testimony before the Senate Foreign Relations Committee during hearings on the US–EC agriculture dispute, February 15, 1983. Ironically, the United States coupled its subsidized wheat flour exports with the requirement, dictated by the Cargo Preference Act, that half the wheat be shipped on high-cost (even though subsidized) US vessels—with the net result that the preference for US shipping partially offset the price advantage conferred through the subsidy on wheat flour. *Journal of Commerce*, 10 March 1983, p. 1.

The Community responded to the US action with a GATT complaint demanding trade compensation of $30 million and with a threat to increase the EC wheat flour subsidy and to subsidize the sale of wheat to traditional US markets. In fact, in February 1983, the European Community sold one million tons of wheat to China, assisted by the "normal" EC subsidy of $75 per ton and a "supplemental" subsidy of $5.60 per ton.[18]

In short, subsidies on agricultural exports remain virtually free of international discipline. The only effective remedy is self-help. At the GATT Ministerial meeting in November 1982, the United States vigorously raised the agricultural issue, only to secure agreement on a two-year study.[19] There is little indication that the study will make a breakthrough where other efforts have so frequently failed.

Differential Treatment of Developing Countries

The GATT has traditionally allowed developing countries special freedom in the pursuit of their commercial policies. This freedom, reflected in GATT Articles XVI and XVIII, in Part IV of the GATT, and in code Article 14, is rationalized by a generalized appeal to the infant-industry argument. According to this argument, a particular industry may not be competitive on world markets today, but, if encouraged by protective government policies, that industry may be competitive within a reasonable period of time.

In the context of subsidies policy, developing-country spokesmen urge, on infant-industry grounds, that their nations should be free to subsidize exports at least down to the world price (Organization of American States 1977; Bela Balassa 1978; Vijay Laxman Kelkar July–August 1980). In addition to infant-industry considerations, export subsidies further are justified as a means of offsetting distortions arising, for example, from overvalued exchange rates; expensive, domestically produced capital goods; high tariffs on imported capital goods; or excessively high wages in relation to local productivity levels.

In response both to infant-industry arguments and to distortion arguments, the code excuses developing-country signatories from the flat prohibition on export subsidies. Instead, the code requires a complaining signatory to show adverse effects as a prerequisite to multilateral authorization of relief. This burden of proof suggests that developed country signatories will bring few cases against developing-country export subsidies under Track II of the code.

It is seldom easy to show that developing-country subsidies have displaced the sales of a developed country firm. When palpable displacement exists in the

---

18. Bureau of National Affairs, *US Export Weekly*, 8 March 1983, p. 891. Also see *Washington Post*, 17 March 1983, p. E1.

19. *New York Times*, 30 November 1982, p. A1.

home market of the complaining firm, it may be only slightly harder for that firm to show material injury and seek unilateral relief under Track I of the code. In short, complaining signatories will probably invoke the code only against developing-country signatories that use export subsidies to capture large chunks of third-country markets.

In the US view, the higher trade-impact standard applied to developing-country signatories under Track II of the code was to be balanced by commitments of those signatories to phase out or at least freeze their export subsidies. If these commitments were not followed, then other signatories could appeal to the nullification or impairment doctrine, particularly GATT Article XXIII:l(c), or the nationally administered material injury standard for relief.

Brazil, the first developing-country signatory to the code, agreed to phase out an extensive range of subsidies.[20] Thereafter, commitments from other countries descended from phase-out clauses to freeze clauses to best-endeavors clauses, that is to say, from meaningful clauses to hortatory statements. (The commitments are reproduced in appendix B.)

One reason for this range in commitments was that the European Community, Japan, and Canada generally viewed the export subsidies of developing countries as mere irritants to the trading system.[21] Another reason was that US enthusiasm for a strong commitments policy weakened in 1980 when the Carter administration, searching for ways to improve relations with Pakistan in the wake of the Afghanistan invasion, accepted a purely hortatory commitment as Pakistan's admission ticket to the code.[22]

Finally, US policy on commitments from developing countries collapsed in 1981 after a skirmish with India on the most-favored-nation question. India had challenged the US policy of applying the code "conditionally"—that is, requiring code signature (in the case of developed countries) or a commitment on subsidies (in the case of developing countries) in return for a US injury test on subsidized imports. India argued that the most-favored-nation provision of GATT Article I requires that trade concessions, including the injury test, be granted unconditionally to all GATT members, and certainly to all code signatories, whether or not they undertake a separate commitment to limit their subsidies. Rather than risk losing the issue before a GATT panel, the Reagan administration acknowl-

---

20. Among early developing-country adherents to the code, Uruguay, like Brazil, agreed to phase out an extensive range of subsidies. Korea declared it had no subsidies, with the possible exception of short-term export credits.

21. The Europeans and Japanese took a more relaxed attitude toward developing-country subsidies in part because they have alternative administrative techniques for dealing with unwanted imports. The less intensive use of countervailing duties by Europe and Japan is no proof of their dedication to free trade.

22. The Pakistan commitment was reached bilaterally with the United States; it was not officially communicated to the Subsidies Code Committee.

edged Indian membership in the code on the basis of a modest best-endeavors agreement.[23]

The collapse of meaningful standards in the commitments process left the United States somewhat exposed in its bilateral negotiations with Mexico. The US executive branch has long wanted to fashion some discipline on aggressive Mexican subsidies. Key US senators adamantly insist that Mexican subsidies must be curbed. In the context of an International Monetary Fund (IMF) stabilization package negotiated in fall 1982, Mexico substantially devalued the peso and withdrew tax-rebate benefits offered under the Certificado de Devolución de Impuesto (CEDI) program. However, Mexico has not been willing to accept a general freeze or phase-out of its industrial subsidies. The United States finds it difficult to exact a precise commitment from Mexico, not only because best endeavors are accepted from industrially sophisticated India, but also because Mexico is America's third largest trading partner, is a large net importer of US goods and services, and since 1981 has suffered acute economic distress.

Conclusion

As a result of the give and take of political compromise, far too many trade-impact standards have been devised, and simplification would be most welcome. However, the escape clause test, substantial cause of serious injury, should not necessarily be the prerequisite for relief in unfair trade cases. Our suggestion is that national relief measures in subsidy cases should all require a finding of material injury (including the threat of material injury) caused by the subsidized trade, meaning an absolute decline in sales, profits, or employment from levels that would otherwise have been achieved. We would apply the material injury test to actions seeking national relief against the loss of markets abroad as well as at home.

In the case of the United States, these suggestions would require a material injury test in the countervailing duty statute as applied to imports from countries that are not signatories to the code. (The history of differential treatment for nonsignatories is discussed further in chapter 5.) These suggestions would also

---

23. In 1982, Uruguay pleaded changed circumstances as a justification for delaying its original schedule of phase-out commitments. It remains to be seen how the code committee will deal with changes in commitments, and how such changes will be viewed in the event national countervailing duty actions are brought. Again, in 1982, differences of opinion emerged between the United States and Brazil as to what incentive programs were covered under the Brazilian declaration, and whether Brazil could stretch out the timetable for eliminating its export subsidies. In parallel with the 1982 GATT Ministerial meeting, the United States accepted Brazil's position in exchange for Brazilian agreement that services trade would be put on the agenda for future GATT discussions. See US General Accounting Office (1983), pp. 13–16.

require a material injury test in the application of section 301 of the Trade Act of 1974 (an omnibus relief provision also discussed in chapter 5).

By contrast, a somewhat lower trade-impact standard should suffice for relief measures authorized multilaterally. The reason for a different and lower trade-impact standard is that the authorization of multilateral countermeasures will presumably receive closer scrutiny and proceed on a more deliberate pace than the authorization of national countermeasures. Each country to the dispute should have reasonable discovery rights, monitored by the GATT Secretariat, with respect to the commercial experience of the other country. If a country were unwilling to supply appropriate information, allegations on that point would be taken against it.

Furthermore, adverse impact, defined in terms of lost sales or lower prices, for particular firms, should provide the touchstone for multilateral relief. The burden to prove or disprove adverse impact should depend on the type of subsidy in question and the share of the relevant market accounted for by the subsidizing country. For example, adverse impact would be presumed to exist, subject to rebuttal, for all export subsidies (that is to say, subsidies that preferentially favor foreign over domestic sales). In addition, adverse impact would be presumed to exist for any other subsidy if the subsidizing country accounts for more than, say, 20 percent of the relevant market.

In all other instances, the complaining country should bear the burden of proving an adverse impact. This suggestion would replace the test now applied that distinguishes between developed and developing countries. Instead, the distinction would be made in terms of market share. If a country takes only a small share of the relevant market, then positive proof would be required of adverse impact. On the other hand, if the country takes a big share of the relevant market, then the subsidy would be presumed to have an adverse impact, subject to rebuttal.

To illustrate, if crankshaft sales to country A by firm X (located in country B) accounted for 20 percent of country A's market, and if country A brought a complaint against country B's subsidization of its crankshaft industry, that subsidy would be presumed to have an adverse impact on country A. To prepare its case, country A could inquire as to firm X's sales experience and country B's subsidy programs. Similarly, country B could obtain data on crankshaft sales within country A.

The Definition and Discipline
of Export Subsidies

As early as 1776, Adam Smith condemned export bounties as another wasteful expedient of the mercantile system.[1] But the exercise of defining and limiting "export subsidies," namely government incentive programs that favor export sales over domestic sales, did not begin until the nineteenth century. This task was originally inspired not by high-minded notions of comparative advantage but by the mercantile notion that subsidies might undercut "legitimate" tariffs.

The most offensive practice of the time was the widespread European custom of giving excessive rebates for indirect taxes or duty drawbacks upon the export of merchandise. The treaty of 1862 between France and the German Zollverein was perhaps the first treaty to contain an antibounty provision. In the next sixty years, some 29 bilateral commercial treaties were negotiated with similar clauses (Jacob Viner 1923, pp. 166–67). The Brussels Sugar Convention, signed in 1902, was an early multilateral attempt to limit export subsidies (Peter Buck Feller 1969, p. 21).

Unilateral steps were also taken. In 1890, the United States enacted a flat rate countervailing duty to offset bounties paid on the exportation of sugar. The US statute was amended in 1897 to cover all exports and to equate the duty with the subsidy. The statute was reenacted in 1909 and 1913 without alteration. In 1922 the statute was amended to cover subsidies on manufacture or production, as well as on exportation (Viner 1923, p. 169; Feller 1969, pp. 22–23). Meanwhile, India, British South Africa, Switzerland, Spain, France, Japan, and other countries enacted similar legislation.

After World War II, the development of international standards defining both permissible and impermissible practices began in earnest. Article VI:3 of the General Agreement on Tariffs and Trade (GATT), drafted in 1947, sanctioned the national imposition of countervailing duties "for the purpose of offsetting

---

1. Adam Smith, *An Inquiry into the Nature and Causes of the Wealth of Nations*, vol. 2, ed. J. Rogers (1869), p. 80, cited in Peter Buck Feller (1969, p. 20).

any bounty or subsidy bestowed, directly or indirectly, upon the manufacture, production, or export of any merchandise." However, Article VI:6(a) required, as a prerequisite to the imposition of a countervailing duty, that the subsidization must "cause or threaten material injury to an established domestic industry, or . . . retard materially the establishment of a domestic industry."

Article VI:4 specified that the exemption of exported products from duties or taxes "borne by the like product" domestically is not a subsidy. By implication, exemption of taxes not borne by the like product (for example, direct taxes on producer income) would entail a subsidy. A note to Article VI stated that multiple currency practices could entail an export subsidy. Article XVI:1 imposed a notification requirement for any subsidy "which operates directly or indirectly to increase exports . . . or to reduce imports," and provided that, if the subsidy causes "serious prejudice," the party granting the subsidy shall discuss "the possibility of limiting the subsidy."

In 1955, section B of Article XVI, consisting of paragraphs 2, 3, 4, and 5, was opened for acceptance by members of the GATT. By 1957, these provisions were accepted by most of the developed country signatories to GATT. Not until November 19, 1960, however, was a declaration signed giving effect to the new provisions, and the declaration did not enter into force until November 1962.[2] Signatories to section B of Article XVI agreed not to grant export subsidies, other than on primary products.[3]

The new Article XVI:4 improved upon the old Article XVI:1, but unfortunately the new language articulated a test adapted from the classic definition of dumping, namely the bilevel pricing test, as a means of identifying export subsidies. Under the bilevel pricing test, the hallmark of an export subsidy is the sale of goods abroad at a lower price than the sale of the same goods at home. This test proved unworkable, both because subsidies can appear in forms other than price competition and because published trade and production statistics seldom permit a detailed comparison between domestic and export prices. Such data are closely held by individual companies, and GATT members have no means to compel discovery of these commercial secrets from one another.

In 1960, a Working Party Report (GATT Secretariat 1961) designated certain practices as export subsidies, falling within the realm of Article XVI:4, and implicitly downgraded the bilevel pricing test for the enumerated items. Just as the countervailing duty language of Article VI tracked the US statute, so too a

---

2. For the legal history, see E. Bruce Butler (1969, pp. 90–91); John H. Jackson (1969, section 15.3); Feller (1969, pp. 54–57).

3. A number of countries accepted section B of Article XVI with reservations. For example, the US acceptance of Article XVI:4 contained a reservation with respect to export subsidies paid to cotton textile manufacturers to offset the high domestic cost of cotton resulting from the US price support program. US cotton sold on world markets was, at that time, priced below the support price level. See GATT Doc. PROT/2/Rev. 3, para. 42.01 (1967).

number of items in the 1960 Working Party Report reflected earlier US counter-vailing duty decisions (Matthew J. Marks and Harald B. Malmgren 1975).

In 1979, the Illustrative List to the Subsidies Code embellished and updated the 1960 Working Party List. The Subsidies Code essentially abandoned the bilevel pricing test for enumerated export subsidies. Nevertheless, the test may linger on for those export subsidies that are prohibited solely by virtue of the catchall item (l) in the list (see the next section).

International negotiators attempting to define and discipline subsidies have all faced the same basic questions:

☐ What practices are permitted?

☐ What practices are proscribed, only if they have a significant trade impact (potentially troublesome subsidies)?

☐ What practices are proscribed per se (export subsidies)?

Drawing a line between permitted practices and practices that are proscribed only when they have a significant trade impact comes down to defining objectionable *domestic* subsidies. This question is addressed in chapter 4. By contrast, the enumeration of practices that are proscribed per se (as well as when they have a trade impact) comes down to defining objectionable *export* subsidies, the subject of this chapter.

The Bilevel Pricing Test

As mentioned earlier, GATT Article XVI:4 labels, as objectionable export subsidies, those fiscal subventions that result in lower export prices than home prices. This so-called bilevel pricing test proved exceptionally difficult to apply in practice. Neither the 1979 Code on Subsidies and Countervailing Duties nor its Illustrative List refers to the bilevel pricing criterion of GATT Article XVI:4. Textual silence does not mean that the role of bilevel pricing as a litmus test for identifying objectionable export subsidies was ignored.

Some delegations, notably the United States, argued in the 1979 code nego-tiations that the bilevel pricing criterion should be dropped, because the existence of a differential between home and export prices is often difficult to prove. In the negotiations, other delegations, including the European Community, strongly supported the bilevel pricing criterion, on the grounds that differential pricing is the hallmark of an export subsidy. However, the European Community suc-cessfully downplayed the importance of the bilevel pricing test in its complaint against the US Domestic International Sales Corporation (DISC). The conflict between the US and EC positions made an explicit resolution of the bilevel pricing test impossible.

In the face of silence in the 1979 code and its Illustrative List, we interpret the code in the following manner. As to practices enumerated in the Illustrative List, including the first catchall provision, item (a), which lists "direct subsidies to a firm or an industry contingent upon export performance," the burden of disproving bilevel pricing has *at least* been shifted to the proponent of the practice. This approach would be consistent with the 1976 GATT panel reports on the DISC and related tax practices.[4] This approach would also be consistent with the proposition contained in note 26 to code Article 8 that the burden of disproving the "adverse trade effects" of a violation of a code obligation rests with the country operating the scheme in question.

Under this interpretation, code signatories have contracted away any claim they might have had under GATT Article XVI:4 to require the complaining party to demonstrate bilevel pricing with respect to the enumerated items on the Illustrative List. Indeed, it is possible that signatories have even contracted away the right to demonstrate the *absence* of bilevel pricing as an affirmative defense against the charge that a particular practice is an export subsidy.

However, for practices falling within the last catchall provision, item (l) of the Illustrative List, which refers to "any other charge on the public account constituting an export subsidy in the sense of Article XVI of the General Agreement," the standards of Article XVI:4 are possibly retained. As to practices that are condemned only by virtue of item (l), it could well be argued that—consistent with Article XV1:4—the complaining party must offer a positive demonstration of bilevel pricing in order to sustain a charge that a particular practice entails an export subsidy. Another possibility, however, is that the reference to Article XVI is only a reference to the ancestral GATT concept of an export subsidy set forth in Article XVI:1, and that the ancestral concept does not include the bilevel pricing test of Article XVI:4, which was only opened for signature in 1955 (Jackson 1969, p. 371).

Practices That Are Not Prohibited: Can They Be Potentially Troublesome Subsidies?

In the evolutionary development of GATT subsidy standards, some practices were judged not to be export subsidies, and some practices were judged not to

---

4. The panels on DISC and related tax matters grappled with the interpretation of bilevel pricing in the context of Article XVI:4. The panels noted that the Contracting Parties adhering to the 1960 Working Party List had agreed that the practices "generally are to be considered subsidies" and therefore could be presumed to result in bilevel pricing. The panel concluded that the burden of disproving the existence of bilevel pricing was, by implication, shifted to the country providing the subsidy. Jackson (1978), among other observers, has criticized the panel reasoning for erecting this presumption against the DISC.

be potentially troublesome subsidies. As an example of the latter category, the precept that the nonexcessive remission of indirect taxes is not a potentially troublesome subsidy was extended to cover value-added taxes (VAT) by item (g) of the 1979 Illustrative List. The rule in item (g) represents an outgrowth of GATT Article VI and the 1960 Working Party Report, both of which in turn codified long-accepted practice that distinguished between excessive and nonexcessive tax remissions.

But other practices that are defined by the Illustrative List *not* to be prohibited export subsidies are not necessarily excluded from the broader category of potentially troublesome subsidies. Four such practices are noteworthy in the Illustrative List:

☐ in respect of item (d), the provision of goods for use in the manufacture of exports on terms less favorable than the world market price, but still subsidized

☐ in respect of item (i), the allowance of duty drawback on identical goods of domestic origin that are incorporated in exports

☐ in respect of item (j), the provision of credit guarantees or exchange risk insurance on terms inadequate, but not "manifestly" inadequate, to cover operating costs of insurance programs

☐ in respect of item (k), the provision of export credits at rates below the cost of money to government, but equal to or above the interest rate norms in the Organization for Economic Cooperation and Development [OECD] Arrangement or the OECD Ships Understanding.

In terms of conferring a benefit on the receiving industry, each of the enumerated practices involves a subsidy. But by GATT definition, none of the practices involves a prohibited export subsidy.

Just because a practice confers a benefit and might be defined in academic circles as a subsidy does not mean it is potentially troublesome. On the other hand, just because a practice is not a prohibited export subsidy does not exclude it from the realm of potentially troublesome subsidies. Specific practices must be put in their proper categories as cases arise. Practices that are defined as potentially troublesome, even though they do not qualify as export subsidies, are liable to the national imposition of countervailing duties upon a showing of material injury. Further, as jurisprudence evolves, potentially troublesome subsidies that deprive a country of third-country markets should eventually be subject to both national and multilateral retaliation.

The drafters of the 1979 code were unable to agree on a general definition of potentially troublesome subsidies. Fine points, such as the overlap between practices permitted and proscribed by the Illustrative List, and the definition of the more general category of all potentially troublesome subsidies, are simply not addressed in the text of the 1979 code. A distinction should be drawn, however, between such practices as duty-drawback provisions and border tax adjustments, which are permitted by the Illustrative List and have enjoyed long international acceptance, and more recent practices such as the provision of official export credits or exchange risk insurance, which were simply not sufficiently egregious to warrant the label of prohibited export subsidy. Practices of the former type would seem not to be potentially troublesome subsidies at all and thus should not be liable to countervailing duties. Practices of the latter type would seem to fall within the definition of potentially troublesome subsidies, and thus should be liable to countervailing duties. Whether national and international jurisprudence evolves along these lines remains to be seen.[5]

Prohibited Export Subsidies and Permitted Export Incentives

Another unresolved issue is the relation between proscribed and permitted practices in the Illustrative List. What is the status of a practice that is implicitly permitted by the language of one item on the list but explicitly forbidden by the language of another item?

Suppose a country administers its export inflation insurance scheme—namely a scheme to compensate exporters for domestic cost inflation that occurs between the time the order is booked and the goods are manufactured—through the tax system. A company wishing to join the scheme pays an additional tax. When the company has a claim, it simply takes a credit against its direct tax liability.

Suppose further that the premiums collected through the tax system are not "manifestly" inadequate to cover the long-term operating costs and losses of the insurance program. Is this scheme permitted under paragraph (j) of the Illustrative List, which relates to government-supported export inflation insurance? Or is this scheme proscribed under paragraph (e), which limits direct tax incentives?

---

5. A similar overlap exists between practices permitted by the Illustrative List and proscribed by the Antidumping Code. In such cases, it seems clear that the Antidumping Code takes precedence. For example, as we previously noted, item (d) of the Illustrative List permits governments to provide goods or services at world prices to their exporters. Thus, for example, governments may subsidize the price of steel used in export production by a margin equal to the difference between the domestic and world price of steel. However, to the extent that this leads to differential pricing of finished products between home and export markets, the practice squarely offends Article 2(a) of the Antidumping Code:
For the purposes of this Code a product is considered as being dumped . . . if the export price of the product exported from one country to another is less than the comparable price . . . for the like product when destined for consumption in the exporting country.

The drafters of the Illustrative List were unable to agree on a hierarchical scheme to resolve such potential inconsistencies. But in light of the disciplinary intent of the Illustrative List, the better view would give priority to the prohibitive, rather than the permissive, item in the list. Signatories should not be allowed to claim that their practices are the "functional equivalent" of a permitted export incentive. If they want the benefits of the permitted practice, they should enact it into law. Otherwise, it would prove more difficult to set meaningful boundaries on export subsidy practices.

Border Tax Adjustments

The exercise in drawing lines between permitted and proscribed export incentives historically started with the attempt to define permissible border tax adjustments. Border tax adjustment rules identify which taxes may be rebated on exports and imposed on imports.

Defining the permissible exemption, remission, or deferral of taxation on export activities has provided entertainment in GATT circles for three decades and no end of scholarly literature (see, for example, Feller 1969; Butler 1969; George N. Carlson, Gary Clyde Hufbauer, and Melvin B. Krauss 1976; Jackson 1978; Thomas Kwako 1980; Edwin S. Cohen and Michael D. Hawkin 1982). It is worth reflecting a moment on the possible border tax adjustment rules that might have been adopted.

At one extreme, nations might have agreed to prohibit the rebate of all taxes and duties. This extreme would be associated with the strict *origin* principle for border tax adjustments. (Under the strict origin principle, taxes are collected only by the country in which the goods are produced.)[6] Or the opposite path could have been taken, and nations might have permitted adjustment at the border for all taxes. This extreme would be associated with a full *destination* principle for border tax adjustments. (Under the full destination principle, taxes are collected only in the country in which goods are consumed.)[7] The current international

---

6. Under a strict origin principle, the taxing authority for traded goods would rest exclusively with the country of production. Thus, any charges levied by a national government in pursuit of its domestic policies would be reflected in the prices of its exported goods. No border adjustments for taxes or duties, no free trade zones, and no offshore assembly provisions would be permitted. Under a strict origin principle, any government practice that directly or indirectly resulted in an export price lower than the domestic price would be subject to offsetting measures by importing countries.

7. Under a full destination principle, the taxing authority for internationally traded goods would rest exclusively with the country of consumption. The exporting country would rebate, and the importing country would levy, all direct and indirect taxes on goods traded internationally at the same rate as the taxes levied on goods produced domestically.

system falls between the extremes of the strict origin and the full destination principles.

At the core of the current system is a compromise—a partial adoption of the destination principle for border tax adjustments. Adjustment is permitted only for duties and indirect taxes "borne by the like product" when sold domestically (GATT Article VI:4), not for direct taxes or *"taxes occultes."* By way of definition, direct taxes are taxes imposed on the income of firms and individuals. *Taxes occultes* are taxes imposed on various components of production costs. Indirect taxes are taxes imposed on products. (The distinction between *taxes occultes* and indirect taxes is discussed further in the next section.) Like the GATT, the European Common Market also permits the rebate of indirect taxes on intra-EC trade, but not direct taxes or *taxes occultes.*[8]

Under this partial destination principle, the authority to tax traded goods lies primarily in the country of consumption, not in the country of production. Indirect taxes and duties may be levied by the country of consumption and may be rebated on exports and imposed on imports. But direct taxes and social welfare charges can be assessed only in the country of production and may not be rebated on exports or imposed on imports.

Under the partial destination principle of taxation—applied to indirect taxes and duties—domestic and imported goods are taxed in the country of consumption at the same rate and in the same manner, thus avoiding discrimination between producers located at home and producers located abroad. Similarly, exports are excused from indirect taxes and duties so that domestic producers for the international market are not hampered in their efforts to sell abroad. However, partial adoption of the destination principle means that direct taxes can neither be imposed on imports nor rebated on exports.

Partial adoption of the destination principle is carried out by Article VI:4 of the GATT, which permits adjustments for internal taxes "borne by the like product" (for example, taxes levied on the sale of products). Article VI:4 provides that the exemption or refund for exported goods of taxes "borne by the like product" when consumed internally shall not give rise to antidumping or countervailing duties:

4. No product of the territory of any contracting party imported into the territory of any other contracting party shall be subject to anti-dumping or countervailing duty by reason of the exemption of such product from duties or taxes borne by the like product when destined for consumption in the country of origin or exportation, or by reason of the refund of such duties or taxes.

---

8. Article 96, Treaty of Rome, 298 UNTS. See Feller (1969, pp. 57–58).

Moreover, the note to GATT Article XVI specifically declares that the exemption or remission of taxes "borne by the like product" is not a subsidy:

The exemption of an exported product from duties or taxes borne by the like product when destined for domestic consumption, or the remission of such duties or taxes in amounts not in excess of those which have accrued, shall not be deemed to be a subsidy.

On the other hand, Article VI:4 does not permit border adjustments for internal taxes not borne by the product (for example, taxes levied on firms and individuals). The implicit GATT distinction between taxes "borne by the like product" and other taxes was made explicit in items (e), (f), (g), and (h) of the 1979 Illustrative List. Thus, the exemption of exports from direct taxes and *taxes occultes*, and the levy of such taxes on imports, is prohibited. Further, the 1979 Illustrative List classifies as a subsidy:

(f) The allowance of special deductions directly related to exports or export performance, over and above those granted in respect to production for domestic consumption, in the calculation of the base on which direct taxes are charged.

In other words, if a country allowed tax depreciation at a more rapid rate for equipment engaged in export production than for equipment engaged in domestic production, that practice would offend item (f).[9] But this restriction only applies to direct taxes. Item (g) specifically permits border adjustments for value-added and other final stage indirect taxes levied on goods entering international commerce. These provisions illustrate the fundamental dichotomy in the international treatment of direct and indirect taxes.

By common assumption, border tax adjustments on the import and export side should be symmetrical, but nowhere in the GATT is this assumption spelled out. In other words, the GATT rules allow, but do not require, symmetry. Articles II and III, governing national treatment of internal taxes, provide that:

Article II

2. Nothing in this Article shall prevent any Contracting Party from imposing at any time on the importation of any product:

---

9. In 1983, in response to criticism over Japan's huge trade surplus, the Japanese finance ministry ended a provision that allows companies to deduct 28 percent of income derived from exports of technology developed under a foreign license. At the same time, the finance ministry ended another provision that allowed 1.22 percent of export sales income to be set aside in tax-exempt reserves. These two provisions offended items (f) and (e) of the Illustrative List, respectively. They enabled corporate tax savings of 27 billion yen in 1981 (about $108 million, at $1.00 = 250 yen). *Asahi Evening News*, 8 July 1983.

(a) a charge equivalent to an internal tax imposed consistently with the provisions of paragraph 2 of Article III in respect of the like domestic product or in respect of an article from which the imported product has been manufactured or produced in whole or in part; . . .

Article III

2. The products of the territory of any Contracting Party imported into the territory of any other Contracting Party shall not be subject, directly or indirectly, to internal taxes in excess of those applied, directly or indirectly, to like domestic products. Moreover, no Contracting Party shall otherwise apply internal taxes or other internal charges to imported or domestic products in a manner which affords protection to domestic production.

In principle, a GATT member could impose its domestic indirect taxes on imported goods but not rebate them on exported goods, or vice versa. In practice, most GATT members do both.

The GATT distinction between direct and indirect taxes, and between types of indirect taxes, was at one time thought to correspond to the economic incidence of the respective taxes in an economy closed to international trade. Conventional wisdom held that indirect taxes are largely shifted forward to consumers, while direct taxes are largely shifted backward to producers. More recent analysis suggests that the incidence of various taxes is not so straightforward. Direct, as well as indirect, taxes can be shifted either forward or backward in a closed economy. The outcome depends on the response of factor supplies and product demand to the imposition of the tax.

More importantly, in an economy open to international trade, rules on tax adjustment at the border can themselves have a strong effect on how a tax is shifted. If the economy is small relative to the world market, it will be a "price-taker" for internationally traded goods. In these circumstances, if a levy is imposed on imports and rebated on exports, and if that levy corresponds, for example, to the corporate income tax, then internal prices for internationally traded goods produced by the corporate sector will rise to reflect the tax. As a result of border tax adjustments, the corporate income tax—a direct tax—will be fully shifted forward to domestic consumers. Conversely, if no border adjustment is made for a sales tax, then domestic firms facing price competition from abroad will simply have to absorb the tax. In other words, workers and owners in the industry will have to accept lower earnings. As a result, the sales tax will be shifted back to labor and capital in the industry. From an economic standpoint, border tax adjustment rules determine the nature and extent of tax shifting for traded goods, rather than vice versa (Carlson, Hufbauer, and Krauss 1976).

The difficulty of drawing valid economic distinctions between types of taxes has led to continuing international dispute over appropriate border tax adjustment rules. The United States, which relies more heavily on direct taxes as a proportion of total taxes than Japan and Europe, has argued that current international practice disadvantages US trade, since direct taxes may not be adjusted at the border.

It is difficult to substantiate the claim that US exports are permanently reduced, or that US imports are permanently increased, by the current border adjustment rules. Overall, any general trade advantage initially enjoyed by countries using indirect taxes is likely, over a period of years, to be offset by general adjustment mechanisms, notably domestic price level and exchange rate changes. (Exchange rate changes can take place continuously under a flexible rate system or in discrete steps under an adjustable peg system.) For the same reason, it would be difficult for Europe to argue that full adoption of the destination principle would confer a permanent advantage to US exports and a permanent disadvantage to European exports. Again, general adjustment mechanisms would largely offset any initial impact.

Even after general adjustment mechanisms have come into play, however, particular sectors may be permanently advantaged or disadvantaged by border tax adjustment rules, simply because the level of taxation is not uniform for all sectors. In reality, therefore, the battle over appropriate border tax adjustment rules is a microeconomic contest between competing industries, not a macroeconomic contest over the balance of trade. Heavily taxed industries benefit most when maximum tax adjustments are made at the border. Lightly taxed industries benefit most when minimum tax adjustments are made at the border.

In light of these observations, how should international rules be designed to regulate border tax adjustments? We believe that countries should enjoy a wide degree of "fiscal sovereignty," in the sense that they should be free to tax certain activities heavily and other activities lightly, either through direct or indirect taxation. Countries should also be free to choose the type of tax imposed without necessarily subjecting their heavily taxed sectors to withering international competition. Under the present GATT rules, however, if a country chooses to impose heavy direct taxation on an industry, no border adjustment can be made. As a consequence, that industry will shrink in the face of untaxed foreign competition. The prospect of this outcome may improperly influence a country's choice of tax policy.

In order to restore fiscal sovereignty to its members, the international community should embrace the full destination principle as a *permissible* (not *mandatory*) method of border tax adjustment, for both direct and indirect taxes. Individual countries could then determine the extent to which they wish to shelter or expose their industries to the international consequences of high (and low) direct taxation. If a country wished to shelter its industries from the consequences of high taxation, it would provide destination principle adjustments for those taxes, whether applied directly or indirectly. If a country did not wish to shelter its industries, but instead wished to encourage the expansion or con-traction of particular sectors through the tax burden imposed, it would apply the origin principle both to direct and indirect taxes.

As supplementary rules, a country should be required to apply the same border adjustment rules to a given tax for all its industries. In other words, the border adjustment rules should be tax specific, not industry specific. Moreover, notifi-cation of any change in the status of a tax from origin to destination principle border adjustment (or vice versa) should be given well in advance to other GATT members, and other members should be allowed consultation rights as to appro-priate means of calculating border adjustments. These supplementary rules are meant to lend stability to the international system. Without some such restraints, countries might have a difficult time monitoring a variegated and shifting inter-national array of border tax adjustment rules, and planning their own investment programs and tax policies accordingly. (For further development of these themes, see Thomas Horst and Hufbauer 1983.)

Taxes Occultes

An obscure issue relating to border tax adjustments concerns the distinction between indirect taxes "borne by the like product" and all other indirect taxes, which are labeled *taxes occultes*. Nations generally agree that any final stage indirect tax is "borne by the like product" and therefore may be rebated when the product is exported. Nations do not agree, however, which indirect taxes levied on purchased inputs prior to the final stage are "borne by the like product." The disputed category of taxes includes, for example, indirect taxes on raw materials, components, fuel and electricity, advertising, and transport. To the extent these taxes are not considered to be "borne by the like product," they are labeled *taxes occultes* and, under present GATT rules, they may not be rebated on exports.

In the absence of a definitive international interpretation, the US Treasury Department, in administering the countervailing duty law before 1979, and the US Department of Commerce, since 1979, have followed the "physical incor-poration" principle to distinguish between indirect taxes borne by the like prod-uct and *taxes occultes*. The physical incorporation principle permits the rebate of indirect taxes on inputs that are physically incorporated in the final product. Physical incorporation is defined to include the raw materials and components actually incorporated in the final product (with a margin for waste and scraps), catalysts, and electricity used, for example, in electrolysis.

By contrast, sales, excise, stamp, and kindred indirect taxes on machinery, on fuel and electricity used to power machinery, and on other inputs not physically incorporated in the exported product, have been designated *taxes occultes*. Their rebate has been subject to countervailing duties under US law. The US approach to *taxes occultes* was adopted in item (h) of the Illustrative List, which embraced the physical incorporation test. Thus the rebate of "prior stage cumulative indirect taxes" is designated an export subsidy unless the inputs in question are physically incorporated in the exported product.

The physical incorporation test produces an anomaly in the treatment of prior stage indirect taxes that arise under a cascade tax system by comparison with a value-added tax system. In a cascade system, a sales tax is levied at each stage on the value of production. No credit is allowed for taxes paid at prior stages. In a VAT system, a tax is imposed at each stage on the value of production, but a credit is allowed at each stage for all prior stage taxes paid on purchased inputs. Thus, the tax burden in a VAT system only falls on the difference between realized proceeds and the cost (including taxes) of purchased inputs, that is to say, on value added in the enterprise.

Under GATT rules, the entire final stage VAT may be rebated (or exempted) upon export of the product. In addition, the exporter can collect the normal credit for all prior stage taxes paid on inputs. By contrast, under GATT rules, the final stage cascade tax may also be rebated, but only those taxes levied on inputs physically incorporated at a prior stage may be rebated. The distinction between rules applied to prior stage value-added taxes and cascade taxes is supposedly justified by the administrative inconvenience of verifying the calculation of cascade taxes on exported products. As if to emphasize the point, US authorities have recently insisted that any rebates paid on the export of an item must be justified, at the time of the rebate, by a reasonable calculation of the prior stage taxes (see *Certain Fasteners from India*, 45 Fed. Reg. 48607, 21 July 1980; *Industrial Fasteners Group, Etc. v. United States*, 525 F. Supp. 885, USCC 1981).

The physical incorporation test is inconsistent with the principle of "fiscal sovereignty" discussed earlier. Administrative convenience is an important issue, however, in apportioning both direct taxes and *taxes occultes* to units of output. The basic purpose of the physical incorporation test could be satisfactorily met by a test expressed in terms of the tax accounts maintained by governments. So long as the tax accounting system enables a government to trace the amount of indirect taxes (and direct taxes) levied at various stages of production, no administrative inconvenience should arise in rebating (or verifying the rebate of) the entire amount of tax on exports, and imposing the same tax on imports.

The DISC and Related Practices

In an attempt to mitigate the perceived tax disadvantages facing US exporters and the effects of an overvalued dollar, the United States adopted legislation in 1971 providing for the preferential taxation of export earnings, through a special status corporation known as the Domestic International Sales Corporation.[10] The DISC provides partial relief from the US corporate income tax levied on export profits, in the form of indefinite tax deferral on an interest-free basis. The lower effective tax rate was intended to compensate for the rebate of value-added and sales taxes received by exporters in many competing countries. According to US Treasury estimates, in DISC year 1981, the revenue cost of DISC was $1,650 million, while additional exports stimulated ranged between $7 billion and $11 billion.[11]

The United States believed that DISC was an answer to the advantages of a territorial tax system. Under the territorial approach, certain countries, such as France, Belgium, and the Netherlands, either exempt the earnings of their foreign subsidiaries from taxation or tax those earnings at a preferentially lower rate. While the territorial approach prevents the double taxation of foreign source earnings, it also exempts from taxation some portion of the sales income of exporters, when exports are routed (on paper) through tax haven subsidiaries. (For surveys of tax practices affecting exports, see Hufbauer 1975; US Senate Committee on the Budget 1975; John Mutti 1982; Cole and Corette 1982.)

The 1960 GATT Working Party agreed that the concept of export subsidy, as defined by Article XVI:4, includes "the remission, calculated in relation to exports, of direct taxes or social welfare charges on industrial or commercial enterprises." But the Working Party did not specifically address the question whether deferral of taxes on export earnings or the exemption of certain types of foreign source income from taxation would entail an export subsidy.

In 1972, the European Community and Canada charged that the DISC legislation violated the GATT prohibition on export subsidies. They argued that the indefinite deferral of taxes under the DISC was comparable to the total exemption of export earnings from taxation and thus constituted an export subsidy. The United States countered with the argument that the territorial tax practices of France, Belgium, and the Netherlands also acted as a subsidy on exports (Jackson 1978). A GATT panel in 1976 concluded that each country's tax practices violated Article XVI:4. As to the DISC:[12]

. . . the Panel considered that if the corporation income tax was reduced with respect to export related activities and was unchanged with respect to domestic activities for the internal market, this would tend to lead to an expansion of export activity. Therefore the DISC would result in more

---

10. For descriptive surveys, see Hufbauer (1980); Cohen and Hawkin (1982); and US Treasury Department (DISC Report). The Western Hemisphere Trade Corporation and the Export Trade Corporation were statutory precursors of the DISC; see Feller (1969, p. 45).

11. US Treasury Department (1983, DISC Report). DISC Year 1981 refers to activity reported in tax returns for years ending between July 1, 1980 and June 30, 1981.

12. This and subsequent quotations appear in GATT Documents L/4422–4425 (2 November 1976).

resources being attracted to export activities than would have occurred in the absence of such benefits for exports.

As to the tax practices of France and Belgium, the panel found that:

However much the practices may have been an incidental consequence of French (and Belgian) taxation principles rather than a specific policy intention, they nonetheless constituted a subsidy on exports because the . . . benefits to exports did not apply to domestic activities for the internal market.

The tax practices of the Netherlands also were found to violate Article XVI:

In circumstances where different tax treatment in different countries resulted in a smaller total tax bill in aggregate being paid on exports than on sales in the home market, the Panel concluded that there was a partial exemption from direct taxes since the Netherlands did not levy a tax on profits from export sales by foreign branches or subsidiaries when these were subject to tax abroad irrespective of whether these tax rights were exercised.

In order to clarify the international standard, the 1979 Illustrative List set forth the following positive statement of an export subsidy:

(e) The full or partial exemption, remission, or deferral specifically related to exports, of direct taxes[1] or social welfare charges paid or payable by industrial or commercial enterprises.[2]

1. For the purpose of this Agreement: the term "direct taxes" shall mean taxes on wages, profits, interest, rents, royalties, and all other forms of income, and taxes on the ownership of real property; . . . .

2. The signatories recognize that deferral need not amount to an export subsidy where, for example, appropriate interest charges are collected. The signatories further recognize that nothing in this text prejudges the disposition by the CONTRACTING PARTIES of the specific issues raised in GATT document L/4422 [The DISC Panel Report] . . . .

Footnote 2 goes on to state that the failure to charge arms-length prices can also give rise to a complaint under the Subsidies Code. The use of export sales subsidiaries located in tax haven countries is not directly attacked, but shipments to such subsidiaries at less than an arm's length price is proscribed.

Two academic commentators, Thomas Kwako (1980) and Dan Muchow (1981), concluded on the basis of the Illustrative List and the negotiating history then on the public record that the DISC was an export subsidy under the terms of item (e) of the 1979 Subsidies Code. This same conclusion was in fact stated in a confidential protocol to the Subsidies Code (the so-called "Hufbauer Agreement;" see appendix C). For domestic political reasons, US Trade Representative

(USTR) Reubin O'D. Askew later renounced the protocol (Kevin M. Harris 1983).
With respect to the tax systems of other countries, the United States has no doubt that the exemption, remission, or deferral of direct taxes constitutes a subsidy under US countervailing duty law.[13] Since US countervailing duty decisions have exerted considerable influence on the evolution of GATT standards, those decisions would seem to have some bearing on the definition of an export subsidy. Indeed, in the last months of the Carter administration and continuing in to the early months of the Reagan administration, behind-the-scenes efforts were made to negotiate a DISC settlement on the basis of the renounced protocol. Finally, on December 6, 1981, the panel reports were accepted by the GATT Council with this qualifying statement:

The Council adopts these reports on the understanding that with respect to these cases, and in general, economic processes (including transactions involving exported goods) located outside the territorial limits of the exporting country need not be subject to taxation by the exporting country and should not be regarded as export activities in terms of Article XVI:4 of the General Agreement. It is further understood that Article XVI:4 requires that arm's-length pricing be observed, i.e., prices for goods in transactions between exporting enterprises and foreign buyers under their or the same control should for tax purposes be the prices which would be charged between independent enterprises acting at arm's length. Furthermore, Article XVI:4 does not prohibit the adoption of measures to avoid double taxation of foreign source income.

Still, reaching a settlement of the DISC dispute and the underlying issues proved exceedingly difficult. Important US exporting firms feel they were bested on six occasions:

☐ when the original GATT was drafted to permit the rebate of taxes "borne by the like product" but not direct taxes

☐ when the European Community subsequently adopted a value-added tax and exempted exports from taxation

☐ when the US Supreme Court, in deciding *Zenith Radio v. United States* (437 US 443, 1978), upheld the long-standing US administrative practice that the rebate of an indirect tax is not a subsidy under US law

☐ when the US Treasury Department, in the wake of the *Zenith* case, defined the rebate of value-added taxes as not a subsidy, an approach that was ratified in item (g) of the 1979 Illustrative List

---

13. See, for example, *Certain Electronic Products from Japan*, 40 Fed. Reg. 5378, 5 February 1975; *Certain Scissors and Shears from Brazil*, 42 Fed. Reg. 8634, 11 February 1977; *Ceramic Tile from Mexico*, 47 Fed. Reg. 20012, 10 May 1982.

☐ when the GATT panel, after assigning the burden of disproving bilevel pricing and adverse effects to the United States, found DISC a presumptive subsidy to the extent that interest was not charged on deferred taxes

☐ when the GATT panel's holding was codified as item (e) in the 1979 Illustrative List.

Reflecting the acute discontent of US firms, USTR General Counsel Donald E. deKieffer stated flatly, in May 1982, that DISC is not a subsidy.[14] According to the extraordinary doctrine advanced by way of explanation, the reference point for measuring an export subsidy is the territorial tax system. If DISC provides a lesser tax benefit than a territorial tax system, then DISC is simply not a subsidy at all.

The "functional equivalent" doctrine advanced by deKieffer might be admissible, if the purpose of GATT discipline were to strike an overall balance on subsidies provided by different national systems. But that has not been the GATT approach for three good reasons:

☐ In the grander assignment of instruments to targets, the goal of overall balance has been assigned to exchange rate movements.

☐ Precise measurement of each country's use of permitted export incentives is quite difficult.

☐ An overall balance approach could well stimulate a race to the bottom, defeating the purpose of the GATT and code.

The "functional equivalent" doctrine, if extended to other export subsidies, would have far-reaching consequences. One country's refund of social security taxes on its exports could be justified as the functional equivalent of another country's VAT exemption.[15] Or, to take a devastating extension of the argument, Brazil might justify a whole range of subsidies as the functional equivalent of an exchange rate devaluation.

In short, the functional equivalent argument would open the door to justifying a considerable range of subsidies by an appeal to general equilibrium analysis—finding a "second-best" solution in a "third-best" world. If such justifications could be offered for particular subsidies, then arguments advanced by imaginative

---

14. Bureau of National Affairs, *Daily Tax Report*, 6 May 1982, p. G–1. The "functional equivalent" argument advanced by deKieffer was considered and rejected by the DISC panel; see GATT Doc. L/4422 (2 November 1976).

15. A respectable case can be made that the value-added tax is just as much a direct tax on the firm as the corporate income tax or the social security tax. All three kinds of taxes are measured with respect to the earnings of capital and labor employed in the industry.

trade lawyers and economists would quickly dissolve the fabric of international discipline.

The better justification for DISC is that it represents a step towards full adoption of the destination principle of border adjustments for direct taxes. This justification, however, depends on international acceptance of the full destination principle, an acceptance which remains to be achieved.

Returning to the main story, in 1982 Canada asked the United States to notify DISC as a subsidy under code Article 7. At the time, the United States was grumbling about Canadian performance requirements imposed by the Foreign Investment Review Agency (FIRA). Moreover, shortly after the US Commerce Department announced its preliminary countervailing duty decisions in the European steel cases, the European Community asked GATT to sanction compensatory measures covering some $2 billion of US exports to Europe in retaliation against the DISC.[16]

Evidently, both the European Community and Canada found advantage in keeping the DISC issue alive to quell excessive US enthusiasm against *their* subsidies and related practices. Conceivably, a US decision to conform the DISC to the code would strengthen the US hand in the drive to limit subsidies through multilateral discipline. (See Jeffrey J. Schott 1982 for further development of this theme.)[17]

In fact, the United States could conform DISC to the GATT standard, with little reduction in tax benefits to US exporters, simply by exempting from tax the foreign source portion of export earnings and taxing at normal rates the domestic source portion. A proposal to this effect was circulated by the Reagan administration in March 1983.[18] The proposal was reduced to draft statutory language and a bill submitted by Congressmen Dan Rostenkowski (D-Ill.) and Barber B. Conable, Jr. (R-NY) in August 1983.[19]

Basically the administration's proposal calls for the creation of foreign sales corporations (FSC) with a corporate presence outside the United States. The export income of these firms (labeled "foreign-trade income" or FTI) would not be subject to US tax. In other words, the United States would adopt a territorial system of taxation for export profits. To ensure that this new system of export tax relief entails no greater revenue cost than the present DISC, the amount of tax-exempt FTI would be limited by formula to the larger of 17 percent of the combined taxable income of the foreign corporation and its related US supplier,

---

16. The steel cases were subsequently settled with a US–EC voluntary export restraint agreement, discussed in chapter 4.

17. In this connection, consider the Japanese elimination in 1983 of two tax incentives, referenced in note 9.

18. See *Tax Notes*, 14 March 1983 and 18 June 1983; *Collado Report*, November 1982.

19. Bureau of National Affairs, *Daily Reporter*, 4 August 1983.

or 1.35 percent of gross sales (but not more than 34 percent of combined taxable income).

The administration's proposal represents a useful interim measure, while the international community explores the adoption of the full destination principle for border tax adjustments. If and when this principle is fully accepted, countries could rebate all corporate income, social security, and other direct taxes incurred in the production of goods for export, and impose those same direct taxes on imports.

Duty-Drawback Provisions

Remitting duties on imported inputs, used to manufacture goods for export, enjoys long standing. In the United States, the duty-drawback provision was established in 1789 by the second statute enacted by Congress. As carried forward into the Tariff Act of 1930 (as amended), the law permits the rebate of "the full amount of the duties paid upon the merchandise . . . less one per centum of such duties," when goods using imported inputs are exported from the United States (19 USC § 1313). To obtain a duty drawback, a producer must export the final good within five years after the input is imported. Most other trading nations also use duty-drawback provisions to enable their domestic producers to acquire traded inputs free of tariff, thereby helping them compete in export markets.

Duty drawbacks not exceeding the amount of duty actually levied on the imported product are explicitly permitted by the GATT. Article VI:4 provides that:

4. No product of the territory of any contracting party imported into the territory of any other contracting party shall be subject to anti-dumping or countervailing duty by reason of the exemption of such product from duties or taxes borne by the like product when destined for consumption in the country of origin or exportation, or by reason of the refund of such duties or taxes.

The overrebate of duties, however, was characterized by the 1960 GATT Working Party as a subsidy liable to countervailing duties, in item (d) of the Working Party List, reproduced in appendix D. According to Feller (1969, p. 41):

The practice of granting tax rebates and customs duty drawbacks which exceed the exporter's tax or duty liability has frequently been used as a subsidy device. In a sense such overcompensation is nothing more than a direct subsidy payment in the guise of an otherwise legitimate border tax adjustment; but since it is typically used to hide subsidy elements behind sometimes complex and circuitous regulatory arrangements, it is accorded separate treatment.

Whether some of the duty drawbacks practiced today might have been characterized as overrebates under the 1960 Working Party's standards is an interesting question. For example, a US manufacturer may substitute *domestic* inputs for *imported* inputs in producing goods destined for export and still receive a refund of duty paid on the imported inputs. But such substitution is permitted only if those imported inputs are "of the same kind and quality as the domestic inputs . . . notwithstanding the fact that none of the imported merchandise may actually have been used in the manufacture or production of the exported articles" (19 USC § 1313). However, the producer must have used some of the imported merchandise within three years of its importation or forfeit the duty drawback for that merchandise. Moreover, as in the case of all other merchandise eligible for duty drawbacks, the producer must export the final good containing domestic substitute inputs "within five years after importation of the imported merchandise" (ibid.).

The United States first adopted the domestic substitution provision in the Tariff Act of 1930. Coverage initially was limited to sugar, nonferrous metals, and ores containing nonferrous metals. The provision responded to complaints of manufacturers that they could not use the existing duty drawback (at that time restricted to imported merchandise), due to the difficulty of maintaining separate inventories for domestic and imported merchandise.

In 1951, and again in 1956, a number of other fungible commodities were included in the domestic substitution provision. In 1958, the provision was expanded to cover all equivalent goods. Among the products that significantly benefit from the domestic substitution provision are petroleum and petrochemicals, followed by steel and motor vehicle stampings and assemblies.

In Japan, duty drawback is used for single import and reexport transactions. However, a manufacturer who intends to utilize imported inputs in continuous production of goods destined for export may apply to the ministry of finance to register the production facility as a bonded manufacturing warehouse. If approved (and most applications are), registration remains valid for two years. This method allows the manufacturer to avoid duty payment altogether on the imported inputs. This aspect of Japan's duty-drawback system resembles a tax-free trade zone.

In the European Community, duty-drawback provisions closely resemble United States practice. Virtually all goods are eligible for duty drawback, and domestic substitution is permitted. Duty drawback generally is not permitted in the European Community on goods eligible for preferential duty treatment under other statutes. For example, if goods are characterized under EC rules of origin as made in the European Community, although a portion actually represents components made elsewhere, they are not eligible for duty drawback.

From the standpoint of disciplining subsidies, it would have been better to forbid domestic substitution. Modern methods of accounting have made it much easier to distinguish between imported and domestically produced inventories. Only because domestic substitution provisions had become widespread in the United States, the European Community, the Nordic countries, and elsewhere, was the practice explicitly sanctioned in the Illustrative List to the 1979 Subsidies Code. Thus, item (i) permits the substitution:

. . . of home market goods equal to, and having the same quality and characteristics as, the imported goods . . . if the import and the corresponding export operations both occur within a reasonable time period, normally not to exceed two years.

By comparison with the international standard, "normally not to exceed two years," the US statute permits domestic substitution over a three-year period.

Offshore Assembly Provisions

The tariff schedules of nearly all developed countries provide for the assessment of duty solely on the foreign value added in those imports that contain domestically produced components. Under these provisions, duty is assessed only on the value of foreign processing or assembly, at the same tariff rate that would apply to the finished good, whether or not the finished good contained domestic value added.

Such provisions are based on the premise that duty should not be levied on domestic goods that enter into international trade for a limited time and are ultimately consumed in the country of production. (See J. M. Finger 1975, 1976, 1977; Joseph Grunwald and Kenneth Flamm forthcoming 1984.) While such provisions are premised on a theory of duty relief for domestic goods, they also contain an element of export incentive. (Duty relief is conditioned on the use of domestic rather than third-country components.)

In the United States, sections 806.30 and 807.00 of the tariff schedule govern the duty treatment of imports from offshore processing and assembly operations. Section 806.30 provides for the partial reduction of the dutiable value of nonprecious metals that are exported for processing and reimported into the United States for further processing. Duty assessment is based on the actual cost of the foreign processing to the US importer. Section 806.30 has continued in force without significant amendment since its enactment as part of the Tariff Act of 1930. Of the two tariff provisions, it is by far the less significant.

Section 807.00, the more important provision, was adopted in 1963 as part of a new US tariff schedule. This section had no actual statutory predecessor, but the basic principle became well established following a 1954 Customs Court decision (CD 1628, June 29, 1954). Section 807.00 provides that duty shall be assessed upon the full value of the imported article, less the cost or value of components originating in the United States. Thus, duty is levied only on the foreign value added in a finished product, not on the value of components fabricated in the United States.

There are two significant restrictions placed on the use of section 807.00. First, the component in question must be traceable to a US manufacturer. (This is enforced administratively by means of a certification procedure.) Second, the US component must not lose its physical identity during the assembly operation. (A US component in a finished product assembled abroad may be painted, for example, but it may not be altered in form.)

The tariff schedules of most of the EC countries and Japan contain provisions similar to, although generally more limited than, the US offshore processing and assembly provisions. In Japan, for example, goods must be licensed prior to exportation for assembly or processing abroad. Those goods are eligible for duty exemption, only if reimported by Japan during the one year following licensing. The United Kingdom also maintains strict eligibility requirements. Only a limited range of assembly and processing operations may be performed on British produced components, if the final product is to qualify for reduced import duties.

Canada offers normal duty reduction for offshore operations, but has carried the concept a huge step further. As described by Butler (1969, p. 104):

In 1963, Canada instituted an import duty remission plan in which automobile manufacturers who increased their exports of automobiles were granted rebates of import duties on a comparable value of imported automotive parts. These remissions were not related to the drawback of import duties imposed on the specific component parts of the exported article . . . .

The 1963 Canadian plan prompted a countervailing duty petition by a US manufacturing firm (29 Fed. Reg. 7249, 3 June 1964). The petition triggered latent US discontent over Canadian trade practices in the automotive industry. Eventually on March 9, 1965, the petition led to the United States-Canadian Automotive Products Agreement, commonly known as the Auto Pact (17 UST 1372, TIAS 6093; also see Feller 1969, p. 42; Butler 1969, p. 104; and Stanley D. Metzger 1967).

In the context of the Auto Pact, Canada replaced its duty-remission plan with a different form of export performance requirement (Butler 1969, p. 105). Some years later, however, the spirit of the old duty-remission plan reappeared. In September 1978, Canada formally instituted a new duty-remission plan applicable solely to Volkswagen's trade in automotive parts and finished vehicles.[20]

The Volkswagen plan provides for a reduction in the dutiable value of all

20. Nissan Motor Company of Japan and Bavarian Motor Works of Germany also agreed to negotiate duty-remission plans with Canada, similar to the 1978 Volkswagen plan.

passenger automobiles imported into Canada by Volkswagen from any source. The amount of reduction in dutiable value is determined by the Canadian value of automotive components purchased in and exported from Canada by, or on behalf of, Volkswagen. The Canadian value of parts exported from Canada by Volkswagen during a model year is credited against the dutiable value of Volkswagen autos imported into Canada during that same model year, whether or not the imported Volkswagens actually contain Canadian parts. A formula, with a threshold level for parts exports, has been developed to govern the total amount of credit and subsequent duty reduction.

The Canadian Volkswagen scheme could be viewed as an export performance requirement (see below). For present purposes, it is worth contrasting the scheme with offshore assembly provisions provided by other nations. The offshore assembly provisions adopted by the United States, the EC states, Japan, and other developed countries are quite distinct from the Canadian duty-remission plan. Unlike the Canadian duty-remission plan, all other offshore assembly provisions stipulate that the domestically produced component be incorporated in the finished import. Since the primary aim of such provisions is to forgive duty on goods produced in the importing country, it seems logical that those goods be present in the imported product.

Neither the 1960 Working Party List nor the 1979 Illustrative List specifically covers offshore assembly provisions. Allowable duty and indirect tax rebates are phrased in terms of inputs in the manufacture of exports, not in terms of the subsequent use of an exported product as an imported good. Since all offshore assembly provisions contain an element of export incentive vis-à-vis third-country suppliers, it could be argued that they all offend the concept in the 1960 Working Party List of:

(b) the provision by governments of direct subsidies to exporters

or the concept in the 1979 Illustrative List of:

(a) the provision by governments of direct subsidies to a firm or an industry, contingent on exports.

Such a position would be extreme, however, given the principal purpose of the provisions. A more moderate position would distinguish between those offshore provisions that follow a physical tracing principle and those which, like the Canadian plan, condition a lower import duty on the export of goods that are never required to find their way back to the exporting country.

Shortly after introduction of Canada's auto duty-remission scheme, the United States complained to Canada and vaguely considered taking the case to GATT. Had such action been taken and a GATT decision been rendered, an international standard for offshore assembly provision might have been established. As it is, the definitive determination whether offshore assembly provisions are all proscribed, are all permitted, or are distinguished one from another, still awaits a panel decision under GATT auspices.

Meanwhile, a Canadian scheme similar to the Volkswagen plan, enacted in April 1980 and applicable to front-end loading construction equipment produced by manufacturers located in Canada, is now being challenged under section 301 of the US Trade Act of 1974. The challenger is a US manufacturer that does not qualify for Canada's duty remission, the J.I. Case Company of Wisconsin. In a July 1982 petition to the US Trade Representative's office, the J.I. Case Company argued that the Canadian practice acts as a subsidy on Canadian exports. That case awaits resolution under US law.

Officially Supported Export Credits

The evolution of discipline over official export credits has been ably chronicled by Axel Wallen and John M. Duff (1981), Orit Frenkel and Claude G.B. Fontheim (1981), Michael Czinkota (1982), and John L. Moore (forthcoming 1984). Here we can only touch on the main contours.

A Tour of GATT and OECD Understandings

The 1960 Working Party Report listed three export credit measures considered as subsidies (see appendix D):

(f) In respect of government export credit guarantees, the charging of premiums at rates which are manifestly inadequate to cover the long-term operating costs and losses of the credit institutions;

(g) The grant by governments (or special institutions controlled by governments) of export credits at rates below those which they have to pay in order to obtain the funds so employed;

(h) The government bearing all or part of the costs incurred by exporters in obtaining credit.

That these practices were unofficially proscribed did not prevent their open, widespread use during the 1960s and 1970s. No nation brought a GATT complaint, in part because GATT dispute settlement procedures are notoriously slow. Thus, the discipline of export credit practices was consigned first to the Berne Union (a group of export credit agencies) and then, in the 1960s and 1970s, to the Organization for Economic Cooperation and Development (OECD). Gradually, a system of discipline arose that involved international norms with respect to maturities, interest rates, down payments, and other dimensions, plus the positive obligation to notify derogations from those norms. The system also involved the all important opportunity for self-help, namely the right to offer a matching export credit subsidy.[21]

Building on the Berne Union experience (Moore forthcoming 1984; Butler 1969, p. 110), an International Arrangement on Guidelines for Officially Supported Export Credits (originally styled a "Consensus" or "Gentlemen's Agreement") was negotiated between major nations in 1975. The arrangement was revised in 1978, updated as to interest rates in 1980 and 1981, and substantially revised in 1982. (Appendix G contains the 1982 version.) All OECD nations now subscribe to this arrangement.

The arrangement sets forth a uniform schedule of minimum interest rates, minimum down payment levels, maximum maturities, and other "floor" terms for the extension of officially supported export credits.[22] If one exporting country proposes to derogate below the floor terms, it must first notify all other arrangement participants, thereby affording them an opportunity to offer matching terms. The prospect of terms being matched somewhat deters participants from derogating from the Arrangement. To be sure, a participant with a deep pocket might take the cynical view that it can outlast the others, but most derogations involve attempts to capture an order by modest concessions negotiated in a darkened room. The prospect of open notification and matching terms works against cozy cloakroom alliances.

The floor terms set forth in the Arrangement permit a degree of export credit subsidy, at least as measured by the standards of the 1960 Working Party Report. In fact, since the interest rates are uniform across exporting countries and currencies, it is almost inevitable that, at any given time, some participants can offer the minimum rates only on a subsidized basis. Nevertheless, the Acquinian approach of a just and uniform price appears to have supplanted, in day-to-day practice, the GATT antisubsidy standard. This could foreshadow developments in other export subsidy areas.

Item (k) of the Subsidies Code

Although the OECD export credit framework was far more effective than the GATT framework in disciplining export credit subsidies, the OECD norms on

---

21. Apart from the OECD exercise, countries within the European Community have agreed to limit their official export credit programs, as applied to sales *within* the Common Market, to the provision of credit guarantees only. This agreement serves to make the Common Market free of export credit subsidies provided by EC countries. Unfortunately, the European Community has objected to an extension of this principle to all industrial country members of the OECD Arrangement.

22. Floor interest rates apply to direct loans, not guarantees. Thus, low interest rate countries, such as Switzerland, Germany, and Japan, can guarantee private export credits in their respective currencies at interest rates below the OECD Arrangement floors without breeching the arrangement.

interests rates were considerably more lenient than the GATT Working Party standard of "cost of money to governments." The negotiators in the Tokyo Round thus faced the historical fact that the principal code of discipline in the sphere of export credits had been crafted within the OECD, but the OECD norms entailed a lower standard than the 1960 Working Party Report. By 1979, many countries were unwilling to condemn as export subsidies those practices condoned in the OECD. The Subsidy Code draftsmen thus agreed to incorporate the OECD Arrangement and the OECD Ships Understanding by reference, as a limited exemption from the cost of money to governments standard.

The language that accomplished this objective appears in item (k) of the Illustrative List:

(k) The grant by governments (or special institutions controlled by and/or acting under the authority of governments) of export credits at rates below those which they actually have to pay for funds so employed (or would have to pay if they borrowed on international capital markets in order to obtain funds of the same maturity and denominated in the same currency as the export credit), or the payment by them of all or part of the costs incurred by exporters or financial institutions in obtaining credits, in so far as they are used to secure a material advantage in the field of export credit terms.

Provided, however, that if a signatory is a party to an international undertaking on official export credits to which at least twelve original signatories to this Agreement are parties as of 1 January 1979 (or a successor undertaking which has been adopted by those original signatories), or if in practice a signatory applies the interest rate provisions of the relevant undertaking, an export credit practice which is in conformity with those provisions shall not be considered an export subsidy prohibited by this Agreement.

The precise wording of item (k) accomplished several objectives:

☐ It limited the exemption to "the interest rate provisions" of the OECD Arrangement and the OECD Ships Understanding.

☐ It enabled countries not members of the OECD Arrangement and the OECD Ships Understanding to avail themselves, for GATT purposes, of the same safe harbors.

☐ It provided for the future updating of the safe harbors, an event that has already happened in the OECD Arrangement.

☐ It provided for a weak injury test ("secure a material advantage") in the event of a departure from the basic GATT standard.

However, the drafting of item (k) left for future resolution several important questions. Two examples will illustrate the definitional questions still to be answered regarding export credits.

When Is the Safe Harbor Available?

Under what circumstances is a government applying the interest rate provisions of the OECD Arrangement and thus exempted, by the terms of item (k), from the higher GATT standard of cost of money to governments?

This question arose in concrete form when the New York Metropolitan Transportation Authority (MTA) invited bids on subway cars. In addition to a bid from the Budd Company from Troy, Michigan, bids were submitted from the Bombardier Company of Montreal, Canada, and from Francorail of Paris, both supported by official export credits. In each case, the official export credits were offered at 9.7 percent, an interest rate well below the OECD Arrangement norm then applicable of 11.25 percent.

These bids raised the question whether either of the following export credit financing practices constitutes an export subsidy:

☐ rates below the OECD Arrangement rate but notified in advance

☐ rates below the OECD Arrangement rate but in competition with another derogating country.

If notified in advance in accordance with the arrangement (as both France and Canada did), or if offered to match a prior derogation as permitted by the arrangement (Canada claims France was the first to derogate; France points the finger at Canada), each export credit practice is arguably consistent with a broad interpretation of the "interest rate provisions" of the arrangement, especially when (as happened in this case) no advance objection was lodged by the United States.[23]

These arguments, however, would enlarge the concept of interest rate provisions very substantially, an enlargement that is inappropriate for three reasons.

---

23. This case had an interesting history. At first, the Budd Company asked the US Treasury to authorize the US Eximbank to provide competitive financing for its bid. The US Treasury declined to take action on the ground that, even with competitive financing, Budd would have lost the order. Then, on June 24, 1982, Budd petitioned the US Commerce Department to impose countervailing duties. The Commerce Department reached a preliminary determination of subsidy on November 29, 1982 (47 Fed. Reg. 53760). Subsequently, apparently for business reasons, Budd withdrew its petition, and New York City reached a 51 percent buy-American agreement with three US unions that intervened in the proceedings (*Wall Street Journal,* 11 February 1983; *US Import Weekly,* 1 December 1982).

First, if the drafters of the GATT standard had meant to incorporate the entire OECD Arrangement, they would have omitted the phrase interest rate provisions in the language of item (k). Second, as a practical matter, the possibility of notifying a derogation or matching a derogation is not open to nonparticipants of the arrangement. The GATT standard should apply equally to participants and nonparticipants. Third, the main reason for using the interest rate provisions was to provide all code signatories with a plain, visible but confined safe harbor. That harbor would become much larger and less well defined, if the notification and matching provisions of the arrangement were read into the GATT standard.

Another aspect of the same question is to what extent the narrowly defined interest rate provisions of the arrangement are to serve as a touchstone for *all* export credits. For example, if a government provides short-term export credits at the arrangement rate, but the arrangement specifically does not include credits for a period of less than two years, can the short-term credits come within the safe harbor? Logic and the negotiating history of the code itself suggest that the safe harbor provision should be limited to the sectors and credit maturities enumerated in the arrangement.[24] An extension of the safe harbor to all sectors and maturities would completely bypass the hard bargaining that went into that OECD Arrangement.

What Is the Standard of No Subsidy?

Even though it is defined not to entail an export subsidy, an official export credit may nevertheless involve a potentially troublesome subsidy under either of two standards:

□ if the official export credit is provided at an interest rate at or above the OECD Arrangement rate but below the cost of money to governments

□ if the official export credit is provided at an interest rate at or above the cost of money to governments but below the commercial rate otherwise available to the exporting firm.

Official export credits provided under the first standard almost certainly belong to the potentially troublesome category. That a practice is defined not to be an export subsidy by virtue of a safe harbor (namely, providing an export credit at OECD Arrangement rates) does not mean the practice was defined not to be a potentially troublesome subsidy. Obviously, the arrangement norms can differ considerably from the cost of money to government standard. There is no record

---

24. The Korean commitment, reproduced in appendix B, extended the safe harbor provision to cover short-term credits. In our view, this extension was inappropriate.

in negotiating history that extensions of credit at arrangement rates would be absolutely excused from penalty duties, particularly if they had a harmful trade impact.

It is doubtful, however, that official export credits made available at rates above the cost of money to government standard belong in the potentially troublesome category. To be sure, in the *Ceramic Tile from Mexico* case (47 Fed. Reg. 20012, 10 May 1982), the US Commerce Department decided that Mexico's export credit subsidy was best measured by reference to the commercial rate, not the cost of money to the Mexican government.[25] This decision followed a line of cases decided by the US Treasury and the US Commerce Department that measured an export credit subsidy by reference to the financing alternatives available to the exporter.[26] The US approach fits in naturally with an opportunity cost measure of a subsidy: the difference between the subsidized cost to the firm and the cost that would have been incurred, if the resource were obtained from an alternative market source.

In terms of international acceptance, however, the US approach seems to involve an overreaching extension of the concept of potentially troublesome subsidies, for three reasons. First, potentially troublesome subsidies have generally been defined in terms of cost, not in terms of the price available from an alternate source. Second, the cost of money to government standard has been enunciated in GATT circles since 1960. Third, the cost standard has enormous administrative convenience: it is readily ascertained and is the same for all users of government credit, while the commercial market standard may not be easily determined and necessarily varies between firms.[27]

The debate on the correct standard for deciding whether official export credits are potentially troublesome raises a larger issue. Should the amount of a subsidy

---

25. For additional detail on this case, see the US Department of Commerce Memorandum to Gary N. Horlick, Acting Assistant Secretary for Trade Administration, "Ceramic Tile from Mexico—Final Countervailing Duty Determination," May 3, 1982. In their regulations implementing the Subsidies Code, both the European Community and Canada have followed a commercial rate standard in assessing the amount of subsidy inherent in export credits. However, as a policy matter, the European Community seems to prefer the "cost of money to government" standard.

26. See, for example, *Certain Pig Iron from Brazil*, 44 Fed. Reg. 67554, 26 November 1979; *Ferroalloys from Spain*, 45 Fed. Reg. 25, 2 January 1980; *Leather Wearing Apparel from Argentina*, 46 Fed. Reg. 23009, 23 April 1982.

27. An underlying question is whether the calculation of subsidy should be tailored to the individual circumstances of each beneficiary—for example, whether it has a high credit rating or a low credit rating. From an administrative standpoint, it would be desirable to use a single benchmark for all firms. However, it is questionable whether a "subsidy" exists for that part of the estimated amount that exceeds the benefit actually received by a particular firm. If a "cost of money to government" standard were used, very few firms could claim that their own potential borrowing costs were lower than that cost. By contrast, any "average" commercial rate is likely to be higher than the alternative cost of money to some firms in the industry.

(by contrast with the existence of a subsidy) be measured by reference to its *cost* to government or by reference to the *benefit* conferred on industry?

The US Commerce Department has adopted a benefit standard in evaluating not only official export credits but also other preferential government financing schemes. (See appendix H, which reproduces the methodological appendices to *Certain Steel Products from Belgium* (47 Fed. Reg. 39304, 7 September 1982). Note, however, that the US Commerce Department does *not* apply the benefit standard in evaluating all subsidies, a point illustrated by *Certain Softwood Products from Canada* (48 Fed. Reg. 24159, 31 May 1983). By contrast, the EC authorities have consistently endorsed the cost standard. It remains to be seen which standard other signatories to the Subsidies Code will accept.

Further Progress on Export Credit Discipline

For the foreseeable future, the working norms for minimum export credit standards will be developed in the OECD framework rather than the GATT. At most, the GATT will play a backstop role for sectors and maturity terms not covered by the OECD Arrangement. The GATT will also function as a reference point for national actions against imports financed with subsidized export credits.[28]

In late 1981, mid-1982, and mid-1983, the OECD, led by Axel Wallen, chairman of the OECD Arrangement, achieved major breakthroughs in bringing arrangement rates closer to market rates and in devising sector agreements for large aircraft and nuclear power equipment sales. (The arrangement, as renegotiated in mid-1982, appears in appendix G.)

The reforms of 1982 (effective July 6, 1982) and 1983 (effective October 15, 1983) entailed the following major changes:[29]

☐ an increase in the interest rates charged Category I (rich) countries from between 11.0 percent and 11.25 percent (depending on maturity term) to between 12.15 percent and 12.40 percent.

☐ a reclassification of borrowing countries, based on the World Bank Development Report final 1979 data, to include in Category I all nations with per capita GNP of over $4,000. This reclassification brings the USSR, Czechoslovakia, the German Democratic Republic, Spain, Ireland, and Greece into Category I.

---

28. For example, in the May 1982 meeting of the GATT Subsidies Committee, the United States notified Export-Import Bank programs as a subsidy. The notification was a prelude to possible action against the export credit programs maintained by other countries.

29. US Treasury Department 1982; *Journal of Commerce,* 13 October 1983, p. 1A; 17 October 1983, p. 1A.

☐ an increase in the interest rates charged Category II (intermediate countries) from between 10.5 percent and 11.0 percent (depending on maturity term) to between 10.85 percent and 11.35 percent. (On October 15, 1983, this class of rates was reduced to between 10.35 percent and 10.7 percent, depending on maturity term.)

☐ a redefinition of Category II to include all nations other than rich nations in Category I and poor nations eligible for credits from the International Development Association (IDA, the "soft-loan" window of the World Bank). In other words, Category III (poor) countries will be confined to IDA countries, most of which are not major users of official export credits. (Indonesia and the Philippines are, however, examples of major users of official export credits in Category III.)

☐ retention of the Category III interest rates at 10.0 percent. (On October 15, 1983, this rate was reduced to 9.5 percent.)

☐ a provision that export credits extended in low interest currencies can differ from the foregoing minimums. This provision was originally crafted to deal with low Japanese market interest rates. Under the summer 1982 compromise, the yen rate represents a blend of public and private rates, but it cannot be less than 0.30 percent above the prevailing long-term yen prime interest rate (with a long term rate of 8.2 percent, this minimum sets a floor of 8.5 percent). Similar flexibility provisions have since been applied to Germany and other countries with low market interest rates.

☐ agreement by the participants not to derogate with respect to maturity term or interest rate. (Both the United States and Canada have derogated with respect to maturity terms in the past.)

☐ no mixed credits (that is, financing that combines official export credits and concessional aid) that contain a grant element of less than 20 percent. This provision is designed to ensure that economic aid is truly aid, and not export credit in disguise.[30]

☐ interest rate commitments in new offers to last only six months (to facilitate a flexible transition to future changes).

☐ under the October 1983 agreement, automatic adjustment of minimum rates every six months to reflect changes in market long-term bond rates in the United States, Germany, the United Kingdom, France, and Japan, provided that the weighted interest rate movement is at least 50 basis points since the preceding charge.

---

30. Despite this provision the use of aid as an export subsidy is still intense. For one example of a subsidy battle fought with aid, see the saga of the Colombian metro, *Financial Times*, 10 August 1983, p. 6.

Owing to the combination of disinflation and the Wallen provisions, the subsidy element of official export credits declined dramatically between 1981 and 1983. Moreover, the so-called "differential rate system,"[31] represented in nascent form by the "yen provisions" of the 1982 Wallen compromise, has since blossomed into fuller flower, as special benchmark rates have been negotiated for such low interest rate currencies as the Swiss franc, the German mark, the Dutch guilder, and the Austrian schilling. Finally, and perhaps most significantly, the 1983 agreement appears to have introduced a degree of automatic change into the schedule of minimum rates. With changes in minimum rates linked to market rates, the possibility that truly huge subsidies will once again creep into the system is much reduced.

With these very substantial accomplishments, it can almost be said that a regime of international discipline has been successfully applied to export credits. However, two additional important reforms can be envisaged. First, the OECD Arrangement countries could ultimately agree to denominate their export credit transactions in a single unit of account, for example, the Special Drawing Right (SDR) (a proposal made in October 1980 by C. Fred Bergsten 1981, p. 33). The single unit of account would overcome the problem of "interest rate illusion"[32] and enable each export credit agency to offer the same package of exchange risk and interest rate to potential buyers.

Second, export credit discipline should be extended to cover agricultural goods and to cover all mixed credits in which the grant element is less, say, than 35 percent. Coverage for agricultural goods is especially important. Like other subsidies associated with agricultural exports, very little discipline is now applied to agricultural export credits. Traditionally, most exporting nations kept their agricultural credits short term, and priced them at commercial interest rates. Since 1980, however, terms have lengthened (three-year credits are now commonly extended), credit subsidies have increased, and the volume of agricultural export credit has expanded. In fiscal year 1983, for example, the US Export Credit Guarantee program rose from an originally planned level of $2.8 billion to nearly $4.8 billion, after supplemental authority was enacted to cover credits to Mexico and "blended" (subsidized) credits to various competitive markets.[33]

---

31. Under a full-blown differential rate system, the minimum level of export credit rates would differ from currency to currency and would adjust automatically to reflect market rates.

32. Interest rate illusion refers to the supposed borrower indifference to a credit denominated in yen, lira, or any other currency, as long as the nominal interest rate is identical. Whether or not interest rate illusion exists in the minds of borrowers, the possibility that it exists creates very real competition between export credit agencies.

33. *Journal of Commerce*, 7 October 1983, p. 12A.

Tax-free Trade Zones

Free (known in the United States as "foreign") trade zones have existed since the earliest days of commercial relations. More than 225 tax-free trade zones, free ports, and similar areas currently are in operation worldwide, offering a broad range of services to traders.[34] Goods imported into a customs-free zone may be stored, repackaged, and processed.

One of the most common activities is the assembly of imported components with domestic goods, using domestic labor and facilities. Generally, the finished goods are then exported. As a result of this physical transformation, however, the imported components may qualify for a lower duty rate on shipment into the adjacent customs territory than the potential duty rate on the goods that originally entered the free trade zone.[35]

Operating essentially as an enclave within a surrounding customs territory, a free trade zone represents a pure form of adjustment for trade policies that would otherwise hinder exports. All zones offer a temporary or permanent exemption from import duties and customs regulations on goods entering the zone. The extent of the exemption depends on whether those goods ultimately are imported into the adjacent customs territory or are reexported to another country. Import quotas generally do not apply to free trade zones. Upon entry into a zone, domestic goods are generally eligible for any refund, duty drawback, or export incentive otherwise available to exports. Most free trade zones are also designed to exempt goods in process from excise or other indirect taxes. These various adjustments enable producers to obtain traded inputs at world prices and to compete in world markets on the basis of underlying factor costs.

In addition, free trade zones increasingly are established in conjunction with industrial parks or other facilities that offer a wide variety of services and incentives to free trade zone users. Infrastructure improvements that are "generally available" to a broad class of industries are usually not regarded as potentially troublesome subsidies.[36] But incentives that are targeted on the export sector, such as the preferential taxation of income and real property located in a free trade zone, may belong to the realm of potentially troublesome practices and could violate either item (a) or item (l) of the 1979 Illustrative List.

---

34. Walter H. Diamond and Dorothy B. Diamond (1977); *Journal of Commerce*, 8 November 1982.

35. In fact, about 70 percent of the $3 billion of goods that leave US foreign trade zones annually enter domestic US commerce. This particular use of foreign trade zones has prompted considerable criticism from the Electronics Industries Association and the American Iron and Steel Institute (*Washington Tariff Trade Letter*, 6 June 1983, p. 3).

36. The test of "general availability" is suggested by Article 11:3 of the code. The Department of Commerce has followed this test in a number of recent cases. See, for example, *Certain Softwood Products from Canada* (48 Fed. Reg. 24159, 31 May 1983).

A case could be made for the international legitimacy of the preferential taxation of income and real property in free trade zones. Just as a free trade zone falls outside the normal customs jurisdiction of a government, so a free trade zone can also fall outside the government's normal taxing jurisdiction. In a sense, income earned in a free trade zone could be compared to foreign source income, which is exempt from taxes altogether or otherwise preferentially taxed when earned by the residents of many home countries.

These possible arguments are outweighed, however, by item (e) of the 1979 Illustrative List, which prohibits the preferential exemption, remission, and deferral of direct taxes (including property taxes) with respect to export activities. No exception was made for free trade zones in the Illustrative List.

As a practical matter, efforts to limit the rebate of direct taxes would be badly undermined if countries could simply skirt the restrictions by declaring parts of the country free trade zones, exempt from taxation to the extent goods made in the zone are exported from the national customs territory. This would amount to a full embrace of the destination principle for border tax adjustments. We would applaud that embrace. But if that is intended, then item (e) of the Illustrative List should simply be dropped. Countries should not need to enact free trade zone legislation to achieve this laudable result.

Export Incentives to Agricultural and Primary Goods

As noted earlier, international guidelines on export incentives for agricultural and other primary products have lagged far behind those for trade in manufactured goods. In 1961, a GATT panel on subsidies found that "although some subsidies exist on nonprimary products, the great bulk of the subsidization measures relate to primary products."[37] The panel uncovered widespread export subsidies on dairy, meat, and cereals products, and found that domestic production subsidies on agricultural products were even more commonplace than export subsidies. Since then, agricultural subsidies have blossomed, particularly in Europe, but also in the United States and Japan.

Estimates of the cost of agricultural support programs to consumers and national treasuries vary, but there is no doubt that the cost of such programs has increased in recent years as a consequence of bountiful harvests and depressed world prices. One analyst has estimated that agricultural support programs in the United States, the European Community, and Japan cost nearly $75 billion between 1979 and 1980 (Sanderson in Japan Economic Institute 1983).

---

37. GATT, 10th Supp. *Basic Instruments and Selected Documents* 201–3 (1962). See also Kenneth W. Dam (1970, ch. 15) for an extensive discussion of international attempts to regulate domestic agricultural policies.

According to an analysis by Kym Anderson and Rodney Tyers (1983), if the European Community were to liberalize completely its trade in grain and meat products—in other words, abandon both its variable levy on imports and its sliding subsidies on exports—then international prices for wheat, coarse grain, and ruminant meat would rise by about 15 percent to 18 percent. Further, the instability of world prices, measured by the coefficient of variation, would drop by one-third to one-half. International trade volumes would increase by about 28 million metric tons annually for grains and 5.4 million metric tons for meat.

As reflected in these various estimates, permissive GATT standards have accommodated the widespread subsidization of agricultural production. GATT Article XVI:3 discourages, but does not prohibit, direct or indirect subsidies to primary product exports. The language of Article XVI:3 offers wide latitude for all manner of agricultural programs that would clearly violate GATT rules if aimed at manufactured goods.[38]

In addition, Article VI:7 accords a special defense to price stabilization programs for primary commodities. An export price lower than the home market price "shall be presumed not to result in material injury" provided: (1) that the program also at some time has resulted in export prices higher than domestic prices, and (2) that the program does not operate to stimulate exports unduly or otherwise seriously prejudice other exporters. Similarly, a note to Article XVI:3 exculpates primary commodity stabilization schemes, funded by their own profits, provided that they sometimes result in lower domestic prices than export prices, and provided that they do not unduly stimulate the exports of the product.

The 1979 Subsidies Code made some progress in narrowing the acceptable range of subsidies on primary products. The OECD Agreement tightens the definition of "primary product" as it relates to subsidies by removing minerals from the list of commodities exempt from the GATT's general prohibitions on subsidies. Further, Article 10:3 of the agreement adds a price dimension to international standards governing trade in agriculture:

Signatories . . . agree not to grant export subsidies on exports of certain primary products to a particular market in a manner which results in prices materially below those of other suppliers to the same market.

This provision recognizes, for the first time, the rights of third-country suppliers in a particular market. The agreement also enlarges the list of relevant criteria

---

38. Article XVI:3 states in part:
. . . contracting parties should seek to avoid the use of subsidies on the export of primary products. If, however, a contracting party grants directly or indirectly any form of subsidy which operates to increase the export of any primary product from its territory, such subsidy shall not be applied in a manner which results in the contracting party having more than an equitable share of world export trade in that product.

for injury determination in agricultural cases. Among the factors signatories may take into account during their injury investigations under Article 6:3 is "whether there has been an increased burden on government support programmes." In other words, injury to the importing country's treasury, as well as injury to private producers, is now a relevant factor.

While the 1979 code may have dented part of the armor protecting agricultural exports from international discipline, national governments can largely ignore the external consequences of their internal agricultural policies. The United States had approached the 1982 GATT Ministerial with the hope of discussing ways to rein in some of the more trade distortive agricultural policies. The European Community's variable import levies, quantitative restrictions, preferential bilateral agreements, and "restitution payments" on agricultural exports, and Japan's import quotas, selectively high tariffs, and nontariff barriers were all on the US negotiating list.

US agricultural policies caused equal concern among foreign competitors: import quotas on a variety of products, generous price support programs leading to oversupply, pressures for "giveaway" programs in the world market, and obscure marketing orders (Marsha A. Echols 1982). In the end, little progress was made. The GATT ministers merely commissioned a two-year study on the impact of national agricultural policies on international trade (Schott 1983).

Various explanations have been offered for the widespread reluctance to impose tighter discipline over agricultural policies. One explanation is that farmers are typically overrepresented in national legislative bodies. Another is that self-sufficiency in agriculture has become a matter of national security. Still a third explanation is that, since agricultural prices historically have fluctuated much more over the economic cycle than industrial prices, governments want to buffer the agricultural sector from cyclical adversity.

Whatever the explanation, the time is at hand for national governments to accept greater international discipline over the use of subsidies in promoting agricultural exports. In particular, subsidies that result in export prices below domestic prices should be subject to discipline whenever a complaining country can show lost sales in an individual market. This standard may have seemed hopelessly impractical in 1982, a year of large carryover stocks and agricultural surpluses. But the agricultural cycle has not been banished, as the 1983 drought in the United States so forcefully demonstrates. When shortages return, conceivably the large exporters of temperate agricultural products—Australia, Canada, the European Community, and the United States—could negotiate a framework of tighter discipline.

Performance Requirements and Associated Investment Incentives

The most familiar performance requirements are local value-added requirements, local ownership requirements, and export requirements (for example, the Canadian Volkswagen scheme discussed earlier). Such performance requirements clearly intrude on management discretion. Firms accept that intrusion mainly because it is accompanied by inducements, such as permission to establish operations in an attractive market or eligibility for fiscal incentives (Barber 1982).

These export performance requirements and associated inducements raise assorted GATT issues (Labor-Industry Coalition for International Trade 1981; Fontheim and R. Michael Gadbaw 1982; Jacobsen 1983). In particular, export performance requirements raise the question: under what conditions does the linkage of a performance requirement and an inducement amount to an export subsidy?

As Fontheim and Gadbaw (1982) have noted, the vice of export performance requirements and associated measures is that, individually, the elements of the policy package may be innocuous, but collectively they can badly distort export markets. Under presently accepted GATT rules, no country can object if another country offers a wide range of "generally available" incentives to promote new and existing lines of production. Further, if a country respects its GATT obligations, its level of tariff and nontariff protection (a level that importantly affects the profitability of private enterprise) cannot be a matter of foreign reproach.

In the absence of a bilateral treaty providing the right of establishment, moreover, no country can object if another country limits entry by domestic or foreign firms into particular lines of business. Finally, there is nothing inherently repugnant about official exhortations to further private exports. But when those export exhortations are linked to government investment incentives or access to a lucrative and protected home market, then the international community may well be faced with an objectionable policy package.

Certain parts of the GATT and the Subsidies Code arguably bear on export performance requirements and related measures. In instances where "direct subsidies . . . contingent upon export performance" are paid to the firm, the entire package can be condemned by the Subsidies Committee under item (a) of the 1979 Illustrative List. When no such direct subsidies are paid (probably the more common situation), any condemnation by the Subsidies Committee might require a demonstration of bilevel pricing in order to come within the scope of catchall item (1) (which refers back to GATT Article XVI). In fact, condemnation may be avoided altogether (even when bilevel pricing can be shown), if the GATT Subsidies Committee accepts the argument that the grant of licensing privileges (for example, the right of establishment or the right to apply for investment incentives) does not entail a "charge on the public account" (to use the phrase of item [1] of the 1979 Illustrative List).

Some of the issues raised by performance requirements were illuminated by the disposition of the US case against Canada's Foreign Investment Review Act, brought under GATT Articles III and XVII. In that case, the United States asserted that export performance requirements contravened Article XVII:1 relating to permissible state trading practices. Article XVII:1 calls upon a state trading enterprise to "act in a manner consistent with the general principles of nondiscriminatory treatment prescribed in this agreement for governmental measures affecting imports or exports by private traders" and to "make any such purchases or sales solely in accordance with commercial considerations . . . ." The United States also asserted that Canadian buy-local performance requirements denied imported goods the right of national treatment provided under Article III:4. Article III:4 requires that the products of each Contracting Party "be accorded treatment no less favorable than that accorded to like products of national origin . . . ."

The GATT panel decided, in July 1983, that Canadian practices violated Article III relating to national treatment of imports, but not Article XVII. With respect to the Article XVII complaint, the panel found:[39]

> 5.18. . . . when allowing foreign investments on the condition that the investors export a certain amount or proportion of their production, Canada does not, in the view of the Panel, act inconsistently with any of the principles of nondiscriminatory treatment prescribed by the General Agreement for governmental measures affecting export by private traders. . . .

The Subsidies Code was not invoked in this proceeding. It remains to be seen whether the code furnishes more discipline against export performance requirements than GATT Article XVII.

Apart from GATT discipline, national authorities could take countervailing duty action against export performance requirements and associated inducements, when the exports result in material injury. The imposition of countervailing duties would require that national authorities, in administering their own law, find that some subsidy is inherent in licensing privileges and other "intangible" incentives.

Further, the countervailing duty action would have a more salutary impact if the national authorities attributed the offensive subsidy solely to induced exports and not to all exports or all production. For example, if the performance requirement explicitly calls for, and in fact compels, the firm to increase its exports by 100 units, if the firm would in any event have exported 200 units, and if the firm's total production for domestic and foreign markets (including the new

---

39. GATT Doc. L/5504 (25 July 1983). The panel report is reproduced in Bureau of National Affairs, *U.S. Export Weekly*, 23 August 1983, pp. 767–80.

exports) is 1,000 units, then the calculated subsidy should be allocated to the incremental exports of 100 units, not to total exports of 300 units, or to total production of 1,000 units.

Finally, given the opaque nature of many performance requirements and associated incentives, the burden should fall on the exporting firm and its government to rebut the petitioning industry's allegations, both as to the existence and amount of subsidies linked to export performance requirements, and as to the geographic direction of induced exports (Hufbauer 1981).

In addition to whatever discipline can be fashioned under national laws, the time may well be at hand to negotiate new multilateral restraints. The process of defining export subsidies has already progressed through three stages. The first stage focused on cash payments from government, typified by excessive duty drawbacks. Later, the focus expanded to cover exemption from tax obligations, in other words, absence of a rightful cash payment to government. Still later, the focus broadened further to cover government provision of services at bargain prices, for example, export credits or rail facilities. Perhaps now the concept of export subsidies should extend even further to cover the provision of licensing rights conditioned on export performance, such as the right of establishment or the right to apply for fiscal incentives.

This conceptual extension would require international negotiation. In the negotiating process, many countries are likely to raise the defense that export performance requirements and associated incentives are simply used to offset the inordinate preference exhibited by some multinational enterprises (MNEs) to buy within the corporate group and to divide markets regardless of comparative advantage. Many nations may be unwilling to accept greater discipline on government actions, as long as MNEs are allowed to operate free of public scrutiny. Thus, the negotiations could ultimately lead to greater public surveillance of the buying and selling practices of MNEs.

Miscellaneous Export Incentives

Beyond the practices already outlined, a number of other private and governmental measures may act as export incentives. Some of those practices, such as currency schemes and preferential transportation charges, are specifically addressed in the GATT. Others are addressed in the 1960 Working Party List and the 1979 Illustrative List.

Currency Practices

The GATT itself envisages a joint GATT and International Monetary Fund (IMF) role in regulating national currency practices as they affect trade (Jackson 1969, pp. 479–95). GATT Article XV:4 states:

Contracting parties shall not, by exchange action, frustrate the intent of the provisions of this agreement nor, by trade action, the provisions of the Articles of Agreement of the International Monetary Fund.

References to currency and exchange practices scattered throughout the GATT and IMF articles originally gave rise to doubt concerning the appropriate role of each body in disciplining multiple exchange rate practices. With the passage of time, however, it became increasingly clear that the IMF would play the lead role in regulating all exchange rate practices.

Nevertheless, GATT retains a role in assessing the consequences of multiple currency practices. Note 2 in the Ad to Articles VI:2 and VI:3 of the GATT advises signatories that "multiple currency practices can in certain circumstances constitute a subsidy to exports which may be met by countervailing duties." However, note 1 to Ad Article XVI, Section B states: "Nothing in Section B shall preclude the use by a contracting party of multiple rates of exchange in accordance with the Articles of Agreement of the International Monetary Fund."

In other words, if the IMF tolerates a multiple currency practice, the GATT is not likely to view that practice as an export subsidy. Conversely, if the IMF condemns a multiple currency practice, the GATT *is* likely to view that practice as an export subsidy. However, the language of the note to GATT Article VI would seemingly permit the national imposition of countervailing duties (upon a showing of material injury) against exports benefiting from a multiple exchange rate system, even though the multiple exchange rate country is in conformity with the IMF articles.

The GATT, moreover, retained an interest in other currency practices with a decided export subsidy flavor. The 1979 Illustrative List, like the 1960 Working Party List, prohibits "currency retention schemes or similar practices which involve a bonus on exports or reexports." This formulation precludes schemes that allow exporters to retain, for their own import needs or for sale to other importers, foreign exchange that carries an implicit scarcity premium.

In several pre–World War II cases involving German multiple exchange rates, and in one small postwar case involving a Uruguayan preferential export rate, the US Treasury (then responsible for administering the US countervailing duty law) and the US courts found that countervailable bounties flowed from these schemes.[40] For the most part, however, multiple exchange rates have attracted surprisingly little attention in circles concerned with export subsidies. This may soon change.

---

40. See T.D. 48, 360, 69 Treas. Dec. 1009 (1936); T.D. 49, 719, 74 Treas. Dec. 193 (1938); T.D. 49, 821, 74 Treas. Dec. 389 (1939); *F.W. Woolworth Co. v. United States*, 115 F.2d 309 (CCPA 1940); T.D. 53257 (1963); *Energetic Worsted Corp. v. United States*, 224 F. Supp. 606 (USCC 1963), reversed on other grounds, 53 CCPA 36 (1966). Also see Butler (1969, pp. 97–102); Feller (1969, pp. 46–50).

In 1983, the American Textile Manufacturers Institute and affiliated textile unions filed a countervailing duty petition against textile and apparel imports from China.[41] The most important subsidy alleged in the petition was the difference between the "internal settlement rate" of 2.8 yuan to the US dollar paid by exporting firms and the official exchange rate of 1.9939 yuan to the US dollar. After an extensive public hearing on the question under what circumstances and to what extent multiple exchange rate practices can give rise to an export subsidy, the Commerce Department ducked the basic issues. Instead, the textile case was settled when the American Textile Manufacturers Institute withdrew its petition in return for an administration commitment to embrace a system of global textile quotas and special "anti-surge" measures (*Wall Street Journal*, 14 December 1983). However, the basic exchange rate questions raised in the textile petition have since featured in subsequent petitions filed by different industries against other exporting nations. In its preliminary negative decisions in *Carbon Steel Wire Rod from Poland* (49 Fed. Reg. 6768, 23 February 1984) and *Carbon Steel Wire Rod from Czechoslovakia* (49 Fed. Reg. 6773, 23 February 1984), the department refused to conduct a serious investigation of the multiple currency charges. However, it seems unlikely that the Commerce Department can continue to avoid these issues much longer.

Equally important, the Subsidies Committee should seek a common understanding as to which multiple exchange rate practices will be considered export subsidies, and how the subsidy will be calculated.

Transportation Charges

Article V of the GATT—Freedom of Transit—is the only article dealing with transportation charges. It does not go beyond the treatment of goods shipped through a signatory's territory in transit to another country (Jackson 1969, pp. 506–11). Thus, Article V does not address differential transportation charges for exported goods and goods sold internally.

However, item (c) of the 1979 Illustrative List, following the 1960 Working Party List, classifies "internal transport and freight charges on export shipments on terms more favorable than for domestic shipments" as a prohibited export subsidy. This is another example, like export credits, in which GATT discipline has been extended to cover ancillary services that are directly related to international trade in goods. But few, if any, cases have been brought against export-biased transportation charges.

41. American Textile Manufacturers Institute, et al., *Textiles, Apparel, and Related Products from the People's Republic of China,* petition filed with the Department of Commerce, September 12, 1983.

Delivery of Goods and Services at World Prices

The 1979 Illustrative List, like the 1960 Working Party List, covers the practice adopted by some governments of providing inputs of goods or services at preferential prices for use in making exported goods. Under certain circumstances, this practice can give rise to a prohibited export subsidy, as defined by the Illustrative List:

(d) The delivery by governments or their agencies of imported or domestic products or services for use in the production of exported goods, on terms or conditions more favourable than for delivery of like or directly competitive products or services for use in the production of goods for domestic consumption, if (in the case of products) such terms or conditions are more favourable than those commercially available on world markets to their exporters.

The principal offense addressed by item (d) is the maintenance of a dual price system on industrial inputs—charging higher prices for inputs used in production for the domestic market than for the same inputs used in production for the export market. By implication, the last clause in item (d) permits a government (or its agencies or nationalized firms) to deliver products (but not services), whether of domestic or foreign origin, at world prices to its exporting firms, even though the world price may be well below the sheltered domestic price. Thus, a government faced with domestic costs of manufacturing steel of $400 per ton, when the world price was $300 per ton, could charge $400 per ton for steel used in the manufacture of household durables sold domestically. At the same time, that government could subsidize steel used in the manufacture of exported household durables to the extent of $100 per ton, without granting a proscribed export subsidy.

Although permitted by item (d), the subsidy in this example might well lead to two-tier pricing for exported household durables and household durables consumed domestically. In turn, the two-tier pricing could give rise to a dumping charge. Antidumping duties could then be levied, upon a finding of material injury. Further, even though the practice illustrated by the example does not involve a proscribed export subsidy, it could involve a potentially troublesome subsidy.

In the European steel cases however (see appendix H), the subsidization of coal production and its provision to the European industry at or above world prices was not regarded by the US Department of Commerce as a subsidy to steel production. The department accepted the argument that, in this instance, any benefits of subsidization remained with the coal industry and were not passed on to the steel industry.

We agree with the Department of Commerce interpretation. It closely adheres to one of the four fundamental principles that underpin existing international rules on subsidies: producers in each nation should have access to internationally traded inputs at "world" prices for use in export production. National policies that enable such access are properly accepted by the international community. And, in this case, foreign steel sales were not a vehicle for exporting subsidized domestic coal, since European steel producers were not required to purchase European coal.

Export Inflation and Exchange Risk Insurance

The widespread adoption of floating exchange rates and the great inflation of the 1970s prompted the introduction of government-supported exchange risk and export inflation insurance programs. Exchange risk insurance protects exporters against losses sustained in transactions denominated in a foreign currency when the value of that currency depreciates relative to the domestic currency, either prior to the delivery of the export product (in a cash sale) or during the repayment period (in a credit sale). Export inflation insurance shields exporters from infla-tion-related increases in the cost of producing goods after the contract is signed but prior to their shipment for export.

A 1977 GATT Working Party was unable to agree whether export inflation insurance programs are compatible with GATT provisions.[42] The same Working Party chose not to address exchange risk insurance programs. However, item (j) of the 1979 Illustrative List establishes a standard for both types of programs. Item (j) holds in part that the provision by governments of inflation and exchange risk insurance "at premium rates, which are manifestly inadequate to cover the long-term operating costs and losses of the programmes" falls within the list of prohibited export subsidies.[43]

The definition in item (j) raises important questions. At what point are pre-miums "manifestly inadequate" to cover "long-term" costs and losses? Does long-term refer to 3 years, 5 years, or 10 years? Can the test of manifestly inadequate be met on the basis of expert projections submitted by insurance actuaries or is only past evidence admissible? Answers to such questions may, in time, make an interesting panel report. At present, these schemes have become less prominent and thus a smaller irritant to the trading system.

---

42. GATT Doc. L/4552 (22 November 1977).

43. Item (j) of the 1979 Illustrative List also applies the manifestly inadequate test to premiums on export credit guarantees. Out of regard for this provision, and its underlying belief that export credit insurance schemes should not become back-door export subsidies, Hermes (the German export credit insurance agency) raised its premium rates in 1983 by some 40 percent to offset higher claims stemming from nonpayment by developing countries. Also in 1983, ECGD (the British export credit insurance agency) reported heavy losses and was considering an increase in premium rates. *Financial Times*, 16 September 1983, p. 18.

Lease of Equipment at Bargain Prices

What happens when a state-owned company that manufactures capital goods, such as airplanes or heavy earth-moving equipment, offers to lease that equipment to foreign users at rents that involve a substantial loss? What happens when an official institution buys equipment made by a domestic private firm and leases that equipment, again at a loss, to a foreign user?

The threshold question is whether leases are even covered by the Subsidies Code or national legislation. The USTR General Counsel stated, in a letter to the Boeing Corporation, that leases are not covered either by the code or the US countervailing duty statute.[44] Under this view, the question whether the lease rate is subsidized is simply not addressed. Since the distinction between a lease and a sale depends only on the fineness of the lawyer's pen, this view will probably be challenged in the appropriate case.

Lease arrangements should, in our view, be subject to the same scrutiny as sales. A lease negotiated or supported by an official institution that does not include a reasonable allowance for depreciation, applicable operating costs, and a return at market interest rates on the capital committed should entail an actionable subsidy.

---

44. Donald deKieffer, USTR General Counsel, letter to J.R.L. Pierce, Treasurer of the Boeing Corporation, December 14, 1982.

4

The Definition and Discipline of Domestic Subsidies

Just beyond the well-established principles concerning export subsidies, embodied in the Subsidies Code and elsewhere, are large gray areas where nations have failed to agree on common rules. In negotiating the Subsidies Code, much less effort was devoted to defining and setting forth methods of calculating potentially troublesome subsidies (apart from the subclass of export subsidies) than to defining the requisite trade impact. But since the Tokyo Round, these issues have come to the forefront of subsidy concerns for two reasons.

First, the definition and calculated amount of potentially troublesome subsidies should influence the determination of whether, in fact, subsidized imports caused the requisite trade impact (material injury or otherwise). To be sure, in *Carbon Steel Wire from Brazil and Trinidad and Tobago* (47 Fed. Reg. 47452, 26 October 1982), a majority of the US International Trade Commission (USITC) stated:

> The statute does not direct the Commission to consider the amount of net subsidy in determining whether there is material injury . . . . The relationship of the net subsidy to material injury should not be dispositive of the issue of causation.

Indeed, in October 1982, the USITC found material injury in two German steel cases, even when subsidies of "0.000" were determined by the US Department of Commerce. Notwithstanding this learning from the USITC, it would seem more logical to link injury (or threat of injury or retardation of an industry) with imports subsidized to the extent of 30 percent than to the extent of 10 percent.

Second, the definition and calculation of potentially troublesome subsidies is important because, once the requisite trade impact is found, the scope of the remedy can extend (and some would say should extend) up to the amount of the calculated subsidy.

Therefore, an important topic for the international trading community is to define a broader class of potentially troublesome subsidies (in addition to the subclass of export subsidies), and to set forth methods for calculating their amount. In other words, which practices, out of the vast range of government intervention measures, should qualify as potentially troublesome subsidies?[1] And how should the amount of potentially troublesome subsidy be related to exports?

To set forth a crisp definition of "potentially troublesome subsidies" and then categorize practices and measure subsidies by reference to that definition would, of course, be appealing. But the definition itself is still being written as individual cases are decided. For the foreseeable future, each country will be free to announce its own definitions and methods of calculating potentially troublesome subsidies. Probably for the rest of this decade, international discipline on national countermeasures will depend on internationally agreed trade-impact tests, not on internationally agreed standards for defining and calculating potentially troublesome subsidies. Nevertheless, some observations can be made about emerging standards—principally announced by the United States—for identifying potentially troublesome subsidies.

Polar Positions

Two extreme definitions of potentially troublesome subsidies have been articulated and rejected. Under one definition, almost any government interference must be regarded as an actionable subsidy.[2] This position was echoed in Harald B. Malmgren's comprehensive definition of a subsidy (1977, p. 22):

For working purposes, a subsidy might therefore be considered to be any government action which causes a firm's, or a particular industry's, total net private costs of production to be below the level of costs that would have been incurred in the course of producing the same level of output in the absence of government action.

Under the other definition, only export subsidies are troublesome to the international order. Indeed, prior to 1973, the administrative practice of the US Treasury reflected this view (Matthew J. Marks and Malmgren 1975, pp. 348–49; Daniel K. Tarullo forthcoming 1984, pp. 25–27). In 1969, Peter Buck Feller could write (1969, p. 27):

---

1. Ethnocentricity tempts some observers to define potentially troublesome subsidies as all forms of intervention not practiced by their own governments. This approach would be too crass to be taken seriously, were it not for the various statements made by US officials in defense of the Domestic International Sales Corporation (DISC).

2. A famous line of dicta in *Downs v. United States* (187 US 496, 515, 1903), seemed to endorse the broad interpretation: "When a tax is imposed on all sugar produced, but is remitted upon all sugar exported, then by whatever process, or in whatever manner, or under whatever name it is disguised, it is a bounty upon exportation." This apparent endorsement was reversed in *Zenith Radio v. United States* (437 US 443, 1978).

There is no evidence, however, that countervailing duties have been levied against foreign practices which were not plainly export subsidies, or which were not intended to increase exports, or which did not result in an increase in exports.

More recently, in administering the countervailing duty law, the US view of objectionable practices has included preferential subsidies that result in selectively favorable treatment for particular regions, industries, or firms. US law began shifting toward this new, somewhat broader, interpretation of an actionable subsidy in the celebrated *Michelin* case (*X-Radial Belted Tires from Canada*, 38 Fed. Reg. 1018, 8 January 1973). In the *Michelin* case, a Canadian regional assistance program was defined as a countervailable subsidy (Robert V. Guido and Michael F. Morrone 1974). The US Treasury's transition from its prior view, which labeled only explicit export subsidies as objectionable, was made easier in the *Michelin* case because 75 percent of the output was shipped to the United States. Two years later, in the *Float Glass* cases (40 Fed. Reg. 2718, 15 January 1975), the US Treasury announced a "rule of reason": regional subsidies that were merely designed to offset local disadvantages, or were provided to firms with limited exports, or were of *de minimis* extent, were not countervailed because they did not create a "trade distortion."

After a certain amount of hostile comment from the courts and the US Congress,[3] the rule of reason approach was narrowed, in the Subsidies Code and in US law, to emphasize the tailoring of subsidies to particular enterprises. Code Article 11:3 refers to "subsidies granted with the aim of giving an advantage to certain enterprises." In the recitation of possible types of domestic subsidies, section 771(5) of the Trade Agreements Act of 1979 lists benefits paid or bestowed directly or indirectly to a "specific enterprise or industry, or group of enterprises or industries . . . ." Both formulations recall the concept of "special favor, benefit, advantage, or inducement" argued by the US Treasury Department brief in the famous *Downs v. United States* case (187 US 496, 1903, record at 236, quoted in Craig M. Brown 1977, p. 1238):

. . . any special favor, benefit, advantage, or inducement conferred by the government, even if it is given as a release from the burden and is not a direct charge on the Treasury, is fairly included in the idea and meaning of an indirect bounty.

---

3. Congress disavowed the regional offset calculations in the Trade Act of 1979; see S. Rep. No. 249, 96th Cong., lst sess. 45 (1979). Thus in *Ceramic Tile from Mexico* (47 Fed. Reg. 20012, 10 May 1982) a Mexican regional subsidy, Certificados de Promoción Fiscal (CEPROFI) was countervailed. However, since an export purpose was not shown, the CEPROFI was prorated over the entire production of the benefited firms. With respect to pre-1973 US law, the Court of Customs and Patent Appeals struck down the US Treasury's "trade distortions" test. *ASG Industries, Inc. v. United States,* 610 F.2d 770 (CCPA 1980), reversing 467 F. Supp. 1187 (Cust. Ct. 1979).

The special favor concept now appears to serve as Ockham's razor to eliminate a wide range of government programs from the sphere of international concern. Under the current US Department of Commerce view, "generally available" subsidies for rail or electric service, manpower training programs, uniform tax credits, and similar broad-brush measures do not qualify as potentially troublesome subsidies. The US Court of International Trade embraced this position in deciding a case of first impression, *Carlisle Tire and Rubber Company v. United States,* (Slip Op. 83–49, May 18, 1983):[4]

What is more, adoption of Carlisle's literal view that generally available benefits are a bounty or grant would, if taken to its logical extreme, lead to an absurd result. Thus, included in Carlisle's category of countervailable benefits would be such things as public highways and bridges, as well as a tax credit for expenditures on capital investment even if available to all industries and sectors.

The court went on to quote from John J. Barcelo (1977, p. 836), who had earlier argued that generally available subsidies should not be countervailed:

These [types of generally available] subsidies have such a widespread effect on production that countervailing duties, were they allowed in such cases, could be imposed on almost every product which enters international commerce. Moreover, measurement of the exact extent of the net subsidy falling on any given product line would be unusually difficult. In any given case the amount of offsetting duty levied could be quite arbitrary.

The emerging distinction between general subsidies and targeted subsidies does not, of course, settle all questions. How general is generally available? Does a program, which on its face is open to all regions or all industries, in fact confer special favors, if in practice or intent the program is used by only a few regions or a few industries?

While these details remain to be spelled out, the Commerce Department seems to insist that to qualify as generally available, a subsidy should be widely available in principle and spread among many industries in practice. Our own view is that the generally available label should be used sparingly to excuse only those incentives that in practice and design are used by a broad range of industries and geographic areas. Otherwise, the international community risks taking countermeasures against little subsidies while big subsidies run free.

Other examples of gray areas in the definition of potentially troublesome subsidies include upstream subsidies, equity in public enterprises, and research

---

4. For an adverse comment see *Washington Business* (supplement to the *Washington Post*), 11 July 1983, p. 22.

and development (R&D) incentives. In the sections that follow, we assume in each case that the incentives are not generally available.

Upstream Subsidies

Under what circumstances should an "upstream subsidy," namely a subsidy on an input purchased by the exporting industry, be regarded as a potentially troublesome subsidy to that exporting industry and thus subject to remedial action, if exports cause the requisite level of trade impact? Under what circumstances should an upstream subsidy be regarded as an outright export subsidy?

The broad view is that any upstream subsidy qualifies as potentially troublesome. Under this view, any upstream subsidy on inputs used by an export industry really amounts to an export subsidy. The narrow view is that upstream subsidies seldom act as export subsidies. Under this view, an upstream subsidy is potentially troublesome only when it results in the provision of inputs at a cheaper price than the price prevailing on world markets.

Under the US Commerce Department view, an upstream subsidy does not confer a potentially troublesome benefit on a downstream industrial purchaser, provided that the two firms are not related and deal with each other at arm's length, unless:

(1) The government imposes conditions on the subsidized industry that require it to sell at bargain prices to the downstream industry;

Or unless:

(2) The government takes measures that prevent foreign downstream purchasers from enjoying access to the subsidized input at the same price as domestic downstream purchasers.

Steel Cases

The proper treatment of upstream subsidies became a particularly lively issue in the context of countervailing duty cases brought by US firms against European steel firms (see appendix H). The European steel firms conceded that, if European coking coal were sold principally to the steel industry and if European coal subsidies led to a delivered price of coking coal at Louvain that was lower than the cheapest alternative coking coal shipped from, say, Baltimore, then to the extent of the price difference, a potentially troublesome subsidy might exist. However, if the price of European coal was equal to or higher than the alternative price of Baltimore coal, no benefit was received and no subsidy was conferred on the steel industry, regardless of whether the European coal actually used was cheaper than it would have been without the subsidy.

According to the US steel industry, the amount of coal subsidy should be imputed to the cost of production of steel, regardless of whether coking coal was used by a wide range of industries and regardless of the delivered price of Baltimore coal.

In its final decision in the European carbon steel cases, the Department of Commerce essentially accepted the European view.[5] Subsidies on the production of European coking coal were not imputed to the production of steel, because they did not result in a price for coal lower than the world price and because the coal and steel firms were unrelated enterprises.

Pasta from the European Community

When does an upstream subsidy amount to an export subsidy? The United States raised this question in a case brought to the Subsidies Committee involving EC pasta exports. The manufacture of pasta in Europe is not itself subsidized. However, pasta is made from European wheat, and European wheat is protected by a variable levy. When the pasta is exported, a rebate is allowed to the extent of the variable levy, thus bringing the cost of the wheat input down to world levels.[6] (The European Community is implementing a similar rebate on barley incorporated in Scotch and Irish single malt whiskey.)

Does the rebate on wheat violate EC code obligations? The panel decided that pasta is not a primary product entitled to the lower trade-impact standard of code Article 10.[7] Thus, if the use of subsidized wheat amounts to an upstream export subsidy for pasta, the EC practice stands condemned, almost regardless of trade impact.

The European Community argued that the rebate on wheat used in exported pasta simply brings the European wheat price down to the world price. The rebate, therefore, comes within the exception implied by the last phrase of item (d) on the 1979 Illustrative List:

(d) The delivery by governments or their agencies of imported or domestic products or services for use in the production of exported goods, on terms or conditions more favorable than for the delivery of like or directly competitive products or services for use in the production of goods for domestic consumption, *if (in the case of products) such terms or conditions are more favorable than those*

---

5. Relevant extracts appear in appendix H; also see Bureau of National Affairs, *US Import Weekly,* 1 September 1982, pp. 663–66.

6. This system is analogous to the US scheme operated in the 1950s for reducing the cost of cotton to US textile mills. When the United States accepted Article XVI:4 in 1957, it took a reservation for the cotton subsidy scheme, thereby acknowledging that the scheme derogated from the standard of Article XVI:4.

7. Bureau of National Affairs, *US Import Weekly,* 27 April 1983, p. 181.

commercially available on world markets to their exporters. [Emphasis supplied.]

The US rebuttal stressed that "commercially available" means *actually* available. According to this analysis, the designation of prohibited export subsidy would turn on whether the export industry (say pasta) is, *in fact,* free to purchase the subsidized upstream input (say wheat) from foreign sources. If it is free, and if local goods are furnished at prices not lower than world prices, then no subsidy should arise when the export industry chooses to buy local goods. If the export industry (pasta) is not free to purchase from whatever source it pleases, then it has become a conduit for enlarging the size of the subsidized activity (wheat). This practice should then be branded as an export subsidy.

In April 1983, the General Agreement on Tariffs and Trade (GATT) panel apparently accepted the US position, but the Subsidies Committee, responding to objections raised by the European Community and other nations, had not by March 1984 accepted the panel report.[8] Confronted with this delay, the US National Pasta Association called for unilateral US action. At this writing, the outcome remains in doubt. In our view, acceptance of the panel report would have a salutary impact. Governments would be less tempted to use finished products as a conduit for the subsidized export of raw materials and components.

Pricing Natural Resources

Closely related to the upstream subsidy question is the proper pricing of natural resources owned or controlled by government. Can government pricing of natural resources for use in downstream processing lead to a subsidy? This question arises in two basic contexts. In one context, the government imposes price controls on private transactions. The controlled prices are below either the world market price or an equilibrium price that would clear the domestic market. In the other context, the government as landlord sells resources under its control at bargain prices for downstream processing.

Over the past few years, three important natural resource pricing cases have arisen. In the first case, the European Community charged that the United States was subsidizing petrochemical exports by virtue of its price controls on crude petroleum and natural gas. This case was negotiated to a compromise without a resolution on the merits.

In the second case, an association of 250 US lumber mills, representing about 20 percent of the US industry, charged in 1982 that Canada was subsidizing the

---

8. The GATT panel decisions are not yet public; see, however, *Washington Tariff and Trade Letter,* 20 June 1983, p. 2.

cutting and subsequent exporting of logs. In terms of trade coverage, this was the largest countervailing duty suit ever filed, affecting US imports of some $2 billion.[9] At the time of the petition, US mills were paying an average of $138 for 1,000 board feet of lumber cut from US Forest Service land, while Canadian mills were paying an average of $24 to the Canadian government. The difference reflected to some extent differences in methods of auctioning cutting rights. More basically, the difference also reflected the boom in cutting rights that occurred in the United States in the late 1970s. Whatever the origins of the differential in stumpage fees, the policy question is whether firms in one country can attack as unfair the practices of a government in another country in setting such charges.

Royalty rates set by governments inevitably reflect a variety of circumstances: when contracts were let; the pace at which the government wants to exploit its natural resources; the desire of the government to promote or retard the extraction industries. Can a principled distinction be made between policies affecting the pace of exploitation of natural resources and policies affecting the pace of development of any other industry? Possibly not.

In practical terms, the consequences of extending the concept of potentially troublesome subsidies to cover the bargain sale of natural resources would be enormous. The lease of rangeland at bargain rents, the construction of irrigation works and the subsequent provision of water at bargain prices, the restricted leasing of mineral lands to companies preferred because of their environmental attitudes—all these practices would be suspect. Moreover, in the case of non-transportable natural resources, there is no ready standard of a world price, or even a well-defined national price, to use as a benchmark to determine whether, in fact, a bargain sale is present.

In its preliminary and final determinations, the Commerce Department was able to avoid this thicket of conceptual issues by finding that the Canadian stumpage rates are generally available to all firms in the wood-products industries and further that, even if they are provided to a "specific enterprise or industry," the stumpage rates are not applied preferentially among Canadian users:[10]

Further, stumpage programs do not confer a countervailable domestic subsidy for the following reasons. First we determine that stumpage programs are not provided only to a "specific enterprise or industry, or group of enterprises or industries." Rather, they are available within Canada on similar terms regardless of the industry or enterprise of the recipient. The only limitations as to the types of industries that use

9. *Washington Post*, 20 February 1983, p. H1; Bureau of National Affairs, *US Import Weekly*, 9 March 1983.

10. *Certain Softwood Products from Canada; Final Negative Countervailing Duty Determinations*, 48 Fed. Reg. 24159, 24167, 31 May 1983; also see the *Preliminary Negative Countervailing Duty Determinations*, 98 Fed. Reg. 24159, 11 March 1983.

stumpage reflect the inherent characteristics of this natural resource and the current level of technology. As technological advances have increased the potential users of standing timber, stumpage has been made available to the new users. Any current limitations on use are not due to the activities of the Canadian governments.

Even if stumpage programs were being provided to a "specific group of . . . industries," we determine that they would not confer a domestic subsidy. In this regard, we determine that Canadian stumpage programs, except for certain aspects of those in Ontario and Quebec, do not confer a domestic subsidy, because they do not provide goods at preferential rates to the producers of the products under investigation within the meaning of subsection 771(5)(B)(ii) . . . .

The standard contained in subsection (ii) is "preferential," which normally means only more favorable to some within the relevant jurisdiction than to others within that jurisdiction.[3] In this context, it does not mean "inconsistent with commercial considerations," a distinct term used in subsection 771(5)(B)(i) (which is not applicable with regard to stumpage programs in general because they do not involve the provision of capital, loans, or loan guarantees).

3. There may be other cases in which the number of users of a good or service may be so limited that the preferentiality test may need to be examined further. In addition, as the Department and the Department of the Treasury have recognized in prior cases, "different" does not necessarily mean "preferential."

The third case involving natural resource pricing concerned natural gas feedstock supplied by Petroleos Mexicanos (PEMEX) to Mexican industrial users, *Anhydrous and Aqua Ammonia from Mexico* (48 Fed. Reg. 14729, 5 April 1983). In this case, PEMEX supplied natural gas to domestic industry at a price below the price charged for household consumption and below the export price. The effects on ammonia trade were summarized by Richard R. Rivers, testifying on behalf of the US Domestic Nitrogen Producers' Ad Hoc Committee (1983):

In recent years, a disturbing development has emerged in the nitrogen fertilizer industry. Increasingly, foreign producers located in countries with large reserves of natural gas are entering the world nitrogen fertilizer market. These producers, however, are presenting a new and very troubling form of competition for private producers. *They are state-owned enterprises—government monopolies—and their governments are making natural gas feedstocks available virtually without cost to turn into nitrogen fertilizer to be sold in the US market at whatever price can be obtained.* Here is a step-by-step description of the process and its result:

First, a foreign government undertakes to exploit its reserves of natural gas by creating a modern, state-owned petrochemical industry, targeted at export markets.

Second, the government provides the natural gas to the state-owned ammonia producer on virtually a cost-free basis *or* at an artificial price which is intentionally set below its real market value.

Third, because these plants are owned by governments which are hard-pressed for foreign exchange, they are built to supply export markets and they are operated to supply a fixed quantity to those markets each year.

Fourth, the government in question having little or no current notion of its costs of production offers its ammonia at whatever price at which a private producer can hope to compete.

In other words, these governments are saying to their producers, "Sell 1,000,000 tons of ammonia this year (or whatever amount was designated that year in their economic plan) in the United States at whatever price you can get." The US producer, on the other hand, knowing it costs him, for example, $160 per ton to produce ammonia and it takes another $20 per ton to return the investment in plant (assuming a reasonable rate of production) says, "Sell the most ammonia you can at $180 per ton or better if you can get it, but don't sell for less than $180."

The Commerce Department did not explore these assertions in its preliminary decision. Instead, citing section 771(5)(B)(ii) of the statute, the Department of Commerce found that cheap gas is not provided to a "specific enterprise or industry, or group of enterprises or industries." In other words, since the Mexican government chooses to supply a natural resource at bargain prices to a wide range of industrial users, no subsidy arose that would trigger the US counter-vailing duty law. By implication, if the Mexican government had chosen to supply natural gas at a bargain price to only a few industries, there would be an actionable subsidy.

In our view, neither in practice nor intent were cheap stumpage rights in Canada and cheap natural gas in Mexico generally available. In both cases, a few resource-intensive industries were able to best take advantage of the bounty of nature and the promotion policies of the government.

Nevertheless, in our view, the pricing of *nontransportable* natural resources should not be subject to international scrutiny. If a country chooses to develop certain industries quickly by selling nontransportable resources "cheaply," that decision should not be regarded as "unfair," and thus subject to the imposition of countervailing duties abroad. By definition, no international market and no futures market exists for nontransportable natural resources. The rights are only sold in a series of local markets bounded in space and time. Who is to say that a government's choice of a particular price, and hence a particular rate of development, is too fast or too slow? Probably not Arthur D. Little & Co., and certainly not the US Commerce Department. Accordingly, harmful trade consequences in cases involving nontransportable natural resources are better left to the escape clause statute and its trade-impact standard of "substantial cause of serious injury."

On the other hand, when a government furnishes *transportable* natural resources at bargain prices, either by selling its own rights or by imposing price controls on private owners, a potentially troublesome subsidy is conferred on the purchasing industry. The subsidy measurement received can be measured by reference to world prices. In our view, such cases should be addressed through the imposition of coutervailing duties.

Calculating the Subsidy Derived from a Grant

It is generally conceded that government grants amount to subsidies. The question is over what period of time, and therefore over what units of output, government grants should be apportioned in order to calculate the subsidy per unit of output. The US Commerce Department considered this question in the context of the European carbon steel cases (see appendix H and Shannon Stock Shuman and Charles Owen Verrill 1984) and modified its previous position.[11]

Grants for operating expenses and small grants are simply allocated to output in the year of the grant. Larger grants, associated with upgrading or acquiring equipment, are prorated over the life of the equipment. However, the amount of subsidy per year is adjusted to reflect the present value of money. The following example (as explained by Mr. B. Kelly) demonstrates the Commerce Department's method (also see appendix H).

Suppose a company receives a $1,000 grant in 1979. The average life of equipment for the industry is 10 years. Thus, the grant is prorated over 10 years. The government borrowing rate is 5 percent. What is the amount of annual subsidy?

Let:

$$\text{Grant amount present value} = PV = \$1,000$$
$$\text{Number of years} = N = 10$$
$$\text{Discount rate} = k = .05$$
$$\text{Annual subsidy} = X$$

The purpose of the exercise is to calculate an annual subsidy X so as to countervail the total amount of $1,000, in 1979 dollars, over a period of 10 years, starting in the year of grant receipt, 1979, and going through 1988.

The basic formula used by the Department of Commerce is:

---

11. Under previous Department of Commerce practice, capital subsidies were prorated on a straight-line basis over one-half of the useful life of capital equipment in the industry. No interest charge was made for the time-value of money.

(1) $PV = X/(1 + k)^0 + X/(1 + k)^1 + X/(1 + k)^2 + \ldots + X/(1 + k)^{n-1}$

Or, taking the sum of the geometric series:

(2) $PV = X((1 + k) - (1 + k)^{1-n})/k$

Substituting the values given above into the formula:

(3) $\$1,000 = X((1.05) - (1.05)^{-9})/.05$

(4) $X = 50/((1.05) - (1.05)^{-9}) = \$123.34$

Thus, the Department of Commerce would apply a countervailing duty of $123.34 per year from 1979 through 1988. The total nominal amount of countervailing duties would be $1,233.40. The total present value, in 1979 dollars, of the duties would be $1,000.

By contrast with the US approach, the European Community views a government grant as containing a subsidy only to the extent of the interest rate on government debt. In other words, the Community would not attempt to apportion the principal amount of the government grant over the life of the equipment, or any other period of time. Whether other countries will adopt the US or EC approach for evaluating the subsidy element in a government grant remains to be seen.

Equity and Loans to State-owned Enterprises

In the recent steel cases, the characterization of equity and loans to state-owned enterprises became a leading issue in the definition of domestic subsidies. The antidistortion school was quick to point out that equity ownership by the state opens up vistas of potential subsidization opaque both to the taxpaying public and to foreign competitors, involving outright coverage of operating losses, cross-subsidization among products, and informal targeting of the export market (Kenneth D. Walters and R. Joseph Monsen 1979). This specter raised several issues, for example:

☐ Under what circumstances is the government purchase of equity or extension of credit a potentially troublesome subsidy?

☐ How should the subsidy be allocated to activities and types of output?

Broadly speaking, the Commerce Department analyzed these cases from the perspective of the benefit conferred on the firm, in light of its alternative means of raising finance. (For a thorough discussion of equity finance questions, see Charlene Barshefsky, Alice L. Mattice, and William L. Martin 1983.) By contrast, the benefit theory was *not* employed in choosing an appropriate interest rate for valuing the subsidy component of a government grant. Instead, the risk-free government rate, or "cost of money to government" standard was used in the present value calculation.

When Is The Purchase of Equity or Extension of Credit a Potentially Troublesome Subsidy?

Some state-owned firms proposed that government purchases of equity and extensions of credit should be condemned as subsidies only if they fail the "business judgment" test: was there a valid business reason at the time of the investment for the equity purchase? The business judgment test specifically averts the glare of hindsight.

By contrast, US competitors of state-owned enterprises proposed that, to the extent that the private market would not have made the investment on the same terms and conditions as the government, there was a subsidy. According to this view, the business judgment test is simply too tolerant of ad hoc justifications served up by foreign governments.

In its decision in the European steel cases (see appendix H and Shuman and Verrill 1984), the Department of Commerce took a middle position. It held that equity purchases do not entail a subsidy per se, unless the government purchases the shares from the company itself at prices higher than prevailing market prices (a test that is only relevant when a private market exists for the shares).

Apart from these infrequent instances of a subsidy per se, the Department of Commerce held that government purchases of equity entailed a subsidy to the extent that subsequent earnings were less than the average return on equity investment for the country as a whole. This is a fairly rigorous test since, at any given time, approximately half the industrial firms in the country will be earning less than the average return on equity.

The decision also announced, however, that the amount of subsidy would in no event exceed an amount that would be calculated, if an outright grant had been given instead of the purchase of equity, using the present value allocation methods described earlier.

In the case of loans and loan guarantees, the Department of Commerce distinguished between creditworthy and uncreditworthy companies. Government loans to private firms made at commercial rates and guarantees to a creditworthy company were deemed not to entail a subsidy. Government loans to a creditworthy company at a rate less than the commercial interest rate were deemed to entail a subsidy to the extent of the difference. In the case of loans to creditworthy companies, two different benchmarks were used for the "commercial" rate. For broad national programs, such as export credit support and generally available public credit to small enterprises, a national average commercial rate served as the benchmark. For credit programs targeted on a specific sector, the alternative rate of interest paid by companies in that sector was the preferred benchmark.

By contrast, loans to an uncreditworthy company were regarded as the equivalent of a contribution of equity. The annual amount of subsidy was calculated in the same manner as an equity contribution, with the limitation that the calculated amount of subsidy would not exceed the grant equivalent of the original loan. In choosing this approach, the Commerce Department rejected methods that would look at the alternative borrowing rate available to distressed firms.

The Department of Commerce methods of calculating the amount of subsidy is, of course, not the only possible method for dealing with government purchases of equity and extensions of credit to an industrial firm. In the view of the European Community, the subsidy should be calculated with reference to the government's cost of money—completely ignoring the commercial financing alternatives available to the firm. The EC authorities take the position that government finance provided at or above the government's cost of money simply does not entail a subsidy. They cite the GATT standard of cost of money to government, applied to official export credits, in support of their position. Further, in the EC view, loans and other means of finance that are extended by government with instructions that the firm undertake programs (for example, shifting production to a depressed area) should not be counted as subsidies at all. In these situations, the burden of the instruction is thought to offset the benefit of the loan.

Allocating the Subsidy to Activities and Types of Output

Can the government's contribution of equity or loan capital be traced to a particular use, not involving the production of exported goods? For example, can a subsidy be allocated entirely to the expense of closing a plant, to manufacturing goods strictly for the domestic market, or to funding research for future products? Alternatively, can a subsidy be allocated entirely to exported products on the presumption that, without a subsidy, the firm would not have been able to reach the export market?

The Department of Commerce takes the position, which we regard as sensible, that equity and loan capital are normally available for all corporate purposes. Accordingly, the party asserting that the subsidy should be allocated to less than all products must meet a heavy burden of proof. However, if an enterprise can show, for example, that government funds are earmarked for plant closing, then, in our view, exports should not be penalized for a socially desirable adjustment policy. (See Barshefsky, Mattice, and Martin 1983, for a criticism of the Commerce Department's decision on this issue.)

Research and Development Subsidies

Government sponsorship of research and development raises some of the same issues as government purchases of equity, for example:

□ When is a government contribution to R&D a potentially troublesome subsidy?

□ How should an R&D subsidy be allocated over units of output and over time?

When is R&D Support a Potentially Troublesome Subsidy?

The emerging standard seems to regard government assistance at the product development stage as a potentially troublesome subsidy. But government support for basic research or government support for R&D by way of generally favorable tax treatment is not potentially troublesome. In the lead US case, *Liquid Optic Level Sensing Systems from Canada* (44 Fed. Reg. 1728, 8 January 1979), the Canadian R&D grant was awarded *after* the patent had been obtained. It was thus deemed more "development" than "research" and hence an objectionable subsidy.

The "basic" versus "applied" distinction used in the *Liquid Optic Level Sensing Systems* case fits naturally into customary R&D labels. In practice, however, these are the wrong labels for defining an unfair trade practice, not only because it is hard to demarcate basic from applied research, but more importantly because what counts in the industrial setting is whether the government *concentrates* its R&D effort on particular industries, and whether it *delays*, even temporarily, the dissemination of the R&D findings to foreign firms. US biogenetic and semiconductor firms do not much care about the basic or applied nature of R&D financed by the Japanese government. They are more concerned with the targeting of those industries for government assistance and the slow dissemination of research results outside Japan. The US Department of Commerce, in its final determination in the European carbon steel cases, did not explore the R&D question in depth, but took the general position that targeted R&D assistance may come to be viewed as a potentially troublesome subsidy (see the introductory section of Department of Commerce Appendix 2, reproduced in appendix H).

Allocating the R&D Subsidy

Over what time period, and to which kinds of output, should an R&D subsidy be allocated? Consider: a small R&D subsidy might help build a formidable export capability several years later. If the R&D subsidy is apportioned over cumulative output from the time of the initial grant to the date when a complaint is brought, the calculated countervailing duty per unit of exports could be trivial. But if the

R&D subsidy is allocated entirely to exports, the contribution of R&D to production for the domestic market is somehow forgotten. Because this debate goes to the nature of the remedy, we shall defer further discussion until chapter 5.

Regional Offsets

Should a reduction in the countervailing duty or other countermeasure be mandated on account of a nation's companion practices or policies that increase the costs of the allegedly subsidized industry? For example, if a government requires an industry to locate in a high-cost, depressed part of the country as a condition for access to a regional subsidy, should the calculation of a countervailing duty take into account the industry's higher costs?

At one time, the US Treasury tried to develop a system of calculating permissible offsets to domestic subsidies, invoking a rule of reason to distinguish between "trade distorting" subsidies and other subsidies. The US Treasury was evidently seeking parallels, in the realm of domestic subsidies, with the long-standing administrative rule that the nonexcessive remission of indirect taxes is not an export subsidy.

These efforts were rebuffed by the US Congress, which feared that all manner of practices might creep into the calculation of offsets. In a sense, the Congress endorsed the argument of the antidistortion school that theoretical justifications of subsidies are likely to be abused. Congress accordingly defined permissible offsets quite narrowly in the Trade Agreements Act of 1979, section 771(6):

(6) Net Subsidy.—For the purpose of determining the net subsidy, the administering authority may subtract from the gross subsidy the amount of—

(A) any application fee, deposit, or similar payment paid in order to qualify for, or to receive, the benefit of the subsidy,

(B) any loss in the value of the subsidy resulting from its deferred receipt, if the deferral is mandated by Government order, and

(C) export taxes, duties, or other charges levied on the export of merchandise to the United States specifically intended to offset the subsidy received.

Possibly the Congress took too hostile a view of regional subsidies. There may be circumstances in which a country can convincingly show that its subsidies do in fact correct a regional distortion specific to a particular industry, and that the distortion could not have been corrected by an exchange rate adjustment or a more general subsidy. In such cases, it would seem reasonable for countries, by agreement, to define a permissible level of subsidy that would not attract countermeasures.[12]

Investment Incentives

Government grants, loans, preferential tax treatment, and many other incentives aimed at inducing private firms to locate facilities in a particular country or region loom as a major irritant in trade relations. H. Peter Gray and Ingo Walter (1983) have documented, for example, that investment incentives are widespread in the petrochemical industry.

For many firms, the practice of playing one government off against another in the bidding competition for the location of new plants has become a way of life. A recent illustration was Britain's offer of various incentives, totaling some 85 percent of investment costs, to attract Hyster, a Portland, Oregon, manufacturer of forklift trucks. Belgium and the Netherlands complained, for fear that Hyster would eliminate 1,800 jobs in their countries.[13]

The European Community has machinery for investigating complaints between its member states. Some 200 inquiries, like the Hyster case, were opened in 1981 and 1982.[14] The Organization for Economic Cooperation and Development (OECD) has also established a weak notification system for keeping track of investment incentives. But many other steps must be taken and many other issues resolved before the international community can effectively control the investment incentive game.

First, there is the problem of identifying government practices that involve "abnormal" incentives and thus are offensive. Possible definitional criteria may be envisaged. Incentives that are freely available to all investors and do not have a "cradle robbing" character should, for the most part, prove inoffensive. For example, such measures as tax deductions and credits for research and development, general investment tax credits, and general provisions for the establishment of free trade zones would seem to be acceptable (assuming that the particular practices by themselves do not offend agreed international rules). On the other hand, a targeted, ad hoc government grant to one company to help offset R&D or training costs, or tax-free status offered to one firm in return for the firm's construction of a plant in a particular location, would seem to fall within the range of offensive measures.

---

12. Bilateral agreements to this effect, while much more practical than multilateral agreements, would raise the most-favored-nation issue: can a regional subsidy be regarded as an offset when granted by country A but not when granted by country B?

13. *Wall Street Journal*, 24 June 1983, p. 26.

14. Ibid.

Second, there is the question whether a complaint must await the emergence of trade flows—at a time when the facts of the original investment decision may be "old and cold" and any distortions resulting from the international bidding game have already occurred—or whether a complaint may be mounted at the time the bidding takes place. In a recent case, *Commuter Aircraft from France and Italy* (47 Fed. Reg. 31632, 21 July 1982), the US International Trade Commission held that trade must flow before a threat of injury can be found. This decision accords with code Article 4:3, which holds that the complaining signatory should find that "through the effects of the subsidy, the subsidized imports are causing injury," before it imposes countervailing duties. This approach means, however, that in most investment incentive cases relief will be delayed; and relief delayed may be relief denied. By contrast, the European Community investigates, and occasionally acts upon, complaints between its own member states well before trade begins to flow.

A third question concerns the attribution of fault. When two nations bid against one another for a particular plant, is the chief wrongdoer the nation that wins the plant, the nation that both wins the plant and grants the largest amount of offensive subsidies, or the nation that offers the largest amount of offensive subsidies? Under the first standard, a country that awarded a small grant in the face of larger offers might nevertheless be subject to international discipline upon winning the plant. Under the second standard, if a country offering a smaller package of incentives won the plant, it would not offend international standards, while a country that lost the plant would never be criticized, regardless of the level of the incentives offered. Under the third standard, a loser in the bidding could still offend international standards by offering the largest package of incentives.

A fourth question concerns the measurement of offending subsidies. Presumably, all subsidies would be expressed, by some agreed arithmetic, in present value standards. Once that calculation is performed, is the offense simply measured as the margin by which the winning government tops the losing government? Or is the entire package of subsidies subject to countermeasures?

Finally, a politically difficult issue faces federal systems, in particular, the United States, Canada, and Australia. Note 22 to code Article 7 imposes upon signatories "the international consequences that may arise under this Agreement as a result of the granting of subsidies within their territories." But to what extent can these federal governments muster the strength to discipline offensive practices that originate at subfederal levels?[15] The European Community has faced

15. For a good discussion of federalism problems in the context of state export credit programs, see Bureau of National Affairs, *US Export Weekly*, 30 August 1983, Special Supplement, "State Efforts to Establish Export Financing Facilities Meet with Local Opposition, Administration Ambivalence."

the same problem with respect to its member states, and, so far, has enjoyed little success in curbing subsidies.[16]

Undoubtedly other obstacles will arise, but these five issues give some indication of the hurdles that await international negotiations to limit investment incentives.

Targeted Industries

"Industrial targeting" by foreign governments is gaining considerable attention in trade circles. It promises to be a concept both difficult to define and to answer with appropriate remedies. (See the articles by Richard Corrigan 1983; the US Senate Banking Committee hearings July 1983; and the major study by the US International Trade Commission October 1983.) At the heart of the debate is the belief that certain foreign governments, especially the Japanese and the French, but also the Canadians, Germans, and others, select particular industries for favored treatment. Alan Wm. Wolff (1983, pp. 7–8) describes the Japanese strategy this way:

> The general pattern of the strategy is as follows: The home market is closed as part of a conscious strategy to establish an industry. Together, government and selected firms choose a few high-volume product lines for specialization. With the help of government grants and loans, and the cooperation of the banking system, large new investments are made in advanced production equipment. If the product is one requiring technological breakthroughs, research and development is funded by the government. Antimonopoly laws are waived to smooth the way toward agreed objectives. An "entering wedge" export drive, characterized by extremely aggressive pricing, is launched with the objective of obtaining market dominance. Then, once a beachhead is established in a broad commodity product area, the product ladder is scaled to obtain a commanding position in the market. Reluctantly, protection of the home market can then be relaxed, as the major objectives have been achieved.

> This is a sound strategy. It worked in the competition between Japan and the United States to produce computer memory chips. Japan has won—so far.

Among the industries said to be targeted by Japan and other countries are computers, microelectronics, robotics, machine tools, and aerospace (Jack Baranson and Malmgren 1981; Robert W. Galvin 1983; William L. Givens 1982; US International Trade Commission September and October 1983). According

---

16. *Wall Street Journal,* 24 June 1983, p. 26.

to Wolff and like-minded observers, the favored industries receive government nourishment in at least five major ways:

☐ They are assured government procurement at favorable prices.

☐ The private domestic market is protected by a variety of tariff and especially nontariff barriers.

☐ The field of new entrants is winnowed out, thereby saving the survivors a costly competitive race.

☐ The government may finance cooperative R&D projects, may extend credit to high-risk ventures at normal commercial rates, and may offer other subsidies.

☐ Regulations that might impose heavy costs on a new industry, relating, for example, to working conditions or the general environment, may be relaxed.

The first, second, and third practices, no matter how decisive in catapulting an industry to world scale, are not now regarded as subsidies that merit countermeasures.[17] Only the fourth, and possibly the fifth group, fall within the normal range of countervailable measures. The limited scope of customary remedies, in the face of targeting practices, has prompted Washington trade lawyers to seek novel forms of relief.

In May 1982, Houdaille Industries, a US producer of numerically controlled machines, filed a petition with the US Trade Representative setting forth in abundant detail Japanese practices over several decades allegedly designed to encourage the Japanese machine tool industry first to capture the domestic market, and second to march upon the world (Houdaille Industries 1982). A subsequent study by the US International Trade Commission (September 1983, p. ix) concluded that: "The increases in Japan's machine tool production during 1977–1982 were, in part, a result of more than 20 years of government intervention in the machine tool industry."

Houdaille (at the suggestion of Covington and Burling, a Washington law firm) sought a novel remedy: invocation by the president of section 103 of the US Revenue Act of 1971. Under this provision, the president can deny US investment tax credits for the purchase of foreign goods, when the offending country "engages in discriminatory or other acts (including tolerance of international cartels) or policies unjustifiably restricting United States commerce."

---

17. At a press conference in Tokyo on 30 March 1983, Representative Sam M. Gibbons (D-Fla.) suggested that the first three practices should be considered subsidies when used to promote a stronger export industry. Reuters tape, 30 March 1983, 30258. Later in 1983, his suggestions were embodied in a bill circulated to the House Ways and Means Committee. Bureau of National Affairs, *US Import Weekly*, 28 September 1983, pp. 1009–13.

After a year-long interagency battle, the president decided not to grant the relief sought for three reasons. First, Houdaille was unable to point to specific Japanese practices that ran contrary to international agreements. Second, the proposed remedy would contradict the most-favored-nation requirement of GATT in that only Japanese machine tools would be denied tax benefits. Third, US actions might trigger a rash of similar actions abroad. Instead, the administration opened talks with Japan on its industrial policies and suggested that Houdaille might wish to pursue the standard approach of filing a section 301 petition.[18] However, as currently structured, section 301 is not necessarily a promising avenue for obtaining relief against potentially objectionable foreign government practices. As Clyde Prestowitz observed, a section 301 petition, if carried to its conclusion, can put the president in the position of condemning another country's domestic policies. Foreign policy considerations are likely to be paramount in such cases, so that the domestic petitioner is unlikely to be awarded relief, even if he makes a showing that unfair trade practices result from domestic policies in the foreign country.[19] This thought is echoed by Clements (1983, p. 50; see discussion of section 301 below).

The administration also unveiled a plan to permit US high technology firms to cooperate on R&D efforts in order to improve their own international competitive position. One group of firms, joined together in the Microelectronics and Computer Technology Corporation and aided by a large grant from the Department of Defense, already has been granted an antitrust exemption.[20] The US Justice Department also has proposed that US antitrust laws be modified to exempt corporate joint R&D ventures from liability for treble damages in civil suits. (Such joint R&D ventures would still be liable for actual damages.)[21]

In contrast to the Houdaille petition, the US semiconductor industry has taken a different approach (orchestrated by the Washington law firm of Verner, Liipfert, Bernard, and McPherson). Rather than seeking administrative relief in the first instance, the industry embarked on a campaign to "educate" the administration and Congress on methods used by Japan to limit the intrusion of foreign producers in the Japanese market while at the same time acquiring a larger share of world markets for Japanese producers (see Semiconductor Industry Association 1983; Wolff 1983; Galvin 1983; and Clements 1983). In an informal way,

---

18. Bureau of National Affairs, *US Import Weekly*, 27 April 1983; *Washington Post*, 26 April 1983, p. D7; *Congressional Quarterly*, 29 January 1983, pp. 211–14; William Clements (1983). For a description of the bureaucratic politics, see *Washington Post*, 15 August 1983, p. A1.

19. Comments made by Clyde Prestowitz, Counselor to the Secretary of Commerce for Japanese Affairs, before the Marketing and International Trade Committee of the President's Commission on Industrial Competitiveness, December 1, 1983.

20. *Science*, 17 June 1983, pp. 1256–57; *Washington Post*, 11 May 1983, p. D7.

21. *Washington Post*, 30 March 1983, p. D8.

the US semiconductor industry has suggested that the Japanese government should assure foreign suppliers a minimum share of the Japanese market.

It is hard to imagine a simple solution to the problem of targeted industries. The definition of targeting practices is imprecise. The trade effects may appear years or even decades after the government initiatives have been withdrawn. Elements of targeting can be found in a vast array of government procurement and other policies, and traditional offset remedies somehow do not seem equal to the grievance. In 1983, Representative Sam M. Gibbons (D-Fla.) sponsored the Trade Remedies Reform Act (H.R. 4784) which included new approaches to deal with novel unfair trade practices.[22] Among other proposals, Gibbons would create an office in the USITC to monitor foreign targeting practices. Further, he would add to the list of actionable practices under the US countervailing duty law "targeting subsidies," defined as "any government plan or scheme consisting of coordinated actions, whether carried out severally or jointly or in combination with any other subsidy, that are bestowed on a specific enterprise, industry, or group thereof, the effect of which is to assist the beneficiary to become more competitive in the export of any class or kind of merchandise." He also would give final decision-making authority to the US Trade Representative (USTR) in order to mitigate the larger foreign policy considerations that invariably enter into decisions made by the president.

We believe that progress to limit targeting most likely will come by precisely defining and addressing offensive individual practices, such as export exhortations coupled with fiscal incentives. Perhaps the Gibbons bill will lead in this direction.[23] In any event, we would prefer that the United States undertake a focused response to specific targeting practices rather than embark on its own uncharted voyage in the sea of industrial intervention.

---

22. Bureau of National Affairs, *US Import Weekly*, 28 September 1983, pp. 1009–13.

23. For a critique of the Gibbons bill (which was approved by the Trade Subcommittee of the House Ways and Means Committee on February 29, 1984), see US Chamber of Commerce (1983).

5

Remedies

While a great deal of effort was lavished in the Tokyo Round on defining the appropriate level of trade impact required to designate a subsidy an offensive subsidy, and some attention was paid to defining export subsidies, very little attention was paid to designing effective remedies. Ideally, remedies would serve several functions: redress the adverse trade impact; offset the distortion; avoid harm to innocent parties; prompt the subsidizing country to alter its policies; avert an escalating spiral of retaliation; not provide a platform for unwarranted protection; and not require the complaining country to spend public monies. Few, if any, remedies meet all criteria. The design of effective remedies is further complicated, since remedies must address the impact of subsidies in three quite different settings:

☐ in the domestic market of the complaining country

☐ in the domestic market of the subsidizing country

☐ in a third-country market.

This chapter examines the functions of various remedies and their success in different settings.

Countervailing Duties

The countervailing duty, when applied to the home market of the complaining country under procedures that lead to its acquiescence by the subsidizing country, meets some of the criteria for an ideal remedy. Article 4 of the Subsidies Code sets forth a number of safeguards designed to avert excessive countervailing duties. In particular:

1. . . . It is desirable that the imposition be permissive in the territory of all signatories and the duty be less than the total amount of the subsidy if such lesser duty would be adequate to remove the injury to the domestic industry.

111

2. No countervailing duty shall be levied[14] on any imported product in excess of the amount of the subsidy found to exist, calculated in terms of subsidization per unit of the subsidized and exported product.[15]

3. When a countervailing duty is imposed in respect of any product, such countervailing duty shall be levied, in the appropriate amounts, on a non-discriminatory basis on imports of such product from all sources found to be subsidized and to be causing injury, except as to imports from those sources which have renounced any subsidies in question or from which undertakings under the terms of this Agreement have been accepted . . . .

5. (a) Proceedings may[16] be suspended or terminated without the imposition of provisional measures or countervailing duties, if undertakings are accepted under which:

    (i) the government of the exporting country agrees to eliminate or limit the subsidy or take other measures concerning its effects; or

    (ii) the exporter agrees to revise its prices so that the investigating authorities are satisfied that the injurious effect of the subsidy is eliminated. Price increases under undertakings shall not be higher than necessary to eliminate the amount of the subsidy . . . .

---

14. As used in this Agreement "levy" shall mean the definitive or final legal assessment or collection of a duty or tax.
15. An understanding among signatories should be developed setting out the criteria for the calculation of the amount of the subsidy.
16. The word "may" shall not be interpreted to allow the simultaneous continuation of proceedings with the implementation of price undertakings, except as provided in paragraph 5(b) of this Article.

The precatory language of Article 4:1 is designed to avert a countervailing duty that overcompensates for the injurious trade impact. However, Article 4:1 says nothing about undercompensation for injurious trade impact. For example, a subsidy of $10 million might launch a new Japanese industry. The industry might take advantage of a favorable learning curve, and five years later, "invade" the French market. A countervailing duty equal to the amount of the original subsidy, when prorated over total output, might not enable a new French competitor to catch up with its Japanese rival.

Further, the traditional countervailing duty simply does not address trade impacts in the home market of the subsidizing country or in third-country markets. These cases are largely left to ad hoc responses, either multilaterally or nationally. The problem with ad hoc responses is that they take time and negotiation to craft. The uncertain application of an uncertain remedy has little deterrent value.

Equally important are the dangers inherent in some of the substitutes for the countervailing duty remedy. Under code Article 4:5, no countervailing duty need be imposed, if the government of the exporting signatory agrees to limit the subsidy or take "other measures" (for example, an export tax or even quantitative export restraints) that offset the effects of the subsidy, or if the private exporter agrees to revise its price structure upwards to eliminate the effect of the subsidy.[1] This provision was essentially incorporated in the US countervailing duty statute (section 704 of the Trade Agreements Act of 1979). In addition, under US law, a petitioner can simply withdraw his complaint, and thereby terminate the inquiry. The petitioner can then use this withdrawal privilege as leverage to induce the US government to negotiate an accord with the foreign government.

Suspension agreements are used with increasing frequency to terminate countervailing duty proceedings under US law. In 1980, three cases were settled with suspension agreements. In 1982, some fifteen cases were settled in this manner. Generally speaking, however, US firms are not enthusiastic about foreign governmental promises to impose export taxes to offset the subsidy, or foreign producer promises to raise prices on sales to the US market. US firms view such "price assurances" as ineffective and simply not as rewarding as a countervailing duty or a quota. Thus, in settlement talks, US firms have often tried to seek a quantitative remedy.

Practical experience with quantitative settlement provisions, in the context of cases brought against European steel producers, suggests that this alternative to the countervailing duty can badly distort the efficient location of production. Indeed, the remedy can prove worse than the original subsidy.

Thus, in October 1982, the US government and the European Community, after an arduous series of discussions, agreed on steel quotas as a basis for withdrawal of the countervailing duty cases by petitioning US firms. Among other side effects, these quotas have restricted shipments from efficient, unsubsidized German producers.[2] Further, the US-EC arrangement contemplates reme-

---

1. For example, in 1982 the US Commerce Department suspended its investigation of steel plate imports from Brazil following Brazil's agreement to levy an export tax that completely offsets the subsidy on its plate exports to the United States. The subsidy itself remains in place, however. See 47 Fed. Reg. 39394, 7 September 1982; 48 Fed. Reg. 11190, 16 March 1983.

The Trade Remedies Reform Act sponsored by Representative Sam M. Gibbons (D-Fla.) would sharply curtail the administration's flexibility in settling countervailing duty cases. The use of "offsets" such as export taxes would be precluded. Quantitative restrictions and the withdrawal of petitions due to a bilateral restraint agreement also would be prohibited, unless the president determined that their effect on consumers would be less adverse than imposition of countervailing duties.

2. The multiple exchange of letters constituting the steel agreement, generally dated October 21, 1982, may be obtained from the US Commerce Department. German government resistance to the quotas nearly scuttled the entire agreement: only at the eleventh hour did German officials acquiesce in the EC plan to manage steel trade with the United States. See Bureau of National Affairs, *US Import Weekly,* 27 October 1982, pp. 99–101.

dial action (by either the United States or the European Community) in the event that European exports of steel products *not* covered by the quotas show a significant increase and threaten the arrangement's protective aims. Finally, consultations are contemplated, if imports from third countries appear to be replacing imports from the Community. The ultimate goal of such consultations is unclear, but during the US-EC talks, the negotiators apparently considered side understandings to limit imports of Korean, Taiwanese, and Japanese steel (Charles Trozzo 1982). In short, the US-EC arrangement looks uncomfortably like the foundation stone for a Multi-Steel Agreement that might, in time, come to resemble the notoriously restrictive Multi-Fiber Arrangement.

Section 30I, US Trade Act of 1974

In the Trade Act of 1974, the US Congress attempted to improve the ability of the United States to respond to certain "unfair" trade practices. Section 301 of that act permits presidential retaliation against "unreasonable" and "unjustified" foreign import restrictions, export subsidies, or other practices that "burden, restrict or discriminate against United States commerce" either in the home market or in third-country markets. "Unjustifiable" means restrictions that are inconsistent with international obligations. "Unreasonable" means restrictions that are not necessarily illegal but discriminate against or burden US commerce. The law covers international trade in services as well as merchandise.[3] Among other uses, section 301 can serve as the vehicle for domestic implementation of a General Agreement on Tariffs and Trade (GATT) Article XXIII recommendation (involving "nullification or impairment") or a GATT Subsidies Committee recommendation (involving, for example, an export subsidy with the requisite "adverse effects" on trade). In addition, the president can use his section 301 powers even in the absence of a GATT recommendation.

In short, section 301 codifies latent US executive branch powers to impose economic countermeasures against foreign countries. Other nations quietly exercise similar but uncodified powers. Since section 301 is not subject to the US Administrative Procedures Act (which lays out notice and hearing requirements), the US Trade Representative (USTR), like its counterparts abroad, also enjoys some discretion to pursue US commercial goals in a quiet and flexible manner. (For description and criticism of the workings of section 301, see Shirley A. Coffield 1981; US General Accounting Office 1983; William Clements 1983.)

---

3. The trade coverage of section 301 is somewhat broader than the coverage of GATT. The GATT coverage is limited to merchandise trade, although in recent years GATT pronouncements have extended to certain ancillary services, such as export finance. Section 301 covers all services associated with international trade. Thus, section 301 actions have been invoked on behalf of insurance underwriters, an area which GATT is not yet prepared to explore.

In practice, the USTR usually makes a staff finding that countervailing and antidumping duties are inadequate before opening a section 301 case. Countervailing duties could be found inadequate for a number of reasons:

☐ The lost markets could be in the subsidizing country or in third-country markets.

☐ The practices in question may seem harmful and unfair to the complaining firm, but they may not entail potentially troublesome subsidies as defined by the Department of Commerce, or cause material injury.

☐ The amount of subsidy, when prorated over cumulative sales, may be trivial and not reflect the injurious loss of market owing to "learning curve" effects.

In theory, a wide variety of interventionist foreign measures, including assorted means of encouraging domestic industry to displace imports and penetrate export markets, could be subject to offsetting US remedies under section 301. In practice, between the passage of the Trade Act of 1974 (in January 1975) and the Trade Agreements Act of 1979 (in July 1979), some eighteen petitions were filed under section 301. No retaliatory action was taken in any of these cases. Six cases were referred to GATT panels; four cases were the subject of bilateral consultations under GATT auspices; and eight cases were never involved in the GATT process. As Clements observed (1983, p. 50):

The shortcomings of Section 301 stem from the political nature of the process. The petitioner must successfully argue against the countervailing foreign policy considerations in order to convince the Executive Branch to retaliate against the trade practices of the foreign government. The difficulty of prevailing in such an argument is amply evidenced by the fact that the US has never taken retaliatory action in response to a 301 petition. Indeed the USTR "considers retaliation a tool of *very last resort.*" Thus the very best that can be expected when bringing a section 301 complaint is a successful (from the standpoint of the petitioner) bilateral negotiation between the United States and the exporting country.

Some commentators have suggested that the United States use section 301 more aggressively as a "sword" to strike at new and subtle forms of subsidies. This suggestion presumes that hard questions about the appropriate scope of industrial policies could best be answered in combat over individual cases. That presumption is not self-evident. A case could be made that merely threatening to use section 301 might prompt serious international review of industrial policies that now fall in the shadows of GATT rules. But if the United States were to strike unilaterally against foreign government practices that parallel US practices, or against practices that the international community has not yet judged unacceptable, the risk of retaliation could be great. At French insistence, the European

Community is considering adoption of a "New Commercial Policy Instrument" that would confer on Brussels much the same wide-ranging powers found in section 301. If adopted, the new instrument might well be used as a shield against unwelcome US initiatives.

The Export Credit Approach: Matching Subsidy with Subsidy

The Arrangement on Guidelines for Officially Supported Export Credits provides a unique means of retaliation against nonconforming export credit practices. Two clauses are central to the arrangement's operation:

☐ Participating governments must notify other participants at least 10 days before offering an export credit that does not meet the guidelines established by the arrangement.

☐ All participants then have the right first to request consultations, and second to compete either by matching the terms of the nonconforming credit or by offering other nonconforming terms.

This system of matching credit terms provides each country an opportunity to protect its economic interests in third markets by offering, on a timely basis, export credit terms at least equal to the most generous (and subsidized) credit terms then available. This threat of matching provides a strong deterrent to initial derogations from the norms of the arrangement.

The Export-Import Bank Act of 1978 provided a similar countermeasure for predatory export credit sales to the US market. The secretary of the treasury may authorize the Export-Import Bank to finance the sale of *domestic* goods for *domestic* use, in response to competing imports that are supported by credits not in conformity with international arrangements.[4] Despite some close cases, this threat has not yet been invoked. In 1983, the US Congress considered statutory language that would *require* the Export-Import Bank to provide matching terms of credit, upon a finding that foreign export credit practices are a significant competitive factor.

The export credit matching approach has many desirable features. It retaliates in a precisely focused manner. It minimizes harm to innocent parties. It reaches

---

4. The US Treasury Department's investigation of New York City's purchase of subway cars from Canada hinged on whether or not such authority should be used. The US Treasury ultimately determined that the Canadian firm would have won the contract even in the absence of nonconforming export credits and therefore did not authorize the use of Export-Import Bank funds. In a countervailing duty petition, however, the US Commerce Department found that the Canadian subway cars were subsidized. The USITC also made a preliminary finding of reasonable indication of injury to the domestic producer, the Budd Company (Bureau of National Affairs, *US Import Weekly*, 4 August 1982, p. 537). Subsequently, the Budd Company withdrew its petition.

into third-country markets. When successful, it instantly redresses the adverse trade impact of the subsidy. The one great drawback is that matching the terms of subsidized credit at home or abroad entails a heavy budget outlay. The heavy budget outlay is a major consideration for President Reagan, as it was for President Carter.

Countervailing Subsidies

One remedy that might be given wider and more automatic application to offset subsidies on traded goods is the countervailing subsidy. This is the remedy now used in the export credit arena under the label of matching. Like matched export credits, a countervailing subsidy would impose heavy budget costs on the complaining country. Unlike matched export credits, however, countervailing subsidies are not yet an internationally accepted form of retaliation. Their use therefore runs a greater danger of prompting escalation. These defects became evident following the US decision to subsidize the sale of wheat flour to Egypt. The wheat flour subsidy not only cost the United States a good deal of money; it also prompted the European Community, at French urging, to retaliate with subsidized sales of wheat flour to US markets in China and Latin America.

The defects of the countervailing subsidy might be mitigated. For example, budget costs could be defrayed if the complaining country raised monies by imposing a low-rate duty on all imports from the subsidizing country. Indeed, a suggestion along these lines was offered many years ago by Alexander Hamilton, who urged in 1791 that special duties be imposed on subsidized imports and turned over to those domestic industries that the United States wanted to nourish for infant-industry reasons.[5] In modern circumstances, when third-country markets are at stake, authorization for any low-rate duty should be obtained in advance from the Subsidies Committee of the GATT. The prior authorization procedure would enhance the acceptability of the measure and might even lead to a withdrawal of the initial subsidy.

Administrative Remedies in Third-Country Markets

The loss of third-country markets because of subsidies, especially in agricultural goods, presents a particularly difficult problem. After all, third-country importers are generally delighted to buy from the cheapest source. Countervailing subsidies are one possible answer.

---

5. Alexander Hamilton, *Report on Manufactures*, in *State Papers and Speeches*, vol. 1, ed. F. Taussig (1893), cited in Peter Buck Feller (1969), p. 20.

Another answer is to institute administrative proceedings in third countries, a suggestion offered by John J. Barcelo (1980). GATT provides a basis for such proceedings in Articles VI:6(b) and (c):

(b) The CONTRACTING PARTIES may . . . permit a contracting party to levy an antidumping or countervailing duty on the importation of any product for the purpose of offsetting dumping or subsidization which causes or threatens material injury to an industry in the territory of another contracting party exporting the product concerned to the territory of the importing contracting party . . . .

(c) In exceptional circumstances, however, where delay might cause damage which would be difficult to repair, a contracting party may levy a countervailing duty for the purpose referred to in subparagraph (b) of this paragraph without the prior approval of the CONTRACTING PARTIES; *provided* that such action shall be reported immediately to the CONTRACTING PARTIES and that the countervailing duty shall be withdrawn promptly if the CONTRACTING PARTIES disapprove.

Individual GATT members could build on Article VI:6(c) and allow one another ready access to their administrative proceedings "in exceptional circumstances." The burden would then fall on the subsidizing country to persuade the GATT Contracting Parties to disallow the action.

This approach, however, would face two difficulties, one juridical and one practical. On the juridical side, GATT Article VI:7 creates a presumption that commodity price stabilizing schemes do *not* cause material injury, if they are operated so that domestic prices can be lower as well as higher than export prices, and if they do not "stimulate exports unduly or otherwise seriously prejudice the interests of other Contracting Parties." Only in severe cases would a complaining country be able to overcome these protective presumptions.

The practical difficulty with the Article VI:6(b) approach is more formidable. Remedies in third-country markets are most needed in agricultural trade. The few countries that keep their agricultural markets open do so because they are delighted to pay the lowest possible prices, whether or not dumping or subsidization exists. These countries are not likely to welcome the imposition of penalty duties that would deny their consumers cheap foodstuffs and other materials.

Yet even these countries might have some third-country markets that they would like to insulate from unfair trade practices. Thus, it might be possible to craft a limited "package" agreement that covered selected agricultural commodities together with some industrial products. For example, Switzerland might grant American firms access to its administrative remedies for poultry in exchange for access to US remedies for watches.

Is the Remedy Adequate?

Some US observers are concerned that trade injury does not set a floor to the extent of the remedy. These observers have the following scenario in mind. A research and development (R&D) grant helps create a mighty foreign enterprise. The domestic industry seeks relief. After extensive hearings, a countervailing duty is imposed. But, when the initial R&D grant is apportioned over cumulative units of output, the resulting duty is trivial. The countervailing duty simply does not compensate for the government-sponsored head start enjoyed by the foreign enterprise. By earning very high profits on its initial sales, the foreign enterprise began to grow and then, thanks to learning curve effects, it continued to earn high profits, while progressively cutting its prices one step ahead of the domestic competition.

This scenario is not limited to R&D grants. Other policies can, and often do, serve the same promotional function. Government procurement practices (France with computers, Japan with telecommunications), licensing restrictions (Brazil with minicomputers, France with data flows), and technical standards (Japan with drugs) can all nourish new industries. Indeed, the United States itself has often applied infant-industry principles to high-technology industries through its military procurement budget and national security regulations.

As a factual matter, this scenario might or might not occur with any regularity. But even if the scenario does recur, countervailing measures imposed unilaterally seem ill-suited to serve the goal of protecting emerging or rapidly evolving high-growth industries against foreign competitors that were given a head start by their own governments.

For one thing, it is difficult to measure the importance of government intervention in the commercial success of many ventures. Many of those who seek a level playing field for emerging and high-growth industries argue that relief should be tailored to offset not only the subsidy but also all subsequent fruits of the initial bounty. The difficulty of drawing a line between benefits flowing indirectly from prior government incentives and benefits flowing from an industry's own efforts seems nearly insurmountable. Unilateral decisions as to the proper dividing line would almost surely prompt retaliation.

If the United States is genuinely worried about its leadership in new industries, perhaps it should develop its own programs to support the particular industries of most concern. Or perhaps the United States should take the lead in attempting to define policies that are impermissible when applied by advanced industrial countries. The two approaches are not mutually exclusive. As indicated earlier, the most promising avenue ultimately lies in international negotiations to define and limit government support for emerging industries, which the international community collectively judges to be undesirable. While unilateral action by the United States carries with it the risk of retaliation, such action might be required in one or two cases to provide sufficient incentive to other nations to negotiate seriously on this issue.

Most-Favored-Nation Principle

Must a country apply remedies uniformly against all its trading partners? Or can it single out one or two trading partners for remedies? To what extent should the most-favored-nation (MFN) principle govern the application of counter-measures?

Long ago governments began to apply countervailing duties to the products of a single country without violating MFN clauses in bilateral commercial treaties (E. Bruce Butler 1969, p. 85). The question today is whether the *standards* for determining whether to apply countervailing duties should differ among countries. This question has arisen in two specific contexts. First, to what extent must the United States apply the injury test to the subsidized imports from GATT members that are not code signatories, or from GATT members that have signed the code but have not undertaken commitments agreeable to the United States? Second, to what extent must national authorities define potentially troublesome subsidies in the same manner for code signatories and for other GATT members?

The jurisprudence of GATT experience with the most-favored-nation principle sheds some light on these questions. The most-favored-nation principle comes in two varieties:

□ *conditional* (under which a privilege that country X grants to country Y, in exchange for a concession from country Y, will also be extended to country Z, but only if country Z offers a comparable concession to country X)

□ *unconditional* (under which a privilege that country X grants to country Y will be extended automatically to country Z).

The cornerstone of the GATT itself is the *unconditional* most-favored-nation principle of Article I. Yet the history of GATT agreements relating to export incentives has been a history of conditional most-favored-nation discipline that naturally ripened into conditional most-favored-nation benefits. Some examples illustrate this point. In 1955, only a subset of GATT members accepted the disciplines of Article XVI:4. A comparative handful of countries participated in drafting the 1960 Working Party Report that made a first attempt at codifying a list of export subsidies. Only 30 nations (out of a GATT membership of some 87 countries) have so far associated themselves with the 1979 Code on Subsidies and Countervailing Duties. Most developing countries still remain outside the code. Further, the "Gentlemen's Agreement" or "Consensus" on Official Export Credits was originally negotiated among the "Big Seven," completely outside

GATT auspices, and only later was it extended to all Organization for Economic Cooperation and Development (OECD) countries. Even today, such countries as Brazil, India, and Korea remain outside the basic framework of export credit arrangements.

The 1979 Subsidies Code both imposed discipline on, and conveyed benefits to, its signatories. Signatories are entitled to consultation privileges and to an injury test that meets prescribed evidentiary standards before other signatories may impose countervailing duties on their exports. (In fact, only the United States in its domestic law limits the injury test to code signatories and countries that undertake obligations equivalent to those set forth in the code.)

Under the code, the less developed country signatories have the further advantage that their export subsidies may not be presumed, in a multilateral case heard before the Subsidies Committee, to create adverse trade effects. Rather, in those cases, the burden of proof remains with the complaining party. Finally, signatories are likely to have the largest say concerning the future evolution of international rules on subsidies. These assorted benefits of the 1979 code are, however, available only on a conditional most-favored-nation basis.

The policy argument for a conditional MFN approach is straightforward. The fabric of international discipline over national subsidies would never become very strong, if nations could rest on their unconditional MFN claims, could enjoy whatever benefits might flow from international agreements, but could escape the disciplines that might be imposed (Gary Clyde Hufbauer, Joanna Shelton Erb, and H.P. Starr 1980). This problem is known as the "free-rider" effect. Some nations may not undertake a commitment, if the benefits of the agreement can be enjoyed at no cost by a free ride on a vehicle provided by other countries.

Whatever the policy merits of a conditional MFN argument, policy considerations alone cannot answer the legal claims for unconditional MFN treatment that may be raised on the basis of GATT Article I (which asserts the principle of unconditional most-favored-nation treatment between GATT members) or on the basis of bilateral trade agreements that contain an unconditional MFN clause. If a conditional MFN approach is to prevail, it must have legal as well as policy footings.

The strongest legal argument that can be made, invoking the language of the GATT, against an unconditional MFN claim is that countervailing and anti-dumping duties and other countermeasures against unfair trade practices are inherently applied on a "case-by-case" basis. In addition, a legal argument could be made that the application of these measures is governed not by the strict MFN standard of Article I, but rather by the looser MFN standard of Article XX. Article XX specifically permits measures:

. . . necessary to secure compliance with laws or regulations which are not inconsistent with the provisions of this Agreement, including those relating to customs enforcement . . . [provided that] . . . such measures are not applied in a manner which would constitute a means of arbitrary or unjustifiable discrimination between countries where the same conditions prevail . . . .

If Article XX governs countermeasures against unfair trade practices, it could be argued that it is not "arbitrary or unjustifiable" for a signatory to distinguish between GATT members that accept the discipline of an agreement, such as the Subsidies Code, and those that do not. Similarly, in the case of many bilateral treaties, it could be argued that their unconditional MFN articles apply to normal tariffs and customs procedures rather than to countermeasures against unfair trade practices.

Whatever the merits of these legal arguments, they were badly (and perhaps deliberately) undercut, at least so far as the United States is concerned. The US Trade Agreements Act of 1979 (see appendix E), on the one hand, granted the injury test to seven countries (the so-called "seven dwarfs," because they were small trading nations) that had bilateral treaties with the United States but were *not* GATT members. The Act, on the other hand, denied the injury test to any GATT member that was not a signatory to the Subsidies Code.[6] In other words, while selected *nonmembers* of GATT were granted an unconditional injury test, all GATT *members*—countries that had accepted the obligations of the GATT and had obtained the supposed benefit of GATT Article I—were denied the unconditional injury test. As a legal matter, the United States could not very well contend in the halls of GATT that GATT members should be treated less favorably than non-GATT members.

Nevertheless, the MFN debate seemed likely to be joined when the United States initially invoked the nonapplication provision of code Article 19 in connection with India's membership. The United States refused to recognize India as a code member, because India had not, on joining the code, undertaken a sufficiently strong commitment to phase out export subsidies. India objected to the US position and invoked Article I of the GATT.

Ultimately the United States backed off from the confrontation. In September 1981 the United States acknowledged Indian membership and India's eligibility for the US injury test, on the basis of a weak Indian commitment to discipline its export subsidies. What was behind the US change of mind? Perhaps it was the previous US decision to accept Pakistan's membership on the basis of a weak commitment to discipline its export subsidies (a commitment that was accepted in the wake of the USSR invasion of Afghanistan); perhaps the change of administration in the United States; or perhaps the weakness of the US international legal case, in light of the statutory treatment of the "seven dwarfs." In

---

6. For further analysis, see Hufbauer, Shelton Erb, and Starr (1980). The "seven dwarfs" provision was inserted in the statute at the urging of the State Department.

any event, a clear resolution of the MFN issue by the GATT awaits another case and another day.

Apart from the injury test, the MFN question arises in the day-to-day practice of national authorities as they define the broader class of potentially troublesome subsidies and the narrower class of export subsidies. For example, should the 1979 Illustrative List to the Subsidies Code define export subsidies for signatories alone or for nonsignatories as well? Under pre-code standards, an export credit offered at terms below government borrowing rates would constitute a clear subsidy on exports. Under code norms, however, if such a credit conforms to the Arrangement for Guidelines on Officially Supported Export Credits, it is not considered an export subsidy. Which standard prevails for nonsignatories? In the *Ceramic Tile from Mexico* case (47 Fed. Reg. 20012, 10 May 1982), the US Department of Commerce listed Mexico's nonmembership in the code as one reason for not applying code standards to Mexican export credits. However, the issue remains to be more fully explored as additional cases arise.

In summary, no clear-cut GATT decisions have been made that authorize a conditional MFN approach or that mandate an unconditional MFN approach to disciplining subsidies. As a practical matter, past US actions have all but conceded that the injury test should be applied on an unconditional basis, regardless whether the exporting country is a code signatory. We believe the time has come for the United States to recognize that fact, and to sign appropriate bilateral agreements on relatively "easy" terms with countries that are not code signatories. But we also believe that a conditional MFN approach may be required to make meaningful progress in new fields, such as limiting agricultural subsidies or performance requirements.

6

Agenda for the Future

In this final chapter, we summarize our major conclusions and suggest some larger issues that the international community should further consider.

The Standards of Trade Impact

Substantial improvement could be made in the existing, loosely structured, relief system by harmonizing the trade-impact standards associated with the various countermeasures that may be taken against subsidized trade. Unilateral national relief measures—whether taken under a countervailing duty statute or some version of the omnibus US section 301 statute—should require a finding that subsidized imports caused material injury, defined in terms of a decline in sales, profits, or employment. Further, the time has come for the Secretariat of the General Agreement on Tariffs and Trade (GATT), working with the Subsidies Committee, to issue periodic reports that evaluate national findings of material injury, with a view to harmonizing the standards applied by different nations.

By contrast, we favor a much lower trade-impact standard for relief authorized multilaterally against export subsidies and other prohibited practices. Based on past GATT experience both in applying Article XXIII and in evaluating claims of serious prejudice, we think the GATT machinery works very poorly in judging trade impact. GATT is better at building international case law that articulates permitted and prohibited practices than in sifting the intricacies of injury determinations. Thus, a low threshold of trade impact—namely "adverse impact," defined in terms of lost sales or lower prices—should provide the key to relief authorized by GATT. Further, once the complaining country shows an offensive practice and demonstrates that the subsidizing country accounts for more than a certain share, say 20 percent, of the relevant market, the subsidizing country should show that its exports have not displaced other suppliers and have not depressed prices.

Most importantly, the trade-impact standard applied to agricultural subsidies should be conformed more closely with the trade-impact standard applied to other goods. At most, the complaining country should be required to demonstrate bilevel pricing (the GATT Article XVI:4 standard). The respondent country should then be required to demonstrate that its subsidies have no adverse trade impact.

The Definition of Export Subsidies

Under this heading, we have offered a number of highly specific suggestions.

□ The disciplinary side of international efforts to limit subsidies should be given greater emphasis than the permissive side. Specifically, many practices that escaped the label of "export subsidy" in the 1979 Illustrative List should be regarded as candidates for the roster of potentially troublesome subsidies. Some examples would include the substitution of domestic goods for imported goods when seeking duty drawback; the compulsory purchase of domestic inputs at subsidized prices (but not below world prices) by industrial firms that use the inputs in making exported goods; and the provision of export credit guarantees at inadequate (but not "manifestly inadequate") rates.

□ When a particular practice could be regarded either as a prohibited export subsidy or as a first cousin of a permitted practice, we would assign the practice to the prohibited category. An example would be tax credits with respect to interest charged on commercial export credits used by an exporting firm. Such practices may be highly similar to permitted practices—in this instance, official export credits. But discipline over export subsidies might soon break down if the "functional equivalent" argument were accepted as a justification for "first cousin" practices.

□ The principle of "fiscal sovereignty" should govern border tax adjustments. Acceptance of this principle would entail a change in present GATT rules so that adjustments could be made, at the border, for direct taxes and *taxes occultes* as well as indirect taxes. This new approach would require considerable attention to mechanical features—for example, appropriate methods of allocating direct taxes and *taxes occultes* to units of product.

More importantly, this change would greatly enlarge the range of taxes that could be adjusted at the border, thereby enabling nations to alter their tax systems with less concern about the repercussions on trade flows. As with indirect taxes, the new adjustments would be permissive, not mandatory. However, countries would be required to give timely advance notice of proposed changes in their border tax adjustment practices.

□ Offshore assembly statutes should limit duty relief to domestic goods, previously exported, that are actually incorporated in the imported goods. These statutes should not be used to promote the exports of collateral products.

◻ While considerable progress has been made in disciplining the subsidy component of official export credits, three further steps should be taken. First, export credit discipline should be extended to cover agricultural goods. Second, mixed credits should be further restrained. Third, and in the more distant future, all official credits should eventually be denominated in a single unit of account.

◻ Free trade zones could provide a backdoor mechanism for adoption of the destination principle of border tax adjustments with respect to direct taxes on exports. We believe that straightforward acceptance of the destination principle would prove more conducive to international harmony and would provide a better opportunity for reaching international agreement on a new regime for border tax adjustments. Free trade zones should not become a backdoor vehicle for relieving exports from direct taxation.

◻ The largest and least disciplined area of subsidization involves agricultural trade. Practices that result in lower prices abroad than at home should be labeled export subsidies. Those practices should be subject to countermeasures, unless the subsidizing country can show that the practices exert no adverse impact on other suppliers to the world market.

◻ The granting or withholding of noncash benefits, conditioned on export performance, should be defined as an export subsidy, subject to the same prohibitions as other export subsidies. Other performance requirements should be regarded as potentially troublesome subsidies.

◻ The link between multiple exchange rate systems and export subsidization needs intensive examination. In particular, agreement should be reached as to the circumstances in which multiple exchange rates give rise to export subsidies and how those subsidies should be calculated.

The Definition of Domestic Subsidies

A major effort should be undertaken to reach international agreement on the definition and calculation of potentially troublesome domestic subsidies. This work could be patterned after the 1960 Working Party Report and the 1979 Illustrative List that sought to define export subsidies. We would offer several suggestions for this exercise.

◻ The work should focus on the demarcation line between "generally available" and "industry-specific" incentive measures, with the understanding that the first category should be excluded from the definition of potentially troublesome subsidies. This exclusion would respect the sovereignty of domestic macroeconomic policy choices. For example, accelerated tax depreciation for all investment in capital goods, or a tax credit for all R&D expenditure would be deemed generally available. However, measures that in theory are available to all industries, but in practice are used by only a few sectors, should not be regarded as generally available.

☐ International rules should condemn the subsidization of one product when that product is required to be purchased for incorporation in the manufacture of another product that is then exported. In other words, a sharp distinction should be made between situations where, through a subsidy, an input is simply made available to local producers at world market prices, and situations where the local producers of an exported product are required (through import restrictions or direct guidance) to buy a subsidized input from local suppliers, whether that input is sold at, above, or below world prices.

☐ The international conferees must consider the pricing of national resources. We would take a fairly relaxed attitude toward the pricing of *nontransportable* natural resources, as long as national pricing practices do not have an overt export bias. In most circumstances, there is simply no recognized standard for establishing a "correct" price for nontransportable resources. On the other hand, we would apply the normal rules to *transportable* natural resources, such as cut timber or iron ore.

☐ The measurement of subsidies inherent in official finance and guarantees is a sure topic. We prefer to use the "cost of money to government" as the standard for measuring various forms of credit subsidy. We realize that the cost of money to government does not reflect the amount of the subsidy in an opportunity-cost sense. However, the certainty and administrative convenience provided by the cost of money to government standard outweigh its imperfections as a benchmark.

☐ As still another part of the exercise in defining potentially troublesome domestic subsidies, attention must be paid to acceptable levels of regional offsets, namely subsidies to compensate for the disadvantage of locating industry in particular regions. In addition, safehavens should be defined for structural adjustment subsidies that are positively linked with the programmed reduction of a declining industry.

☐ Last, but still important, is the growing question of performance requirements. In our view, all manner of performance requirements, investment incentives, and practices designed to encourage particular industries in a targeted fashion should be regarded as potentially troublesome subsidies, even though those incentives and practices have no overt export emphasis.

Effective Remedies

The proper design of effective remedies can do much to limit the incidence and scope of subsidies worldwide. For example, if a government seeking to launch a subsidized infant industry on world markets knew in advance that restrictions against that industry's exports would be imposed, the government might well restrain the extent of its subsidies in the first place. Advanced warning of this sort is contained in Australia's preferential trade agreements with Papua New Guinea.

Despite progress made in the GATT and later in the Subsidies Code, the fashioning of effective remedies in response to a wide variety of novel but potentially offensive trade practices remains an ad hoc matter. The effort is made more difficult with the proliferation of "industrial policies" of all description, ranging from targeted encouragement of private firms to government operation of particular industries. The appropriate international response to the increasingly blurred distinction between public and private enterprise may prove to be the central dilemma facing policymakers in the coming decades.

There are many dimensions to the question of how to fashion effective remedies. A few of our earlier conclusions deserve repetition.

□ Remedies in the form of quantitative restraints should be avoided. Such remedies—which usually border on government-sponsored cartels—are simply too attractive to producers, and too punitive on consumers. Their economic costs usually outweigh whatever administrative convenience they offer.

□ Private firms should not be compelled to depend on the ebb and flow of international diplomacy in their search for appropriate relief. By way of reform of present procedures, private firms should be given standing to bring cases before the Subsidies Committee. (Some mechanism would be required to prevent a proliferation of frivolous cases brought in that forum.) In these actions, the private parties would largely control the presentation of evidence and the pace of proceedings. Unlike governments, they would not be so easily subject to pressure on broad foreign policy grounds.

□ The countervailing subsidy, a remedy used under the name of "matching" in the realm of official export credits, should be used more widely to counteract foreign subsidy practices, both as they affect home and third-country markets. Further, we suggest that countervailing subsidies be financed by low-rate tariffs imposed on imports from the subsidizing country. This step should not, however, be taken without prior multilateral authorization, because it carries the risk of triggering a round of harmful escalation.

□ Other remedies may help limit subsidization that affects third-country markets. The most promising alternative approach would involve an agreement, within the framework of GATT Article VI, that signatories open their regular administrative proceedings to foreign petitioners who assert they have been wrongfully deprived of export markets.

□ Remedies should continue to be scaled to offset the subsidy, not the injury. The extent of injury should at most (as under the code) set a ceiling on the countermeasure, not a floor. Efforts to redress the injury allegedly caused, for example, by an R&D subsidy that inspires a dramatic industrial advance, would be too open-ended for the unfair trade statutes as currently structured. This problem is better addressed by negotiated international responses to national industrial policies, rather than by countermeasures applied in response to specific subsidy policies.

□ The conditional most-favored-nation approach in regard to remedies may well prove necessary for further progress in international negotiations aimed at disciplining subsidies, particularly in such areas as performance requirements and agricultural subsidies. The United States relied on a conditional MFN approach in fashioning its domestic legislation to enact the Subsidies Code. This strategy helped bring forth a stronger code, and induced more countries to sign it, than otherwise might have happened.

Conclusion

The main precept which emerges from our analysis is that the powerful quest for international harmonization of national trade practices, the long search for an elusive level playing field, cannot be ignored. The progress made within the framework of the Subsidies Code has so far been quite modest (US General Accounting Office 1983). Either the GATT points the way toward harmonization at lower levels by restraining subsidies, or disadvantaged countries on their own initiative will harmonize trade practices at higher levels by introducing new subsidies.

If Europe, Canada, the United States, Japan, and the growing number of newly industrialized countries do not agree to greater discipline over their subsidies, all are likely to increase their programs of fiscal subvention when the next turn of the fiscal wheel favors a more liberal approach toward government spending. The tepid approach of many nations toward the 1982 GATT Ministerial makes it rather more likely that nations will "harmonize up" than "harmonize down." But the health of the international system would be better served if the GATT could point the way toward tighter discipline over subsidies and countervailing measures.

The Tokyo Round dealt for the first time with practices that were once considered strictly within the domain of sovereign governments—government procurement, product standards, and even domestic subsidies. That experience provides precedent for further progress on the international discipline of subsidies in the late 1980s and the 1990s.

Appendices

A Code on Subsidies and Countervailing Duties and Key Articles of the GATT

Agreement on Interpretation and Application of Articles VI, XVI and XXIII of the General Agreement on Tariffs and Trade

---

The signatories[1] to this Agreement,

Noting that Ministers on 12–14 September 1973 agreed that the Multilateral Trade Negotiations should, *inter alia*, reduce or eliminate the trade restricting or distorting effects of non-tariff measures, and bring such measures under more effective international discipline,

Recognizing that subsidies are used by governments to promote important objectives of national policy,

Recognizing also that subsidies may have harmful effects on trade and production,

Recognizing that the emphasis of this Agreement should be on the effects of subsidies and that these effects are to be assessed in giving due account to the internal economic situation of the signatories concerned as well as to the state of international economic and monetary relations,

Desiring to ensure that the use of subsidies does not adversely affect or prejudice the interests of any signatory to this Agreement, and that countervailing measures do not unjustifiably impede international trade, and that relief is made available to producers adversely affected by the use of subsidies within an agreed international framework of rights and obligations,

Taking into account the particular trade, development and financial needs of developing countries,

Desiring to apply fully and to interpret the provisions of Articles VI, XVI and XXIII of the General Agreement on Tariffs and Trade[2] (hereinafter referred to as "General Agreement" or "GATT") only with respect to subsidies and countervailing measures and to elaborate rules for their application in order to provide greater uniformity and certainty in their implementation,

Desiring to provide for the speedy, effective and equitable resolution of disputes arising under this Agreement,

Have agreed as follows:

Part I

Article 1   Application of Article VI of the General Agreement[3]

Signatories shall take all necessary steps to ensure that the imposition of a countervailing duty[4] on any product of the territory of any signatory imported into the territory of another signatory is in accordance with the provisions of Article VI of the General Agreement and the terms of this Agreement.

Article 2   Domestic Procedures and Related Matters

1. Countervailing duties may only be imposed pursuant to investigations initiated[5] and conducted in accordance with the provisions of this Article. An investigation to determine the existence, degree and effect of any alleged subsidy shall normally be initiated upon a written request by or on behalf of the industry affected. The request shall include sufficient evidence of the existence of (a) a subsidy and, if possible, its amount, (b) injury within the meaning of Article VI of the General Agreement as interpreted by this Agreement[6] and (c) a causal link between the subsidized imports and the alleged injury. If in special circumstances the authorities concerned decide to initiate an investigation without having received such a request, they shall proceed only if they have sufficient evidence on all points under (a) to (c) above.

2. Each signatory shall notify the Committee on Subsidies and Countervailing Measures[7] (a) which of its authorities are competent to initiate and conduct investigations referred to in this Article and (b) its domestic procedures governing the initiation and conduct of such investigations.

3. When the investigating authorities are satisfied that there is sufficient evidence to justify initiating an investigation, the signatory or signatories, the products of which are subject to such investigation and the exporters and importers known to the investigating authorities to have an interest therein and the complainants shall be notified and a public notice shall be given. In determining whether to initiate an investigation, the investigating authorities should take into account the position adopted by the affiliates of a complainant party[8] which are resident in the territory of another signatory.

4. Upon initiation of an investigation and thereafter, the evidence of both a subsidy and injury caused thereby should be considered simultaneously. In the event the evidence of both the existence of subsidy and injury shall be considered simultaneously (a) in the decision whether or not to initiate an investigation and (b) thereafter during the course of the investigation, starting on a date not later than the earliest date on which in accordance with the provisions of this Agreement provisional measures may be applied.

5. The public notice referred to in paragraph 3 above shall describe the subsidy practice or practices to be investigated. Each signatory shall ensure that the investigating authorities afford all interested signatories and all interested parties[9] a reasonable opportunity, upon request, to see all relevant information that is not confidential (as indicated in paragraphs 6 and 7 below) and that is used by the investigating authorities in the investigation, and to present in writing, and upon justification orally, their views to the investigating authorities.

6. Any information which is by nature confidential or which is provided on a confidential basis by parties to an investigation shall, upon cause shown, be treated as such by the investigating authorities. Such information shall not be disclosed without specific

permission of the party submitting it.[10] Parties providing confidential information may be requested to furnish non-confidential summaries thereof. In the event such parties indicate that such information is not susceptible of summary, a statement of reasons why summarization is not possible must be provided.

7. However, if the investigating authorities find that a request for confidentiality is not warranted and if the party requesting confidentiality is unwilling to disclose the information, such authorities may disregard such information unless it can otherwise be demonstrated to their satisfaction that the information is correct.[11]

8. The investigating authorities may carry out investigations in the territory of other signatories as required, provided they have notified in good time the signatory in question and unless the latter objects to the investigation. Further, the investigating authorities may carry out investigations on the premises of a firm and may examine the records of a firm if (a) the firm so agrees and (b) the signatory in question is notified and does not object.

9. In cases in which any interested party or signatory refuses access to, or otherwise does not provide, necessary information within a reasonable period or significantly impedes the investigation, preliminary and final findings,[12] affirmative or negative, may be made on the basis of the facts available.

10. The procedures set out above are not intended to prevent the authorities of a signatory from proceeding expeditiously with regard to initiating an investigation, reaching preliminary or final findings, whether affirmative or negative, or from applying provisional or final measures, in accordance with relevant provisions of this Agreement.

11. In cases where products are not imported directly from the country of origin but are exported to the country of importation from an intermediate country, the provisions of this Agreement shall be fully applicable and the transaction or transactions shall, for the purposes of this Agreement, be regarded as having taken place between the country of origin and the country of importation.

12. An investigation shall be terminated when the investigating authorities are satisfied either that no subsidy exists or that the effect of the alleged subsidy on the industry is not such as to cause injury.

13. An investigation shall not hinder the procedures of customs clearance.

14. Investigations shall, except in special circumstances, be concluded within one year after their initiation.

15. Public notice shall be given of any preliminary or final finding whether affirmative or negative and of the revocation of a finding. In the case of an affirmative finding each such notice shall set forth the findings and conclusions reached on all issues of fact and law considered material by the investigating authorities, and the reasons and basis therefor. In the case of a negative finding each notice shall set forth at least the basic conclusions and a summary of the reasons therefor. All notices of finding shall be forwarded to the signatory or signatories the products of which are subject to such finding and to the exporters known to have an interest therein.

16. Signatories shall report without delay to the Committee all preliminary or final actions taken with respect to countervailing duties. Such reports will be available in the GATT secretariat for inspection by government representatives. The signatories shall also submit, on a semi-annual basis, reports on any countervailing duty actions taken within the preceding six months.

Article 3   Consultations

1. As soon as possible after a request for initiation of an investigation is accepted, and in any event before the initiation of any investigation, signatories the products of which

may be subject to such investigation shall be afforded a reasonable opportunity for consultations with the aim of clarifying the situation as to the matters referred to in Article 2, paragraph 1 above and arriving at a mutually agreed solution.

2. Furthermore, throughout the period of investigation, signatories the products of which are the subject of the investigation shall be afforded a reasonable opportunity to continue consultations, with a view to clarifying the factual situation and to arriving at a mutually agreed solution.[13]

3. Without prejudice to the obligation to afford reasonable opportunity for consultation, these provisions regarding consultations are not intended to prevent the authorities of a signatory from proceeding expeditiously with regard to initiating the investigation, reaching preliminary or final findings, whether affirmative or negative, or from applying provisional or final measures, in accordance with the provisions of this Agreement.

4. The signatory which intends to initiate any investigation or is conducting such an investigation shall permit, upon request, the signatory or signatories the products of which are subject to such investigation access to non-confidential evidence including the non-confidential summary of confidential data being used for initiating or conducting the investigation.

Article 4   Imposition of Countervailing Duties

1. The decision whether or not to impose a countervailing duty in cases where all requirements for the imposition have been fulfilled and the decision whether the amount of the countervailing duty to be imposed shall be the full amount of the subsidy or less are decisions to be made by the authorities of the importing signatory. It is desirable that the imposition be permissive in the territory of all signatories and that the duty be less than the total amount of the subsidy if such lesser duty would be adequate to remove the injury to the domestic injury.

2. No countervailing duty shall be levied[14] on any imported product in excess of the amount of the subsidy found to exist, calculated in terms of subsidization per unit of the subsidized and exported product.[15]

3. When a countervailing duty is imposed in respect of any product, such countervailing duty shall be levied, in the appropriate amounts, on a non-discriminatory basis on imports of such product from all sources found to be subsidized and to be causing injury, except as to imports from those sources which have renounced any subsidies in question or from which undertakings under the terms of this Agreement have been accepted.

4. If, after reasonable efforts have been made to complete consultations, a signatory makes a final determination of the existence and amount of the subsidy and that, through the effects of the subsidy, the subsidized imports are causing injury, it may impose a countervailing duty in accordance with the provisions of this section unless the subsidy is withdrawn.

5. (a) Proceedings may[16] be suspended or terminated without the imposition of provisional measures or countervailing duties, if undertakings are accepted under which:

   (i) the government of the exporting country agrees to eliminate or limit the subsidy or take other measures concerning its effects; or

   (ii) the exporter agrees to revise its prices so that the investigating authorities are satisfied that the injurious effect of the subsidy is eliminated. Price increases under undertakings shall not be higher than necessary to eliminate the amount of the subsidy. Price undertakings shall not be sought or accepted from exporters unless the importing signatory has first (1) initiated an investigation in accordance with the provisions of Article 2 of this Agreement and (2) obtained the consent of the exporting signatory. Undertakings offered need not be accepted if the authorities of the importing signatory consider their acceptance impractical, for example if the number of actual or potential exporters is too great, or for other reasons.

(b)   If the undertakings are accepted, the investigation of injury shall nevertheless be completed if the exporting signatory so desires or the importing signatory so decides. In such a case, if a determination of no injury or threat thereof is made, the undertaking shall automatically lapse, except in cases where a determination of no threat of injury is due in large part to the existence of an undertaking; in such cases the authorities concerned may require that an undertaking be maintained for a reasonable period consistent with the provisions of this Agreement.

(c)   Price undertakings may be suggested by the authorities of the importing signatory, but no exporter shall be forced to enter into such an undertaking. The fact that governments or exporters do not offer such undertakings or do not accept an invitation to do so, shall in no way prejudice the consideration of the case. However, the authorities are free to determine that a threat of injury is more likely to be realized if the subsidized imports continue.

6. Authorities of an importing signatory may require any government or exporter from whom undertakings have been accepted to provide periodically information relevant to the fulfillment of such undertakings, and to permit verification of pertinent data. In case of violation of undertakings, the authorities of the importing signatory may take expeditious actions under this Agreement in conformity with its provisions which may constitute immediate application of provisional measures using the best information available. In such cases definitive duties may be levied in accordance with this Agreement on goods entered for consumption not more than ninety days before the application of such provisional measures, except that any such retroactive assessment shall not apply to imports entered before the violation of the undertaking.

7. Undertakings shall not remain in force any longer than countervailing duties could remain in force under this Agreement. The authorities of an importing signatory shall review the need for the continuation of any undertaking, where warranted, on their own initiative, or if interested exporters or importers of the product in question so request and submit positive information substantiating the need for such review.

8. Whenever a countervailing duty investigation is suspended or terminated pursuant to the provisions of paragraph 5 above and whenever an undertaking is terminated, this fact shall be officially notified and must be published. Such notices shall set forth at least the basic conclusions and a summary of the reasons therefor.

9. A countervailing duty shall remain in force only as long as, and to the extent necessary to counteract the subsidization which is causing injury. The investigating authorities shall review the need for continued imposition of the duty, where warranted, on their own initiative or if any interested party so requests and submits positive information substantiating the need for review.

Article 5   Provisional Measures and Retroactivity

1. Provisional measures may be taken only after a preliminary affirmative finding has been made that a subsidy exists and that there is sufficient evidence of injury as provided for in Article 2, paragraph 1(a) to (c). Provisional measures shall not be applied unless the authorities concerned judge that they are necessary to prevent injury being caused during the period of investigation.

2. Provisional measures may take the form of provisional countervailing duties guaranteed by cash deposits or bonds equal to the amount of the provisionally calculated amount of subsidization.

3. The imposition of provisional measures shall be limited to as short a period as possible, not exceeding four months.

4. The relevant provisions of Article 4 shall be followed in the imposition of provisional measures.

5. Where a final finding of injury (but not of a threat thereof or of a material retardation of the establishment of an industry) is made or in the case of a final finding of threat of injury where the effect of the subsidized imports would, in the absence of the provisional measures, have led to a finding of injury, countervailing duties may be levied retroactively for the period for which provisional measures, if any, have been applied.

6. If the definitive countervailing duty is higher than the amount guaranteed by the cash deposit or bond, the difference shall not be collected. If the definitive duty is less than the amount guaranteed by the cash deposit or bond, the excess amount shall be reimbursed or the bond released in an expeditious manner.

7. Except as provided in paragraph 5 above, where a finding of threat of injury or material retardation is made (but no injury has yet occurred) a definitive countervailing duty may be imposed only from the date of the finding of threat of injury or material retardation and any cash deposit made during the period of the application of provisional measures shall be refunded and any bonds released in an expeditious manner.

8. Where a final finding is negative any cash deposit made during the period of the application of provisional measures shall be refunded and any bonds released in an expeditious manner.

9. In critical circumstances where for the subsidized product in question the authorities find that injury which is difficult to repair is caused by massive imports in a relatively short period of a product benefiting from export subsidies paid or bestowed inconsistently with the provisions of the General Agreement and of this Agreement and where it is deemed necessary, in order to preclude the recurrence of such injury, to assess countervailing duties retroactively on those imports, the definitive countervailing duties may be assessed on imports which were entered for consumption not more than ninety days prior to the date of application of provisional measures.

Article 6   Determination of Injury

1. A determination of injury[17] for purposes of Article VI of the General Agreement shall involve an objective examination of both (a) the volume of subsidized imports and their effect on prices in the domestic market for like products[18] and (b) the consequent impact of these imports on domestic producers of such products.

2. With regard to volume of subsidized imports the investigating authorities shall consider whether there has been a significant increase in subsidized imports, either in absolute terms or relative to production or consumption in the importing signatory. With regard to the effect of the subsidized imports on prices, the investigating authorities shall consider whether there has been a significant price undercutting by the subsidized imports as compared with the price of a like product of the importing signatory, or whether the effect of such imports is otherwise to depress prices to a significant degree or prevent price increases, which otherwise would have occurred, to a significant degree. No one or several of these factors can necessarily give decisive guidance.

3. The examination of the impact on the domestic industry concerned shall include an evaluation of all relevant economic factors and indices having a bearing on the state

of the industry such as actual and potential decline in output, sales, market share, profits, productivity, return on investments, or utilization of capacity; factors affecting domestic prices; actual and potential negative effects on cash flow, inventories, employment, wages, growth, ability to raise capital or investment and, in the case of agriculture, whether there has been an increased burden on Government support programmes. This list is not exhaustive, nor can one or several of these factors necessarily give decisive guidance.

4. It must be demonstrated that the subsidized imports are, through the effects[19] of the subsidy, causing injury within the meaning of this Agreement. There may be other factors[20] which at the same time are injuring the domestic industry, and the injuries caused by other factors must not be attributed to the subsidized imports.

5. In determining injury, the term "domestic industry" shall, except as provided in paragraph 7 below, be interpreted as referring to the domestic producers as a whole of the like products or to those of them whose collective output of the products constitutes a major proportion of the total domestic production of those products, except that when producers are related[21] to the exporters or importers or are themselves importers of the allegedly subsidized product the industry may be interpreted as referring to the rest of the producers.

6. The effect of the subsidized imports shall be assessed in relation to the domestic production of the like product when available data permit the separate identification of production in terms of such criteria as: the production process, the producers' realization, profits. When the domestic production of the like product has no separate identity in these terms the effects of subsidized imports shall be assessed by the examination of the production of the narrowest group or range of products, which includes the like product, for which the necessary information can be provided.

7. In exceptional circumstances the territory of a signatory may, for the production in question, be divided into two or more competitive markets and the producers within each market may be regarded as a separate industry if (a) the producers within such market sell all or almost all of their production of the product in question in that market, and (b) the demand in that market is not to any substantial degree supplied by producers of the product in question located elsewhere in the territory. In such circumstances injury may be found to exist even where a major portion of the total domestic industry is not injured provided there is a concentration of subsidized imports into such an isolated market and provided further that the subsidized imports are causing injury to the producers of all or almost all of the production within such market.

8. When the industry has been interpreted as referring to the producers in a certain area, as defined in paragraph 7 above, countervailing duties shall be levied only on the products in question consigned for final consumption to that area. When the constitutional law of the importing signatory does not permit the levying of countervailing duties on such a basis, the importing signatory may levy the countervailing duties without limitation, only if (a) the exporters shall have been given an opportunity to cease exporting at subsidized prices to the area concerned or otherwise give assurances pursuant to Article 4, paragraph 5, of this Agreement, and adequate assurances in this regard have not been promptly given, and (b) such duties cannot be levied only on products of specific producers which supply the area in question.

9. Where two or more countries have reached under the provisions of Article XXIV:8(a) of the General Agreement such a level of integration that they have the characteristics of a single, unified market the industry in the entire area of integration shall be taken to be the industry referred to in paragraphs 5 to 7 above.

Part II

Article 7   Notification of Subsidies[22]

1. Having regard to the provisions of Article XVI:1 of the General Agreement, any signatory may make a written request for information on the nature and extent of any subsidy granted or maintained by another signatory (including any form of income or price support) which operates directly or indirectly to increase exports of any product from or reduce imports of any product into its territory.
2. Signatories so requested shall provide such information as quickly as possible and in a comprehensive manner, and shall be ready, upon request, to provide additional information to the requesting signatory. Any signatory which considers that such information has not been provided may bring the matter to the attention of the Committee.
3. Any interested signatory which considers that any practice of another signatory having the effects of a subsidy has not been notified in accordance with the provisions of Article XVI:1 of the General Agreement may bring the matter to the attention of such other signatory. If the subsidy practice is not thereafter notified promptly, such signatory may itself bring the subsidy practice in question to the notice of the Committee.

Article 8   Subsidies—General Provisions

1. Signatories recognize that subsidies are used by governments to promote important objectives of social and economic policy. Signatories also recognize that subsidies may cause adverse effects to the interests of other signatories.
2. Signatories agree not to use export subsidies in a manner inconsistent with the provisions of this Agreement.
3. Signatories further agree that they shall seek to avoid causing, through the use of any subsidy:
   (a) injury to the domestic industry of another signatory,[23]
   (b) nullification or impairment of the benefits accruing directly or indirectly to another signatory under the General Agreement,[24] or
   (c) serious prejudice to the interests of another signatory.[25]
4. The adverse effects to the interests of another signatory required to demonstrate nullification or impairment[26] or serious prejudice may arise through
   (a) the effects of the subsidized imports in the domestic market of the importing signatory,
   (b) the effects of the subsidy in displacing or impeding the imports of like products into the market of the subsidizing country, or
   (c) the effects of the subsidized exports in displacing[27] the exports of like products of another signatory from a third country market.[28]

Article 9   Export Subsidies on Products Other than Certain Primary Products[29]

1. Signatories shall not grant export subsidies on products other than certain primary products.
2. The practices listed in points (a) to (1) in the Annex are illustrative of export subsidies.

Article 10   Export Subsidies on Certain Primary Products

1. In accordance with the provisions of Article XVI:3 of the General Agreement, signatories agree not to grant directly or indirectly any export subsidy on certain primary products in a manner which results in the signatory granting such subsidy having more than an equitable share of world export trade in such product, account being taken of the shares of the signatories in trade in the product concerned during a previous representative period, and any special factors which may have affected or may be affecting trade in such product.
2. For purposes of Article XVI:3 of the General Agreement and paragraph 1 above:
   (a) "more than equitable share of world export trade" shall include any case in which the effect of an export subsidy granted by a signatory is to displace the exports of another signatory bearing in mind the developments on world markets;
   (b) with regard to new markets traditional patterns of supply of the product concerned to the world market, region or country, in which the new market is situated shall be taken into account in determining "equitable share of world export trade";
   (c) "a previous representative period" shall normally be the three most recent calendar years in which normal market conditions existed.
3. Signatories further agree not to grant export subsidies on exports of certain primary products to a particular market in a manner which results in prices materially below those of other suppliers to the same market.

Article 11   Subsidies Other than Export Subsidies

1. Signatories recognize that subsidies other than export subsidies are widely used as important instruments for the promotion of social and economic policy objectives and do not intend to restrict the right of signatories to use such subsidies to achieve these and other important policy objectives which they consider desirable. Signatories note that among such objectives are:
   (a) the elimination of industrial, economic and social disadvantages of specific regions,
   (b) to facilitate the restructuring, under socially acceptable conditions, of certain sectors, especially where this has become necessary by reason of changes in trade and economic policies, including international agreements resulting in lower barriers to trade,
   (c) generally to sustain employment and to encourage re-training and change in employment,
   (d) to encourage research and development programmes, especially in the field of high-technology industries,
   (e) the implementation of economic programmes and policies to promote the economic and social development of developing countries,
   (f) redeployment of industry in order to avoid congestion and environmental problems.
2. Signatories recognize, however, that subsidies other than export subsidies, certain objectives and possible form of which are described, respectively, in paragraphs 1 and 3 of this Article, may cause or threaten to cause injury to a domestic industry of another signatory or serious prejudice to the interests of another signatory or may nullify or impair benefits accruing to another signatory under the General Agreement, in particular where such subsidies would adversely affect the conditions of normal competition. Signatories shall therefore seek to avoid causing such effects through the use of subsidies. In particular, signatories, when drawing up their policies and practices

in this field, in addition to evaluating the essential internal objectives to be achieved, shall also weigh, as far as practicable, taking account of the nature of the particular case, possible adverse effects on trade. They shall also consider the conditions of world trade, production (e.g. price, capacity utilization etc.) and supply in the product concerned.

3. Signatories recognize that the objectives mentioned in paragraph 1 above may be achieved, *inter alia*, by means of subsidies granted with the aim of giving an advantage to certain enterprises. Examples of possible forms of such subsidies are: government financing of commercial enterprises, including grants, loans or guarantees; government provision or government financed provision of utility, supply distribution and other operational or support services or facilities; government financing of research and development programmes; fiscal incentives; and government subscription to, or provision of, equity capital.

Signatories note that the above form of subsidies are normally granted either regionally or by sector. The enumeration of forms of subsidies set out above is illustrative and non-exhaustive, and reflects these currently granted by a number of signatories to this Agreement.

Signatories recognize, nevertheless, that the enumeration of forms of subsidies set out above should be reviewed periodically and that this should be done, through consultations, in conformity with the spirit of Article XVI:5 of the General Agreement.

4. Signatories recognize further that, without prejudice to their rights under this Agreement, nothing in paragraphs 1–3 above and in particular the enumeration of forms of subsidies creates, in itself, any basis for action under the General Agreement, as interpreted by this Agreement.

Article 12 Consultations

1. Whenever a signatory has reason to believe that an export subsidy is being granted or maintained by another signatory in a manner inconsistent with the provisions of this Agreement, such signatory may request consultations with such other signatory.

2. A request for consultations under paragraph 1 above shall include a statement of available evidence with regard to the existence and nature of the subsidy in question.

3. Whenever a signatory has reason to believe that any subsidy is being granted or maintained by another signatory and that such subsidy either causes injury to its domestic industry, nullification or impairment of benefits accruing to it under the General Agreement, or serious prejudice to its interests, such signatory may request consultations with such other signatory.

4. A request for consultations under paragraph 3 above shall include a statement of available evidence with regard to (a) the existence and nature of the subsidy in question and (b) the injury caused to the domestic industry or, in the case of nullification or impairment, or serious prejudice, the adverse effects caused to the interests of the signatory requesting consultations.

5. Upon request for consultations under paragraph 1 or paragraph 3 above, the signatory believed to be granting or maintaining the subsidy practice in question shall enter into such consultations as quickly as possible. The purpose of the consultations shall be to clarify the facts of the situation and to arrive at a mutually acceptable solution.

Article 13 Conciliation, Dispute Settlement and Authorized Countermeasures

1. If, in the case of consultations under paragraph 1 of Article 12, a mutually acceptable solution has not been reached within thirty days[30] of the request for consultations,

any signatory party to such consultations may refer the matter to the Committee for conciliation in accordance with the provisions of Part VI.

2. If, in the case of consultations under paragraph 3 of Article 12, a mutually acceptable solution has not been reached within sixty days of the request for consultations, any signatory party to such consultations may refer the matter to the Committee for conciliation in accordance with the provisions of Part VI.

3. If any dispute arising under this Agreement is not resolved as a result of consultations or conciliations, the Committee shall, upon request, review the matter in accordance with the dispute settlement procedures of Part VI.

4. If, as a result of its review, the Committee concludes that an export subsidy is being granted in a manner inconsistent with the provisions of this Agreement or that a subsidy is being granted or maintained in such a manner as to cause injury, nullification or impairment, or serious prejudice, it shall make such recommendations[31] to the parties as may be appropriate to resolve the issue and, in the event the recommendations are not followed, it may authorize such countermeasures as may be appropriate, taking into account the degree and nature of the adverse effects found to exist, in accordance with the relevant provisions of Part VI.

Part III

Article 14   Developing Countries

1. Signatories recognize that subsidies are an integral part of economic development programmes of developing countries.

2. Accordingly, this Agreement shall not prevent developing country signatories from adopting measures and policies to assist their industries, including those in the export sector. In particular the commitment of Article 9 shall not apply to developing country signatories, subject to the provisions of paragraphs 5 through 8 below.

3. Developing country signatories agree that export subsidies on their industrial products shall not be used in a manner which causes serious prejudice to the trade or production of another signatory.

4. There shall be no presumption that export subsidies granted by developing country signatories result in adverse effects, as defined in this Agreement, to the trade or production of another signatory. Such adverse effects shall be demonstrated by positive evidence, through an economic examination of the impact on trade or production of another signatory.

5. A developing country signatory should endeavour to enter into a commitment[32] to reduce or eliminate export subsidies when the use of such export subsidies is inconsistent with its competitive and development needs.

6. When a developing country has entered into a commitment to reduce or eliminate export subsidies, as provided in paragraph 5 above, countermeasures pursuant to the provisions of Parts II and VI of this Agreement against any export subsidies of such developing country shall not be authorized for other signatories of this Agreement, provided that the export subsidies in question are in accordance with the terms of the commitment referred to in paragraph 5 above.

7. With respect to any subsidy, other than an export subsidy, granted by a developing country signatory, action may not be authorized or taken under Parts II and VI of this

Agreement, unless nullification or impairment of tariff concessions or other obligations under the General Agreement is found to exist as a result of such subsidy, in such a way as to displace or impede imports of like products into the market of the subsidizing country, or unless injury to domestic industry in the importing market of a signatory occurs in terms of Article VI of the General Agreement, as interpreted and applied by this Agreement. Signatories recognize that in developing countries, governments may play a large role in promoting economic growth and development. Intervention by such governments in their economy, for example through the practices enumerated in paragraph 3 of Article 11, shall not, *per se*, be considered subsidies.

8. The Committee shall, upon request by an interested signatory, undertake a review of a specific export subsidy practice of a developing country signatory to examine the extent to which the practice is in conformity with the objectives of this Agreement. If a developing country has entered into a commitment pursuant to paragraph 5 of this Article, it shall not be subject to such review for the period of that commitment.

9. The Committee shall, upon request by an interested signatory, also undertake similar reviews of measures maintained or taken by developed country signatories under the provisions of this Agreement which affect interests of a developing country signatory.

10. Signatories recognize that the obligations of this Agreement with respect to export subsidies for certain primary products apply to all signatories.

Part IV

Article 15   Special Situations

1. In cases of alleged injury caused by imports from a country described in NOTES AND SUPPLEMENTARY PROVISIONS to the General Agreement (Annex I, Article VI, paragraph 1, point 2) the importing signatory may base its procedures and measures either
   (a) on this Agreement, or, alternatively
   (b) on the Agreement on Implementation of Article VI of the General Agreement on Tariffs and Trade.

2. It is understood that in both cases (a) and (b) above the calculation of the margin of dumping or of the amount of the estimated subsidy can be made by comparison of the export price with
   (a) the price at which a like product of a country other than the importing signatory or those mentioned above is sold, or
   (b) the constructed value[33] of a like product in a country other than the importing signatory or those mentioned above.

3. If neither prices nor constructed value as established under (a) or (b) of paragraph 2 above provide an adequate basis for determination of dumping or subsidization then the price in the importing signatory, if necessary duly adjusted to reflect reasonable profits, may be used.

4. All calculations under the provisions of paragraphs 2 and 3 above shall be based on prices or costs ruling at the same level of trade, normally at the ex factory level, and in respect of operations made as nearly as possible at the same time. Due allowances shall be made in each case, on its merits, for the difference in conditions and terms of sale or in taxation and for the other differences affecting price comparability, so that the method of comparison applied is appropriate and not unreasonable.

Part V

Article 16   Committee on Subsidies and Countervailing Measures

1. There shall be established under this Agreement a Committee on Subsidies and Countervailing Measures composed of representatives from each of the signatories to this Agreement. The Committee shall elect its own Chairman and shall meet not less than twice a year and otherwise as envisaged by relevant provisions of this Agreement at the request of any signatory. The Committee shall carry out responsibilities as assigned to it under this Agreement or by the signatories and it shall afford signatories the opportunity of consulting on any matters relating to the operation of the Agreement or the furtherance of its objectives. The GATT secretariat shall act as the secretariat to the Committee.
2. The Committee may set up subsidiary bodies as appropriate.
3. In carrying out their functions, the Committee and any subsidiary bodies may consult with and seek information from any source they deem appropriate. However, before the Committee or a subsidiary body seeks such information from a source within the jurisdiction of a signatory, it shall inform the signatory involved.

Part VI

Article 17   Conciliation

1. In cases where matters are referred to the Committee for conciliation failing a mutually agreed solution in consultations under any provision of this Agreement, the Committee shall immediately review the facts involved and, through its good offices, shall encourage the signatories involved to develop a mutually acceptable solution.[34]
2. Signatories shall make their best efforts to reach a mutually satisfactory solution throughout the period of conciliation.
3. Should the matter remain unresolved, notwithstanding efforts at conciliation made under paragraph 2 above, any signatory involved may, thirty days after the request for conciliation, request that a panel be established by the Committee in accordance with the provisions of Article 18 below.

Article 18   Dispute Settlement

1. The Committee shall establish a panel upon request pursuant to paragraph 3 of Article 17.[35] A panel so established shall review the facts of the matter and, in light of such facts, shall present to the Committee its findings concerning the rights and obligations of the signatories party to the dispute under the relevant provisions of the General Agreement as interpreted and applied by this Agreement.
2. A panel should be established within thirty days of a request therefor[36] and a panel so established should deliver its findings to the Committee within sixty days after its establishment.
3. When a panel is to be established, the Chairman of the Committee, after securing the agreement of the signatories concerned, should propose the composition of the panel.

Panels shall be composed of three or five members, preferably governmental, and the composition of panels should not give rise to delays in their establishment. It is understood that citizens of countries whose governments[37] are parties to the dispute would not be members of the panel concerned with that dispute.

4. In order to facilitate the constitution of panels, the Chairman of the Committee should maintain an informal indicative list of governmental and non-governmental persons qualified in the fields of trade relations, economic development, and other matters covered by the General Agreement and this Agreement, who could be available for serving on panels. For this purpose, each signatory would be invited to indicate at the beginning of every year to the Chairman of the Committee the name of one or two persons who would be available for such work.

5. Panel members would serve in their individual capacities and not as government representatives, nor as representatives of any organization. Governments would therefore not give them instructions with regard to matters before a panel. Panel members should be selected with a view to ensuring the independence of the members, a sufficiently diverse background and a wide spectrum of experience.

6. To encourage development of mutually satisfactory solutions between the parties to a dispute and with a view to obtaining their comments, each panel should first submit the descriptive part of its report to the parties concerned, and should subsequently submit to the parties to the dispute its conclusions, or an outline thereof, a reasonable period of time before they are circulated to the Committee.

7. If a mutually satisfactory solution is developed by the parties to a dispute before a panel, any signatory with an interest in the matter has a right to enquire about and be given appropriate information about that solution and a notice outlining the solution that has been reached shall be presented by the panel to the Committee.

8. In cases where the parties to a dispute have failed to come to a satisfactory solution, the panels shall submit a written report to the Committee which should set forth the findings of the panel as to the questions of fact and the application of the relevant provisions of the General Agreement as interpreted and applied by this Agreement and the reasons and bases therefor.

9. The Committee shall consider the panel report as soon as possible and, taking into account the findings contained therein, may make recommendations to the parties with a view to resolving the dispute. If the Committee's recommendations are not followed within a reasonable period, the Committee may authorize appropriate countermeasures (including withdrawal of GATT concessions or obligations) taking into account the nature and degree of the adverse effect found to exist. Committee recommendations should be presented to the parties within thirty days of the receipt of the panel report.

Part VII

Article 19   Final Provisions

1. No specific action against a subsidy of another signatory can be taken except in accordance with the provisions of the General Agreement, as interpreted by this Agreement.[38]

2. (a) This Agreement shall be open for acceptance by signature or otherwise, by governments contracting parties to the GATT and by the European Economic Community.

   (b) This Agreement shall be open for acceptance by signature or otherwise by governments having provisionally acceded to the GATT, on terms related to the effective application of rights and obligations under this Agreement, which take into account rights and obligations in the instruments providing for their provisional accession.

   (c) This Agreement shall be open to accession by any other government on terms, related to the effective application of rights and obligations under this Agreement, to be agreed between that government and the signatories, by the deposit with the Director-General to the CONTRACTING PARTIES to the GATT of an instrument of accession which states the terms so agreed.

   (d) In regard to acceptance, the provisions of Article XXVI:5(a) and (b) of the General Agreement would be applicable.

RESERVATIONS

3. Reservations may not be entered in respect of any of the provisions of this Agreement without the consent of the other signatories.

ENTRY INTO FORCE

4. This Agreement shall enter into force on 1 January 1980 for the governments[39] which have accepted or acceded to it by that date. For each other government it shall enter into force on the thirtieth day following the date of its acceptance or accession to this Agreement.

NATIONAL LEGISLATION

5. (a) Each government accepting or acceding to this Agreement shall take all necessary steps, of a general or particular character, to ensure, not later than the date of entry into force of this Agreement for it, the conformity of its laws, regulations and administrative procedures with the provisions of this Agreement as they may apply to the signatory in question.

   (b) Each signatory shall inform the Committee of any changes in its laws and regulations relevant to this Agreement and in the administration of such laws and regulations.

REVIEW

6. The Committee shall review annually the implementation and operation of this Agreement taking into account the objectives thereof. The Committee shall annually inform the CONTRACTING PARTIES to the GATT of developments during the period covered by such reviews.[40]

AMENDMENTS

7. The signatories may amend this Agreement having regard, *inter alia*, to the experience gained in its implementation. Such an amendment, once the signatories have con-

curred in accordance with procedures established by the Committee, shall not come into force for any signatory until it has been accepted by such signatory.

WITHDRAWAL

8. Any signatory may withdraw from this Agreement. The withdrawal shall take effect upon the expiration of sixty days from the day on which written notice of withdrawal is received by the Director-General to the CONTRACTING PARTIES to the GATT. Any signatories may upon such notification request an immediate meeting of the Committee.

NONAPPLICATION OF THIS AGREEMENT BETWEEN PARTICULAR SIGNATORIES

9. This Agreement shall not apply as between any two signatories if either of the signatories, at the time either accepts or accedes to this Agreement, does not consent to such application.

ANNEX

10. The annex to this Agreement constitutes an integral part thereof.

SECRETARIAT

11. This Agreement shall be serviced by the GATT secretariat.

DEPOSIT

12. This Agreement shall be deposited with the Director-General to the CONTRACTING PARTIES to the GATT, who shall promptly furnish to each signatory and each contracting party to the GATT a certified copy thereof and of each amendment thereto pursuant to paragraph 7, and a notification of each acceptance thereof or accession thereto pursuant to paragraph 2, and of each withdrawal therefrom pursuant to paragraph 8 of this Article.

REGISTRATION

13. This Agreement shall be registered in accordance with the provision of Article 102 of the Charter of the United Nations.

Done at Geneva this twelfth day of April nineteen hundred and seventy-nine in a single copy, in the English, French and Spanish languages, each text being authentic.

Notes

1. The term "signatories" is hereinafter used to mean Parties to this Agreement.

2. Wherever in this Agreement there is reference to "the terms of this Agreement" or the "articles" or "provisions of this Agreement" it shall be taken to mean, as the context requires, the provisions of the General Agreement as interpreted and applied by this Agreement.

3. The provisions of both Part I and Part II of this Agreement may be invoked in parallel: however, with regard to the effects of a particular subsidy in the domestic market of the importing country, only one form of relief (either a countervailing duty or an authorized countermeasure) shall be available.

4. The term "countervailing duty" shall be understood to mean a special duty levied for the purpose of off-setting any bounty or subsidy bestowed directly or indirectly upon the manufacture, production or export of any merchandise, as provided for in Article VI:3 of the General Agreement.

5. The term "initiated" as used hereinafter means procedural action by which a signatory formally commences an investigation as provided in paragraph 3 of this Article.

6. Under this Agreement the term "injury" shall, unless otherwise specified, be taken to mean material injury to a domestic industry, threat of material injury to a domestic industry or material retardation of the establishment of such an industry and shall be interpreted in accordance with the provisions of Article 6.

7. As established in Part V of this Agreement and hereinafter referred to as "the Committee."

8. For the purposes of this Agreement "party" means any natural or juridical person resident in the territory of any signatory.

9. Any "interested signatory" or "interested party" shall refer to a signatory or a party economically affected by the subsidy in question.

10. Signatories are aware that in the territory of certain signatories disclosures pursuant to a narrowly drawn protective order may be required.

11. Signatories agree that requests for confidentiality should not be arbitrarily rejected.

12. Because of different terms used under different systems in various countries the term "finding" is hereinafter used to mean a formal decision or determination.

13. It is particularly important, in accordance with the provisions of this paragraph, that no affirmative finding whether preliminary or final be made without reasonable opportunity for consultations having been given. Such consultations may establish the basis for proceeding under the provisions of Part VI of this Agreement.

14. As used in the Agreement "levy" shall mean the definitive or final legal assessment or collection of a duty or tax.

15. An understanding among signatories should be developed setting out the criteria for the calculation of the amount of the subsidy.

16. The word "may" shall not be interpreted to allow the simultaneous continuation of proceedings with the implementation of price undertakings, except as provided in paragraph 5(b) of this Article.

17. Determinations of injury under the criteria set forth in this Article shall be based on positive evidence. In determining threat of injury the investigating authorities, in examining the factors listed in this Article, may take into account the evidence on the nature of the subsidy in question and the trade effects likely to arise therefrom.

18. Throughout this Agreement the term "like product" ("produit similaire") shall be interpreted to mean a product which is identical, i.e. alike in all respects to the product under consideration or in the absence of such a product, another product which although not alike in all respects, has characteristics closely resembling those of the product under consideration.

19. As set forth in paragraphs 2 and 3 of this Article.

20. Such factors include *inter alia*, the volume and prices of non-subsidized imports of the product in question, contraction in demand or changes in the pattern of consumption, trade restrictive practices of and competition between the foreign and domestic producers, developments in technology and the export performance and productivity of the domestic industry.

21. The Committee should develop a definition of the word "related" as used in this paragraph.

22. In this Agreement, the term "subsidies" shall be deemed to include subsidies granted by any government or any public body within the territory of a signatory. However, it is recognized that for signatories with different federal systems of government, there are different divisions of powers. Such signatories accept nonetheless the international consequences that may arise under this Agreement as a result of the granting of subsidies within their territories.

23. Injury to the domestic industry is used here in the same sense as it is used in Part I of this Agreement.

24. Benefits accruing directly or indirectly under the General Agreement include the benefits of tariff concessions bound under Article II of the General Agreement.

25. Serious prejudice to the interests of another signatory is used in this Agreement in the same sense as it is used in Article XVI:1 of the General Agreement and includes threat of serious prejudice.

26. Signatories recognize that nullification or impairment of benefits may also arise through the failure of a signatory to carry out its obligations under the General Agreement or this Agreement. Where such failure concerning export subsidies is determined by the Committee to exist, adverse effects may, without

prejudice to paragraph 9 of Article 18 below, be presumed to exist. The other signatory will be accorded a reasonable opportunity to rebut this presumption.

27. The term "displacing" shall be interpreted in a manner which takes into account the trade and development needs of developing countries and in this connection is not intended to fix traditional market shares.

28. The problem of third country markets so far as certain primary products are concerned is dealt with exclusively under Article 10 below.

29. For purposes of this Agreement "certain primary products" means the products referred to in Note Ad Article XVI of the General Agreement, Section B, paragraph 2, with the deletion of the words "or any mineral."

30. Any time periods mentioned in this Article and in Article 18 may be extended by mutual agreement.

31. In making such recommendations, the Committee shall take into account the trade, development and financial needs of developing country signatories.

32. It is understood that after this Agreement has entered into force, any such proposed commitment shall be notified to the Committee in good time.

33. Constructed value means cost of production plus a reasonable amount for administration, selling and any other costs and for profits.

34. In this connexion, the Committee may draw signatories' attention to those cases in which, in its view, there is no reasonable basis supporting the allegations made.

35. This does not preclude, however, the more rapid establishment of a panel when the Committee so decides, taking into account the urgency of the situation.

36. The parties to the dispute would respond within a short period of time, i.e. seven working days, to nominations of panel members by the Chairman of the Committee and would not oppose nominations except for compelling reasons.

37. The term "governments" is understood to mean governments of all member countries in cases of customs unions.

38. This paragraph is not intended to preclude action under other relevant provisions of the General Agreement, where appropriate.

39. The term "governments" is deemed to include the competent authorities of the European Economic Community.

40. At the first such review, the Committee shall, in addition to its general review of the operation of the Agreement, offer all interested signatories an opportunity to raise questions and discuss issues concerning specific subsidy practices and the impact on trade, if any, of certain direct tax practices.

Annex   Illustrative List of Export Subsidies

(a) The provision by governments of direct subsidies to a firm or an industry contingent upon export performance.

(b) Currency retention schemes or any similar practices which involve a bonus on exports.

(c) Internal transport and freight charges on export shipments, provided or mandated by governments, on terms more favourable than for domestic shipments.

(d) The delivery by governments or their agencies of imported or domestic products or services for use in the production of exported goods, on terms or conditions more favourable than for delivery of like or directly competitive products or services for use in the production of goods for domestic consumption, if (in the case of products) such terms or conditions are more favourable than those commercially available on world markets to their exporters.

(e) The full or partial exemption, remission, or deferral specifically related to exports, of direct taxes[1] or social welfare charges paid or payable by industrial or commercial enterprises.[2]

(f) The allowance of special deductions directly related to exports or export performance, over and above those granted in respect to production for domestic consumption, in the calculation of the base on which direct taxes are charged.

(g) The exemption or remission in respect of the production and distribution of exported products, of indirect taxes[1] in excess of those levied in respect of the production and distribution of like products when sold for domestic consumption.

(h) The exemption, remission or deferral of prior stage cumulative indirect taxes[1] on goods or services used in the production of exported products in excess of the exemption, remission or deferral of like prior stage cumulative indirect taxes on goods or services used in the production of like products when sold for domestic consumption; provided, however, that prior stage cumulative indirect taxes may be exempted, remitted or deferred on exported products even when not exempted, remitted or deferred on like products when sold for domestic consumption, if the prior stage cumulative indirect taxes are levied on goods that are physically incorporated (making normal allowance for waste) in the exported product.[3]

(i) The remission or drawback of import charges[1] in excess of those levied on imported goods that are physically incorporated (making normal allowance for waste) in the exported product; provided, however, that in particular cases a firm may use a quantity of home market goods equal to, and having the same quality and characteristics as, the imported goods as a substitute for them in order to benefit from this provision if the import and the corresponding export operations both occur within a reasonable time period, normally not to exceed two years.

(j) The provision by governments (or special institutions controlled by governments) of export credit guarantees or insurance programmes, of insurance or guarantee programmes against increases in the costs of exported products[4] or of exchange risk programmes, at premium rates, which are manifestly inadequate to cover the long-term operating costs and losses of the programmes.[5]

(k) The grant by governments (or special institutions controlled by and/or acting under the authority of governments) of export credits at rates below those which they actually have to pay for the funds so employed (or would have to pay if they borrowed on international capital markets in order to obtain funds of the same maturity and denominated in the same currency as the export credit), or the payment by them of all or part of the costs incurred by exporters or financial institutions in obtaining credits, in so far as they are used to secure a material advantage in the field of export credit terms.

Provided, however, that if a signatory is a party to an international undertaking on official export credits to which at least twelve original signatories[6] to this Agreement are parties as of 1 January 1979 (or a successor undertaking which has been adopted by those original signatories), or if in practice a signatory applies the interest rates provisions of the relevant undertaking, an export credit practice which is in conformity with those provisions shall not be considered an export subsidy prohibited by this Agreement.

(l) Any other charge on the public account constituting an export subsidy in the sense of Article XVI of the General Agreement.

Notes

1. For the purpose of this Agreement:

The term "direct taxes" shall mean taxes on wages, profits, interest, rents, royalties, and all other forms of income, and taxes on the ownership of real property;

The term "import charges" shall mean tariffs, duties, and other fiscal charges not elsewhere enumerated in this note that are levied on imports;

The term "indirect taxes" shall mean sales, excise, turnover, value added, franchise, stamp, transfer, inventory and equipment taxes, border taxes and all taxes other than direct taxes and import charges;

"Prior stage" indirect taxes are those levied on goods or services used directly or indirectly in making the product;

"Cumulative" indirect taxes are multi-staged taxes levied where there is no mechanism for subsequent crediting of the tax if the goods or services subject to tax at one stage of the production are used in a succeeding stage of production;

"Remission" of taxes includes the refund or rebate of taxes.

2. The signatories recognize that deferral need not amount to an export subsidy where, for example, appropriate interest charges are collected. The signatories further recognize that nothing in this text prejudges the disposition by the CONTRACTING PARTIES of the specific issues raised in GATT document L/4422. The signatories reaffirm the principle that prices for goods in transactions between exporting enterprises and foreign buyers under their or under the same control should for tax purposes be the prices which would be charged between independent enterprises acting at arm's length. Any signatory may draw the attention of another signatory to administrative or other practices which may contravene this principle and which result in a significant saving of direct taxes in export transactions. In such circumstances the signatories shall normally attempt to resolve their differences using the facilities of existing bilateral tax treaties or other specific international mechanisms, without prejudice to the rights and obligations of signatories under the General Agreement, including the right of consultation created in the preceding sentence.

Paragraph (e) is not intended to limit a signatory from taking measures to avoid the double taxation of foreign source income earned by its enterprises of the enterprises of another signatory.

Where measures incompatible with the provisions of paragraph (e) exist, and where major practical difficulties stand in the way of the signatory concerned bringing such measures promptly into conformity with the Agreement, the signatory concerned shall, without prejudice to the rights of other signatories under the General Agreement or this Agreement, examine methods of bringing these measures into conformity within a reasonable period of time.

In this connexion the European Economic Community has declared that Ireland intends to withdraw by 1 January 1981 its system of preferential tax measures related to exports, provided for under the Corporation Tax Act of 1976, whilst continuing nevertheless to honour legally binding commitments entered into during the lifetime of this system.

3. Paragraph (h) does not apply to value-added tax systems and border-tax adjustment in lieu thereof; the problem of the excessive remission of value-added taxes is exclusively covered by paragraph (g).

4. The signatories agree that nothing in this paragraph shall prejudge or influence the deliberations of the panel established by the GATT Council on 6 June 1978 (C/M/126).

5. In evaluating the long-term adequacy of premium rates, costs and losses of insurance programmes, in principle only such contracts shall be taken into account that were concluded after the date of entry into force of this Agreement.

6. An original signatory to this Agreement shall mean any signatory which adheres *ad referendum* to the Agreement on or before 30 June 1979.

Article VI of the General Agreement on Tariffs and Trade

Anti-dumping and Countervailing Duties

1. The contracting parties recognize that dumping, by which products of one country are introduced into the commerce of another country at less than the normal value of the products, is to be condemned if it causes or threatens material injury to an established industry in the territory of a contracting party or materially retards the establishment of a domestic industry. For the purposes of this Article, a product is to be considered as being introduced into the commerce of an importing country at less than its normal value, if the price of the product exported from one country to another
   (a) is less than the comparable price, in the ordinary course of trade, for the like product when destined for consumption in the exporting country, or,
   (b) in the absence of such domestic price, is less than either
      (i) the highest comparable price for the like product for export to any third country in the ordinary course of trade, or
      (ii) the cost of production of the product in the country of origin plus a reasonable addition for selling cost and profit.
   Due allowance shall be made in each case for differences in conditions and terms of sale, for differences in taxation, and for other differences affecting price comparability.
2. In order to offset or prevent dumping, a contracting party may levy on any dumped product an anti-dumping duty not greater in amount than the margin of dumping in respect of such product. For the purposes of this Article, the margin of dumping is the price difference determined in accordance with the provisions of paragraph 1.
3. No countervailing duty shall be levied on any product of the territory of any contracting party imported into the territory of another contracting party in excess of an amount equal to the estimated bounty or subsidy determined to have been granted, directly or indirectly, on the manufacture, production or export of such product in the country of origin or exportation, including any special subsidy to the transportation of a particular product. The term "countervailing duty" shall be understood to mean a special duty levied for the purpose of offsetting any bounty or subsidy bestowed, directly or indirectly, upon the manufacture, production or export of any merchandise.
4. No product of the territory of any contracting party imported into the territory of any other contracting party shall be subject to anti-dumping or countervailing duty by reason of the exemption of such product from duties or taxes borne by the like product when destined for consumption in the country of origin or exportation, or by reason of the refund of such duties or taxes.
5. No product of the territory of any contracting party imported into the territory of any other contracting party shall be subject to both anti-dumping and countervailing duties to compensate for the same situation of dumping or export subsidization.
6. (a) No contracting party shall levy any anti-dumping or countervailing duty on the importation of any product of the territory of another contracting party unless it determines that the effect of the dumping or subsidization, as the case may be, is such as to cause or threaten material injury to an established domestic industry, or is such as to retard materially the establishment of a domestic industry.
   (b) The CONTRACTING PARTIES may waive the requirement of sub-paragraph (a) of this paragraph so as to permit a contracting party to levy an anti-dumping or countervailing duty on the importation of any product for the purpose of offsetting

dumping or subsidization which causes or threatens material injury to an industry in the territory of another contracting party exporting the product concerned to the territory of the importing contracting party. The CONTRACTING PARTIES shall waive the requirements of sub-paragraph (a) of this paragraph, so as to permit the levying of a countervailing duty, in cases in which they find that a subsidy is causing or threatening material injury to an industry in the territory of another contracting party exporting the product concerned to the territory of the importing contracting party.

   (c)   In exceptional circumstances, however, where delay might cause damage which would be difficult to repair, a contracting party may levy a countervailing duty for the purpose referred to in sub-paragraph (b) of this paragraph without prior approval of the CONTRACTING PARTIES; *Provided* that such action shall be reported immediately to the CONTRACTING PARTIES and that the countervailing duty shall be withdrawn promptly if the CONTRACTING PARTIES disapprove.

7. A system for the stabilization of the domestic price or of the return to domestic producers of a primary commodity, independently of the movements of export prices, which results at times in the sale of the commodity for export at a price lower than the comparable price charged for the like commodity to buyers in the domestic market, shall be presumed not to result in material injury within the meaning of paragraph 6 if it is determined by consultation among the contracting parties substantially interested in the commodity concerned that:

   (a)   the system has also resulted in the sale of the commodity for export at a price higher than the comparable commodity price charged for the like commodity to buyers in the domestic market and,

   (b)   the system is so operated, either because of the effective regulation of production, or otherwise, as not to stimulate exports unduly or otherwise seriously prejudice the interests of other contracting parties.

Note to Article VI

Paragraph 1

1. Hidden dumping by associated houses (that is, the sale by an importer at a price below that corresponding to the price invoiced by an exporter with whom the importer is associated, and also below the price in the exporting country) constitutes a form of price dumping with respect to which the margin of dumping may be calculated on the basis of the price at which the goods are resold by the importer.

2. It is recognized that, in the case of imports from a country which has a complete or substantially complete monopoly of its trade and where all domestic prices are fixed by the State, special difficulties may exist in determining price comparability for the purposes of paragraph 1, and in such cases importing contracting parties may find it necessary to take into account the possibility that a strict comparison with domestic prices in such a country may not always be appropriate.

Paragraphs 2 and 3

1. As in many other cases in customs administration, a contracting party may require reasonable security (bond or cash deposit) for the payment of anti-dumping or countervailing duty pending final determination of the facts in any case of suspected dumping or subsidization.

2. Multiple currency practices can in certain circumstances constitute a subsidy to exports which may be met by countervailing duties under paragraph 3 or can constitute a form of dumping by means of a partial depreciation of a country's currency which may be met by action under paragraph 2. By "multiple currency practices" is meant practices by governments or sanctioned by governments.

Paragraph 6(b)

Waivers under the provisions of this sub-paragraph shall be granted only on application by the contracting party proposing to levy an anti-dumping or countervailing duty, as the case may be.

Article XVI of the General Agreement on Tariffs and Trade

Subsidies

Section A   Subsidies in General

1. If any contracting party grants or maintains any subsidy, including any form of income or price support, which operates directly or indirectly to increase exports of any product from, or to reduce imports of any product into, its territory, it shall notify the CONTRACTING PARTIES in writing of the extent and nature of the subsidization, of the estimated effect of the subsidization on the quantity of the affected product or products imported into or exported from its territory and of the circumstances making the subsidization necessary. In any case in which it is determined that serious prejudice to the interest of any other contracting party is caused or threatened by any such subsidization, the contracting party granting the subsidy shall, upon request, discuss with the other contracting party or parties concerned, or with the CONTRACTING PARTIES, the possibility of limiting the subsidization.

Section B   Additional Provisions on Export Subsidies

2. The contracting parties recognize that the granting by a contracting party of a subsidy on the export of any product may have harmful effects for other contracting parties, both importing and exporting, may cause undue disturbance to their normal commercial interests, and may hinder the achievement of the objectives of this Agreement.

3. Accordingly, contracting parties should seek to avoid the use of subsidies on the export of primary products. If, however, a contracting party grants directly or indirectly any form of subsidy which operates to increase the export of any primary product from its territory, such subsidy shall not be applied in a manner which results in that contracting party having more than an equitable share of world export trade in that product, account being taken of the shares of the contracting parties in such trade in the product during a previous representative period, and any special factors which may have affected or may be affecting such trade in the product.

4. Further, as from 1 January 1958 or the earliest practicable date thereafter, contracting parties shall cease to grant either directly or indirectly any form of subsidy on the export of any product other than a primary product which subsidy results in the sale of such product for export at a price lower than the comparable price charged for the like product to buyers in the domestic market. Until 31 December 1957 no contracting party shall extend the scope of any such subsidization beyond that existing on 1 January 1955 by the introduction of new, or the extension of existing, subsidies.

5. The CONTRACTING PARTIES shall review the operation of the provisions of this Article from time to time with a view to examining its effectiveness, in the light of actual experience, in promoting the objectives of this Agreement and avoiding subsidization seriously prejudicial to the trade or interests of contracting parties.

Note to Article XVI

The exemption of an exported product from duties or taxes borne by the like product when destined for domestic consumption, or the remission of such duties or taxes in amounts not in excess of those which have accrued, shall not be deemed to be a subsidy.

Section B

1. Nothing in Section B shall preclude the use by a contracting party of multiple rates of exchange in accordance with the Articles of Agreement of the International Monetary Fund.

2. For the purposes of Section B, a "primary product" is understood to be any product of farm, forest or fishery, or any mineral, in its natural form or which has undergone only such processing as is customarily required to prepare it for marketing in substantial volume in international trade.

Paragraph 3

1. The fact that a contracting party has not exported the product in question during the previous representative period would not in itself preclude that contracting party from establishing its right to obtain a share of the trade in the product concerned.

2. A system for the stabilization of the domestic price or of the return to domestic producers of a primary product independently of the movements of export prices, which results at times in the sale of the product for export at a price lower than the comparable price charged for the like product to buyers in the domestic market, shall be considered not to involve a subsidy on exports within the meaning of paragraph 3 if the CONTRACTING PARTIES determine that:

    (a) the system has also resulted, or is so designed as to result, in the sale of the product for export at a price higher than the comparable price charged for the like product to buyers in the domestic market; and

(b) the system is so operated, or is designed so to operate, either because of the effective regulation of production or otherwise, as not to stimulate exports unduly or otherwise seriously to prejudice the interests of other contracting parties. Notwithstanding such determination by the CONTRACTING PARTIES, operations under such a system shall be subject to the provisions of paragraph 3 where they are wholly or partly financed out of government funds in addition to the funds collected from producers in respect of the product concerned.

Paragraph 4

The intention of paragraph 4 is that the contracting parties should seek before the end of 1957 to reach agreement to abolish all remaining subsidies as from 1 January 1958; or, failing this, to reach agreement to extend the application of the standstill until the earliest date thereafter by which they can expect to reach such agreement.

Article XXIII of the General Agreement on Tariffs and Trade

Nullification or Impairment

1. If any contracting party should consider that any benefit accruing to it directly or indirectly under this Agreement is being nullified or impaired or that the attainment of any objective of the Agreement is being impeded as the result of
   (a) the failure of another contracting party to carry out its obligations under this Agreement, or
   (b) the application by another contracting party of any measure, whether or not it conflicts with the provisions of the Agreement, or
   (c) the existence of any other situation,
   the contracting party may, with a view to the satisfactory adjustment of the matter, make written representations or proposals to the other contracting party or parties which it considers to be concerned. Any contracting party thus approached shall give sympathetic consideration to the representations or proposals made to it.

2. If no satisfactory adjustment is effected between the contracting parties concerned within a reasonable time, or if the difficulty is of the type described in paragraph 1(c) of this Article, the matter may be referred to the CONTRACTING PARTIES. The CONTRACTING PARTIES shall promptly investigate any matter so referred to them and shall make appropriate recommendations to the contracting parties which they consider to be concerned, or give a ruling on the matter, as appropriate. The CONTRACTING PARTIES may consult with contracting parties, with the Economic and Social Council of the United Nations and with any appropriate inter-governmental organization in cases

where they consider such consultation necessary. If the CONTRACTING PARTIES consider that the circumstances are serious enough to justify such action, they may authorize a contracting party or parties to suspend the application to any other contracting party or parties of such concessions or other obligations under this Agreement as they determine to be appropriate in the circumstances. If the application to any contracting party of any concession or other obligation is in fact suspended, that contracting party shall then be free, not later than sixty days after such action is taken, to give written notice to the Executive Secretary to the CONTRACTING PARTIES of its intention to withdraw from this Agreement and such withdrawal shall take effect upon the sixtieth day following the day on which such notice is received by him.

B Unilateral Declarations and Exchanges of Letters with Selected Signatories to the Code on Subsidies and Countervailing Duties

Australia

Embassy of Australia
Washington, DC

Ambassador   25 September 1981
Sir Nicholas Parkinson

Dear Ambassador Brock,

With reference to bilateral discussions between representatives of the Government of the United States of America and the Government of Australia regarding acceptance by the Government of Australia of the Agreement on Interpretation and Application of Articles VI, XVI and XXIII of the General Agreement on Tariffs and Trade done at Geneva on 12 April 1979 (called "The Code") and regarding the basis on which each Government will apply provisionally to the other the rights and obligations of the Code when it enters into force between them, I wish to inform you that the following represents the understanding of my Government of the outcome of those discussions.

1. The Government of Australia will accept the Code by 29 September 1981 on which occasion it will lodge the statement at Annex A with the GATT Secretariat, for circulation to the parties to the Code and to other GATT Contracting Parties.
2. The rights and obligations of the Code will apply between our two Governments subject to the right of each Government to terminate the application of the Code to the other Government if its expectations, as set out below, are not realised. This right will not prejudice the right of withdrawal under Article 19.8 of the Code.
3. While recognising that the Government of the United States of America is not in a position to commit itself with respect to the following the Government of Australia has the expectation:
   (I) That the Government of the United States of America will not operate a Domestic International Sales Corporation System (DISC) in a manner inconsistent with the Code beyond a reasonable time, which in the view of the Government of Australia will be no later than 30 June 1983, and
   (II) That the DISC will not be modified to increase the value of benefits available that are not in conformity with the Code over those available under existing criteria.

4. In addition, the Government of Australia has the expectation:
   (I)   That the Government of the United States of America will not introduce any new export incentive schemes, the use of which is proscribed by the Code.
   (II) That the Government of the United States of America will recognise Australia as a "country under the Agreement" in terms of the United States countervailing duty law and will accord Australian exports the benefit of a material injury test in any countervailing duty investigations affecting these exports, and
   (III) That our two Governments will co-operate in the Code in the development of disciplines relating to agricultural export subsidies which are substantially equivalent to those adopted in respect of products other than certain primary products as defined in the Code.
5. Similarly, while recognising that the Government of Australia is not in a position to commit itself to the following, the Government of the United States of America has the expectation:
   (I)   That the Government of Australia will not operate an Export Expansion Grants (EEG) Scheme or an Export Market Development Grants (EMDG) Scheme in a manner inconsistent with the Code beyond a reasonable time which in the view of the Government of the United States of America will be no later than 30 June 1983, and
   (II) That the EEG and EMDG schemes will not be modified to increase the value of benefits available that are not in conformity with the Code over those available under existing criteria. In this connection, the "value of benefits" means the rate of assistance expressed *inter alia* as a maximum amount payable and/or as a percentage. In addition, neither scheme will be modified to permit new sectors or products that would not be eligible under existing legislation to qualify for benefits proscribed by the Code.
6. In addition, the Government of the United States of America has the expectation:
   (I)   That the Government of Australia will not introduce any new export incentive schemes, the use of which is proscribed by the Code, and
   (II) That our two Governments will co-operate in the Code in the development of disciplines relating to agricultural export subsidies which are substantially equivalent to those adopted in respect of products other than certain primary products as defined in the Code.
7. Our two Governments will consult prior to any proposed termination of the application of the Code to one another.
8. Each of our Governments will lodge with the Director-General of the GATT, as depositary of the Code, the relevant statement set out in Annex B.
9. I should be grateful to have your confirmation that the understanding of your Government conforms with the foregoing.

The Honourable William Brock,   Yours sincerely,
US Trade Representative,
Suite 209,   /s/
600 17th Street, NW,
Washington, DC 20506   Nicholas Parkinson

Annex A Statement by the Government of Australia on Acceptance of the Agreement on the Interpretation and Application of Articles VI, XVI and XXIII of the GATT

It is a matter of regret to the Government of Australia that participants in the MTN were unable to develop more effective disciplines on the use of agricultural export subsidies. The Agreement on the Interpretation and Application of Articles VI, XVI and XXIII of the GATT is heavily imbalanced as between its provisions relating to agricultural and to industrial products.

Notwithstanding the disappointing result, the Government of Australia has decided to accept the Agreement on the expectation that within a reasonable time GATT Contracting Parties will develop disciplines relating to agricultural export subsidies which are substantially equivalent to those adopted in respect of export subsidies on products other than certain primary products (as defined in the Agreement).

In respect of Australian measures which may exist within the purview of the illustrative list at the time of acceptance by the Government of Australia of the Agreement and where major practical difficulties stand in the way of the Government of Australia bringing such measures promptly into conformity with the Agreement, the Government of Australia will, without prejudice to the rights of other signatories under the General Agreement or this Agreement, examine methods of bringing these measures into conformity within a reasonable time.

In any event the Government of Australia will be reviewing its position in relation to the Agreement in the light of experience.

Annex B

I. Formal Notification by the United States on the Subsidy Code

Until such time as the United States Government otherwise notifies the Director General to the CONTRACTING PARTIES to the GATT, the United States will provisionally apply to Australia all rights and obligations of the Agreement on the Interpretation and Application of Articles VI, XVI and XXIII of the General Agreement on Tariffs and Trade.

II. Formal Notification by Australia on the Subsidy Code

Until such time as the Government of Australia otherwise notifies the Director General to the CONTRACTING PARTIES to the GATT, Australia will provisionally apply to the United States all rights and obligations of the Agreement on the Interpretation and Application of Articles VI, XVI and XIII [sic] of the General Agreement on Tariffs and Trade.

September 25, 1981

Dear Mr. Ambassador:

I refer to your letter of today's date, which reads as follows:

With reference to bilateral discussions between representatives of the Government of the United States of America and the Government of Australia regarding acceptance by the Government of Australia of the Agreement on Interpretation and Application of Articles VI, XVI and XXIII of the General Agreement on Tariffs and Trade done at Geneva on 12 April 1979 (called "The Code") and regarding the basis on which each Government will apply provisionally to the other the rights and obligations of the Code when it enters into force between them, I wish to inform you that the following represents the understanding of my Government of the outcome of those discussions.

1. The Government of Australia will accept the Code by September 29, 1981 on which occasion it will lodge the statement at Annex A with the GATT Secretariat, for circulation to the parties to the Code and to other GATT Contracting Parties.

2. The rights and obligations of the Code will apply between our two Governments subject to the right of each Government to terminate the application of the Code to the other Government if its expectations, as set out below, are not realised. This right will not prejudice the right of withdrawal under Article 19.8 of the Code.

3. While recognising that the Government of the United States of America is not in a position to commit itself with respect to the following, the Government of Australia has the expectation:

   (I)   That the Government of the United States of America will not operate a Domestic International Sales Corporation system (DISC) in a manner inconsistent with the Code beyond a reasonable time, which in the view of the Government of Australia will be no later than 30 June 1983, and

   (II) That the DISC will not be modified to increase the value of benefits available that are not in conformity with the Code over those available under existing criteria.

4. In addition, the Government of Australia has the expectation:

   (I)   That the Government of the United States of America will not introduce any new export incentive schemes, the use of which is proscribed by the Code.

   (II) That the Government of the United States of America will recognise Australia as a "country under the Agreement" in terms of the United States countervailing duty law and will accord Australian exports the benefit of a material injury test in any countervailing duty investigations affecting these exports, and

   (III) That our two Governments will co-operate in the Code in the development of disciplines relating to agricultural export subsidies, which are substantially equivalent to those adopted in respect of products other than certain primary products, as defined in the Code.

5. Similarly, while recognising that the Government of Australia is not in a position to commit itself to the following, the Government of the United States of America has the expectation:

(I) That the Government of Australia will not operate an Export Expansion Grants (EEG) Scheme or an Export Market Development Grants (EMDG) Scheme in a manner inconsistent with the Code beyond a reasonable time, which in the view of the Government of the United States of America will be no later than 30 June 1983, and

(II) That the EEG and EMDG Schemes will not be modified to increase the value of benefits available that are not in conformity with the Code over those available under existing criteria. In this connection, the "value of benefits" means the rate of assistance expressed *inter alia* as a maximum amount payable and/or as a percentage. In addition, neither scheme will be modified to permit new sectors or products that would not be eligible under existing legislation to qualify for benefits proscribed by the Code.

6. In addition, the Government of the United States of America has the expectation:

(I) That the Government of Australia will not introduce any new export incentive schemes, the use of which is proscribed by the Code, and

(II) That our two Governments will co-operate in the Code in the development of disciplines relating to agricultural export subsidies which are substantially equivalent to those adopted in respect of products other than certain primary products, as defined in the Code.

7. Our two Governments will consult prior to any proposed termination of the application of the Code to one another.

8. Each of our Governments will lodge with the Director General of the GATT, as depositary of the Code, the relevant statement set out in Annex B.

9. I should be grateful to have your confirmation that the understanding of your Government conforms with the foregoing.

I wish to confirm that the foregoing conforms to the understanding of my Government.

Honorable Sir Nicholas Parkinson   Very truly yours,
Ambassador of Australia
Embassy of Australia   /s/
1601 Massachusetts Avenue, NW
Washington, DC 20036   William E. Brock

Brazil

General Agreement on
Tariffs and Trade

1 January 1980

Limited Distribution
Original: English

Agreement on Implementation and Application of Articles VI, XVI and XXIII of the General Agreement on Tariffs and Trade

Declaration by Brazil

In the context of his signature on 28 December 1979 of the Agreement on Implementation and Application of Articles VI, XVI and XXIII of the General Agreement on Tariffs and Trade, the representative of Brazil deposited the following Declaration of Acceptance by Brazil with the request that it be circulated as a GATT document.

Declaration of Acceptance by Brazil

In view of the provisions of Article 14:5 of Part III of the Agreement on Interpretation and Application of Articles VI, XVI and XXIII of the General Agreement on Tariffs and Trade:

1. The Government of Brazil has decided to eliminate the IPI and ICM credit rates according to the following schedule:

Date	Cumulative reduction of IPI and ICM credit rates
1 March 1979	10 percent
30 June 1979	15 percent
31 December 1979	30 percent
31 December 1980	50 percent
31 December 1981	70 percent
31 December 1982	90 percent
30 June 1983	100 percent

2. During the period of reduction and elimination of export subsidies—as provided in paragraph 1 above—the Government of Brazil will not increase the overall level of export subsidies in a way that offsets this phase-out commitment.
3. The Government of Brazil understands that, if an export subsidy is found to exist in a manner which is inconsistent with the terms of this commitment, countermeasures, pursuant to the provisions of Part II of the Agreement on Interpretation and Application of Articles VI, XVI and XXIII of the General Agreement on Tariffs and Trade, may be

authorized in relation to such subsidy, subject to the provisions of Article 14:4 of Part III of that Agreement.

4. The Government of Brazil understands that, in the light of the above decisions, it will not be subject to the review procedures mentioned in Article 14:8 of Part III of the Agreement on Interpretation and Application of Articles VI, XVI and XXIII of the General Agreement on Tariffs and Trade, as regards export subsidies, for a period of eight years from the initial date of implementation of this commitment (1 March 1979). The Government of Brazil recognizes however that after 30 June 1983, countermeasures pursuant to Part II of that Agreement may be authorized for other signatories thereof in relation to export subsidies, subject to the provisions of Article 14:4 of Part III of the same Agreement.

India

Permanent Mission of India
to the United Nations Offices
9, Rue du Valais
1202 Geneva

B.L. Das,
Ambassador   September 25, 1981

No. GEN/PMI/GATT/204/23/81

Dear Ambassador Smith,

With respect to the recent discussions between our two countries relating to the matter of subsidies and countervailing duties, I have been authorized by my Government to agree with the US on the following actions, all to become effective or to be taken simultaneously:

1. India will apply the provisions of the attached Text to the United States. At the same time, the US will extend to India the benefits of Articles 14.6 and 14.8 of the AGREEMENT ON INTERPRETATION AND APPLICATION OF ARTICLES VI, XVI AND XXIII OF THE GENERAL AGREEMENT ON TARIFFS AND TRADE.

2. India will initiate informal consultations on the attached Text with members of the Committee with a view to achieving its acceptance under Article 14.5 of the AGREEMENT. The Government of India expects that, based on these consultations, the Committee will take formal action in the near future with respect to this Text, thereby securing for India from other Committee members the rights contained in Articles 14.6 and 14.8 of the AGREEMENT. Should this not be the case, India shall nevertheless continue to apply the provisions of the text with respect to the US and the US shall continue to extend to India the benefits of Articles 14.6 and 14.8 of the AGREEMENT.

3. The US will inform the Director-General, GATT, and the Committee Chairman of its withdrawal of its invocation of non-application with respect to India pursuant to Article

19.9 of the AGREEMENT and will also designate India as a "country under the AGREEMENT" under US law.

4. India will withdraw its GATT complaint against the US with respect to the non-extension to India of the injury criteria in US Countervailing Duties Law.

I would suggest that the above take place on September 25, 1981.

I would be grateful for a formal confirmation from you that the above is acceptable to your Government.

His Excellency Mr. Michael B. Smith,   Yours sincerely,
United States Trade Representative,
USTR's Office,   /S/
Botanic Building,
Geneva   B.L. Das

Text

1. The Government of India recognizes that restrictive use of export subsidies is desirable. Therefore, it is the Government of India's policy to reduce or eliminate export subsidies whenever the use of such subsidies is inconsistent with its competitive or development needs.
2. The Government of India does not intend to substantially modify its export assistance programme. The major program utilized by the Government of India for export assistance is the cash compensatory support program (CCS). The CCS is designed basically to compensate for the indirect taxes borne by the product, including those levied on goods and services used in production of exports. After obtaining data from the Export Promotion Councils, the CCS rate is determined for individual products by calculating the incidence of indirect taxes, and by taking into consideration the existence of other disincentives to exports, the competitive need of the product and the development needs of India. Exporters do not have a right to the CCS. Any export assistance under CCS is given on a selective basis for limited periods, and is subject to periodic reviews.
3. It is the policy of the Government of India to use CCS restrictively. Reflecting this, less than three years ago, the CCS applied to about 660 products/product categories as against about 400 now. Also, the trend of expenditures under the program has declined over the last three years, a trend anticipated to continue. Furthermore, a CCS in excess of indirect taxes is ordinarily not sanctioned for traditional manufactured and non-manufactured exports.
4. At present, over 60 percent of India's exports have no CCS. Where CCS is used, the extent of the CCS payment is in many cases less than the indirect taxes borne by the like product when destined for domestic consumption. It is the policy of the Government of India that excesses above the incidence of indirect taxes are provided temporarily only when fully justified by competitive or development needs.
5. It is the overall policy of the Government of India with respect to products where CCS payments are now made not to increase the excess over indirect taxes, if any exists, not to introduce any excess if one does not exist, and to reduce any such excess with a view to eventual elimination consistent with Government of India policy.

6. For products which are not included in the CCS program at present, but may in future be brought within its purview, it is the Government of India's policy to continue its current restrictive use of the CCS, particularly with regard to the payment of excesses above the incidence of indirect taxes. Any excess over indirect taxes will be notified to the Subsidies Code Committee of the GATT, and the Government of India will be prepared to consult upon request with any other signatory.

7. The Government of India does not maintain nor does it intend to establish any programme inconsistent with the provisions of the GATT Code on Subsidies. With respect to export assistance programmes other than the CCS, the Government of India does not anticipate establishing new export subsidy programmes; the incidence of benefits under the existing programmes is small and no increases are intended.

Permanent Mission of India
to the United Nations Offices
9, Rue du Valais
1202 Geneva

B.L. Das,
Ambassador

September 25, 1981

No. GEN/PMI/204/23/81

Dear Mr. Dunkel,

I would like to inform you that as a result of bilateral consultations between India and USA, the matter relating to the GATT Dispute Panel, established by a decision of the COUNCIL OF REPRESENTATIVES on 10 November 1980, has now been satisfactorily resolved. I would, therefore, request that the proceedings of the Panel be terminated.

We take this opportunity to express through you, our appreciation of the understanding and cooperation shown by Ambassador Ewerlof in his capacity as Chairman of the Panel, and the other members. I would also request you to convey the contents of this letter to them as soon as possible.

Mr. Arthur Dunkel,
Director-General,
GATT,
Centre William Rappard,
154, Rue de Lausanne,
Geneva

Yours sincerely,

/S/

B.L. Das

United States Trade Representative
1–3 Avenue de la Paix
1202 Geneva, Switzerland

September 25, 1981

Dear Ambassador Das:

Thank you for your letter of September 25, 1981. I hereby confirm that the actions set forth in your letter are acceptable to my Government, and agree that they should take place on September 25, 1981.

With respect to the text attached to your letter, it is my expectation that the Government of India will submit the text to the Committee on Subsidies and Countervailing Measures for formal action by the end of this year. Furthermore, I confirm my Government's understanding that, in the unlikely event of the Committee being unable to take formal action on the text, India will still continue to apply the provisions of the text to the United States and the United States will continue to extend to India benefits under Article 14.6 and 14.8 of Articles VI, XVI and XXIII of the General Agreement on Tariffs and Trade (hereinafter the Agreement).

Furthermore, the United States is pleased to note that it is your overall policy not to expand existing subsidies or to introduce new subsidies in a manner inconsistent with your code obligations. We look forward to receiving your timely notification of such programs as the Cash Compensatory Scheme and any modifications thereof, and welcome your willingness to consult upon request concerning issues pertaining to the implementation of the Agreement.

His Excellency Bhagirath Lal Das   Sincerely,
Ambassador
Permanent Mission of India   /s/
9, rue de Valais
1202 Geneva   Michael B. Smith
                                                    Ambassador

United States Trade Representative
1–3 Avenue de la Paix
1202 Geneva, Switzerland

September 25, 1981

Dear Mr. Director-General:

I have been instructed by my authorities to inform you in your capacity as the depositary of the Agreement on Interpretation and Application of Articles VI, XVI, and XXIII of the General Agreement on Tariffs and Trade that, effective September 25, 1981, the United States withdraws its invocation of the provisions of Article 19:9 of the Agreement with respect to India. Accordingly, the United States consents to the application of the afore-mentioned Agreement between the United States and India and therefore considers the rights and obligations of the Agreement to apply between the United States and India, effective September 25, 1981.

A letter to the same effect is being sent to the Chairman of the Committee on Subsidies and Countervailing Measures.

Honorable Arthur Dunkel   Sincerely,
Director-General
General Agreement on Tariffs   /s/
   and Trade
154, rue de Lausanne   Michael B. Smith
Geneva 1211   Ambassador

Korea

1. With regard to the provisions of Article 14 of the Agreement on Subsidies and Countervailing Measures, the Government of Korea grants no aids to domestic producers or exporters which are materially incompatible with the commitment of Article 9, nor does it intend to establish such aids.
2. The Government of Korea understands that, in the light of the above, it will not be subject to the review procedures mentioned in paragraph 8 of Article 14 of the Agreement on Subsidies and Countervailing Measures, as regards export subsidies, for a period of six years from the date of Korean accession to the Agreement.
3. The Government of Korea also understands that, if extraordinary economic conditions lead it to reconsider its position, the signatories would give sympathetic consideration to the establishment of programs consistent with the change in Korea's competitive and development needs.
4. The Government of Korea further understands that as its official export credit rates are above those of the international undertaking mentioned in paragraph (k) of the illustrative list of export subsidies, Korea's present system of short term export credits is compatible with the commitment of Article 9.

New Zealand

New Zealand Embassy
37 Observatory Circle, NW
Washington, DC 20009

16 September 1981

My dear Ambassador Brock,

I have been asked to convey to you the text of the following letter from the New Zealand Minister of Overseas Trade, the Rt. Hon. B.E. Talboys.

Wellington

16 September 1981

My dear Ambassador,

With reference to bilateral discussions between representatives of the United States Government and the Government of New Zealand concerning New Zealand's acceptance of the Agreement on Interpretation and Application of Articles VI, XVI and XXIII of the General Agreement on Tariffs and Trade (the Code) and regarding the basis on which each Government shall apply provisionally to the other the benefits of the Code, I have the honour to inform you of the following undertakings by my Government. The Government of New Zealand accepted the Code on 15 September 1981.

As the United States Government is aware, the Government of New Zealand currently operates a number of export incentive schemes which fall within the purview of certain items of the Code's "illustrative list." These schemes and references to the applicable items of the "illustrative list" are listed in the attachment to this letter. The United States Government is also aware that these schemes were introduced in recent years as part of an integrated strategy to achieve a more outward-looking economy with a greater role in world trade and that these schemes are not intended to be a permanent feature of economic policy.

On accepting the Code, New Zealand sought the agreement of other Code signatories to a reservation to the provisions of Article 19(5)(A) concerning the immediate compatibility of domestic legislation relating to those schemes which are not described in paragraph (E) of the Code's "illustrative list." In the reservation, New Zealand undertakes to examine methods of bringing these schemes into conformity with the Code within a reasonable period of time, without prejudice to the rights of other signatories under the General Agreement or the Code. New Zealand accepts without reservation all other obligations and provisions of the Agreement.

From the date of New Zealand's acceptance of the Code, New Zealand undertakes not to introduce any new export incentive schemes, the use of which is proscribed by the Code. New Zealand shall also not modify any existing schemes to permit new sectors or products to qualify for benefits to exporters proscribed by the Code. It should, however, be noted that some existing schemes permit new companies or products to receive incentives upon fulfilling existing criteria.

Furthermore, New Zealand undertakes not to modify existing export incentive schemes to increase the value of benefits available. In this connection, the "value of benefits" means the rate of subsidisation expressed *inter alia* as a flat amount or as a percentage. It should, however, be noted that under certain programmes, goods or producers can "graduate" from one "rate band" to another. The rate structure and the amount of benefits realised thereunder, however, will not be changed.

The Government of New Zealand in the context of its economic strategy is not in a position to state when it may be able to conform its incentive schemes to the Code. It recognises that the United States Government's provisional application of the benefits of the Code is however based on the United States Government's expectation that the Government of New Zealand shall bring its schemes (which are listed in the attachment hereto) into conformity with the Code not later than the date of their expiration under existing legislation.

The Government of New Zealand agrees that all rights and obligations of the Code shall apply as between New Zealand and the United States, subject to the reservation to Article 19(5)(A) referred to above, and subject to the right of the United States Government to terminate such application between our two Governments if New Zealand is not in a position to fulfill the undertakings in this letter or if the expectation of the United States Government referred to above is not realised. Our two Governments shall consult prior to any such termination of the application of the Code. The Government of New Zealand shall apply the Code to the United States on a provisional basis as long as the United States is applying the Code to New Zealand on the same basis.

Yours sincerely,

B.E. Talboys
Minister of Overseas Trade

I will convey the signed original to you as soon as it arrives.

Ambassador William E. Brock,   Yours sincerely,
United States Trade Representative,
600 17th Street, NW   /s/
Washington, DC 20506

                                                Frank Gill
                                                Ambassador

Attachment

Illustrative list paragraph	New Zealand export incentive schemes	Date current legislation expires
(E)	1. Export Performance Taxation Incentives—tax rebate scheme	3/31/85
(E) (A)	2. Export Market Development Taxation Incentives—tax rebate or refund	3/31/85
(L)	3. Export Programme Grants Scheme—direct grants	3/31/85
(F)	4. Export Manufacturing Investment Allowance—income tax deduction	3/31/85
(E)	5. Increased Exports Taxation Incentive—income tax deduction—replaced by 1	3/31/83
(F)	6. New Markets Increased Exports Taxation—replaced by 1	3/31/83
(L)	7. New Market Development Grant—replaced by 3—grants for market development	3/31/83

Note: The methods of calculating the benefit under each of these schemes are being communicated separately to the United States Government.

The United States Trade Representative
Washington 20506

September 16, 1981

Dear Mr. Minister:

Having regard to your letter of September 16, 1981, I have the honor to inform you that the United States Government agrees that all rights and obligations of the Agreement on the Interpretation and Application of Articles VI, XVI and XXIII of the General Agreement on Tariffs and Trade will apply as between the United States and New Zealand subject to the reservation on the part of New Zealand referred to in your letter and subject to the right of the United States Government to terminate such application between our two governments if the Government of New Zealand is not in a position to fulfill the undertakings in your letter or if the expectations of the United States Government are not realized regarding the dates when the export incentives schemes of New Zealand will be brought into conformity with the Agreement. The United States Government agrees to consult with the Government of New Zealand prior to any termination of the application of the Agreement to New Zealand.

Furthermore, the United States will inform the Director General of the GATT, as depositary of the Agreement, that until such time as the United States Government otherwise notifies the Director General to the CONTRACTING PARTIES to the GATT the United States Government will provisionally apply to New Zealand all rights and obligations of the Agreement on the Interpretation and Application of Articles VI, XVI and XXIII of the General Agreement on Tariffs and Trade.

Rt. Hon. B.E. Talboys   Very truly yours,
Minister of Overseas Trade
Parliament Buildings   /s/
Wellington, New Zealand

                                                    William E. Brock

The United States Trade Representative
Washington 20506

September 16, 1981

Dear Mr. Minister:

I am pleased that we were able to come to a mutually satisfactory accommodation facilitating your government's acceptance of the Agreement on Interpretation and Application of Articles VI, XVI and XXIII of the General Agreement on Tariffs and Trade and allowing my government to designate New Zealand as a country under the Agreement for the purposes of the US countervailing duty law. As we recognized in our bilateral agreement, our provisional application of the Agreement's rights and obligations to New Zealand is subject to potential termination if the Government of New Zealand is not in a position to fulfill its undertakings or if the expectations of the United States Government are not realized.

In our bilateral agreement, the right to terminate such provisional application is expressed as a discretionary option which may or may not be exercised, subject to certain defined conditions being satisfied. Nevertheless, I believe it is only fair for me to inform you that it would be my intention to terminate our provisional application of the Agreement's rights and obligations to New Zealand in the event the Government of New Zealand is not in a position to fulfill its undertakings or if the expectations of the United States Government are not realized. Naturally, I hope that it does not prove necessary for me to consider such an action.

Rt. Hon. B.E. Talboys
Minister of Overseas Trade
Parliament Buildings
Wellington, New Zealand

Very truly yours,

/s/

William E. Brock

Pakistan

There follows text of commitment attached to letter, also dated March 18 [1980] and initialed under same authority by Javed Burki. Begin text:

"It is the policy of the Government of Pakistan to ensure that the export incentives that it provides are consistent with its development and competitive needs.

"The present export regime in Pakistan is substantially made up of two programmes which, consistent with its development and competitive needs, are designed to remove disincentives to export. The programs are available for export-oriented industries or exporters and are, respectively, the raw material replenishment scheme (RMR) and the compensatory rebate scheme. The former is designed to make available imported raw material for the production of goods for export and the latter mainly to offset indirect taxes and other imposts levied on the physical inputs into the commodity concerned.

"The export regime is kept under continuous review by the GOP to ensure that consistent with the policy described in paragraph 1, it continues to serve its development and competitive needs. Such review may lead to modification of the export regime. However, it is not the intention of the Government that the compensatory rebate scheme should be so modified as will reflect amounts which more than offset the amounts of indirect taxes and similar other levies paid on physical inputs.

"Should subsequent review reveal the existence of subsidy elements in existing programmes or should Pakistan's development and competitive needs require an increase in the existing subsidy element, if any, or the introduction of a new export subsidy, any such subsidy element will, as envisaged by Article 14(3) of the code, not be used in a manner which causes serious prejudice to the trade or production of another signatory. Moreover, any export subsidy will be reduced or eliminated whenever it ceases to be consistent with such needs.

"GOP will immediately notify the Committee of signatories of changes in the export regime and consult under the Code if requested by a signatory.
Initialed Javed Burki."
End Text.

Spain

Ambassador William E. Brock
US Trade Representative
Washington, DC

El Embajador de España
Translation
Madrid

April 13th, 1982

Dear Ambassador Brock:

With reference to bilateral discussions between representatives of the United States government and the Government of Spain concerning Spain's acceptance of the Agreement
on Interpretation and Application of Articles VI, XVI and XXIII of the General Agreement
on Tariffs and Trade (the Code) and regarding the basis on which each Government shall
apply provisionally to the other the benefits of the Code, I have the honor to inform you
of the following undertakings by my Government.

The Government of Spain will accept the Code by April 14, 1982, on which occasion it
will seek the agreement of other Code signatories to a reservation to the provisions of
Article 19, 5(A) concerning the conformity of national laws, regulations and administrative
procedures with the Code.

The Government of Spain has initiated the process of bringing its laws, regulations and
administrative procedures into conformity with the Code. The Government of Spain will
undertake all necessary steps in order to ensure that its laws, regulations and administrative
procedures are brought into conformity with the provisions of the Code (in particular, the
provisions of Article 9, Paragraph 2 of the Code and the Annex to the Code) within a
reasonable period of time, and in no case later than December 31, 1984.

The Government of Spain has already taken steps in this direction and intends to modify
further its fiscal system, introducing the value-added tax in the place of the current turnover
tax. This important change in the Spanish fiscal system, and the method of its application,
will require a transition period in order for the Government of Spain to adapt its laws,
regulations and administrative procedures to the new fiscal system. During this transitional
period, if a net overrebate of the turnover tax upon export should be found in any particular
case, both Governments will consult in order to find a mutually acceptable solution in
conformity with the Code, and without prejudice to the application of either Government's
respective legislation.

From the date of Spain's acceptance of the Code, Spain undertakes not to introduce any
new export incentive schemes, the use of which is proscribed by the Code. Spain shall also
not modify any existing schemes to permit new sectors or products to qualify for benefits
to exporters proscribed by the Code. Furthermore, Spain undertakes not to modify its fiscal
system or export incentive schemes so as to increase the value of benefits available.

The Government of Spain recognizes that the United States Government's provisional
application of the benefits of the Code to Spain is based on the United States Government's

expectation that the Government of Spain's laws, regulations and administrative procedures shall be in conformity with the Code no later than December 31, 1984.

The Government of Spain agrees that all rights and obligations of the Code shall apply as between Spain and the United States, subject to the reservation to Article 19, 5(A) referred to above, and subject to the right of the United States Government to terminate such application between our two Governments if Spain is not in a position to fulfill the undertakings in this letter or if the expectation of the United States Government referred to above is not realized. Our two Governments shall consult prior to any such termination of the application of the Code. The Government of Spain shall apply the Code to the United States on a provisional basis as long as the United States is applying the Code to Spain on the same basis. Furthermore, the Government of Spain understands that, during the transitional period, both Governments will consult upon request concerning the rights and obligations of Spain and the United States under the Code.

Therefore, my Government requests that the United States Government designate Spain as a country under the Agreement for purposes of United States countervailing duty law.

Please accept, Dear Ambassador, the assurance of my highest personal consideration.

Juan Antonio García Díez
Vice-President of the
Government and Ministry
of Economy and Commerce

Translation

Spanish Reservation

"With respect to the provisions of Paragraph 2, Article 9 of the Agreement on Interpretation and Application of Articles VI, XVI, and XXIII of the General Agreement on Tariffs and Trade (the Subsidies Code), and to practices outlined in the Annex to the Code, the Government of Spain has initiated the process of bringing its laws, regulations and administrative procedures into conformity with the provisions of the Code.

The Government of Spain has already taken steps in this direction and intends to modify further its fiscal system, introducing the value added tax in the place of the current turnover tax. This important change in the Spanish fiscal system, and the method of its application, will require a transition period in order for the Government of Spain to adapt its laws, regulations and administrative procedures to the new fiscal system.

During this period of transition, the Government of Spain will introduce no new export incentive schemes, the use of which is proscribed by the Code. Neither will the Government of Spain expand or increase existing schemes which may be inconsistent with the Code.

The Government of Spain, therefore, in accepting the Code, reserves its position on the application of the provisions of Paragraphs 5(A), Article 19, inasmuch as, without prejudice to the rights and obligations of any signatories under the General Agreement or the Code, the Government of Spain will undertake all the necessary steps in order to bring its laws, regulations and administrative procedures into conformity with the provisions of the Code within a reasonable period of time, and in no case later than December 31, 1984."

The United States Trade Representative
Washington 20506

April 14, 1982

Dear Mr. Minister:

Having regard to your letter of April 13, I have the honor to inform you that my Government has today designated Spain as a country under the Agreement for the purposes of United States countervailing duty law. This step has been taken on the understanding that the United States Government agrees that all rights and obligations of the Agreement on the Interpretation and Application of Articles VI, XVI and XXIII of the General Agreement on Tariffs and Trade will apply as between the United States and Spain subject to the reservation on the part of Spain referred to in your letter and subject to the right of the United States Government to terminate such application between our two governments if the Government of Spain is not in a position to fulfill the undertakings in your letter or if the expectations of the United States Government are not realized regarding the dates when the export incentives schemes of Spain will be brought into conformity with the Agreement.

The United States Government agrees to consult with the Government of Spain prior to any termination of the application of the Agreement to Spain, or in the event that an overrebate of the turnover tax should be found in any particular case. I also understand that, during the transitional period before December 31, 1984, both governments will consult upon request concerning the rights and obligations of Spain and the United States under the Agreement.

Furthermore, the United States will inform the Director General of the GATT, as depositary of the Agreement, that until such time as the United States Government otherwise notifies the Director General to the CONTRACTING PARTIES to the GATT, the United States Government will provisionally apply to Spain all rights and obligations of the Agreement on the Interpretation and Application of Articles VI, XVI and XXIII of the General Agreement on Tariffs and Trade.

Please accept, Excellency, the assurances of my highest personal consideration.

Very truly yours,

His Excellency, Juan Antonio García Díez
Vice President of the Government of Spain
and Minister of Economy and Commerce
Government of Spain

/s/

David R. Macdonald
Acting

Taiwan

Excellency:

I have the honor to refer to recent discussions concerning our bilateral trade. During those discussions, it was noted that we expect to implement agreements resulting from the Tokyo Round trade negotiations that will benefit your exports, and it was agreed that in consideration of these concessions you will implement measures that will benefit our exports. This letter describes these reciprocal actions more fully.

We expect to include among our Tokyo Round concessions and to implement domestically, on a most-favored-nation basis, tariff concessions that have been discussed between us and that will benefit your exports. We further expect to extend to your exports the benefits of several non-tariff agreements that we may enter into in the Tokyo Round, including agreements on subsidies and countervailing duties, customs valuation, licensing, government procurement, commercial counterfeiting, and technical barriers to trade.

In consideration of the implementation of the above actions on our part, we understand that you will implement the tariff and non-tariff concessions listed in Annexes I and II to this letter, at the same time that we implement our measures described above. We further understand that you will observe obligations substantially the same as those applicable to developing countries set forth in non-tariff agreements concluded in the Tokyo Round, including agreements on subsidies and countervailing duties, customs valuation, licensing, government procurement, commercial counterfeiting, and technical barriers to trade. It is understood that neither your concessions nor ours will be nullified or impaired by actions inconsistent with the provisions of the General Agreement on Tariffs and Trade or the agreements referred to above.

We acknowledge that you and we will continue to grant most-favored-nation treatment to each other's partners.

We are confident that amicable adjustments will be made if necessary to ensure that the bilateral undertakings described in these letters remain appropriately balanced. We understand that only those articles for which you supplied ten percent or more of total US imports in 1976 will be considered in establishing the initial bilateral balance. Thereafter, each side shall have the same rights as those of a GATT Contracting Party with respect to articles referred to in this exchange of letters for which it becomes, or ceases to be, a principal or substantial supplier. Every effort will be made to consult through appropriate channels on any trade matters including those covered by this letter.

It is further understood that both sides will consider favorably incorporating matters covered by this letter into other arrangements at an appropriate time.

Accept, Excellency, renewed assurances of my highest esteem.

Political Vice Minister Yi-ting Wong   Sincerely,
Ministry of Economic Affairs
Taipei, Taiwan   /s/
Republic of China

                                                      Robert S. Strauss

Embassy of the Republic of China
2311 Massachusetts Avenue, NW
Washington, DC 20008

December 29, 1978

Excellency:

I have the honor to acknowledge the receipt of Your Excellency's letter of today's date, which reads as follows:

Excellency:

I have the honor to refer to recent discussions concerning our bilateral trade. During those discussions, it was noted that we expect to implement agreements resulting from the Tokyo Round trade negotiations that will benefit your exports, and it was agreed that in consideration of these concessions you will implement measures that will benefit our exports. This letter describes these reciprocal actions more fully.

We expect to include among our Tokyo Round concessions and to implement domestically, on a most-favored-nation basis, tariff concessions that have been discussed between us and that will benefit your exports. We further expect to extend to your exports the benefits of several non-tariff agreements that we may enter into in the Tokyo Round, including agreements on subsidies and countervailing duties, customs valuation, licensing, government procurement, commercial counterfeiting, and technical barriers to trade.

In consideration of the implementation of the above actions on our part, we understand that you will implement the tariff and non-tariff concessions listed in Annexes I and II to this letter, at the same time that we implement our measures described above. We further understand that you will observe obligations substantially the same as those applicable to developing countries set forth in non-tariff agreements concluded in the Tokyo Round, including agreements on subsidies and countervailing duties, customs valuation, licensing, government procurement, commercial counterfeiting, and technical barriers to trade. It is understood that neither your concessions nor ours will be nullified or impaired by actions inconsistent with the provisions of the General Agreement on Tariffs and Trade or the agreements referred to above.

We acknowledge that you and we will continue to grant most-favored-nation treatment to each other's partners.

We are confident that amicable adjustments will be made if necessary to ensure that the bilateral undertakings described in these letters remain appropriately balanced. We understand that only those articles for which you supplied ten percent or more of total U.S. imports in 1976 will be considered in establishing the initial bilateral balance. Thereafter, each side shall have the same rights as those of a GATT Contracting Party with respect to articles referred to in this exchange of letters for which it becomes, or ceases to be, a principal or substantial supplier. Every effort will be made to consult through appropriate channels on any trade matters including those covered by this letter.

It is further understood that both sides will consider favorably incorporating matters covered by this letter into other arrangements at an appropriate time.

Accept, Excellency, renewed assurances of my highest esteem.

Sincerely,

/s/

Robert S. Strauss

I have the further honor to inform you, on behalf of the Government of the Republic of China, that it concurs with the contents of your letter.

Please accept, Excellency, the renewed assurances of my highest esteem.

Ambassador Robert S. Strauss
Special Representative for
   Trade Negotiations
Executive Office of the President
Washington, DC

Sincerely,

/s/

Yi-ting Wong
Political Vice Minister
Ministry of Economic Affairs

American Institute in Taiwan
1700 N. Moore St.
17th floor
Arlington, Virginia 22209

October 24, 1979

Dear Mr. Shah:

I have the honor to refer to recent discussions concerning our bilateral trade. During those discussions, it was noted that as a result of the Tokyo Round trade negotiations, reductions in United States tariffs are expected that will benefit exports from Taiwan, and it was agreed that in consideration of these concessions, measures will be implemented in Taiwan that will benefit exports from the United States. This letter describes these reciprocal actions more fully.

It is understood that among the Tokyo Round concessions to be made by the United States and to be implemented domestically on a non-discriminatory basis will be included certain tariff concessions which have been discussed among us and which are included in the United States' Schedule XX deposited with the GATT, a copy of which has been furnished to your delegation. Those tariff concessions enumerated in Annex I to this letter will also be implemented in the United States on a non-discriminatory basis. We understand that those items contained in the US Schedule XX for which exports from Taiwan constituted ten percent or more of total US imports in 1976, as well as all articles described in Annex I to this letter, have been considered in establishing the initial bilateral balance. It is further understood that the implementation in the United States of tariff concessions referred to in this letter will begin on January 1, 1980, in accordance with the staging schedules enumerated in Annex I to the United States' Schedule XX and as described in Annex I to this letter.

In consideration of the implementation of the above action, we understand that all tariff and non-tariff measure concessions previously offered affecting trade with the United States will continue in effect in Taiwan, and any concessions not yet implemented, with the exception of those items subject to deferred staging as enumerated in Annex II, will be implemented as of January 1, 1980 in Taiwan. We note with satisfaction that the concessions concerning apples and automobiles have already been implemented.

With regard to tariff measures referred to in this letter, both sides shall have the same rights a GATT Contracting Party would have with respect to articles bound in the GATT for which it becomes or ceases to be a principal or substantial supplier.

We further understand that obligations substantially the same as those applicable to developing countries set forth in certain non-tariff agreements concluded in the Tokyo Round will be observed in Taiwan, i.e., the agreements on subsidies and countervailing measures, customs valuation, licensing, government procurement, and technical barriers to trade as well as the provisions likely to be set forth in an agreement on commercial counterfeiting to be concluded. We expect that the benefits of several non-tariff agreements concluded in the Tokyo Round, i.e., the agreements on subsidies and countervailing measures, customs valuation, licensing, government procurement, and technical barriers to trade as well as benefits likely to be set forth in an agreement on commercial counter-feiting to be concluded, will be extended in the United States to exports from Taiwan.

It is understood that none of these concessions will be nullified or impaired by actions which would be inconsistent with the provisions of the General Agreement on Tariffs and Trade or the agreements referred to above. We believe that these assurances reflect commitments appropriate to Taiwan's stage of development.

We understand that discussions between the two sides will continue at a mutually convenient date, aimed at defining bilateral obligations and an appropriate dispute settlement mechanism for matters falling within the purview of those non-tariff agreements enumerated above.

We are confident that amicable adjustments will be made if necessary to ensure that the bilateral undertakings described in this exchange of letters remain appropriately balanced.

Every effort will be made to consult through appropriate channels on any trade matters, including those covered by this letter.

It is further understood that both sides will consider favorably incorporating matters covered by this letter into other arrangements at an appropriate time.

Sincerely,

Konsin C. Shah, Representative   /s/
Coordination Council for North
  American Affairs   David Dean
5161 River Road   Chairman of the Board
Washington, DC 20016   and Managing Director

Uruguay

General Agreement on
Tariffs and Trade
L/4924

10 January 1980

Limited Distribution

Original: Spanish

Agreement on Interpretation and Application of Articles VI, XVI and XXIII of the General Agreement on Tariffs and Trade

Declaration by Uruguay

The following Declaration, dated 31 December 1979, was deposited by the representative of Uruguay on the occasion of the acceptance by Uruguay of the above-mentioned Agreement.

Declaration Made by Uruguay on the Occasion of Subscribing to the Agreement on Interpretation and Application of Articles VI, XVI and XXIII of the General Agreement on Tariffs and Trade

In the period following the Second World War, Uruguay implemented a growth strategy designed to relieve it of the problems that had beset it during the war years. To that end it defined an import replacement strategy based on:

(a) high tariff protection to domestic industry
(b) differential exchange rates, and
(c) quota restriction of imports.

This programme rapidly yielded the expected results; gross industrial product grew at an annual rate of approximately 6 percent and employment in the subsector at the rate of 5 percent.

As was to be expected, however, given the small size of Uruguay's domestic market (2,800,000 consumers), this strategy became spent, and in 1958 there began a period of marked economic stagnation which continued, with slight variations, up to the end of 1973.

The second phase of the process began with the energy crisis of late 1973 which, as is well known, affected more severely the developing countries that are not petroleum producers.

In addition to the consequences of this energy crisis and the increase in petroleum prices which Uruguay has had to face, the international market price of its principal export product, bovine meat, fell from $1,800 per ton in late 1973 to $600 per ton of "compensated" quarters in 1974.

This crisis obliged Uruguay to adopt an economic policy entirely different from the one pursued to date and based on a gradual opening of the economy toward the rest of the world as a means of achieving self-sustaining economic growth.

Accordingly, in 1974 a number of obstacles were lifted which had been inhibiting the national economy; reform of the sytem was initially concentrated on the financial sector, as the foundation for the present development of our market, with a view to confirming the prestige that Uruguay had formerly enjoyed as a recognized international financial market.

In 1977, basic provisions were published regarding the real scope of the economy, and 1978 represented a major turning-point in respect of everything concerned with the producing sectors:

(a) in August 1978, a market economy policy was approved for the agricultural and livestock sector which for some decades had seen substantial transfers of earnings toward the secondary sector and toward consumption; and
(b) a tariff policy was announced that will gradually reduce the excessive tariff protection granted to domestic industry in the decades of excessive protectionism.

Effective tariff protection—"tariff" being taken to cover any kind of duty, tax or charge applied on the entry of goods into the country—varied between a minimum of 22 percent and a maximum of 600 percent, the average being not less than 60 percent.

In order to deal with this situation and reallocate productive resources through the market mechanism, Uruguay has adopted unilaterally a strategy for gradually reducing tariff protection, without seeking any similar concessions from developed countries, since it recognizes the need to defend the consumer against monopolies and against the sometimes unlimited effects of tariff barriers.

Accordingly, in December 1978 the new tariff policy was adopted which provides over a six-year period for an across-the-board reduction of the basic tariff applicable to all imported products, whether raw materials, intermediate or finished goods, which is to be in all cases at the level of 35 percent.

As from 1 January 1980, the first adjustment of tariff protection will be made, and the differences between the percentage indicated earlier and the nominal protection granted on each product will be reduced by 16.66 percent.

As may be understood, in the context of an import replacement strategy the Uruguayan entrepreneur was in effect tied to the domestic market and because of the excessive tariff protection that he enjoyed, he tended to disregard new technologies, renovation of industrial equipment, and reinvestment.

Adoption of the outward-looking growth strategy has obliged the Uruguayan entrepreneur to develop toward the exterior, to improve his efficiency and productivity and therefore to set out to win markets—a new activity for which he was not prepared.

The Uruguayan Government realized this situation, and in order to avoid any major disruption and exaggerated social costs and considering in particular a new flare-up of protectionism in the industrialized countries, it adopted an incentive policy for exports of non-traditional manufactured goods; in certain cases this led to reimbursement of internal taxes and for other sectors economic and financial incentives were introduced in the form of rebates, applied on the f.o.b. export price.

These rebates are not at a standard rate but on the contrary are paid at different nominal rates, in relation with the input product ratio.

Another of the advantages afforded to non-traditional exporters comprised credit lines at negative interest rates which undoubtedly allowed them to make substantial profits.

Similarly, export earnings were not subject to the income tax applicable to industry and trade, a clear differentiation being thus made between production intended for the domestic market and production for export.

In 1975, a process of reducing the above-mentioned incentives was initiated, starting with percentage reductions of a general character in respect of the rebates granted on non-traditional exports.

In this way, and without any break in continuity, on 1 July of each year a reduction of not less than 10 percent is being made, and the rate has been 15 percent in the last two years.

In the early months of 1979 all subsidies were eliminated on interest rates for export credits and the reform was completed in the same year by making export earnings taxable, so that all producing activities are now on an equal footing, whatever the market in which their goods or services are sold.

This effort, which has been made on an absolutely unilateral basis, represents for a small economy a tremendous sacrifice, the results of which will be reflected in an improvement in the level of activity and, ultimately, the level of employment.

The Uruguayan Government is resolved, and has so announced, to eliminate completely any remaining direct or indirect subsidies in respect of non-traditional exports, notwithstanding tremendous pressure caused by the protectionist policies to which industrialized countries are increasingly having recourse.

To all these considerations must be added another element that affects (and) places in a proper perspective the advantages granted to the non-traditional exporter in Uruguay. Manufacturing output by Uruguay is on such a small scale that, considered in conjunction with the market diversification that has been achieved, it is practically impossible for any country importing our products to show any serious proof of injury.

Notwithstanding this and for reasons of neutral economic policy in the allocation of productive resources, the gradual elimination of all subsidies has been announced on numerous occasions, considering that as from 1982 non-traditional exports, which at present are the sole beneficiaries of a small percentage refund, will be left to their own devices, it being understood that if any residual refunds were still maintained they would be applicable generally for all export activities and would merely take the form of reimbursement of the internal taxes that an exporter has to pay within the country and which, in accordance with the accepted principles in this regard, cannot be the subject of any transfer abroad.

Broadly speaking, that is the situation in regard to Uruguay's producing activities and the commitments entered into by the Government in various international organizations and specialized bodies. It is relevant to underline once more that all these efforts have been made unilaterally in the context of a well-defined economic policy, and without any reciprocal concessions being sought from the industrialized countries.

Geneva, 31 December 1979

C Meeting on 8 June 1979 on Understandings in the Area of Subsidies and Countervailing Measures (*Tax Notes*, Aug. 2, 1982, pp. 453 ff.)

Participants:

Mr. O. Linden, GATT, Chairman
Mr. J. Dugimont, European Communities
Mr. W. E. Culbert, United States
Mr. J. N. Feij, Netherlands
Mr. G. C. Hufbauer, United States
Mr. F. Klein, European Communities
Mr. W. Lavorel, United States
Mr. H. van Tuinen, GATT
Mr. P. Williams, GATT

1. Mr. Hufbauer said that it was the understanding of his Government that the existence and contents of the meeting should not be disclosed or be the subject of international communication unless and until actions were taken by a participant that significantly conflicted with the actions mutually contemplated in the discussions during the meeting. In no circumstances would the meeting be disclosed prior to the adoption of enabling legislation by the principal signatories to the Subsidy and Countervailing Measures Agreement. His Government took the position that the minutes of the Chair should be conclusive as to the subjects discussed and the agreements recorded. Copies of the minutes should be distributed only to the participants in the meeting and only at their request. The purpose of the meeting was to record certain understandings that were informally reached in the context of negotiations on the Subsidy and Countervailing Measures Agreement.

2. His Government believed, Mr. Hufbauer said, that DISC, as presently conceived in the statute, was not consistent with the provisions of item (e) of the Illustrative List of Export Subsidies annexed to the Subsidy and Countervailing Measures Agreement. In particular, under the DISC statute, appropriate interest charges were not collected on taxes foregone, and an arm's length pricing standard was not in all instances required for transactions between a DISC and its parent firm. However, the Government found that major practical difficulties stood in the way of amending the DISC statute to bring it into conformity with item (e), and further that these difficulties would persist during the life of the present Administration which held office through January 1981. Accordingly, his Government understood that the EEC would allow the GATT Panel Report on DISC, L/4422, to remain on the table and not be brought before the GATT Council, at least not until early 1981. While the Panel Report remained on the table, the US Government trusted that the EEC would not take countermeasures against the DISC.

3. Mr. Hufbauer said that his Government understood that neither the GATT Panel Reports L/4423 (France), L/4424 (Belgium), and L/4425 (Netherlands) nor item (e) of the Illustrative List of Export Subsidies should be read as a frontal attack on the territorial system of taxation. For example, the conclusion of Panel Report L/4423, in paragraph 47, had "noted that the particular application of the territoriality principle by France allowed some part of export activities belonging to an economic process originating in the country, to be outside the scope of French taxes." (footnote omitted) The emphasized language was most important, for it clearly distinguished economic processes located in France from economic processes involving the same goods but located in a foreign nation. The former were properly subject to taxation by France; the latter not. Footnote 2 of the Illustrative List read: "The signatories reaffirm the principle that prices for goods in transactions between exporting enterprises and foreign buyers under their or under the same control should for tax purposes be the prices which would be charged between independent enterprises acting at arm's length."

4. Read together, these texts of the Panel Reports and the Illustrative List indicated that territorial tax systems were not per se offensive. Rather, all countries, including those with territorial tax systems, were obliged to ensure that neither advertent nor inadvertent fiscal incentives to export arose on account of prices charged between related enterprises at variance from the arm's length standard. Panel Reports L/4423, L/4424 and L/4425 merely emphasized that such incentives for abuse of the arm's length standard might be keen in the case of territorial tax systems, especially when exported goods were routed on paper or in fact through third country subsidiaries or branches which paid significantly lower direct tax rates than those applied in the country of origin.

5. Mr. Hufbauer noted that his Government understood that the cited Panel Reports could be considered by the GATT Council in the spring of 1980, separate from the Panel Report on DISC, which addressed quite distinct issues and, for reasons already noted, would not be ripe for consideration at so early a date. The United States Government suggested that the Panel Reports might be accepted by the GATT Council on the basis of an interpretative note that territorial tax systems were not impugned by the GATT or by the Subsidy and Countervailing Measures Agreement; rather, countries practising such systems were under a positive duty to ensure that their firms adhered to an arm's length pricing standard, particularly when export goods were routed through third countries that applied significantly lower tax rates than the relevant tax rate applied by the exporting nation.

6. Mr. Klein said that he shared the views of Mr. Hufbauer on the confidential nature of the meeting, on the conclusive character of the Chairman's minutes and on the need not to disclose the conclusions of the meeting until after the adherence of the principal signatories to the Subsidy and Countervailing Measures Agreement.

7. With reference to particular points made by Mr. Hufbauer, Mr. Klein said that he realized that the DISC statute could not be amended before early 1981 and he took note of the fact that the United States trusted that the Communities would not in the meantime take countervailing measures against the DISC. He confirmed that the Communities would not lightheartedly have recourse to countervailing action in such cases. He agreed that a solution had been found to the problem of prices at variance from the arm's length standard through note 2 to item (e) of the Illustrative List annexed to the Subsidy and Countervailing Measures Agreement. He agreed that the Panel Reports made it clear that territoriality was no longer in dispute per se. Mr. Klein, referring to the ideas expressed by Mr. Hufbauer as set out in paras. 3 and 4, said that they were new ideas to which the United States Government would be free to revert in the further proceedings in the GATT.

8. Mr. Klein said that he could confirm the understanding by the United States Government that the Panel Reports on the tax practices of France, Belgium and the Netherlands would be considered by the GATT Council in the spring of 1980 and that the consideration of the Reports would not be linked to the consideration of the DISC Report. As far as the territoriality principle was concerned, it should be possible to dispose of the Panel Reports on the basis of note 2 to item (e) of the Illustrative List.

9. Mr. Feij recalled that his Government had criticised the conclusions of the Report on the tax practices of the Netherlands (L/4425). If, however, it could be generally agreed that this report should be interpreted as stated by Mr. Hufbauer (e.g. that economic processes located in the Netherlands were properly subject to tax by the Netherlands and that economic processes involving the same goods but located in a foreign nation were not) then it should not be difficult to arrive at a satisfactory conclusion of this case in the Council. Such a conclusion should refer to the interpretation as developed by Mr. Hufbauer and—as far as the obligation to respect the arm's length standard was concerned—to footnote 2 of the Illustrative List, which provided a satisfactory procedure.

10. The Netherlands authorities could agree, Mr. Feij said, to the Council considering the Report on Netherlands tax practices in the spring of 1980 separately from the Report on DISC. In view of today's understanding there was no need at this stage to anticipate the detailed drafting of the Council's conclusions.

D 1960 GATT Working Party Report on Subsidies

Subsidies

Provisions of Article XVI:4

Report Adopted on 19 November 1960 (L/1381)

1. The Working Party considered in accordance with its terms of reference what steps should be taken by the CONTRACTING PARTIES to implement the provisions of paragraph 4 of Article XVI of the General Agreement.

2. The Working Party noted that paragraph 4 of Article XVI contains the provision that "as from 1 January 1958 or the earliest practicable date thereafter, contracting parties shall cease to grant either directly or indirectly any form of subsidy on the export of any product other than a primary product which subsidy results in the sale of such product for export at a price lower than the comparable price charged for the like product to buyers in the domestic market." The only question which was thus left open in paragraph 4 of Article XVI was the date from which the prohibition on subsidies on any product other than a primary product should become effective. Since no agreement on that date has so far been reached by contracting parties, the standstill provision contained in paragraph 4 of Article XVI has ceased to be operative, but a number of contracting parties have agreed to extend it beyond that date by means of a declaration.

3. The Working Party was generally of the view that the time had come to put the provisions of Article XVI fully into effect. It furthermore agreed that the most practical and expeditious way in which to implement the prohibition provided for in paragraph 4 of Article XVI would be for the CONTRACTING PARTIES to open for acceptance before the end of the seventeenth session a declaration embodying the agreement of all the parties to prohibit the use of subsidies of the kind referred to in paragraph 4 of Article XVI. Some members of the Working Party, however, explained that for various reasons it was not possible for their respective governments to undertake a commitment to prohibit subsidies at the present time and consequently to accept a declaration along the lines of Annex A.

4. The Working Party then examined the text of a draft declaration prepared by the secretariat on the basis of the proposal submitted by the Government of France. The text of the draft as revised by the Working Party is attached to this report as Annex A.

5. The following detailed list of measures which are considered as forms of export subsidies by a number of contracting parties was referred to in the proposal submitted by the Government of France, and the question was raised whether it was clear that these measures could not be maintained if the provisions of the first sentence of paragraph 4 of Article XVI were to become fully operative:

(a) Currency retention schemes or any similar practices which involve a bonus on exports or re-exports;

(b) The provision by governments of direct subsidies to exporters;

(c) The remission, calculated in relation to exports, of direct taxes or social welfare charges on industrial or commercial enterprises;

(d) The exemption, in respect of exported goods, of charges or taxes, other than charges in connexion with importation or indirect taxes levied at one or several stages on the same goods if sold for internal consumption; or the payment, in respect of exported goods, of amounts exceeding those effectively levied at one or several stages on these goods in the form of indirect taxes or of charges in connexion with importation or in both forms;

(e) In respect of deliveries by government or governmental agencies of imported raw materials for export business on different terms than for domestic business, the charging of prices below world prices;

(f) In respect of government export credit guarantees, the charging of premiums at rates which are manifestly inadequate to cover the long-term operating costs and losses of the credit insurance institutions;

(g) The grant by governments (or special institutions controlled by government) of export credits at rates below those which they have to pay in order to obtain the funds so employed;

(h) the government bearing all or part of the costs incurred by exporters in obtaining credit.

The Working Party agreed that this list should not be considered exhaustive or to limit in any way the generality of the provisions of paragraph 4 of Article XVI. It noted that the governments prepared to accept the declaration contained in Annex A agreed that, for the purpose of that declaration, these practices generally are to be considered as subsidies in the sense of Article XVI:4 or are covered by the Articles of Agreement of the International Monetary Fund. The representatives of governments which were not prepared to accept that declaration were not able to subscribe at this juncture to a precise interpretation of the term "subsidies," but had no objection to the above interpretation being accepted by the future parties to that declaration for the purposes of its application.

6. The Working Party also considered the meaning of the term "primary products" and noted the following interpretation contained in the explanatory note to Article XVI: "For the purposes of Section B, a 'primary product' is understood to be any product of farm, forest or fishery, or any mineral, in its natural form or which has undergone such processing as is customarily required to prepare it for marketing in substantial volume in international trade." Although in the view of the Working Party this interpretation was necessarily of a general character, it was nevertheless felt that it provided sufficient guidance for the CONTRACTING PARTIES to deal, as and when necessary, with specific cases where doubts might arise concerning the applicability of paragraph 4 of Article XVI.

7. As was the case in the previous Declaration extending the standstill, the declaration would only enter into force when a number of industrialized countries has accepted it. The list in paragraph 2 of the draft declaration contains the industrialized countries in Western Europe and North America; these contracting parties indicated that they were in principal ready to accept the declaration drafted on the basis of the French proposal.

8. Some contracting parties, although unable to take a definite stand at this time, had nevertheless indicated their readiness to examine the possibilities of taking early action with a view to becoming parties to the declaration.

9. The Working Party suggests that the CONTRACTING PARTIES should follow the application of this declaration, and in particular should consider the question of how far countries have been able to subscribe to the declaration.

10. The Working Party was therefore of the view that the declaration on the standstill should be extended. The Working Party, however, was of the view that the previous Declaration on the standstill should be modified on various points so as to bring about some further progress towards the abolition of subsidies. A revised draft of the declaration extending the standstill is contained in Annex B to this report. Some members of the Working Party stressed that this declaration, as in the case of the declaration contained in Annex A, was of a voluntary character; they indicated that for various reasons their respective governments were not in a position to accept this declaration at the present time.

11. The Working Party recommends that the CONTRACTING PARTIES open for acceptance the two declarations contained in Annexes A and B to the report.

E Excerpts from the Trade Agreements Act of 1979, Public Law 96–39, July 26, 1979

Title I Countervailing and Antidumping Duties

Sec. 101   Addition of New Countervailing and Antidumping Duties Title to Tariff Act of 1930

The Tariff Act of 1930 is amended by adding at the end thereof the following new title:

Title VII   Countervailing and Antidumping Duties

Subtitle A   Imposition of Countervailing Duties

Sec. 701   Countervailing Duties Imposed

(a) GENERAL RULE.—If—
  (1) the administering authority determines that—
      (A) a country under the Agreement, or
      (B) a person who is a citizen or national of such a country, or a corporation, association, or other organization organized in such a country,
   is providing, directly or indirectly, a subsidy with respect to the manufacture, production, or exportation of a class or kind of merchandise imported into the United States, and
  (2) the Commission determines that—
      (A) an industry in the United States—
          (i)   is materially injured, or
          (ii) is threatened with material injury, or
      (B) the establishment of an industry in the United States is materially retarded, by reason of imports of that merchandise,
   then there shall be imposed upon such merchandise a countervailing duty, in addition to any other duty imposed, equal to the amount of the net subsidy.
(b) COUNTRY UNDER THE AGREEMENT.—For purposes of this subtitle, the term "country under the agreement" means a country—

(1) between the United States and which the Agreement on Subsidies and Countervailing Measures applies, as determined under section 2(b) of the Trade Agreements Act of 1979,

(2) which has assumed obligations with respect to the United States which are substantially equivalent to obligations under the Agreement, as determined by the President, or

(3) with respect to which the President determines that—

    (A) there is an agreement in effect between the United States and that country which—

        (i) was in force on June 19, 1979, and

        (ii) requires unconditional most-favored-nation treatment with respect to articles imported into the United States,

    (B) the General Agreement on Tariffs and Trade does not apply between the United States and that country, and

    (C) the agreement described in subparagraph (A) does not expressly permit—

        (i) actions required or permitted by the General Agreement on Tariffs and Trade, or required by the Congress, or

        (ii) nondiscriminatory prohibitions or restrictions on importation which are designed to prevent deceptive or unfair practices.

(c) CROSS REFERENCE.—For provisions of law applicable in the case of merchandise which is the product of a country other than a country under the Agreement, see section 303 of this Act.

Sec. 702   Procedures for Initiating a Countervailing Duty Investigation

(a) INITIATION BY ADMINISTERING AUTHORITY.—A countervailing duty investigation shall be commenced whenever the administering authority determines, from information available to it, that a formal investigation is warranted into the question of whether the elements necessary for the imposition of a duty under section 701(a) exist.

(b) INITIATION BY PETITION

(1) PETITION REQUIREMENTS.—A countervailing duty proceeding shall be commenced whenever an interested party described in subparagraph (C), (D), or (E) of section 771(9) files a petition with the administering authority, on behalf of an industry, which alleges the elements necessary for the imposition of the duty imposed by section 701(a), and which is accompanied by information reasonably available to the petitioner supporting those allegations. The petition may be amended at such time, and upon such conditions, as the administering authority and the Commission may permit.

(2) SIMULTANEOUS FILING WITH COMMISSION.—The petitioner shall file a copy of the petition with the Commission on the same day as it is filed with the administering authority.

(c) PETITION DETERMINATION.—Within 20 days after the date on which a petition is filed under subsection (b), the administering authority shall—

(1) determine whether the petition alleges the elements necessary for the imposition of a duty under section 701(a) and contains information reasonably available to the petitioner supporting the allegations,

(2) if the determination is affirmative, commence an investigation to determine whether a subsidy is being provided with respect to the class or kind of merchandise described in the petition, and provide for the publication of notice of the determination to commence an investigation in the Federal Register, and

(3) if the determination is negative, dismiss the petition, terminate the proceeding, notify the petitioner in writing of the reasons for the determination, and provide for the publication of notice of the determination in the Federal Register.

(d) NOTIFICATION TO COMMISSION OF DETERMINATION.—The administering authority shall—

(1) notify the Commission immediately of any determination it makes under subsection (a) or (c), and

(2) if the determination is affirmative, make available to the Commission such information as it may have relating to the matter under investigation, under such procedures as the administering authority and the Commission may establish to prevent disclosure, other than with the consent of the party providing it or under protective order, of any information to which confidential treatment has been given by the administering authority.

Sec. 703 Preliminary Determinations

(a) DETERMINATION BY COMMISSION OF REASONABLE INDICATION OF INJURY.— Except in the case of a petition dismissed by the administering authority under section 702(c)(3), the Commission, within 45 days after the date on which a petition is filed under section 702(b) or on which it receives notice from the administering authority of an investigation commenced under section 702(a), shall make a determination, based upon the best information available to it at the time of the determination, of whether there is a reasonable indication that—

(1) an industry in the United States—

(A) is materially injured, or

(B) is threatened with material injury, or

(2) the establishment of an industry in the United States is materially retarded,

by reason of imports of the merchandise which is the subject of the investigation by the administering authority. If that determination is negative, the investigation shall be terminated.

(b) PRELIMINARY DETERMINATION BY ADMINISTERING AUTHORITY.—Within 85 days after the date on which a petition is filed under section 702(b), or an investigation is commenced under section 702(a), but not before an affirmative determination by the Commission under subsection (a) of this section, the administering authority shall make a determination, based upon the best information available to it at the time of the determination, of whether there is a reasonable basis to believe or suspect that a subsidy is being provided with respect to the merchandise which is the subject of the investigation. If the determination of the administering authority under this subsection is affirmative, the determination shall include an estimate of the net subsidy.

(c) EXTENSION OF PERIOD IN EXTRAORDINARILY COMPLICATED CASES

(1) IN GENERAL.—If—

(A) the petitioner makes a timely request for an extension of the period within which the determination must be made under subsection (b), or

(B) the administering authority concludes that the parties concerned are cooperating and determines that—

(i) the case is extraordinarily complicated by reason of—

(I) the number and complexity of the alleged subsidy practices;

(II) the novelty of the issues presented;

(III) the need to determine the extent to which particular subsidies are used by individual manufacturers, producers, and exporters; or

(IV) the number of firms whose activities must be investigated; and

(ii) additional time is necessary to make the preliminary determination, then the administering authority may postpone making the preliminary determination under subsection (b) until not later than the 150th day after the date on which a petition is filed under section 702(b), or an investigation is commenced under section 702(a).

(2) NOTICE OF POSTPONEMENT.—The administering authority shall notify the parties to the investigation, not later than 20 days before the date on which the preliminary determination would otherwise be required under subsection (b), if it intends to postpone making the preliminary determination under paragraph (1). The notification shall include an explanation of the reasons for the postponement. Notice of the postponement shall be published in the Federal Register.

(d) EFFECT OF DETERMINATION BY THE ADMINISTERING AUTHORITY.—If the preliminary determination of the administering authority under subsection (b) is affirmative, the administering authority—

(1) shall order the suspension of liquidation of all entries of merchandise subject to the determination which are entered, or withdrawn from warehouse, for consumption on or after the date of publication of the notice of the determination in the Federal Register,

(2) shall order the posting of a cash deposit, bond, or other security, as it deems appropriate, for each entry of the merchandise concerned equal to the estimated amount of the net subsidy, and

(3) shall make available to the Commission all information upon which its determination was based and which the Commission considers relevant to its injury determination, under such procedures as the administering authority and the Commission may establish to prevent disclosure, other than with the consent of the party providing it or under protective order, of any information to which confidential treatment has been given by the administering authority.

(e) CRITICAL CIRCUMSTANCES DETERMINATIONS

(1) IN GENERAL.—If a petitioner alleges critical circumstances in its original petition, or by amendment at any time more than 20 days before the date of a final determination by the administering authority, then the administering authority shall promptly determine, on the basis of the best information available to it at that time, whether there is a reasonable basis to believe or suspect that—

(A) the alleged subsidy is inconsistent with the Agreement, and

(B) there have been massive imports of the class or kind of merchandise which is the subject of the investigation over a relatively short period.

(2) SUSPENSION OF LIQUIDATION.—If the determination of the administering authority under paragraph (1) is affirmative, then any suspension of liquidation ordered under subsection (d)(1) shall apply, or, if notice of such suspension of liquidation is already published, be amended to apply, to unliquidated entries of merchandise entered, or withdrawn from warehouse, for consumption on or after the date which is 90 days before the date on which suspension of liquidation was first ordered.

(f) NOTICE OF DETERMINATIONS.—Whenever the Commission or the administering authority makes a determination under this section, it shall notify the petitioner, other parties to the investigation, and the other agency of its determination and of the fact and conclusions of law upon which the determination is based, and it shall publish notice of its determination in the Federal Register.

Sec. 704   *Termination or Suspension of Investigation*

(a) TERMINATION OF INVESTIGATION ON WITHDRAWAL OF PETITION.—An investigation under this subtitle may be terminated by either the administering authority or the Commission after notice to all parties to the investigation, upon withdrawal of the petition by the petitioner. The Commission may not terminate an investigation under the preceding sentence before a preliminary determination is made by the administering authority under section 703(b).

(b) AGREEMENTS TO ELIMINATE OR OFFSET COMPLETELY A SUBSIDY OR TO CEASE EXPORTS OF SUBSIDIZED MERCHANDISE.—The administering authority may suspend an investigation if the government of the country in which the subsidy practice is alleged to occur agrees, or exporters who account for substantially all of the imports of the merchandise which is the subject of the investigation agree—

  (1) to eliminate the subsidy completely or to offset completely the amount of the net subsidy, with respect to that merchandise exported directly or indirectly to the United States, within 6 months after the date on which the investigation is suspended, or

  (2) to cease exports of that merchandise to the United States within 6 months after the date on which the investigation is suspended.

(c) AGREEMENTS ELIMINATING INJURIOUS EFFECT

  (1) GENERAL RULE.—If the administering authority determines that extraordinary circumstances are present in a case, it may suspend an investigation upon the acceptance of an agreement from a government described in subsection (b), or from exporters described in subsection (b), if the agreement will eliminate completely the injurious effect of exports to the United States of the merchandise which is the subject of the investigation.

  (2) CERTAIN ADDITIONAL REQUIREMENTS.—Except in the case of an agreement by a foreign government to restrict the volume of imports of the merchandise which is the subject of the investigation into the United States, the administering authority may not accept an agreement under this subsection unless—

    (A) the suppression or undercutting of price levels of domestic products by imports of that merchandise will be prevented, and

    (B) at least 85 percent of the net subsidy will be offset.

  (3) QUANTITATIVE RESTRICTIONS AGREEMENTS.—The administering authority may accept an agreement with a foreign government under this subsection to restrict the volume of imports of merchandise which is the subject of an investigation into the United States, but it may not accept such an agreement with exporters.

  (4) DEFINITION OF EXTRAORDINARY CIRCUMSTANCES

    (A) EXTRAORDINARY CIRCUMSTANCES.—For the purposes of this subsection, the term "extraordinary circumstances" means circumstances in which—

      (i) suspension of an investigation will be more beneficial to the domestic industry than continuation of the investigation, and

      (ii) the investigation is complex.

    (B) COMPLEX.—For purposes of this paragraph, the term "complex" means—

      (i) there are a large number of alleged subsidy practices and the practices are complicated,

      (ii) the issues raised are novel, or

      (iii) the number of exporters involved is large.

(d) ADDITIONAL RULES AND CONDITIONS

  (1) PUBLIC INTEREST; MONITORING.—The administering authority shall not accept an agreement under subsection (b) or (c) unless—

(A) it is satisfied that suspension of the investigation is in the public interest, and

(B) effective monitoring of the agreement by the United States is practicable.

(2) EXPORTS OF MERCHANDISE TO UNITED STATES NOT TO INCREASE DURING INTERIM PERIOD.—The administering authority may not accept any agreement under subsection (b) unless that agreement provides a means of ensuring that the quantity of the merchandise covered by that agreement exported to the United States during the period provided for elimination or offset of the subsidy or cessation of exports does not exceed the quantity of such merchandise exported to the United States during the most recent representative period determined by the administering authority.

(3) REGULATIONS GOVERNING ENTRY OR WITHDRAWALS.—In order to carry out an agreement concluded under subsection (b) or (c), the administering authority is authorized to prescribe regulations governing the entry, or withdrawal from warehouse, for consumption of merchandise covered by such agreement.

(e) SUSPENSION OF INVESTIGATION PROCEDURE.—Before an investigation may be suspended under subsection (b) or (c) the administering authority shall—

(1) notify the petitioner of, and consult with the petitioner concerning, its intention to suspend the investigation, and notify other parties to the investigation and the Commission not less than 30 days before the date on which it suspends the investigation,

(2) provide a copy of the proposed agreement to the petitioner at the time of the notification, together with an explanation of how the agreement will be carried out and enforced (including any action required of foreign governments), and of how the agreement will meet the requirements of subsections (b) and (d) or (c) and (d), and

(3) permit all parties to the investigation to submit comments and information for the record before the date on which notice of suspension of the investigation is published under subsection (f)(1)(A).

(f) EFFECTS OF SUSPENSION OF INVESTIGATION

(1) IN GENERAL.—If the administering authority determines to suspend an investigation upon acceptance of an agreement described in subsection (b) or (c), then—

(A) it shall suspend the investigation, publish notice of suspension of the investigation, and issue an affirmative preliminary determination under section 703(b) with respect to the merchandise which is the subject of the investigation, unless it has previously issued such a determination in the same investigation,

(B) the Commission shall suspend any investigation it is conducting with respect to that merchandise, and

(C) the suspension of investigation shall take effect on the day on which such notice is published.

(2) LIQUIDATION OF ENTRIES

(A) CESSATION OF EXPORTS; COMPLETE ELIMINATION OF NET SUBSIDY.—If the agreement accepted by the administering authority is an agreement described in subsection (b), then—

(i) notwithstanding the affirmative preliminary determination required under paragraph (1)(A), the liquidation of entries of merchandise which is the subject of the investigation shall not be suspended under section 703(d)(1),

(ii) if the liquidation of entries of such merchandise was suspended pursuant to a previous affirmative preliminary determination in the same case with respect to such merchandise, that suspension of liquidation shall terminate, and

(iii) the administering authority shall refund any cash deposit and release any bond or other security deposited under section 703(d)(1).

(B) OTHER AGREEMENTS.—If the agreement accepted by the administering authority is an agreement described in subsection (c), then the liquidation of entries of the merchandise which is the subject of the investigation shall be suspended under section 703(d)(1), or, if the liquidation of entries of such merchandise was suspended pursuant to a previous affirmative preliminary determination in the same case, that suspension of liquidation shall continue in effect, subject to subsection (h)(3), but the security required under section 703(d)(2) may be adjusted to reflect the effect of the agreement.

(3) WHERE INVESTIGATION IS CONTINUED.—If, pursuant to subsection (g), the administering authority and the Commission continue an investigation in which an agreement has been accepted under subsection (b) or (c), then—

(A) if the final determination by the administering authority or the Commission under section 705 is negative, the agreement shall have no force or effect and the investigation shall be terminated, or

(B) if the final determinations by the administering authority and the Commission under such section are affirmative, the agreement shall remain in force, but the administering authority shall not issue a countervailing duty order in the case so long as—

(i) the agreement remains in force,

(ii) the agreement continues to meet the requirements in subsections (b) and (d) or (c) and (d), and

(iii) the parties to the agreement carry out their obligations under the agreement in accordance with its terms.

(g) INVESTIGATION TO BE CONTINUED UPON REQUEST.—If the administering authority, within 20 days after the date of publication of the notice of suspension of an investigation, receives a request for the continuation of the investigation from—

(1) the government of the country in which the subsidy practice is alleged to occur, or

(2) an interested party described in subparagraph (C), (D), or (E) of section 771(9) which is a party to the investigation, then the administering authority and the Commission shall continue the investigation.

(h) REVIEW OF SUSPENSION

(1) IN GENERAL.—Within 20 days after the suspension of an investigation under subsection (c), an interested party which is a party to the investigation and which is described in subparagraph (C), (D), or (E) of section 771(9) may, by petition filed with the Commission and with notice to the administering authority, ask for a review of the suspension.

(2) COMMISSION INVESTIGATION.—Upon receipt of a review petition under paragraph (1), the Commission shall, within 75 days after the date on which the petition is filed with it, determine whether the injurious effect of imports of the merchandise which is the subject of the investigation is eliminated completely by the agreement. If the Commission's determination under this subsection is negative, the investigation shall be resumed on the date of publication of notice

of such determination as if the affirmative preliminary determination under section 703(b) had been made on that date.

(3) SUSPENSION OF LIQUIDATION TO CONTINUE DURING REVIEW PERIOD.— The suspension of liquidation of entries of the merchandise which is the subject of the investigation shall terminate at the close of the 20-day period beginning on the day after the date on which notice of suspension of the investigation is published in the Federal Register, or, if a review petition is filed under paragraph (1) with respect to the suspension of the investigation, in the case of an affirmative determination by the Commission under paragraph (2), the date on which notice of the affirmative determination by the Commission is published. If the determination of the Commission under paragraph (2) is affirmative, then the administering authority shall—

(A) terminate the suspension of liquidation under section 703(d)(1), and

(B) release any bond or other security, and refund any cash deposit, required under section 703(d)(2).

(i) VIOLATION OF AGREEMENT

(1) IN GENERAL.—If the administering authority determines that an agreement accepted under subsection (b) or (c) is being, or has been, violated, or no longer meets the requirements of such subsection (other than the requirement, under subsection (c)(1), of elimination of injury) and subsection (d), then, on the date of publication of its determination, it shall—

(A) suspend liquidation under section 703(d)(1) of unliquidated entries of the merchandise made on or after the later of—

(i) the date which is 90 days before the date of publication of the notice of suspension of liquidation, or

(ii) the date on which the merchandise, the sale or export to the United States of which was in violation of the agreement, or under an agreement which no longer meets the requirements of subsections (b) and (d) or (c) and (d), was first entered, or withdrawn from warehouse, for consumption.

(B) if the investigation was not completed, resume the investigation as if its affirmative preliminary determination under section 703(b) were made on the date of its determination under this paragraph,

(C) if the investigation was completed under subsection (g), issue a countervailing duty order under section 706(a) effective with respect to entries of merchandise the liquidation of which was suspended, and

(D) notify the petitioner, interested parties who are or were parties to the investigation, and the Commission of its action under this paragraph.

(2) INTENTIONAL VIOLATION TO BE PUNISHED BY CIVIL PENALTY.—Any person who intentionally violates an agreement accepted by the administering authority under subsection (b) or (c) shall be subject to a civil penalty assessed in the same amount, in the same manner, and under the same procedure, as the penalty imposed for a fraudulent violation of section 592(a) of this Act.

(j) DETERMINATION NOT TO TAKE AGREEMENT INTO ACCOUNT.—In making a final determination under section 705, or in conducting a review under section 751, in a case in which the administering authority has terminated a suspension of investigation under subsection (i)(1), or continued an investigation under subsection (g), the Commission and the administering authority shall consider all of the merchandise which is the subject of the investigation, without regard to the effect of any agreement under subsection (b) or (c).

(a) FINAL DETERMINATION BY ADMINISTERING AUTHORITY
   (1)   IN GENERAL.—Within 75 days after the date of its preliminary determination under section 703(b), the administering authority shall make a final determination of whether or not a subsidy is being provided with respect to the merchandise.
   (2)   CRITICAL CIRCUMSTANCES DETERMINATIONS.—If the final determination of the administering authority is affirmative, then that determination, in any investigation in which the presence of critical circumstances has been alleged under section 703(e), shall also contain a finding as to whether—
         (A)   the subsidy is inconsistent with the Agreement, and
         (B)   there have been massive imports of the class or kind of merchandise involved over a relatively short period.
(b) FINAL DETERMINATION BY COMMISSION
   (1)   IN GENERAL.—The Commission shall make a final determination of whether—
         (A)   an industry in the United States—
               (i)   is materially injured, or
               (ii) is threatened with material injury, or
         (B)   the establishment of an industry in the United States is materially retarded, by reason of imports of the merchandise with respect to which the administering authority has made an affirmative determination under subsection (a).
   (2)   PERIOD FOR INJURY DETERMINATION FOLLOWING AFFIRMATIVE PRE-LIMINARY DETERMINATION BY ADMINISTERING AUTHORITY.—If the pre-liminary determination by the administering authority under section 703(b) is affirmative, then the Commission shall make the determination required by paragraph (1) before the later of—
         (A)   the 120th day after the day on which the administering authority makes its affirmative preliminary determination under section 703(b), or
         (B)   the 45th day after the day on which the administering authority makes its affirmative final determination under subsection (a).
   (3)   PERIOD FOR INJURY DETERMINATION FOLLOWING NEGATIVE PRELIMI-NARY DETERMINATION BY ADMINISTERING AUTHORITY.—If the prelimi-nary determination by the administering authority under section 703(b) is neg-ative, and its final determination under subsection (a) is affirmative, then the final determination by the Commission under this subsection shall be made within 75 days after the date of that affirmative final determination.
   (4)   CERTAIN ADDITIONAL FINDINGS
         (A)   If the finding of the administering authority under subsection (a)(2) is affirmative, then the final determination of the Commission shall include findings as to whether—
               (i)   there is material injury which will be difficult to repair, and
               (ii) the material injury was by reason of such massive imports of the subsidized merchandise over a relatively short period.
         (B)   If the final determination of the Commission is that there is no material injury but that there is a threat of material injury, then its determination shall also include a finding as to whether material injury is by reason of imports of the merchandise with respect to which the administering author-ity has made an affirmative determination under subsection (a) would have

been found but for any suspension of liquidation of entries of that merchandise.

(c) EFFECT OF FINAL DETERMINATIONS

   (1)   EFFECT OF AFFIRMATIVE DETERMINATION BY THE ADMINISTERING AUTHORITY.—If the determination of the administering authority under subsection (a) is affirmative, then—

      (A)   the administering authority shall make available to the Commission all information upon which such determination was based and which the Commission considers relevant to its determination, under such procedures as the administering authority and the Commission may establish to prevent disclosure, other than with the consent of the party providing it or under protective order, of any information to which confidential treatment has been given by the administering authority, and

      (B)   in cases where the preliminary determination by the administering authority under section 703(b) was negative, the administering authority shall order under paragraphs (1) and (2) of section 703(d) the suspension of liquidation and the posting of a cash deposit bond or other security.

   (2)   ISSUANCE OF ORDER; EFFECT OF NEGATIVE DETERMINATION.—If the determinations of the administering authority and the Commission under subsections (a)(1) and (b)(1) are affirmative, then the administering authority shall issue a countervailing duty order under section 706(a). If either of such determinations is negative, the investigation shall be terminated upon the publication of notice of that negative determination and the administering authority shall—

      (A)   terminate the suspension of liquidation under section 703(d)(1), and

      (B)   release any bond or other security and refund any cash deposit required under section 703(d)(2).

   (3)   EFFECT OF NEGATIVE DETERMINATIONS UNDER SUBSECTIONS (a)(2) AND (b)(4)(A).—If the determination of the administering authority or the Commission under subsection (a)(2) and (b)(4)(A), respectively, is negative, then the administering authority shall—

      (A)   terminate any retroactive suspension of liquidation required under section 703(e)(2), and

      (B)   release any bond or other security, and refund any cash deposit required, under section 703(d)(2) with respect to entries of the merchandise the liquidation of which was suspended retroactively under section 703(e)(2).

(d) PUBLICATION OF NOTICE OF DETERMINATIONS.—Whenever the administering authority or the Commission makes a determination under this section, it shall notify the petitioner, other parties to the investigation, and the other agency of its determination and of the facts and conclusions of law upon which the determination is based, and it shall publish notice of its determination in the Federal Register.

Sec. 706   Assessment of Duty

(a) PUBLICATION OF COUNTERVAILING DUTY ORDER.—Within 7 days after being notified by the Commission of an affirmative determination under section 705(b), the administering authority shall publish a countervailing duty order which—

   (1)   directs customs officers to assess a countervailing duty equal to the amount of the net subsidy determined or estimated to exist, within 6 months after the date on which the administering authority receives satisfactory information upon which the assessment may be based, but in no event later than 12 months after

the end of the annual accounting period of the manufacturer or exporter within which the merchandise is entered, or withdrawn from warehouse, for consumption.

(2) includes a description of the class or kind of merchandise to which it applies, in such detail as the administering authority deems necessary, and

(3) requires the deposit of estimated countervailing duties pending liquidation of entries of merchandise at the same time as estimated normal customs duties on that merchandise are deposited.

(b) IMPOSITION OF DUTIES

(1) GENERAL RULE.—If the Commission, in its final determination under section 705(b), finds material injury or threat of material injury which, but for the suspension of liquidation under section 703(d)(1), would have led to a finding of material injury, then entries of the merchandise subject to the countervailing duty order, the liquidation of which has been suspended under section 703(d)(1), shall be subject to the imposition of countervailing duties under section 701(a).

(2) SPECIAL RULE.—If the Commission, in its final determination under section 705(b), finds threat of material injury, other than threat of material injury described in paragraph (1), or material retardation of the establishment of an industry in the United States, then merchandise subject to a countervailing duty order which is entered, or withdrawn from warehouse, for consumption on or after the date of publication of notice of an affirmative determination of the Commission under section 705(b) shall be subject to the imposition of countervailing duties under section 701(a), and the administering authority shall release any bond or other security, and refund any cash deposit made, to secure the payment of countervailing duties with respect to entries of the merchandise entered, or withdrawn from warehouse, for consumption before that date.

Sec. 707 Treatment of Difference Between Deposit of Estimated Countervailing Duty and Final Assessed Duty Under Countervailing Duty Order

(a) DEPOSIT OF ESTIMATED COUNTERVAILING DUTY UNDER SECTION 703(d)(2).—If the amount of a cash deposit, or the amount of any bond or other security, required as security for an estimated countervailing duty under section 703(d)(2) is different from the amount of the countervailing duty determined under a countervailing duty order issued under section 706, then the difference for entries of merchandise entered, or withdrawn from warehouse, for consumption before notice of the affirmative determination of the Commission under section 705(b) is published shall be—

(1) disregarded, to the extent that the cash deposit, bond, or other security is lower than the duty under the order, or

(2) refunded or released, to the extent that the cash deposit, bond, or other security is higher than the duty under the order.

(b) DEPOSIT OF ESTIMATED COUNTERVAILING DUTY UNDER SECTION 706(a)(3).—If the amount of an estimated countervailing duty deposited under section 706(a)(3) is different from the amount of the countervailing duty determined under a countervailing duty order issued under section 706, then the difference for entries of merchandise entered, or withdrawn from warehouse, for consumption after notice of the affirmative determination of the Commission under section 705(b) is published shall be—

(1) collected, to the extent that the deposit under section 706(a)(3) is lower than the duty determined under the order, or

(2) refunded, to the extent that the deposit under section 706(a)(3) is higher than the duty determined under the order, together with interest as provided by section 778.

Subtitle B Imposition of Antidumping Duties [omitted]

Subtitle C Review of Determinations

Sec. 751 Administrative Review of Determinations

(a) PERIODIC REVIEW OF AMOUNT OF DUTY
    (1) IN GENERAL.—At least once during each 12-month period beginning on the anniversary of the date of publication of a countervailing duty order under this title or under section 303 of this Act, an antidumping duty order under this title or a finding under the Antidumping Act, 1921, or a notice of the suspension of an investigation, the administering authority, after publication of notice of such review in the Federal Register, shall—
        (A) review and determine the amount of any net subsidy,
        (B) review, and determine (in accordance with paragraph (2)), the amount of any antidumping duty, and
        (C) review the current status of, and compliance with, any agreement by reason of which an investigation was suspended, and review the amount of any net subsidy or margin of sales at less than fair value involved in the agreement,
    and shall publish the results of such review, together with notice of any duty to be assessed, estimated duty to be deposited, or investigation to be resumed in the Federal Register.
    (2) DETERMINATION OF ANTIDUMPING DUTIES.—For the purpose of paragraph (1)(B), the administering authority shall determine—
        (A) the foreign market value and United States price of each entry of merchandise subject to the antidumping duty order and included within that determination, and
        (B) the amount, if any, by which the foreign market value of each such entry exceeds the United States price of the entry.
    The administering authority, without revealing confidential information, shall publish notice of the results of the determination of antidumping duties in the Federal Register, and that determination shall be the basis for the assessment of antidumping duties on entries of the merchandise included within the determination and for deposits of estimated duties.
(b) REVIEWS UPON INFORMATION OR REQUEST
    (1) IN GENERAL.—Whenever the administering authority or the Commission receives information concerning, or a request for the review of, an agreement accepted under section 704 or 734 or an affirmative determination made under section 704(h)(2), 705(a), 705(b), 734(h)(2), 735(a), or 735(b), which shows changed circumstances sufficient to warrant a review of such determination, it shall conduct such a review after publishing notice of the review in the Federal Register. In reviewing its determination under section 704(h)(2) or 734(h)(2), the Commission shall consider whether, in the light of changed circumstances, an agreement accepted under section 704(c) or 734(c) continues to eliminate completely the injurious effects of imports of the merchandise.

(2) LIMITATION ON PERIOD FOR REVIEW.—In the absence of good cause shown—
   (A) the Commission may not review a determination under section 705(b) or 735(b), and
   (B) the administering authority may not review a determination under section 705(a) or 735(a), or the suspension of an investigation suspended under section 704 or 734,
   less than 24 months after the date of publication of notice of that determination or suspension.
(c) REVOCATION OF COUNTERVAILING DUTY ORDER OR ANTIDUMPING DUTY ORDER.—The administering authority may revoke, in whole or in part, a counter-vailing duty order or an antidumping duty order, or terminate a suspended investi-gation, after review under this section. Any such revocation or termination shall apply with respect to unliquidated entries of merchandise entered, or withdrawn from warehouse, for consumption on and after a date determined by the administering authority.
(d) HEARINGS.—Whenever the administering authority or the Commission conducts a review under this section it shall, upon the request of any interested party, hold a hearing in accordance with section 774(b) in connection with that review.
(e) DETERMINATION THAT BASIS FOR SUSPENSION NO LONGER EXISTS.—If the determination of the Commission under the last sentence of subsection (b)(1) is negative, the agreement shall be treated as not accepted, beginning on the date of the publication of the Commission's determination, and the administering authority and the Commission shall proceed, under section 704(i) or 734(i), as if the agreement had been violated on that date, except that no duty under any order subsequently issued shall be assessed on merchandise entered, or withdrawn from warehouse, for con-sumption before that date.

Subtitle D   General Provisions

Sec. 771   Definitions; Special Rules

For purposes of this title—
(1) ADMINISTERING AUTHORITY.—The term "administering authority" means the Secretary of the Treasury, or any other officer of the United States to whom the responsibility for carrying out the duties of the administering authority under this title are transferred by law.
(2) COMMISSION.—The term "Commission" means the United States Interna-tional Trade Commission.
(3) COUNTRY.—The term "country" means a foreign country, a political subdivi-sion, dependent territory, or possession of a foreign country, and, except for the purpose of antidumping proceedings, may include an association of 2 or more foreign countries, political subdivisions, dependent territories, or possessions of countries into a customs union outside the United States.
(4) INDUSTRY
   (A) IN GENERAL.—The term "industry" means the domestic producers as a whole of a like product, or those producers whose collective output of the like product constitutes a major proportion of the total domestic production of that product.
   (B) RELATED PARTIES.—When some producers are related to the exporters or importers, or are themselves importers of the allegedly subsidized or dumped merchandise, the term "industry" may be applied in appropriate circumstances by excluding such producers from those included in that industry.

(C) REGIONAL INDUSTRIES.—In appropriate circumstances, the United States, for a particular product market, may be divided into 2 or more markets and the producers within each market may be treated as if they were a separate industry if—

    (i) the producers within such markets sell all or almost all of their production of the like product in question in that market, and

    (ii) the demand in that market is not supplied, to any substantial degree, by producers of the product in question located elsewhere in the United States.

In such appropriate circumstances, material injury, the threat of material injury, or material retardation of the establishment of an industry may be found to exist with respect to an industry even if the domestic industry as a whole, or those producers whose collective output of a like product constitutes a major proportion of the total domestic production of that product, is not injured, if there is a concentration of subsidized or dumped imports into such an isolated market and if the producers of all, or almost all, of the production within that market are being materially injured or threatened by material injury, or if the establishment of an industry is being materially retarded, by reason of the subsidized or dumped imports.

(D) PRODUCT LINES.—The effect of subsidized or dumped imports shall be assessed in relation to the United States production of a like product if available data permit the separate identification of production in terms of such criteria as the production process or the producer's profits. If the domestic production of the like product has no separate identity in terms of such criteria, then the effect of the subsidized or dumped imports shall be assessed by the examination of the production of the narrowest group or range of products, which includes a like product, for which the necessary information can be provided.

(5) SUBSIDY.—The term "subsidy" has the same meaning as the term "bounty or grant" as that term is used in section 303 of this Act, and includes, but is not limited to, the following:

(A) Any export subsidy described in Annex A to the Agreement (relating to illustrative list of export subsidies).

(B) The following domestic subsidies, if provided or required by government action to a specific enterprise or industry, or group of enterprises or industries, whether publicly or privately owned, and whether paid or bestowed directly or indirectly on the manufacture, production, or export of any class or kind of merchandise:

    (i) The provision of capital, loans, or loan guarantees on terms inconsistent with commercial considerations.

    (ii) the provision of goods or services at preferential rates.

    (iii) The grant of funds or forgiveness of debt to cover operating losses sustained by a specific industry.

    (iv) The assumption of any costs or expenses of manufacture, production, or distribution.

(6) NET SUBSIDY.—For the purpose of determining the net subsidy, the administering authority may subtract from the gross subsidy the amount of—

(A) any application fee, deposit, or similar payment paid in order to qualify for, or to receive, the benefit of the subsidy,

(B) any loss in the value of the subsidy resulting from its deferred receipt, if the deferral is mandated by Government order, and

(C) export taxes, duties, or other charges levied on the export of merchandise to the United States specifically intended to offset the subsidy received.

(7) MATERIAL INJURY

(A) IN GENERAL.—The term "material injury" means harm which is not inconsequential, immaterial, or unimportant.

(B) VOLUME AND CONSEQUENT IMPACT.—In making its determinations under sections 703(a), 705(b), 733(a), and 735(b), the Commission shall consider, among other factors—

(i) the volume of imports of the merchandise which is the subject of the investigation,

(ii) the effect of imports of that merchandise on prices in the United States for like products, and

(iii) the impact of imports of such merchandise on domestic producers of like products.

(C) EVALUATION OF VOLUME AND OF PRICE EFFECTS.—For purposes of subparagraph (B)—

(i) VOLUME.—In evaluating the volume of imports of merchandise, the Commission shall consider whether the volume of imports of the merchandise, or any increase in that volume, either in absolute terms or relative to production or consumption in the United States is significant.

(ii) PRICE.—In evaluating the effect of imports of such merchandise on prices, the Commission shall consider whether—

(I) there has been significant price undercutting by the imported merchandise as compared with the price of like products of the United States, and

(II) the effect of imports of such merchandise otherwise depresses prices to a significant degree or prevents price increases, which otherwise would have occurred, to a significant degree.

(iii) IMPACT ON AFFECTED INDUSTRY.—In examining the impact on the affected industry, the Commission shall evaluate all relevant economic factors which have a bearing on the state of the industry, including, but not limited to—

(I) actual and potential decline in output, sales, market share, profits, productivity, return on investments, and utilization of capacity,

(II) factors affecting domestic prices, and

(III) actual and potential negative effects on cash flow, inventories, employment, wages, growth, ability to raise capital, and investment.

(D) SPECIAL RULES FOR AGRICULTURAL PRODUCTS

(i) The Commission shall not determine that there is no material injury or threat of material injury to United States producers of an agricultural commodity merely because the prevailing market price is at or above the minimum support price.

(ii) In the case of agricultural products, the Commission shall consider any increased burden on government income or price support programs.

(E) SPECIAL RULES.—For purposes of this paragraph—

(i) NATURE OF SUBSIDY.—In determining whether there is a threat of material injury, the Commission shall consider such information as may be presented to it by the administering authority as to the nature of the subsidy (particularly as to whether the subsidy is an export subsidy inconsistent with the Agreement) provided by a foreign country and the effects likely to be caused by the subsidy.

(ii) STANDARD FOR DETERMINATION.—The presence or absence of any factor which the Commission is required to evaluate under subparagraph (C) or (D) shall not necessarily give decisive guidance with respect to the determination by the Commission of material injury.

(8) AGREEMENT ON SUBSIDIES AND COUNTERVAILING MEASURES; AGREEMENT.—The terms "Agreement on Subsidies and Countervailing Measures" and "Agreement" mean the Agreement on Interpretation and Application of Articles VI, XVI, and XXIII of the General Agreement on Tariffs and Trade (relating to subsidies and countervailing measures) approved under section 2(a) of the Trade Agreements Act of 1979.

(9) INTERESTED PARTY.—The term "interested party" means—

(A) a foreign manufacturer, producer, or exporter, or the United States importer, of merchandise which is the subject of an investigation under this title or a trade or business association a majority of the members of which are importers of such merchandise,

(B) the government of a country in which such merchandise is produced or manufactured,

(C) a manufacturer, producer, or wholesaler in the United States of a like product,

(D) a certified union or recognized union or group of workers which is representative of an industry engaged in the manufacture, production, or wholesale in the United States of a like product, and

(E) a trade or business association a majority of whose members manufacture, produce, or wholesale a like product in the United States.

(10) LIKE PRODUCT.—The term "like product" means a product which is like, or in the absence of like, most similar in characteristics and uses with, the article subject to an investigation under this title.

(11) AFFIRMATIVE DETERMINATIONS BY DIVIDED COMMISSION
If the Commissioners voting on a determination by the Commission are evenly divided as to whether the determination should be affirmative or negative, the Commission shall be deemed to have made an affirmative determination. For the purpose of applying this paragraph when the issue before the Commission is to determine whether there is—

(A) material injury to an industry in the United States,

(B) threat of material injury to such an industry, or

(C) material retardation of the establishment of an industry in the United States,

by reason of imports of the merchandise, an affirmative vote on any of the issues shall be treated as a vote that the determination should be affirmative.

(12) ATTRIBUTION OF MERCHANDISE TO COUNTRY OF MANUFACTURE OR PRODUCTION.—For purposes of subtitle A, merchandise shall be treated as the product of the country in which it was manufactured or produced without regard to whether it is imported directly from that country and without regard to whether it is imported in the same condition as when exported from that country or in a changed condition by reason of remanufacture or otherwise.

(13) EXPORTER.—For the purpose of determining United States price, the term "exporter" includes the person by whom or for whose account the merchandise is imported into the United States if—

(A) such person is the agent or principal of the exporter, manufacturer, or producer;

(B) such person owns or controls, directly or indirectly, through stock ownership or control or otherwise, any interest in the business of the exporter, manufacturer, or producer;

(C) the exporter, manufacturer, or producer owns or controls, directly or indirectly, through stock ownership or control or otherwise, any interest in any business conducted by such person; or

(D) any person or persons, jointly or severally, directly or indirectly, through stock ownership or control or otherwise, own or control in the aggregate 20 percent or more of the voting power or control in the business carried on by the person by whom or for whose account the merchandise is imported into the United States and also 20 percent or more of such power or control in the business of the exporter, manufacturer, or producer.

(14) SOLD OR, IN THE ABSENCE OF SALES, OFFERED FOR SALE.—The term "sold or, in the absence of sales, offered for sale" means sold or, in the absence of sales, offered—

(A) to all purchasers at wholesale, or

(B) in the ordinary course of trade to one or more selected purchasers at wholesale at a price which fairly reflects the market value of the merchandise,

without regard to restrictions as to the disposition or use of the merchandise by the purchaser except that, where such restrictions are found to affect the market value of the merchandise, adjustment shall be made therefor in calculating the price at which the merchandise is sold or offered for sale.

(15) ORDINARY COURSE OF TRADE.—The term "ordinary course of trade" means the conditions and practices which, for a reasonable time prior to the exportation of the merchandise which is the subject of an investigation, have been normal in the trade under consideration with respect to merchandise of the same class or kind.

(16) SUCH OR SIMILAR MERCHANDISE.—The term "such or similar merchandise" means merchandise in the first of the following categories in respect of which a determination for the purposes of subtitle B of this title can be satisfactorily made:

(A) The merchandise which is the subject of an investigation and other merchandise which is identical in physical characteristics with, and was produced in the same country by the same person as, that merchandise.

(B) Merchandise—
   (i) produced in the same country and by the same person as the merchandise which is the subject of the investigation,
   (ii) like that merchandise in component material or materials and in the purposes for which used, and
   (iii) approximately equal in commercial value to that merchandise.

(C) Merchandise—
   (i) produced in the same country and by the same person and of the same general class or kind as the merchandise which is the subject of the investigation,
   (ii) like that merchandise in the purpose for which used, and
   (iii) which the administering authority determines may reasonably be compared with that merchandise.

(17) USUAL WHOLESALE QUANTITIES.—The term "usual wholesale quantities," in any case in which the merchandise which is the subject of the investigation is sold in the market under consideration at different prices for different quantities, means the quantities in which such merchandise is there sold at the price or prices for one quantity in an aggregate volume which is greater than the aggregate volume sold at the price or prices for any other quantity.

[*Authors' note*: Additional sections, relating to antidumping duties and administration of the statute, are omitted.]

F 1976 OECD Declaration on International Investment and Multinational Enterprises (21st June 1976)

THE GOVERNMENTS OF OECD MEMBER COUNTRIES

CONSIDERING

☐ that international investment has assumed increased importance in the world economy and has considerably contributed to the development of their countries;

☐ that multinational enterprises play an important role in this investment process;

☐ that co-operation by Member countries can improve the foreign investment climate, encourage the positive contribution which multinational enterprises can make to economic and social progress, and minimise and resolve difficulties which may arise from their various operations;

☐ that, while continuing endeavours within the OECD may lead to further international arrangements and agreements in this field, it seems appropriate at this stage to intensify their co-operation and consultation on issues relating to international investment and multinational enterprises through inter-related instruments each of which deals with a different aspect of the matter and together constitute a framework within which the OECD will consider these issues:

DECLARE:

Guidelines for Multinational Enterprises	I.	that they jointly recommend to multinational enterprises operating in their territories the observance of the Guidelines as set forth in the Annex hereto having regard to the considerations and understandings which introduce the Guidelines and are an integral part of them;
National Treatment	II. 1.	that Member countries should, consistent with their needs to maintain public order, to protect their essential security interests and to fulfil commitments relating to international peace and security, accord to enterprises operating in their territories and owned or controlled directly or indirectly by nationals of another Member country (hereinafter referred to as "Foreign-Controlled Enterprises") treatment under their laws, regulations and administrative practices, consistent with international law and no less favourable than that accorded in like situations to domestic enterprises (hereinafter referred to as "National Treatment");

2. that Member countries will consider applying "National Treatment" in respect of countries other than Member countries;

3. that Member countries will endeavour to ensure that their territorial subdivisions apply "National Treatment";

4. that this Declaration does not deal with the right of Member countries to regulate the entry of foreign investment or the conditions of establishment of foreign enterprises;

International Investment Incentives and Disincentives

III. 1. that they recognise the need to strengthen their co-operation in the field of international direct investment;

2. that they thus recognise the need to give due weight to the interests of Member countries affected by specific laws, regulations and administrative practices in this field (hereinafter called "measures") providing official incentives and disincentives to international direct investment;

3. that Member countries will endeavour to make such measures as transparent as possible, so that their importance and purpose can be ascertained and that information on them can be readily available;

Consultation Procedures

IV. that they are prepared to consult one another on the above matters in conformity with the Decisions of the Council relating to Inter-Governmental Consultation Procedures on the Guidelines for Multinational Enterprises, on National Treatment and on International Investment Incentives and Disincentives;

Review

V. that they will review the above matters within three years with a view to improving the effectiveness of international economic co-operation among Member countries on issues relating to international investment and multinational enterprises;

Note: The Turkish Government did not participate in the Declaration and abstained from the Decisions.

Annex to the Declaration of 21st June 1976 by Governments of OECD Member Countries on International Investment and Multinational Enterprises

Guidelines for Multinational Enterprises

1. Multinational enterprises now play an important part in the economies of Member countries and in international economic relations, which is of increasing interest to

governments. Through international direct investment, such enterprises can bring substantial benefits to home and host countries by contributing to the efficient utilisation of capital, technology and human resources between countries and can thus fulfil an important role in the promotion of economic and social welfare. But the advances made by multinational enterprises in organising their operations beyond the national framework may lead to abuse of concentrations of economic power and to conflicts with national policy objectives. In addition, the complexity of these multinational enterprises and the difficulty of clearly perceiving their diverse structures, operations and policies sometimes give rise to concern.

2. The common aim of the Member countries is to encourage the positive contributions which multinational enterprises can make to economic and social progress and to minimise and resolve the difficulties to which their various operations may give rise. In view of the transnational structure of such enterprises, this aim will be furthered by co-operation among the OECD countries where the headquarters of most of the multinational enterprises are established and which are the location of a substantial part of their operations. The guidelines set out hereafter are designed to assist in the achievement of this common aim and to contribute to improving the foreign investment climate.

3. Since the operations of multinational enterprises extend throughout the world, including countries that are not Members of the Organisation, international co-operation in this field should extend to all States. Member countries will give their full support to efforts undertaken in co-operation with non-member countries, and in particular with developing countries, with a view to improving the welfare and living standards of all peoples both by encouraging the positive contributions which multinational enterprises can make and by minimising and resolving the problems which may arise in connection with their activities.

4. Within the Organisation, the programme of co-operation to attain these ends will be a continuing, pragmatic and balanced one. It comes within the general aims of the Convention on the Organisation for Economic Co-operation and Development (OECD) and makes full use of the various specialised bodies of the Organisation whose terms of reference already cover many aspects of the role of multinational enterprises, notably in matters of international trade and payments, competition, taxation, manpower, industrial development, science and technology. In these bodies, work is being carried out on the identification of issues, the improvement of relevant qualitative and statistical information and the elaboration of proposals for action designed to strengthen inter-governmental co-operation. In some of these areas procedures already exist through which issues related to the operations of multinational enterprises can be taken up. This work could result in the conclusion of further and complementary agreements and arrangements between governments.

5. The initial phase of the co-operation programme is composed of a Declaration and three Decisions promulgated simultaneously as they are complementary and interconnected, in respect of guidelines for multinational enterprises, national treatment for foreign-controlled enterprises and international investment incentives and disincentives.

6. The guidelines set out below are recommendations jointly addressed by Member countries to multinational enterprises operating in their territories. These guidelines, which take into account the problems which can arise because of the international structure of these enterprises, lay down standards for the activities of these enterprises in the different Member countries. Observance of the guidelines is voluntary and not legally enforceable. However, they should help to ensure that the operations of these enterprises are in harmony with national policies of the countries where they operate and to strengthen the basis of mutual confidence between enterprises and States.

7. Every State has the right to prescribe the conditions under which multinational enterprises operate within its national jusrisdiction, subject to international law and to the international agreements to which it has subscribed. The entities of a multinational enterprise located in various countries are subject to the laws of these countries.

8. A precise legal definition of multinational enterprises is not required for the purposes of the guidelines. These usually comprise companies or other entities whose ownership is private, state or mixed, established in different countries and so linked that one or more of them may be able to exercise a significant influence over the activities of others and, in particular, to share knowledge and resources with the others. The degree of autonomy of each entity in relation to the others varies widely from one multinational enterprise to another, depending on the nature of the links between such entities and the fields of activity concerned. For these reasons, the guidelines are addressed to the various entities within the multinational enterprise parent companies and or local entities according to the actual distribution of responsibilities among them on the understanding that they will co-operate and provide assistance to one another as necessary to facilitate observance of these guidelines. The word "enterprise" as used in these guidelines refers to these various entities in accordance with their responsibilities.

9. The guidelines are not aimed at introducing differences of treatment between multinational and domestic enterprises; wherever relevant they reflect good practice for all. Accordingly, multinational and domestic industries are subject to the same expectations in respect of their conduct wherever the guidelines are relevant to both.

10. The use of appropriate international dispute settlement mechanisms, including arbitration, should be encouraged as a means of facilitating the resolution of problems arising between enterprises and Member countries.

11. Member countries have agreed to establish appropriate review and consultation procedures concerning issues arising in respect of the guidelines. When multinational enterprises are made subject to conflicting requirements by Member countries, the governments concerned will co-operate in good faith with a view to resolving such problems either within the Committee on International Investment and Multinational Enterprises established by the OECD Council on 21st January 1975 or through other mutually acceptable arrangements.

Having regard to the foregoing considerations, the Member countries set forth the following guidelines for multinational enterprises with the understanding that Member countries will fulfil their responsibilities to treat enterprises equitably and in accordance with international law and international agreements, as well as contractual obligations to which they have subscribed.

General Policies

Enterprises should

1. take fully into account established general policy objectives of the Member countries in which they operate;
2. in particular, give due consideration to those countries' aims and priorities with regard to economic and social progress, including industrial and regional development, the

protection of the environment, the creation of employment opportunities, the promotion of innovation and the transfer of technology;

3. while observing their legal obligations concerning information, supply their entities with supplementary information the latter may need in order to meet requests by the authorities of the countries in which those entities are located for information relevant to the activities of those entities, taking into account legitimate requirements of business confidentiality;

4. favour close co-operation with the local community and business interests;

5. allow their component entities freedom to develop their activities and to exploit their competitive advantage in domestic and foreign markets, consistent with the need for specialisation and sound commercial practice;

6. when filling responsible posts in each country of operation, take due account of individual qualifications without discrimination as to nationality, subject to particular national requirements in this respect;

7. not render—and they should not be solicited or expected to render—any bribe or other improper benefit, direct or indirect, to any public servant or holder of public office;

8. unless legally permissible, not make contributions to candidates for public office or to political parties or other political organisations;

9. abstain from any improper involvement in local political activities.

Disclosure of Information

Enterprises should, having due regard to their nature and relative size in the economic context of their operations and to requirements of business confidentiality and to cost, publish in a form suited to improve public understanding a sufficient body of factual information on the structure, activities and policies of the enterprise as a whole, as a supplement, in so far as necessary for this purpose, to information to be disclosed under the national law of the individual countries in which they operate. To this end, they should publish within reasonable time limits, on a regular basis, but at least annually, financial statements and other pertinent information relating to the enterprise as a whole, comprising in particular:

(i) the structure of the enterprise, showing the name and location of the parent company, its main affiliates, its percentage ownership, direct and indirect, in these affiliates, including shareholdings between them;

(ii) the geographical areas[1] where operations are carried out and the principal activities carried on therein by the parent company and the main affiliates;

(iii) the operating results and sales by geographical area and the sales in the major lines of business for the enterprise as a whole;

(iv) significant new capital investment by geographical area and, as far as practicable, by major lines of business for the enterprise as a whole;

(v) a statement of the sources and uses of funds by the enterprise as a whole;

(vi) the average number of employees in each geographical area;

(vii) research and development expenditure for the enterprise as a whole;

(viii) the policies followed in respect of intra-group pricing;

(ix) the accounting policies, including those on consolidation, observed in compiling the published information.

Competition

Enterprises should, while conforming to official competition rules and established policies of the countries in which they operate,

1. refrain from actions which would adversely affect competition in the relevant market by abusing a dominant position of market power, by means of, for example,
   (a) anti-competitive acquisitions,
   (b) predatory behaviour toward competitors,
   (c) unreasonable refusal to deal,
   (d) anti-competitive abuse of industrial property rights,
   (e) discriminatory i.e. unreasonably differentiated pricing and using such pricing transactions between affiliated enterprises as a means of affecting adversely competition outside these enterprises;
2. allow purchasers, distributors and licensees freedom to resell, export, purchase and develop their operations consistent with law, trade conditions, the need for specialisation and sound commercial practice;
3. refrain from participating in or otherwise purposely strengthening the restrictive effects of international or domestic cartels or restrictive agreements which adversely affect or eliminate competition and which are not generally or specifically accepted under applicable national or international legislation;
4. be ready to consult and co-operate, including the provision of information, with competent authorities of countries whose interests are directly affected in regard to competition issues or investigations. Provision of information should be in accordance with safeguards normally applicable in this field.

Financing

Enterprises should, in managing the financial and commercial operations of their activities, and especially their liquid foreign assets and liabilities, take into consideration the established objectives of the countries in which they operate regarding balance of payments and credit policies.

Taxation

Enterprises should

1. upon request of the taxation authorities of the countries in which they operate, provide, in accordance with the safeguards and relevant procedures of the national laws of these countries, the information necessary to determine correctly the taxes to be assessed in connection with their operations, including relevant information concerning their operations in other countries;
2. refrain from making use of the particular facilities available to them, such as transfer pricing which does not conform to an arm's length standard, for modifying in ways contrary to national laws the tax base on which members of the group are assessed.

Employment and Industrial Relations

Enterprises should, within the framework of law, regulations and prevailing labour relations and employment practices, in each of the countries in which they operate,

1. respect the right of their employees, to be represented by trade unions and other bona fide organisations of employees, and engage in constructive negotiations, either individually or through employers' associations, with such employee organisations with a view to reaching agreements on employment conditions, which should include provisions for dealing with disputes arising over the interpretation of such agreements, and for ensuring mutually respected rights and responsibilities;
2. (a) provide such facilities to representatives of the employees as may be necessary to assist in the development of effective collective agreements,
   (b) provide to representative of employees information which is needed for meaningful negotiations on conditions of employment;
3. provide to representatives of employees where this accords with local law and practice, information which enables them to obtain a true and fair view of the performance of the entity or, where appropriate, the enterprise as a whole;
4. observe standards of employment and industrial relations not less favourable than those observed by comparable employers in the host country;
5. in their operations, to the greatest extent practicable, utilise, train and prepare for upgrading members of the local labour force in co-operation with representatives of their employees and, where appropriate, the relevant governmental authorities;
6. in considering changes in their operations which would have major effects upon the livelihood of their employees, in particular in the case of the closure of an entity involving collective lay-offs or dismissals, provide reasonable notice of such changes to representatives of their employees, and where appropriate to the relevant governmental authorities, and co-operate with the employee representatives and appropriate governmental authorities so as to mitigate to the maximum extent practicable adverse effects;
7. implement their employment policies including hiring, discharge, pay, promotion and training without discrimination unless selectivity in respect of employee characteristics is in furtherance of established governmental policies which specifically promote greater equality of employment opportunity;
8. in the context of bona fide negotiations[2] with representatives of employees on conditions of employment, or while employees are exercising a right to organise, not threaten to utilise a capacity to transfer the whole or part of an operating unit from the country concerned in order to influence unfairly those negotiations or to hinder the exercise of a right to organise;
9. enable authorised representatives of their employees to conduct negotiations on collective bargaining or labour management relations issues with representatives of management who are authorised to take decisions on the matters under negotiation.

Science and Technology

Enterprises should

1. endeavour to ensure that their activities fit satisfactorily into the scientific and technological policies and plans of the countries in which they operate, and contribute to the development of national scientific and technological capacities, including as far as

appropriate the establishment and improvement in host countries of their capacity to innovate;

2. to the fullest extent practicable, adopt in the course of their business activities practices which permit the rapid diffusion of technologies with due regard to the protection of industrial and intellectual property rights;

3. when granting licenses for the use of industrial property rights or when otherwise transferring technology do so on reasonable terms and conditions.

---

[1]For the purposes of the guideline on disclosure of information the term "geographical area" means groups of countries or individual countries as each enterprise determines is appropriate in its particular circumstances. While no single method of grouping is appropriate for all enterprises or for all purposes, the factors to be considered by an enterprise would include the significance of operations carried out in individual countries or areas as well as the effects on its competitiveness, geographic proximity, economic affinity, similarities in business environments and the nature, scale and degree of inter-relationship of the enterprises' operations in the various countries.

[2]Bona fide negotiations may include labour disputes as part of the process of negotiation. Whether or not labour disputes are so included will be determined by the law and prevailing employment practices of particular countries.

Decision of the Council on National Treatment

The Council,

Having regard to the Convention on the Organisation for Economic Co-operation and Development of 14th December, 1960 and, in particular, Articles 2(c), 2(d), 3 and 5(a) thereof;

Having regard to the Resolution of the Council of 21st January, 1975 establishing a Committee on International Investment and Multinational Enterprises and, in particular, paragraph 2 thereof [C(74)/247 (Final)];

Taking note of the Declaration by the Governments of OECD Member countries of 21st June, 1976 on national treatment;

Considering that it is appropriate to establish within the Organisation suitable procedures for reviewing laws, regulations, and administrative practices (hereinafter referred to as "measures") which depart from "National Treatment";

On the proposal of the Committee on International Investment and Multinational Enterprises;

Decides:

1. Measures taken by a Member country constituting exceptions to "National Treatment" (including measure restricting new investment by "Foreign-Controlled Enterprises" already established in their territory) which are in effect on the date of this Decision shall be notified to the Organisation within 60 days after the date of this Decision.

2. Measures taken by a Member country constituting new exceptions to "National Treatment" (including measures restricting new investment by "Foreign-Controlled Enterprises" already established in their territory) taken after the date of this Decision shall be notified to the Organisation within 30 days of the date of their introduction together with the specific reasons therefore and the proposed duration thereof.

3. Measures introduced by a territorial subdivision of a Member country, pursuant to its independent powers, which constitute exceptions to "National Treatment," shall be notified to the Organisation by the Member country concerned, insofar as it has knowledge thereof, within 30 days of the responsible officials of the Member country obtaining such knowledge.

4. The Committee on International Investment and Multinational Enterprises (hereinafter called "the Committee") shall periodically review the application of "National Treatment" (including exceptions thereto) with a view to extending such application of "National Treatment." The Committee shall make proposals as and when necessary in this connection.

5. The Committee shall act as a forum for consultations, at the request of a Member country, in respect of any matter related to this instrument and its implementation, including exceptions to "National Treatment" and their application.

6. Member countries shall provide to the Committee, upon its request, all relevant information concerning measures pertaining to the application of "National Treatment" and exceptions thereto.

7. This Decision shall be reviewed within a period of three years. The Committee shall make proposals for this purpose as appropriate.

Decision of the Council on International Investment Incentives and Disincentives

The Council,

Having regard to the Convention on the Organisation for Economic Co-operation and Development of 14th December, 1960 and, in particular, Articles 2(c), 2(d), 2(e), 3 and 5(a) thereof;

Having regard to the Resolution of the Council of 21st January, 1975 establishing a Committee on International Investment and Multinational Enterprises and, in particular, paragraph 2 thereof (C(74)247/Final);

Taking note of the Declaration by the Governments of OECD Member countries of 21st June 1976 on international investment incentives and disincentives;

On the proposal of the Committee on International Investment and Multinational Enterprises;

Decides:

1. Consultations will take place in the framework of the Committee on International

Investment and Multinational Enterprises at the request of a Member country which considers that its interests may be adversely affected by the impact on its flow of international direct investments of measures taken by another Member country specifically designed to provide incentives or disincentives for international direct investment. Having full regard to the national economic objectives of the measures and without prejudice to policies designed to redress regional imbalances, the purpose of the consultations will be to examine the possibility of reducing such efforts to a minimum.

2. Member countries shall supply, under the consultation procedures, all permissible information relating to any measures being the subject of the consultation.

3. This Decision shall be served within a period of three years. The Committee on International Investment and Multinational Enterprises shall make proposals for this purpose as appropriate.

Decision of the Council on Inter-Government Consultation Procedures on the Guidelines for Multinational Enterprises

The Council,

Having regard to the Convention on the Organisation for Economic Co-operation and Development of 14th December, 1960 and, in particular, to Articles 2(d), 3 and 5(a) thereof;

Having regard to the Resolution of the Council of 21st January, 1975 establishing a Committee on International Investment and Multinational Enterprises and, in particular, to paragraph 2 thereof (C(74)247/Final);

Taking note of the Declaration by the Governments of the OECD Member countries of 21st June, 1976 in which they jointly recommend to multinational enterprises the observance of guidelines for multinational enterprises;

Recognising the desirability of setting forth procedures by which consultations may take place on matters related to these guidelines;

On the proposal of the Committee on International Investment and Multinational Enterprises;

Decides:

1. The Committee on International Investment and Multinational Enterprises (hereinafter called "the Committee") shall periodically or at the request of a Member country hold an exchange of views on matters related to the guidelines and the experience gained in their application. The Committee shall periodically report to the Council on these matters.

2. The Committee shall periodically invite the Business and Industry Advisory Committee to OECD (BIAC) and the Trade Union Advisory Committee to OECD (TUAC) to express

their views on matters related to the guidelines and shall take account of such views in its reports to the Council.

3. On the proposal of a Member country the Committee may decide whether individual enterprises should be given the opportunity, if they so wish, to express their views concerning the application of the guidelines. The Committee shall not reach conclusions on the conduct of individual enterprises.

4. Member countries may request that consultations be held in the Committee on any problem arising from the fact that multinational enterprises are made subject to conflicting requirements. Governments concerned will co-operate in good faith with a view to resolving such problems, either within the Committee or through other mutually acceptable arrangements.

5. This Decision shall be reviewed within a period of three years. The Committee shall make proposals for this purpose as appropriate.

G OECD Arrangement on Guidelines for Officially Supported Export Credits (With effect from July 6, 1982, based on an unofficial text obtained from the US Treasury Department)

Arrangement on Guidelines for Officially Supported Export Credits

Form and Scope of the Arrangement

This informal Arrangement is applicable among the Participants[1] in the form of guidelines, to officially supported export credits with a repayment term of two years or more, regardless of whether they relate to contracts for sale of goods and services or to leases equivalent in effect to such contracts or to pure service contracts.

1. Cash Payments

Participants will require purchasers of exported goods and services to make cash payments at or before the starting point equal to a minimum of 15 percent of the export contract value. Participants will not provide official support for such cash payments other than insurance and guarantees against the usual pre-credit risks.

2. Maximum Repayment Term

(a) Except for the special sectors referred to in Paragraph 4 and countries referred to in footnote 2 to Paragraph 3(a), the maximum repayment term will be 8.5 years for relatively rich and intermediate countries and 10 years for relatively poor countries. The export credit agreement and ancillary document shall not permit the extension of the repayment term. If a Participant intends to support a repayment term longer than 5, and up to 8.5, years for a relatively rich country, the Participant will give prior notification in accordance with the procedure set forth in Paragraph 9(b)(1).

(b) Principal of an export credit which is officially supported by way of direct credit, refinancing, eligibility for an interest subsidy, guarantee, or insurance shall normally be repayable in equal and regular installments not less frequently than every six months, commencing not later than six months after the starting point. If a Participant intends not to follow the normal practice, the Participant will give prior notification in accordance with the procedure set forth in Paragraph

9(b)(1). Such prior notification will not be required in the case of leases if the amount of principal and interest combined is payable in equal and regular installments not less frequently than every six months, commencing not later than six months after the starting point.

3. Minimum Interest Rate

(a) The following minimum rates of interest will apply where Participants are providing official financing support by way of direct credit, refinancing, or interest rate subsidy:

Classification[2] of country	Number of years in maximum repayment terms		
	2–5	5–8.5	Over 8.5–10
I Relatively rich	12.15%	12.40%	N/A
II Intermediate	10.85%	11.35%	N/A[3]
III Relatively poor	10.0%	10.0%	10.0%

(b) It is understood that if commercial lending rates of interest for the national currency in a Participant's country fall below the lowest minimum level at (a) above, any Participant may provide such official financing support for export credit in that currency carrying interest at rates below the above guidelines, provided that the interest rate charged for the export credit which is being financed, as a whole or in part with such official support, is not less than the commercial interest reference rate[4] increased by 0.3 percentage points per annum.

(c) Interest on an export credit which is officially supported by way of direct credit, refinancing, eligibility for an interest subsidy, guarantee or insurance shall normally not be capitalized during the repayment term but shall be payable not less frequently than every six months, commencing not later than six months after the starting point. If a Participant intends not to follow the normal practice, the Participant will give prior notification in accordance with the procedure set forth in Paragraph 9(b)(1).

4. Special Sectors

The following terms shall apply to the sectors listed below:

(a) CONVENTIONAL POWER PLANTS: The terms of this Arrangement shall apply except that the maximum repayment term shall be 12 years. If a Participant intends to support a repayment term longer than 5 years in transactions with relatively rich countries and longer than the relevant maximum set forth in Paragraph 2(a) for other countries, the Participant will give prior notification in accordance with the procedure set forth in Paragraph 9(b)(1).

(b) GROUND SATELLITE COMMUNICATIONS STATIONS: The terms of this Arrangement shall be applicable except that the maximum repayment term to any country may not exceed eight years [as provided for in the OECD Understanding on Export Credits for Ground Satellite Communications Stations].

(c) SHIPS: Participants will apply the terms of this Arrangement to ships not covered by the OECD Understanding on Export Credits for Ships. (See also Paragraph 12(d) of this Arrangement.)

5. *Local Costs*

(a) The following provisions apply to local costs related to those export credits to which this Arrangement applies:
   (1) For credits to intermediate or relatively poor countries, Participants will not finance or insure credit for more than 100 percent of the value of the goods and services exported. Thus the amount of local costs supported on credit terms will not exceed the cash payments. Furthermore, Participants will not grant such support for local costs carrying interest rates (if in the same currency as that of the export credit) or repayment terms more favorable than those supported for the exports to which such local costs are related.
   (2) For credits to relatively rich countries, the provisions of Paragraph 5(a)(1) will apply, provided, however, that any support will be confined to insurance or guarantees.

(b) For the purposes of this Paragraph, and in accordance with the text of the OECD Declarations on local costs of May 15, 1975:
   (1) Local costs means expenditure for the supply from the buyer's country of goods and services (however commissions payable to the exporter's agent in the buying country do not fall within the definition of local costs in the context of the Arrangement) which are necessary either for executing the exporter's contract or for completing the project of which the exporter's contract forms part.
   (2) Exported goods and services includes goods and services supplied by third countries.

6. *Commitments[5] and Prior Commitments*

(a) INDIVIDUAL TRANSACTIONS NOT COVERED BY LINES OF CREDIT. The credit terms and conditions of new commitments shall not be fixed for periods exceeding six months. In the case of changes in the guidelines of the Arrangement, the support of credit conditions not in conformity with the guidelines as modified shall not be justified after a period of six months from the date of modification. Nonconforming commitments still outstanding six months after the date of modification shall be notified to all other Participants immediately, utilizing the standard form set out in Annex B.

(b) LINES OF CREDIT.[6] The credit terms and conditions of a line of credit, whether new or one that is being renewed or prolonged, shall not be fixed for a period exceeding six months. In the case of changes in the guidelines of this Arrangement, the support of credit conditions attributable to the lines of credit which are not in conformity with the modified guidelines shall not be justified after a period of six months from the date of modification. Credit lines, not in conformity with the guidelines as modified, still outstanding six months after the date of modification shall be notified to all other Participants immediately utilizing the standard form set out in Annex A.

(c) MATCHING

    (1) Any Participant has the right to match the terms supported by another Participant under a prior commitment.

    (2) The matching Participant will make reasonable efforts to determine whether nonconforming terms of a prior commitment for an individual transaction or of a prior credit line will be used to support a particular transaction. This Participant will be considered to have made such reasonable efforts if it has informed by telex the Participant assumed to offer such nonconforming terms of its intention to match, but has not been informed within three working days that the prior commitment or prior credit line will not be used to support the transaction in question.

    (3) Insofar as the individual transactions referred to in Paragraph 6(a) are concerned, the matching Participant will follow the procedure set forth in Paragraph 9(b)(2) and (3).

    (4) Insofar as lines of credit referred to in Paragraph 6(b) are concerned, each Participant has the right to match the credit terms offered by another Participant on an individual transaction basis, or by means of another line of credit. If the latter method is adopted, the date of expiry of the matching line of credit shall not surpass the length of commitment made within the framework of the line of credit being matched.

    (5) If a Participant matching a credit line intends to support terms which include any other nonconforming element, the Participant shall follow the prior notification and discussion procedure set forth in Paragraph 9(a)(2)(ii). As soon as a Participant commits itself, it must in all cases immediately inform all other Participants accordingly.

7. *Tied Aid Credits*[7]

If a Participant intends to support a tied aid credit the Participant shall, without prejudice to official development assistance procedures administered by the Development Assistance Committee, give notification in accordance with the procedures set forth in Paragraphs:

(i)   9(a)(1), if the grant element is less than 15 percent;

(ii) 9(b)(1), if the grant element is 15 percent or more, but less than 25 percent;

(iii) 9(c)(1), if the grant element is 25 percent or more.

8. *Best Endeavors*

(a) The guidelines set out in this Arrangement represent the most generous credit terms for which Participants intend in general to give official support. All Participants recognize the risk that in the course of time these guidelines may come to be regarded as norms. They therefore undertake to take, as far as possible, the necessary steps to prevent this risk from materializing.

(b) In particular, they undertake that where, in an individual branch of trade or industrial sector to which this Arrangement applies, terms less generous to buyers than those set out are customary, they will continue to respect such customary terms and will do everything in their power to prevent those terms from being eroded as a result of recourse to the terms set out in this Arrangement.

(c) In keeping with the objectives set forth in subparagraphs (a) and (b) above, Participants recognize the advantage which can accrue if a clearly defined common attitude toward the credit terms for a particular transaction can be achieved and if maximum use is made of the existing arrangements for exchanging information at an early stage. If a Participant informs another Participant of the terms which it envisages supporting for a particular transaction and requests similar information from the other Participant, then, in the absence of a satisfactory reply within seven calendar days, the enquiring Participant may assume that the other will support the transaction on the most favorable terms permitted by these guidelines. In cases of particular urgency, the enquiring Participant may request a more rapid reply.

9. Procedures

(a) DEROGATIONS: PROCEDURE FOR PRIOR NOTIFICATION AND DISCUSSION

(1) *Notification and Discussion.* If a Participant intends to take the initiative to support terms not in conformity with this Arrangement, or to support a tied aid credit having a grant element of less than 15 percent, the Participant will notify all other Participants of the terms it intends to support at least ten calendar days before issuing any commitment. If any other Participant requests a discussion during this period, the initiating Participant will delay an additional ten calendar days before issuing any commitment on such terms. Normally this discussion shall be by telex. In extreme cases face-to-face discussion may be requested and would be arranged, preferably in the country intending to derogate. If the initiating Participant moderates or withdraws its intention to support nonconforming terms, it must immediately inform all other Participants accordingly.

(2) *Matching* (identical or by other support): On and after the expiry of the first ten-day period referred to above if no discussion is requested (or on and after the expiry of the second ten-day period if discussion is requested) and unless the matching Participant has received notice from the initiating Participant that the latter has withdrawn its intention to support nonconforming terms, any Participant shall have the right to support:

(i) With respect to *identical matching*, terms which include the identical nonconforming element but which otherwise conform to the guidelines provided that the matching Participant notifies, as early as possible, its intention to do so; or

(ii) With respect to *other support prompted by the initial derogation*, any other nonconforming element of the terms, provided that the responding Participant introduces a fresh derogation, initiating a five-calendar-day prior notification and five-calendar-day discussion procedure and awaits its completion. This period can run concurrently with that of the prior notification and discussion procedure initiated by the derogating Participant, but cannot elapse before the end of the ten- or twenty-day period referred to under Paragraph 9(a)(1).

(3) *Terms Offered by a Non-Participant*: The Participant which intends to meet nonconforming terms offered by a non-Participant will follow the prior notification and discussion procedure under (1) and (2) above. Before considering meeting nonconforming terms, the Participant shall make every effort to verify that the nonconforming terms are receiving official support. The Participant shall inform all other Participants of the nature and outcome of these efforts.

(4) *Information on Commitment.* As soon as a Participant commits itself to support nonconforming terms, it must in all cases immediately inform all other Participants accordingly.

(b) PROCEDURE FOR PRIOR NOTIFICATION WITHOUT DISCUSSION
    (1) *Notification.* A Participant will notify all other Participants of the terms it intends to support at least ten calendar days before issuing any commitment, if the Participant intends:
        (i) to support a credit with a repayment term of "over 5 to 8.5 years" to a relatively rich country, or
        (ii) not to follow normal payment practices with respect to principal or interest referred to in Paragraphs 2(b) and 3(c), or
        (iii) to support a credit for a conventional power plant with a repayment term longer than the relevant maximum set forth in Paragraph 2(a), or
        (iv) to support a tied aid credit having a grant element of 15 percent or more but less than 25 percent, or
        (v) to support credit conditions for any type of ships to which the existing OECD Understanding applies, which would be more favorable than those credit conditions permitted by this Arrangement.
    (2) If the initiating Participant moderates or withdraws its intention to give such support, it must immediately inform all other Participants accordingly.
    (3) *Matching* (identical or by other support): On and after the expiry of the ten-day period referred to above and unless the matching Participant has received notice from the initiating Participant that the latter has withdrawn its intention to support terms referred to in Paragraph 9(b)(1), any Participant shall have the right to support:
        (i) with respect to *identical matching*, terms which include the identical element referred to in Paragraph 9(b)(1) but which otherwise conform to the guidelines provided that the matching Participant notifies, as early as possible, its intention to do so; or
        (ii) with respect to *other support*, any other element of the terms which does not conform to the guidelines, provided that the responding Participant initiates a five-calendar-day prior-notification procedure without discussion and awaits its completion. This period can run concurrently with that of the prior notification procedure started by the initiating Participant, but cannot elapse before the end of the ten-day period referred to under Paragraph 9(b)(1).
    (4) *Information on Commitment.* As soon as a Participant commits itself, it must in all cases immediately inform all other Participants accordingly.

(c) PROMPT NOTIFICATION PROCEDURE
    (1) *Notification.* As soon as a Participant commits itself to support a tied aid credit having a grant element of 25 percent or more the Participant must notify all other Participants accordingly.
    (2) *Matching.* No prior notification need be given if a Participant supports terms to match a tied aid credit with a grant element of 25 percent or more.
    (3) *Information on Commitment.* As soon as a Participant commits itself, it must in all cases immediately inform all other Participants accordingly.

(d) INFORMATION TO BE SUPPLIED UNDER THE PROCEDURES MENTIONED UNDER (A), (B) AND (C) ABOVE. The notifications called for by the above procedures will be made in accordance with and contain the information set out in the "Standard Form" in Annex C and be copied to the Secretariat of the OECD.

10. *No-Derogation Engagement*

Participants agree not to avail themselves from October 15, 1982 onwards of the possibilities provided under the Arrangement under:

□ Paragraph 9(a)(1) for derogations with respect to maximum repayment terms (whatever the form of support), to minimum interest rates or to the limitation of the validity of commitments to a maximum of six months.

□ Paragraph 9(a)(1) and 9(b)(1)(iv) to support tied aid credits have a grant element of less than 20 percent.

11. *Exceptions*

The guidelines of this Arrangement shall not apply to:

(a) *Military equipment.*
(b) *Agricultural commodities.*
(c) *Aircraft*: The terms of the OECD "standstill" shall apply to officially supported export credit and lease transactions.
(d) *Nuclear Power Plants.* The terms of the OECD "standstill" shall apply.
(e) *Ships covered by the OECD Understandings on Credits for Ships.* (See also Paragraph 12(d) of this Arrangement.)

12. *Definitions and Related Provisions*

(a) For the purposes of this Arrangement:
   (1) *Cash payments* means payments to be received for goods and services exported by the completion of the exporter's contractual obligations, the date of completion being determined by the starting point.

   The quantum of the minimum cash payments is established by reference to the total export contract value except that in the case of a transaction involving some goods or services supplied from outside the exporter's country the total export contract value may be reduced proportionately if the official support from which the exporter benefits does not cover those goods and services.

   Retention payments due after the latest appropriate starting point referred to in Paragraph 12(a)(6) do not count as cash payments for the purpose of conformity with the Guidelines.
   (2) *Commitment* means any arrangement for or declaration on credit conditions, in whatever form, by means of which the intention or willingness to refinance, insure, or guarantee supplier credits or to grant, refinance, insure or guarantee financial credits is brought to the attention of the recipient country, the buyer or the borrower, the exporter, or the financial institution.
   (3) *A line of credit* signifies any understanding or statement, in whatever form, whereby the intention to grant credit benefiting from official support up to a ceiling and in respect of a series of transactions, linked or not to a specific project, is brought to the attention of the recipient country, the buyer or the borrower, or the financial institution.
   (4) *Tied aid credit* means a credit which is provided for development aid purposes and which is financed either exclusively from public funds, or, as a mixed credit, partly from public and partly from private funds. For the purposes of this Arrangement the grant element of the ODA or concessional portion is

calculated in accordance with the method adopted by the Development Assistance Committee of the OECD and that of the export credit portion is considered to be zero. The grant element of a tied aid credit is determined by dividing (i) the sum of the results obtained by multiplying the face value of each credit comprising the tied aid credit by the respective grant element of each credit by (ii) the aggregate face value of the credits.

(5) *Repayment term* means the period of time commencing at the starting point and terminating on the date of the final payment.

(6) *Starting point* is the same as the Berne Union definition currently in use and is as follows:

(i) In the case of a contract for the sale of capital goods consisting of individual items usable in themselves (e.g., locomotives), the starting point is the mean date or actual date when the buyer takes physical possession of the goods in his own country.

(ii) In the case of a contract for the sale of capital equipment for complete plant or factories where the supplier has no responsibility for commissioning, the starting point is the date when the buyer is to take physical possession of the entire equipment (excluding spare parts) supplied under the contract.

(iii) In the case of construction contracts where the contractor has no responsibility for commissioning, the starting point is the date when construction has been completed.

(iv) In the case of any contract where the supplier or contractor has a contractual responsibility for commissioning, the starting point is the date when he has completed installation or construction and preliminary tests to ensure that it is ready for operation. This applies whether or not it is handed over to the buyer at that time in accordance with the terms of the contract and irrespective of any continuing commitment which the supplier or contractor may have, e.g., for guaranteeing its effective functioning or for training local personnel.

(v) In the case of paragraphs (ii), (iii), and (iv) above where the contract involves the separate execution of individual parts of a project, the date of the starting point is the date of the starting point for each separate part, or the mean date of those starting points or, where the supplier has a contract, not for the whole project but for an essential part of it, the starting point may be that appropriate to the project as a whole.

(7) *Interest* excludes:

(i) Any payment by way of premium or other charge for insuring or guaranteeing supplier credits or financial credits;

(ii) Any other payment by way of banking fees or commissions associated with the export credit, other than annual or semiannual bank charges payable throughout the repayment term; and

(iii) Withholding taxes imposed by the importing country.

(8) The *classification of countries* in Paragraph 3(a) is based on the following criteria:

Category I   Countries with a GNP per capita income of over $4000 p.a. according to the definite 1979 figures shown in the 1981 World Bank Atlas.

Category II   Countries not classified with Categories I or III.

Category III   Countries eligible for IDA credits plus any others on the IBRD list of low income countries and other countries or territories, the GNP per capita of which would not exceed the IDA eligibility level.

(b) INTEREST RATE AND OFFICIAL SUPPORT. Apart from agreement on the definition of interest set forth in Paragraph 12(a)(7) it has not proved possible to establish common definitions of interest rate and official support in the light of differences between long-established national systems of export credit and export credit insurance now in operation in the Participating countries. Efforts will be pursued to elaborate solutions for these definitions. While such definitions are being elaborated, these guidelines do not prejudice present interpretations. In order to facilitate these efforts, notes concerning actual practices in this area, including information on annual or semiannual bank charges payable throughout the repayment term and considered as part of interest, as they result from the different national systems, were transmitted to the Secretariat of the OECD and distributed to all the Participants.

(c) ACTION TO AVOID OR MINIMIZE LOSSES. The provisions of this Arrangement are without prejudice to the right of the export credit or insurance authority to take appropriate action after the export credit agreement and ancillary documents become effective to avoid or minimize losses.

(d) APPLICABILITY OF THIS ARRANGEMENT TO SHIPS. Apart from agreement as set forth in Paragraph 4(c) on the applicability of the provisions of this Arrangement to ships not covered by the OECD Understanding on Export Credit for Ships it has not proved possible to establish common provisions for all ships. Efforts will be pursued to arrive at such provisions. Without prejudice to the rules applicable under the OECD Understanding on Export Credits for Ships and until common provisions for all ships are agreed upon, if a Participant intends to support terms for any type of ship to which the existing OECD Understanding applies, which would be more favorable than those terms permitted by this Arrangement, the Participant will notify all other Participants of such terms in accordance with the procedure set forth in Paragraph 9(b)(1). Participants will make maximum use of the existing arrangements for exchanging information.

(e) THE APPLICABLE INTEREST RATE AND REPAYMENT TERM FOR EXPORTS THROUGH A "RELAY COUNTRY." Participants considered that the interest rate and repayment term set out in Paragraphs 2 and 3 corresponding to the country of "final destination" should apply in cases:

   □ where the "relay country" makes payment, if and when received from the country of final destination, to the exporting country on the basis of the latter's portion in the total export value; or
   □ where there is direct guarantee and payment by the country of final destination.

13. *Wider Participation*

Any OECD Member country, which is willing to apply these guidelines, may become a Participant in the Arrangement. Any other country, which is willing to apply these guidelines, may become a Participant upon the prior invitation of the then existing Participants.

14. *Review*

(a) Participants will review, at least annually, the operation in practice of these guidelines.[8] In the review they will examine, *inter alia*, the functioning of the various prior and prompt notification procedures; derogations and questions related to matching (including lines of credit); prior commitments; agriculture credit practices and, without prejudice to the possibility of *ad hoc* consideration of a request to participate in the Arrangement, questions related to wider participation in the Arrangement.

(b) At each annual review Participants will review and decide in the light of the economic and monetary situation prevailing at that time modifications which might prove to be necessary to the minimum interest rate provisions of this Arrangement. The aim would be notably to bring the matrix interest rates closer to market rates.

(c) Each review will be prepared by the OECD Secretariat, based upon information on Participants' experience in respect of the points mentioned above, such information to be provided by Participants not later than 45 days before the date of the review.

15. *Validity and Duration*

The provisions of the present Arrangement are applicable without limit of time, unless revised in accordance with Paragraph 14; however, the provisions laid down on July 6, 1982, are only valid until May 1, 1983.

16. *Withdrawal*

Any Participant may withdraw from this Arrangement upon not less than 60 calendar days prior written notice to the other Participants.

---

[1] See Annex D for the list of Participants.

[2] For criteria underlying the classification cf. Paragraph 12(a)(8).

[3] *Specific provisions for countries which were classified in Category III before 6th July, 1982 but as of this date are classified in Category II:*
(a) The maximum repayment terms will be ten years, the minimum interest rate applicable for repayment terms of over 8.5 to 10 years being the same as that for repayment terms of over 5 to 8.5 years.
(b) Until December 31, 1982, a minimum interest rate of 10.5 percent will be applied for repayment terms of between 2 and 5 years and of 10.75 percent for repayment terms of over 5 to 10 years.

[4] The commercial interest reference rate for Japanese Yen is the long term prime rate (LTPR) for Japan.

[5] For definition cf. Paragraph 12(a)(2).

[6] For definition cf. Paragraph 12(a)(3).

[7] For definition cf. Paragraph 12(a)(4).

[8] The reviews will normally take place in the spring of each year.

Annex A Standard Form for Listing Lines of Credit Regarded as Prior Commitments

1. Name of authority/agency administering support for the line of credit under the Arrangement.
2. "We regard the following line(s) of credit as prior commitment(s) which is (are) not in conformity with the guidelines in effect since. . . ."

The following points to be covered in respect of each and every line of credit:

3. Country of buyers/borrowers.
4. (Where relevant) names and locations of buyers/borrowers.
5. (Where relevant) nature of project/goods covered by the line of credit; location of project.
6. Amount of line of credit in the denominated currency [see also point 10(a) below].
   (a) Initial Amount.
   (b) Amount still available for use on _____.
   (c) The indicative or restrictive nature of the ceiling in the framework of credit lines that also have a date limit.
7. Any minimum contract value in the denominated currency.
8. Details of credit terms which may be supported under the line of credit:
   (a) cash payments;
   (b) repayment term (including starting point of credit, frequency of installments for repaying principal amount of credit, and whether these installments will be equal in amount);
   (c) interest rate;
   (d) support for local costs (including the total amount of local costs expressed as a percentage of the total value of goods and services exported, the terms of repayment, and the nature of the support to be given).
9. Date on which we entered into this prior commitment.
10. (a) Indicate when this prior commitment will lapse, specifying whether the commitment is expressed in terms of a terminal calendar date, or a ceiling amount of credit, or a combination of both these factors.
    (b) Indicate the date on which any of the credit terms of the line of credit may be reviewed or revised.
11. Final date for placing contracts [if different from date given at 10(a)].

Annex B Standard Form for Notifying Prior Commitments for Individual Transactions

Points to be covered in each and every notification:

(1) Name of authority/agency responsible under the Arrangement for making notifications.
(2) Reference number.
(3) "We are notifying in accordance with the provisions of Paragraph 6(a) the following transaction for which the credit terms are not in conformity with the guidelines as modified with effect of . . . ."
(4) Not applicable.

(5) Country or buyer/borrower.

(6) Name and location of buyer/borrower.

(7) Nature of project/goods to be exported; location of project.

(8) Value of the project or contract: *both* total value *and* value of exporter's national share.*

(9) (If relevant) specify any minimum contract value.*

(10) Credit terms which the agency listed in (1) above intends to support:

    (a) cash payments;

    (b) repayment term (including starting point of credit, frequency of installments for repaying principal amount of credit, and whether these installments will be equal in amount);

    (c) interest rate;

    (d) support from local costs (including the total amount of local costs expressed as a percentage of the total value of goods and services exported, the terms of repayment, and the nature of the support to be given).

(11) Dates concerning the prior commitment:

    (a) Date on which this prior commitment was made.

    (b) Date of expiry of this prior commitment.

(12) Any other relevant information (including references to related cases).

---

* Values shall be stated in terms of value ratings in accordance with the following scale in Special Drawing Rights (SDRs):

Category I	up to	600,000 SDRs	
Category II	from	600,000 to	1,000,000 SDRs
Category III	from	1,000,000 to	2,000,000 SDRs
Category IV	from	2,000,000 to	3,000,000 SDRs
Category V	from	3,000,000 to	5,000,000 SDRs
Category VI	from	5,000,000 to	7,000,000 SDRs
Category VII	from	7,000,000 to	10,000,000 SDRs
Category VIII	from	10,000,000 to	20,000,000 SDRs
Category IX	from	20,000,000 to	40,000,000 SDRs
Category X	exceeding	40,000,000 SDRs	

Annex C   Standard Form for Notifications Required Under Paragraph 9

Points to be covered in each and every notification:

(1) Name of authority/agency responsible under the Arrangement for making notifications.

(2) Reference number.

(3) "We are notifying the following transaction/line of credit which we regard as:

    ☐ an outright derogation *or*

    ☐ a derogation justified by the need to match *or*

    ☐ a permissible deviation or required notification as provided for in the Arrangement—(indicate nature)."

(4) "Accordingly we are hereby:
- ☐ initiating the prior notification and discussion procedure *or*
- ☐ giving prior notification without discussion *or*
- ☐ giving prompt notification."

(5) Country of buyer/borrower.

(6) Name and location of buyer/borrower.

(7) Nature of project/goods to be exported; location of project.

(8) Value of line of credit/project/contract: *both* total value *and* value of exporter's national share.*

(9) In the case of a line of credit, specify any minimum contract value.*

(10) Credit terms which the agency listed in (1) above intends to support (or has supported):
- (a) cash payments;
- (b) repayment term (including starting point of credit, frequency of installments for repaying principal amount of credit, and whether these installments will be equal in amount);
- (c) interest rate;
- (d) support for local costs (including the total amount of local costs expressed as a percentage of the total value of goods and services exported, the terms of repayment, and the nature of the support to be given).

(11) Justification, if any, for instance:
- (a) matching—specify competition to be matched.
- (b) permissible deviation or required notification as provided for in the Arrangement—(indicate nature).

(12) Any other relevant information including references to related cases and in the case of a tied aid credit:
- (a) the name of authority/agency responsible for the concessional aid loans;
  the nature of project/goods to be exported under the loan; the location of the project;
  the terms of the aid loan (as under item 10 above);
- (b) the overall grant element of the tied aid credit calculated in accordance with Paragraph 12(a)(4).

---

* Values shall be stated as follows:

(a) The exact value in the denominated currency for a line of credit, and for any minimum contract value under a line of credit.

(b) The value of an individual project or contract should be disclosed in terms of value ratings in accordance with the following scale in Special Drawing Rights (SDRs):

Category I	up to	600,000 SDRs	
Category II	from	600,000 to	1,000,000 SDRs
Category III	from	1,000,000 to	2,000,000 SDRs
Category IV	from	2,000,000 to	3,000,000 SDRs
Category V	from	3,000,000 to	5,000,000 SDRs
Category VI	from	5,000,000 to	7,000,000 SDRs
Category VII	from	7,000,000 to	10,000,000 SDRs
Category VIII	from	10,000,000 to	20,000,000 SDRs
Category IX	from	20,000,000 to	40,000,000 SDRs
Category X	exceeding	40,000,000 SDRs	

Annex D List of Participants

Australia
Austria
Canada
European Economic Community[1]
Finland
Japan
New Zealand

Norway
Portugal
Spain
Sweden
Switzerland
United States

---

1. Composed of the following Member States: Belgium, Denmark, France, Germany, Greece, Ireland, Italy, Luxembourg, Netherlands, United Kingdom.

Country Classification
(Preliminary List)

Category I Countries

Andorra
Australia
Austria
*Bahrain
Belgium
Bermudas
*Brunei
Canada
*Czechoslovakia
Denmark
(a) Continental zone;
(b) Overseas zone:
    Greenland
    Faroe Islands
Finland
France
(a) European zone;
(b) Overseas Departments:
    Guadeloupe
    Guyane
    Martinique
    Réunion
    St. Pierre and Miquelon
(c) Overseas Territories:
    French Antarctic Territories
    New Caledonia
    French Polynesia
    Wallis and Futuna

(d) Mayotte
*German Democratic Republic
German Federal Republic
*Gibraltar
*Greece
Iceland
*Ireland
*Israel
Italy
Japan
Kuwait
Libya
Liechtenstein
Luxembourg
Monaco
Netherlands
(a) European zone
New Zealand
(a) Continental zone;
(b) Overseas zone:
    Cook Islands
    Ross Dependency
    Nive
    Tokelau
Norway
Qatar
San Marino
Saudi Arabia

*Spain
Sweden
Switzerland
United Arab Emirates:
    Abu Dhabi
    Ajman
    Dubai
    Fujairah
    Ras al Khaimah
    Sharjah
    Umm al Qaiwain
United Kingdom
(a) European zone;

(b) Overseas zone:
    1. Central America and the Caribbean:
        Virgin Islands
United States
(a) Member States of the Union;
(b) Overseas zone:
    Guam
    Northern Marianas
    Puerto Rico
    American Samoa
    American Virgin Islands
*USSR
Vatican

Note: The status of a few dependencies is not yet determined.

* Countries now in Category I that were in Category II before July 6, 1982.

Category II Countries

*Albania
*Algeria
Antigua
Argentina
Bahamas
Barbados
*Belize
*Botswana
*Brazil
Bulgaria
*Chile
*Colombia
*Costa Rica
*Cuba
Cyprus
*Dominican Republic
*Ecuador
*Fiji
Gabon
*Guatemala
Hungary
Iraq
Iran
*Ivory Coast
*Jamaica
*Jordan
*Kiribati
*Korea (North)
*Korea (South)
*Lebanon

*Malaysia
Malta
*Mauritius
*Mexico
*Mongolia
*Morocco
Namibia
Nauru
Netherlands
(b) Overseas zone:
    Dutch West Indies
*Nigeria
Oman
Panama
*Papua-New Guinea
*Paraguay
*Peru
Poland
Portugal
(a) European zone:
    Azores
    Madeira
*(b) Overseas zone:
    Macao
Romania
*Seychelles (without Diego Garcia)
Singapore
South Africa
St. Lucia
Surinam

*Syria
*Taiwan
.Trinidad and Tobago
*Tunisia
*Turkey
Trust Territory of the Pacific Islands (US)
United Kingdom
(b) Overseas zone:
   1. Central America and the Caribbean

*Montserrat
4. Asia
   Hong Kong
*Uruguay
Venezuela
West Indian Associated States:
   *St. Kitts-Nevis
Yugoslavia

---

* Countries now in Category II that were in Category III before July 6, 1982.

Category III Countries

Afghanistan
Angola
Bangladesh
Benin (ex Dahomey)
Bhutan
Bolivia
Burma
Burundi
Cameroon
Canton and Enderbury
   (United Kingdom/United States)
Cape Verde Islands
Central African Republic
Chad
China
Comoro Islands
   (Anjouan, Grande Comore, Moheli)
Congo
Djibouti
Dominica
Egypt
El Salvador
Ethiopia
Gambia
Ghana
Grenada
Guinea
Guinea-Bissau
Guinea-Equatorial
Guyana
Haiti
Honduras
India
Indonesia

Kampuchea (ex Cambodia)
Kenya
Laos
Lesotho
Liberia
Madagascar
Malawi
Maldives
Mali
Mauritania
Mozambique
Nepal
New Hebrides (France/United Kingdom)
Nicaragua
Niger
Pakistan
Philippines
Rwanda
São Tomé and Principe
Senegal
Sierra Leone
Solomon Islands
Somalia
Sri Lanka
St. Vincent and the Grenadines
Sudan
Swaziland (Ngwane)
Tanzania
Thailand
Togo
Tonga
Tuvalu (ex Ellice)
Uganda
United Kingdom

(b) Overseas zone:
    1. Central America and the Caribbean:
        Anguilla
        Cayman Islands
        Turks and Caicos
    2. South America:
        Falklands
    3. Africa:
        St. Helena (and dependencies)
    4. Asia:
        British Territory of the
        Indian Ocean
    5. Oceania:
        Central and Southern Line

Gilbert
Pitcairn
Solomon
Upper Volta
Vanuatu
Vietnam
West Indian Associated States:
    Anguilla
Western Samoa
Yemen, Arab Republic (Sanaa)
Yemen, Peoples Democratic Republic
Zaire
Zambia
Zimbabwe

H US Department of Commerce Methodology in the European Steel Cases as Set Forth in Appendices 2, 3, and 4 to the Final Affirmative Countervailing Duty Determinations, Certain Steel Products from Belgium (47 Fed. Reg. 39316, *et seq.*, 7 September 1982)

Appendix 2   Methodology

Several basic issues are common to many of the countervailing duty investigations of certain steel products, initiated by the Department of Commerce ("the Department") on February 1, 1982; *e.g.*, government assistance through grants, loans, equity infusions, loss coverage, research and development projects and labor programs. This appendix describes in some detail the general principles applied by the Department when dealing with these issues as they arise within the factual contexts of these cases. This appendix, although substantially the same as Appendix B to the preliminary determinations (see "Preliminary Affirmative Countervailing Duty Determinations, Certain Steel Products from Belgium" (47 FR 26300)), does describe some changes in methodology. These changes are principally in the areas of the discount rate value, funds for loss coverage, and preferential loans with deferred principal payment.

Grants

Petitioners alleged that respondent foreign steel companies have received numerous grants for various purposes. Under section 771(5)(B) of the Tariff Act of 1930, as amended (the Act) (19 U.S.C. 1677(5)(B)), domestic subsidies are countervailable where they are "provided or required by government action to a *specific* enterprise or industry, or group of enterprises or industries" (emphasis added).

The legislative history of Title VII of the Act states that where a grant is "tied" to—that is, bestowed specifically to purchase—costly pieces of capital equipment, the benefit flowing from the grant should be allocated in relation to the useful life of that equipment. A subsidy for capital equipment should also be "front loaded" in these circumstances; that is, it should be allocated more heavily to the earlier years of the equipment's useful life, reflecting its greater commercial impact and benefit in those years.

Prior to these cases on certain steel products, the Department allocated the face value of the grant, in equal increments, over the appropriate time period. For large capital equipment, we used a period of half the useful life of the equipment purchased with the grant. In each year we countervailed only that year's allocated portion of the total grant. For example, a hypothetical grant of $100 million used to purchase a machine with a 20-year life would have been countervailed at a rate of $10 million per year (allocated over the appropriate [product] group) for 10 years, beginning in the year of receipt.

This allocation technique has been criticized for not capturing the entire subsidy because it ignores the fact that money has a changing value as it moves through time. It has been argued that $100 million today is much more valuable to a grant recipient than $10 million per year for the next 10 years since the present value (the value in the initial year of receipt) of the series of payments is considerably less than the amount if initially given as a lump sum. We agree with this position and, as indicated in the preliminary determinations, have now changed our methodology of grant subsidy calculation to reflect this agreement. As long as the present value (in the year of grant receipt) of the amounts allocated over time does not exceed the face value of the grant, we are consistent with both our domestic law and international obligations in that the amount countervailed will not exceed the total net subsidy.

The present value of any series of payments is calculated using a discount rate. As indicated in the preliminary determinations, we considered using each company's weighted cost of capital at the time of the grant receipt as the appropriate measure of the time value of its funds. However, we lacked sufficient information to do so for the preliminary determinations, and instead used the national cost of long-term corporate debt as a substitute measure of a company's discount rate.

Between the preliminary and final determinations we reviewed the comments and suggestions of various interested parties, principally contained in the pre- and post-hearing briefs. In addition, we sought the advice of an outside consultant with experience in the field of international investment banking.

On the basis of those discussions and that advice, we determine that the most appropriate discount rate for our purposes is the "risk-free" rate as indicated by the secondary market rate for long-term government debt (in the home country of the company under investigation). The basic function of the "present value" exercise is to allocate money received in one year to other years. Domestic interest rates perform this function within the context of an economy. The foundation of a country's interest rate structure is usually its government debt interest rate (the risk-free rate). All other borrowings incorporate this risk-free rate and add interest overlays reflecting the riskiness of the funded investment.

When we allocate a subsidy over a number of years it is not the intention of the Department to comment on nor judge the riskiness of the project undertaken with the subsidized funds nor to evaluate the riskiness of the company as a whole. Nor do we intend to speculate how a project would have been financed absent government involvement in the provision of funds. Rather, we simply need a financial mechanism to move money through time so as to accurately reflect the benefit the company receives. We believe that the best discount rate for our purposes is one which is risk-free and applicable to all commercial actors in the country. Therefore we have used in these final determinations long-term government debt rates (as reflected in the secondary market) as our discount rates.

For costly pieces of capital equipment, we believe that the appropriate time period over which to allocate the subsidy is its entire useful life. In the past, we allocated the subsidy over only half the useful life in order to "front load" the countervailing duties, thereby complying with the legislative intent of the Act. However, so long as we allocate the subsidy [in] equal nominal increments over the entire useful life, it will still be effectively front loaded in real terms (as long as a positive discount rate is used) since money tomorrow is less valuable than money today.

For these steel investigations we have allocated a grant over the useful life of equipment purchased with it when the value of that grant was large (in these investigations, greater than $50 million) and specifically tied to pieces of capital equipment. Where the grant was small (generally less than one percent of the company's gross revenues and tied to items generally expensed in the year purchased, such as wages or purchases of materials), we have allocated the subsidy solely to the year of the grant receipt. We construe that a grant is "tied" when the intended use is known to the subsidy giver and so acknowledged prior to or concurrent with the bestowal of the subsidy. All other grants—the vast majority of those involved in these investigations—are allocated over 15 years, a period of time reflecting the average life of capital assets in integrated steel mills. The 15-year figure is based on Internal Revenue Service studies of actual experience in integrated mills in the U.S. Furthermore, we understand that a 15-year period is a common useful life adopted in some of the countries involved in these investigations for steel capital equipment. We are using this time period because we sought a uniform period of time for these allocations and this was the best available estimate of the average steel asset life worldwide. We could not calculate the average life of capital assets on a company-by-company basis, since different accounting principles, extraordinary write-offs, and corporate reorganizations yield extremely inconsistent results.

Funds to Cover Losses

In the preliminary determinations we did not distinguish funds (either in the form of untied grants or equity infusions) which were available for loss coverage from other grants or equity infusions. We stated that since grants used for loss coverage often have the effect of helping keep the firm in business, we allocated the benefit over 15 years when the funds were in the form of a grant or used the appropriate equity methodology when the loss coverage funds were in the form of equity.

Between the preliminary and final determinations we reviewed the comments and suggestions of various interested parties principally contained in the pre- and post-hearing briefs. In addition, we sought the advice of the Department's accountants and outside consultants on the issue of the appropriate treatment of funds for loss coverage. Based on the above, we have decided not to allocate the subsidy benefit of these funds over time but rather to allocate them to the year of receipt.

We have done so on the advice of these accounting experts in order to reflect the nature of the liabilities giving rise to the loss. These liabilities are generally the basic costs of operations (*e.g.*, wages, materials, certain overhead expenses)—items generally expensed in the year incurred.

We calculated the magnitude of the loss from a company's financial statements beginning with net earnings and working back to a cash based measure of loss. We allocated to loss coverage only those grants and equity infusions which were truly cash inflows into the company and were actually available to cover losses.

In any instances in which infusions were specifically tied to loss coverage, we allocated such infusions accordingly. If infusions were not so tied, we concluded that general, untied grants were a more logical source of loss coverage assistance than general infusions of equity. Accordingly, in making these allocations we treated funds available from grants as the primary source of monies available for loss coverages. We allocated funds available from equity infusions to loss coverage only in the absence of grants or after available grant funds had been exhausted.

We generally treated such cash inflows as covering the losses incurred in the previous fiscal year and allocated the subsidy benefit flowing from such funds to the year of their receipt. An exception was made where losses were continually covered by a special arrangement with the government (as through the use of a special reserve account). In these cases, since the funds for loss coverage were accessible as the losses arose, we allocated the benefit flowing from these funds to the period in which the losses occurred.

Loans and Loan Guarantees for Companies Considered Creditworthy

In these investigations, various loan activities give rise to subsidies. The most common practices are the extension of a loan at a preferential interest rate where the government is either the actual lender or directs a private lender to make funds available at a preferential rate, or where the government guarantees the repayment of the loan made by a private lender. The subsidy is computed by comparing what a company would pay a normal commercial lender in principal and interest in any given year with what the company actually pays on the preferential loan in that year. We determine what a company would pay a normal commercial lender by constructing a comparable commercial loan at the appropriate market rate (the benchmark) reflecting standard commercial terms. If the preferential loan is part of a broad, national lending program, we use a national average commercial interest rate as our benchmark. If the loan program is not generally available—like most large loans to respondent steel companies—the benchmark used instead, where available, is the company's actual commercial credit experience (*e.g.*, a contemporaneous loan to the company from a private commercial lender). If there were no similar loans, the national commercial loan rate is used as a substitute rate. Finally, where a national loan-based interest rate was not available, an average industrial bond rate was used as best evidence.

For loans denominated in a currency other than the currency of the country concerned in an investigation, the benchmark is selected from interest rates (either national or company-specific, as appropriate) applicable to loans denominated in the same currency as the loan under consideration (where possible rates on loans in that currency in the country where the loan was obtained; otherwise, loans in that currency in other countries, as best evidence). The appropriate discount rate remains the risk-free rate as indicated by the secondary market rate for long-term debt obligations of the company's home country government. The subsidy for each year is calculated in the foreign currency and converted at an exchange rate applicable for each year.

After calculating the payment differential in each year of the loan, we then calculated the present value of this stream of benefits in the year the loan was made, using the risk-free rate (as described in the grants section of this appendix) as the discount rate. In other words, we determined the subsidy value of a preferential loan as if the benefits had been bestowed as a lump-sum grant in the year the loan was given. This amount was then allocated evenly over the life of the loan to yield the annual subsidy amounts. We did so with one exception: where the loan was given expressly for the purchase of a costly piece of capital equipment, the present value of the payment differential was allocated over the useful life of the capital equipment concerned.

For loans not tied to capital equipment with mortgage-type repayment schedules, this methodology results in annual subsidies equivalent to those calculated under the methodology previously employed by the Department whereby we considered the difference in total repayments in each year of a loan's lifetime to be the subsidy *in that year*. For loans with constant principal repayments (*i.e.*, declining total repayments), loans with deferral of repayments, and loans for costly capital equipment, the present value method results in even allocations of the subsidy over the relevant period. This effectively front loads countervailing duties on these loan benefits in the same manner as grants are front loaded.

A loan guarantee by the government constitutes a subsidy to the extent the guarantee assures more favorable loan terms than for an unguaranteed loan. The subsidy amount is quantified in the same manner as for a preferential loan.

If a borrowing company preferentially received a payment holiday from a government lending institution or from a private lender at government direction, an additional subsidy arises that is separate from and in addition to the preferential interest rate benefit. The subsidy value of the payment holiday is measured in the same manner as for preferential loans, by comparing what the company pays versus what it would pay on a normal commercial loan in any given year. A payment holiday early in the life of a loan can result in such large loan payments near the end of its term that, during the final years, the loan recipient's annual payments on the subsidized loan may be greater than they would have been on an unsubsidized loan. By reallocating the benefit over the entire life of the loan through the present value methodology described above, we avoid imposing countervailing duties in excess of the net subsidy. Where we have sufficient evidence that deferral of principal is a normal and/or customary lending practice in the country under consideration, then such deferral has not been considered as conferring an additional subsidy.

Loans and Loan Guarantees for Companies Considered Uncreditworthy

In a number of cases petitioners have alleged that certain respondent steel companies were uncreditworthy for purposes of these investigations at the time they received preferential loans or guarantees, and that they could not have obtained any commercial loan without government intervention.

Where the company under investigation has a history of deep or significant continuing losses, and diminishing (if any) access to private lenders, we generally agree with petitioners. This does not mean that such a company is totally uncreditworthy for all purposes. Virtually all companies can obtain limited credit, such as short-term supplier credits, no matter how precarious their financial situation. Our use of the term uncreditworthy means simply that the company in question would not, in our view, have been able to obtain comparable loans in the absence of government intervention. Accordingly, in these situations neither national nor company-specific market interest rates provide an appropriate benchmark since, by definition, an uncreditworthy company could not receive loans on these or any terms without government intervention. Nor have we been able to find any reasonable and practical basis for selecting a risk premium to be added to a national interest rate in order to establish an appropriate interest benchmark for companies considered uncreditworthy. Therefore, we continue to treat loans to an uncreditworthy company as an equity infusion by or at the direction of the government. We believe this treatment is justified by the great risk, very junior status, and low probability of repayment of these loans absent government intervention or direction. To the extent that principal and/or interest is actually paid on these loans, we have adjusted our subsidy calculation (which is performed using our equity methodology, *infra*) to reflect this. We have applied the rate of return shortfall (the amount by which the corporate rate of return on equity was lower than the national average rate of return on equity) only to the outstanding principal in the year which we are measuring subsidization. From this amount, we additionally subtract any interest and fees paid in that year. Moreover, in no case do we countervail a loan subsidy to a creditworthy or uncreditworthy company more than if the government gave the principal as an outright grant.

Short-Term Credits

In all our cases, even the most financially troubled companies regularly receive short-term supplier credits. We find this type of debt different and easily distinguishable from the loans previously discussed. Where a company receives private-sourced supplier credits we have found this countervailable only where they were at preferential rates because of explicit government direction.

Where supplier credits were not given at a preferential rate directed by the government, we found no subsidy. Furthermore, since the risk involved and basis for giving supplier credits is qualitatively different than for long-term loans, we did not interpret the presence of supplier credits as an indication of creditworthiness.

Equity

Petitioners allege that government purchases of equity in respondent steel companies confer a subsidy equal to the entire amount of the equity purchased. Many respondents claim that such equity purchases are investments on commercial terms, and thus do not confer subsidies on these companies.

It is well settled that neither government equity ownership *per se*, nor any secondary benefit to the company reflecting the private market's reaction to government ownership, confers a subsidy. Government ownership confers a subsidy only when it is on terms inconsistent with commercial considerations. An equity subsidy potentially arises when the government makes equity infusions into a company which is sustaining deep or significant continuing losses and for which there does not appear to be any reasonable indication of a rapid recovery. If such losses have been incurred, then we consider from whom the equity was purchased and at what price, or, absent a market value for the equity, we examine the rate of return on the company's equity and compare it to the national average rate of return on equity.

If the government buys previously issued shares on a market or directly from shareholders rather than from the company, there is no subsidy to the company. This is true no matter what price the government pays, since any overpayment benefits only the prior shareholders and not the company.

If the government buys shares directly from the company (either a new issue or corporate treasury stock) and similar shares are traded in a market, a subsidy arises if the government pays more than the prevailing market price. The Department has a strong preference for measuring the subsidy by reference to a market price. This price, we believe, rightly incorporates private investors' perceptions of the company's future earning potential and worth. To avoid any effect on the market price resulting from the government's purchase or speculation in anticipation of such purchase, we used for comparison a market price on a date sufficiently preceding the government's action. Any amount of overpayment is treated as a grant to the company.

It is more difficult to judge the possible subsidy effects of direct government infusions of equity where there is no market price for the shares (as where, for example, the government is already sole owner of the company). Government equity participation can be a legitimate commercial venture. Often, however, as in many of these steel cases, equity infusions follow massive or continuing losses and are part of national government programs to sustain or rationalize an industry which otherwise would not be competitive. We respect the government's characterization of its infusion as equity in a commercial venture. However, to the extent in any year that the government realizes a rate of return on its equity investment in a particular company which is less than the average rate of return on equity investment for the country as a whole (thus including returns on both successful and unsuccessful investments), its equity infusion is considered to confer a subsidy. This "rate of return shortfall" (the difference between the company's rate of return on equity and the national average rate of return on equity) is multiplied by the original equity infusion (less any loss coverage to which the equity funds were applied) to yield the annual subsidy amount. Under no circumstances do we countervail in any year an amount greater than that which is calculated treating the government's equity infusion as an outright grant.

Forgiveness of Debt

Where we have found that the government has forgiven an outstanding debt obligation, we have treated this as a grant to the company equal to the outstanding principal at the time of forgiveness. Where outstanding debt has been converted into equity (*i.e.*, the government receives shares in the company in return for eliminating debt obligations of the company), a subsidy may result. The existence and extent of such subsidies are determined by treating the conversions as an equity infusion in the amount of the remaining principal of the debt. We then calculate the value of the subsidy by using our equity methodology, *supra*.

Coal Assistance

As explained in detail in our notice of "Final Affirmative Countervailing Duty Determinations: Certain Steel Products from the Federal Republic of Germany" in this issue of the

Federal Register, we have analyzed and verified aspects of the German coal subsidy program as it applies to steel. Based upon the verified information in the records of these investigations, we have determined that this particular program does not confer a countervailable benefit on either non-German or German steel producers.

As we stated in some of the preliminary determinations reached on June 10 (47 Fed. Reg. 26309), benefits bestowed upon the manufacturer of an input do not flow down to the purchaser of that input if the sale is transacted at arm's length. In an arm's length transaction, the seller generally attempts to maximize its total revenue by charging as high a price and selling as large a volume as the market will bear.

The application of these principles to sales of German coal outside Germany is as follows. The records of these transactions show that the prices charged for subsidized German coal outside Germany certainly do not undercut the freely available market prices. Therefore, non-German purchasers of subsidized German coal do not benefit from German coal subsidies.

In support of this conclusion, we note that if non-German steel producers did benefit from German coal subsidies, they would attempt to purchase German coal rather than unsubsidized coal from other sources including the US, since there are no restrictions on their ability to do so. The fact that they purchase significant amounts of unsubsidized US coal indicates that the subsidies on German coal do not flow to non-German consumers.

Moreover, it is extremely unlikely that the German government would significantly subsidize non-German coal consumers unless compelled to do so by obligations with respect to the European Communities. Since there is no evidence of such obligation, we conclude that the German government is not in fact subsidizing non-German coal consumers.

For these reasons, we determine that non-German steel producers do not benefit from subsidization of German coal.

Research and Development Grants and Loans

Grants and preferential loans awarded by a government to finance research that has broad application and yields results which are made publicly available do not confer subsidies. Programs of organizations or institutions established to finance research on problems affecting only a particular industry or group of industries (*e.g.*, metallurgical testing to find ways to make cold-rolled sheet easier to galvanize) and which yield results that are available only to producers in that country (or in a limited number of countries) confer a subsidy on the products which benefit from the results of the research and development (R&D). On the other hand, programs which provide funds for R&D in a wide range of industries are not countervailable even when a portion of the funds is provided to the steel sector.

Once we determine that a particular program is countervailable, we calculate the value of the subsidy by reference to the form in which the R&D was funded. An R&D grant is treated as an "untied" grant; a loan for R&D is treated as any other preferential loan.

Labor Subsidies

To be countervailable, a benefit program for workers must give preferential benefits to workers in a particular industry or in a particular targeted region. Whether the program preferentially benefits some workers as opposed to others is determined by looking at both program eligibility and participation. Even where provided to workers in specific industries, social welfare programs are countervailable only to the extent that they relieve the firm of costs it would ordinarily incur—for example, a government's assumption of a firm's normal obligation partially to fund worker pensions.

Labor-related subsidies are generally conferred in the form of grants and are treated as untied grants for purposes of subsidy calculation. Where they are small and expensed by the company in the year received, we likewise allocated them only to the year of receipt. However, where they were more than one percent of gross revenues we allocated them over a longer period of time generally reflecting the program duration.

Comments by Parties to the Proceeding

Grants

COMMENT 1

Respondents claim that the present value methodology used in these investigations does not provide a "real" value and that it is based on assumptions which do not reflect the realities of the manufacture of the products under investigation.

DOC POSITION

The present value concept is a widely recognized tool of financial and economic analysis. Its utility and necessity derive from the fact that money has a time value. For example, as stated above, $100 million today is considerably more valuable to a grant recipient than $10 million per year for the next ten years. To move a sum of money through time without adjusting the nominal amount would seriously understate the value of the money. So long as the present value (in the year of grant receipt) of the amounts allocated over time does not exceed the face value of the grant, the amount countervailed will not exceed the total net subsidy.

COMMENT 2

Petitioners argue that grants and preferential loans awarded expressly for the benefit of products not under investigation should also be considered countervailable benefits for the product(s) under investigation. They base their argument on the contention that aid thus received is fungible.

DOC POSITION

We have not viewed all aid received for any purpose by companies under investigation as fungible, and thus equally beneficial to all products made by the company in question. While the law clearly envisions reaching subsidies which benefit the product under investigation indirectly, as well as directly, it would distort and be inconsistent with the clear intent of the statute, as reflected in its legislative history, to allocate to products under investigation any portion of benefits clearly tied to products not under investigation. This is particularly true since we are compelled to allocate fully to the products actually being investigated any subsidies directly tied to them. To allocate tied subsidies fully to the products to which they are tied and simultaneously to allocate any part of the same subsidies to other products would result in double-counting, which would be inconsistent with both the Act and the Subsidies Code.

Loans and Loan Guarantees for Companies Considered Creditworthy

COMMENT 3

Petitioners allege that the Department has improperly applied offsets to preferential loan benefits by subtracting principal and interest paid on the loans in 1981 and by the use of a "grant cap."

DOC POSITION

In calculating the subsidy flowing from a loan to a creditworthy company, we must take account of principal and interest paid because, by definition, the subsidy is equal to the difference between what the company actually paid and what it should have paid as expressed by our benchmark loan.

When calculating the subsidy arising from a loan to an uncreditworthy company, for purposes of these final determinations, we recognize the effect on the subsidy of principal and interest repayments. We believe it is appropriate to apply the rate of return shortfall only to the outstanding principal in 1981, recognizing that prior year paybacks of principal are equivalent to disinvestment of equity. We then subtract interest paid in 1981 not because it is an offset but because it is a legitimate payment on their debt. These funds, therefore, are not available to benefit the company and should not be included in the gross subsidy amount.

We apply a "grant cap" (the amount of subsidy allocated to the year of review if the original principal had been received as a grant rather than a loan) because a loan cannot be worth more to a company than an outright grant of the same amount. This capping by the grant amount is not distortive, nor does it lead to an understatement of the subsidy because the grant methodology incorporates in it the time value of money.

COMMENT 4

Petitioner argues that respondent steel companies, absent government backing, would not have been able to borrow at "average" or "national" rates and that our use of these rates as benchmarks understates the subsidy.

DOC POSITION

When the Department is measuring the subsidy flowing from a preferential loan, the benchmark rate (our choice of rate which we believe reflects the unsubsidized cost of debt to which this firm has access) of first choice is one which reflects loans of similar magnitude and duration actually received by the firm in a private transaction without government influence. In those situations where comparable private loans were not available, this benchmark rate had to be estimated. We chose a national average rate since we had no evidence a given firm was perceived as more or less risky than the "average" firm by lenders at the time the preferential loan was received.

Loans and Loan Guarantees for Companies Considered Uncreditworthy

COMMENT 5

Respondents argue that the Department's method of determining uncreditworthiness was unfair in that it was based [on] hindsight which was not available to a lender at the time it made a decision whether or not to provide funds to a company.

DOC POSITION

As outlined in each of these notices in which uncreditworthiness was found, all determinations as to the creditworthiness of firms were based upon information reasonably available to a potential lender *at the time a loan was given*. For instance, although British Steel Corporation's financial results for the fiscal year 1976/77 were a major factor pointing to uncreditworthiness, in our final determinations we found it uncreditworthy beginning in fiscal year 1977/78, when the lending company could reasonably have known of the weakness of the firm's financial position in the preceding year. This approach allows the potential lender time to evaluate its behavior in light of the changed circumstances of the firm.

COMMENT 6

Petitioners state that to the extent that the Department calculates the benefit from a loan to an uncreditworthy company as if it were a grant, failure to use a discount rate to reflect the greater risk of providing credit to uncreditworthy firms which could not borrow at any average or national rate leads to an understatement of the true value of the subsidy received.

DOC POSITION

We disagree. Although we used the average national debt rate as the discount rate in the preliminary determinations, we did not intend this to imply that the choice of the discount rate reflected our speculation as to the riskiness of the company or the cost of alternative financing. As discussed in the *Grants* section of this appendix, we view the discount rate as simply a financial tool to move money through time. It is not our intention to embed in this rate any project-specific risk or company risk. For this reason we are changing the discount rate used in these final determinations to the risk-free rate, a rate equally accessible to all companies (including very risky ones) country-wide.

COMMENT 7

Petitioners allege that the provision of supplier credit to an uncreditworthy company constitutes a subsidy because once the firm becomes uncreditworthy, absent government support, suppliers would require cash payments instead of extending credit.

DOC POSITION

Government subsidization of a company does not convey benefits over and above the actual subsidy (whose measurement is described earlier in this appendix). Private supplier credits are countervailable only where they are at a preferential rate due to government guarantees or direction. There is no benefit from rates and terms the petitioner may argue to be preferential resulting from the private sector's commercial reaction to government ownership.

Regarding the presence of supplier credits as it affects the Department's evaluation of creditworthiness, since the risk involved and the basis for giving supplier credits is qualitatively different than for long-term loans, we did not interpret the presence of supplier credits to be an indication of creditworthiness.

COMMENT 8

Petitioners argue that the Department should have used the methods for calculating benefits to uncreditworthy firms which they proposed in their petitions. US Steel had proposed the "Sossin method" and counsel for the Five proposed a "creditworthiness proxy."

DOC POSITION

The Sossin method, developed by Howard B. Sossin of the Columbia University Business School, represents an attempt to adapt the Option Pricing Model for use in valuing loan guarantees. This model has applications in analysis of a number of complex financial transactions, such as measuring the effects of risk on the value of corporate debt, the effect of mergers, acquisitions, scale expansions and spin-offs on the relative values of debt and equity claims on a firm, and the value of commodity options, forward contracts and futures contracts.

The Department decided not to use the Sossin method for several reasons. First, the model itself contains numerous simplifying assumptions which cast doubt on its applicability and non-arbitrariness for these investigations. In addition, we would have had to adapt the method greatly to make it applicable on a firm-specific basis, posing an immense administrative burden given the information and technical expertise necessary to calculate the benefits.

The "creditworthiness proxy" method proposed by counsel for the Five would use the cash-to-debt service ratio for each firm. If a firm under investigation for possible subsidization is granted a loan when its ratio is less than 2:1, the amount by which its income is below twice the debt payments would be considered to be a subsidy in that year.

This method also poses several serious problems. First, as there is no direct relationship in this formula between specific benefits and the calculation of subsidies, its use by the Department would place it in violation of both the Act and the GATT Subsidies Code. Second the ratio chosen is arbitrary and does not represent a reasonable benchmark for uncreditworthiness across companies. While a 2:1 ratio may indeed be a common "rule of thumb" popular in American banking circles, we have no compelling evidence indicating its applicability and general use in each of the nine countries examined in these cases. We cannot and do not intend to impose American standards of banking practice upon foreign firms.

Equity

COMMENT 9

Respondents claim that our determination whether government infusions of equity into a steel company are consistent with commercial considerations must take into account the fact that private stockholders or creditors of companies in financial trouble often inject additional capital into the company in the hopes of recouping as much of their original investment as possible.

DOC POSITION

We agree that government ownership of a company does not confer a subsidy *per se,* and that the government may act based upon commercial considerations with respect to decisions whether to increase its equity ownership in a firm. Our determination whether such action is in fact on terms consistent with commercial considerations necessarily depends upon the facts of each individual case. In our investigations of certain steel products from Luxembourg, for example, we found an instance in which private persons as well as the government invested equity in MMR-A, a Luxembourg steel company which arguably was in financial trouble. In view of the participation of those private persons, we considered the government's action not to confer a subsidy because it was consistent with commercial considerations as evidenced by the private purchasers' behavior. In other situations, however, we think that, based upon the facts presented, no stockholder, governmental or private, would have injected further equity into the company based upon commercial considerations.

COMMENT 10

Respondents argue that the use of an average rate of return on equity in a country sets an unfair standard for measuring the rate of a cyclical industry like steel, because such a standard by definition will indicate subsidization in the troughs of the cycles.

DOC POSITION

The Department's methodology does not penalize firms simply because they are in the trough of a cycle. A subsidy only arises when an original equity investment is unsound, *i.e.,* inconsistent with commercial considerations.

We recognize that steel is a cyclical industry, but neither the Act nor the GATT Subsidies Code immunize subsidies to a company in the bottom of its cycle from countervailing duties. Unsubsidized companies in cyclical industries survive by using revenues from the peak of a cycle to offset the years in the cycle's trough.

COMMENT 11

Respondents argue that premiums paid over market value of stock are common in takeovers where the objective is to gain control of a firm, and that therefore such a payment should not be considered a subsidy.

DOC POSITION

Payment of a premium over market value for stock (including where the objective is to gain control) is a special commercial circumstance which occurs under fairly unique conditions. Payment of such a premium for stock in a firm in weak or distressed financial condition is unlikely, for as a firm approaches near-bankruptcy, its market price of equity falls to the liquidation value range. Furthermore, it is highly unlikely for a control premium to be warranted when the government is the sole bidder for the troubled firm. Therefore in the absence of compelling evidence that a premium payment by a government was warranted and motivated by commercial conditions (as evidenced, for example, by similar competing private bids), the Department has a strong preference for measuring a subsidy by the difference between the market price of the stock and the stock price paid by the government. We believe that this market price correctly incorporates private investors' perceptions of the worth of the stock.

Coal Assistance

COMMENT 12

Petitioners reject the Department's view that a party receiving a benefit on the production of its merchandise is not assumed to share that benefit with an unrelated purchaser. They maintain that a party may market its products at a lower price than it would be able to charge absent the subsidy in order to secure or hold on to a larger share of the market, and thus to increase its profitability by realizing lower unit costs and increased unit sales.

DOC POSITION

We agree that there is more than one way to seek to achieve maximum profitability. In these investigations, in fact, assistance to coal has been provided to enable some coal companies to sell below their cost of production. However, the German coal companies do not sell below the prices of coal as sold in Europe and elsewhere. In fact, German steel producers are required to pay a slight but significant premium for German coal. Under these circumstances, we disagree with petitioners' argument that German steel companies are indirectly subsidized through German coal subsidies.

COMMENT 13

Petitioners argue that the Department should have considered German coal subsidies to subsidize all steel companies purchasing that coal, both German and non-German, because the intent of the coal subsidies is to stabilize coal supplies to the ECSC steel industry and to insure that industry against the risk of adverse price developments on the world market. Petitioners claim that without this subsidized coal, the ECSC steel companies would have had to pay higher world market prices.

DOC POSITION

For the reasons indicated *supra,* we believe that it is too speculative to consider possible effects on world prices for coal in the hypothetical absence of German subsidization of its coal industry. However, if coal prices would rise in that event, we believe that they would rise throughout the world. We do not believe that prices would rise more for European purchasers of coal rather than non-Europeans.

As also indicated in detail *supra,* we believe that the real economic effect of German subsidies is to penalize, not to assist, German steel companies. As a result of the German coal policy, German steel companies are required to pay a slight premium above the world market price for their coal purchases. Non-German purchasers of subsidized German coal similarly receive no demonstrable price advantage.

COMMENT 14

Petitioners argue that the ECSC and the FRG government, through an "intense program of coordinated subsidy financing," have assisted the German coal and steel industries in order to sustain production at cost efficient levels, in significant part by producing for export.

DOC POSITION

Although the arguments seem ambiguous, we believe that petitioners mean to imply that the German and ECSC coal assistance programs constitute an export subsidy for steel. If so, then we disagree, since in both cases coal assistance is provided without the establishment of any condition concerning the exportation of steel produced using that coal.

COMMENT 15

Petitioners object to the Department's alleged requirement that a subsidy on an input be demonstrated to confer an unfair competitive advantage. Petitioners imply that in so doing, the Department is usurping the jurisdiction of the International Trade Commission which is authorized to determine injury.

DOC POSITION

Under the Act, the Department is required to determine whether respondents have received subsidies within the meaning of the Act. To do so, the Department seeks to determine whether or not respondents have received directly or indirectly an economic benefit. Whereas this is relatively easy in the case of the direct bestowal of a grant, it is quite difficult with regard to indirect subsidies allegedly conferred through the subsidization of inputs used in a final product. In this more complex area, we believe it is required for the Department to consider whether there is an economic benefit to foreign manufacturers of the final product of subsidies bestowed on manufacturers of an individual input. This is quite distinct from the ITC's determination whether imports of the final product into the United States injure a US industry. The Department therefore disagrees with petitioners on this issue.

COMMENT 16

Respondents argue that they pay more for their coal than would otherwise be the case if the FRG coal assistance program and import restrictions were not in effect.

DOC POSITION

As indicated in detail *supra*, we agree. Largely on this basis we have determined that FRG assistance to its coal producers does not indirectly subsidize either FRG steel producers or non-German steel producers.

COMMENT 17

Respondents argue that [even] if Germany entered the world market for coal and world coal prices were driven up, they would be the same to all purchasers.

DOC POSITION

We have no firm basis upon which to predict possible effects on world coal prices by cessation of German subsidization of its coal industry.

Labor Subsidies

COMMENT 18

Respondents argue that the Department's treatment of labor programs is not related to possible benefits to the production of the products under investigation, but rather is based on whether programs benefit employees or employers.

Labor programs are countervailable only to the extent that they relieve the company of some or all of its labor-related obligations. Direct assumption of a cost of production, such as absorption in whole or in part of the wage bill, is indeed a subsidy on the products produced by the company.

Appendix 3 Programs Administered by Organizations of the European Communities

I. The ECSC

On April 8, 1965, the three separate European communities—the European Coal and Steel Community ("ECSC"), the European Economic Community ("EEC"), and the European Atomic Energy Community—signed a treaty to merge into the European Communities ("EC"). Article 9 of the merger treaty established the Commission of the European Communities to take the place of the High Authority of each of the formerly independent institutions. The merger became effective in 1967.

The ECSC itself was established by the Treaty of Paris in [1951] to modernize production, improve quality, and assure a supply of coal and steel to the member countries. The Treaty of Paris governs all programs intended directly to affect the steel industry. Funds for these programs flow from two sources: (1) ECSC borrowings on international capital markets, and (2) the ECSC budget.

A. ECSC Programs Determined to Be Subsidies

1. ECSC LOAN GUARANTEES

Under Article 54 of the Treaty of Paris, the ECSC is authorized to guarantee loans from commercial lenders to coal and steel companies. Since these guarantees are intended specifically for the steel industry, we find the resulting benefits to be countervailable. The countervailable benefit is the difference between the interest rate charged by private lenders to commercial customers in the ordinary course of business and the rates available with an ECSC loan guarantee.

2. PROGRAMS FUNDED THROUGH ECSC BORROWINGS

Because of its quasi-governmental nature, the ECSC is able to raise funds at interest rates lower than those which would be available on commercial terms to European steel companies. When the ECSC relends these borrowed funds to a company without increasing the interest rate, any difference between the lower interest rate passed on and the rate otherwise available to the steel company in the commercial financial market (the "benchmark") is a benefit to the company. For this reason, we determine that ECSC loans raised through capital market funding are countervailable insofar as they offer preferential interest rates (*i.e.*, rates which would not be available on commercial terms) to steel companies. Consequently, any loan to a steel company involving ECSC funds borrowed on international capital markets, provided under an ECSC assistance program, confers countervailable benefits to the extent that the loan is made at a preferential interest rate.

a.   ECSC Industrial Investment Loans

Article 54 of the Treaty of Paris authorizes the ECSC to provide loans to steel companies in member countries for reducing production costs, increasing production, or facilitating product marketing. Loans provided under this program are funded exclusively from ECSC borrowings on world capital markets. For the reasons discussed above, we reaffirm our preliminary determination that this program confers countervailable benefits to loan recipients to the extent that the interest rates are preferential.

b.   ECSC Industrial Reconversion Loans

Under Article 56 of the Treaty of Paris, the ECSC provides loans to companies or public authorities for investments in new non-steel ventures in regions of declining steel industry activity. The goal of the loan program is to provide employment for former steel workers in new industries. In our preliminary determinations, we concluded that this program did not appear to benefit steel companies. Therefore, we preliminarily determined that it does not confer subsidies on steel.

However, since our preliminary determinations, we verified that some industrial reconversion loans have been made for use in the iron and steel industry. Therefore, to the extent that such loans were made for steel production, they confer benefits on steel production generally if the loans were untied, and on steel production generally or possibly on particular types of steel products if the loans were tied. Since this program is funded exclusively from ECSC borrowings on world capital markets, we determine, for the reasons discussed above, that these loans to steel producers confer subsidies on steel to the extent that the interest rates are preferential.

3.   PROGRAMS FUNDED THROUGH THE ECSC BUDGET

With respect to programs funded by the ECSC budget, we preliminarily determined that they do not confer countervailable benefits because for 1971–1980 (the last year for which complete data were available) their total amount did not exceed total levies collected from coal and steel producers within the ECSC member states.

Since our preliminary determinations were made we have verified the following facts about the composition of the ECSC budget:

☐ From 1952 through 1956, the ECSC budget was financed exclusively through producer-generated levies.

☐ From 1971 through 1977, the ECSC budget was financed exclusively through producer-generated levies, funds generated from unexpended levies, and other relatively small amounts obtained from steel companies (*e.g.*, fines and late payment fees).

☐ Since 1978, the ECSC budget has been financed by member state contributions to the following extent: 1978, 18.80%; 1979, 16.27%; 1980, 16.22%; and 1981, 20.05%.

☐ Beginning in 1982, the member state contribution is to be used exclusively to fund one particular program, rehabilitation aid provided under Article 56 of the Treaty of Paris.

We continue to believe that programs funded by the ECSC budget through 1977 do not confer countervailable benefits.

However, since 1978 member state contributions have constituted a portion of the ECSC budget. Upon consideration of this newly available information, for the years 1978–1981 we believe it is more reasonable to assume that programs funded by the ECSC budget are subsidized to the extent that the budget derives from member state contributions. To assume to the contrary (*i.e.*, that *all* program assistance derives from levies and levy-generated funds, and that member state contributions are used *exclusively* for expenses other than program assistance) is inappropriate unless member state contributions are expressly earmarked for particular programs. Accordingly, we have treated as a subsidy in 1981 a proportion of the benefits received under programs funded by the ECSC budget.

Although not relevant to the subsidies being determined and measured in these investigations, we note that for 1982, member state contributions have been so earmarked for one particular program rehabilitation aid provided under Article 56 of the Treaty of Paris. If all member state contributions are expended in funding that program, other programs would then be funded by levies and levy-generated funds, not from member state contributions.

a. *ECSC Labor Assistance and Rehabilitation Aids*

Under Article 56 of the Treaty of Paris, the ECSC provides matching grants to member states for programs that assist former steelworkers currently unemployed or in training for a new trade. In our preliminary determinations, we implied that this assistance may confer a subsidy on the industries for which workers are newly trained, but decided that it does not confer a subsidy on steel. However, upon verification we learned that some, though not all of this assistance has been provided to retrain workers for other jobs *within* the *same* industry; and to cover worker unemployment and early retirement expenses, for some of which the employing companies may have been legally responsible. If such assistance has been provided to retrain steel workers for new steel jobs, and/or to cover unemployment and early retirement expenses which steel companies would normally be required to pay, then it benefits the steel industry. To that extent, it is considered a subsidy in these investigations.

This program is funded from the ECSC budget. In view of the relatively small amounts concerned, we are expensing this assistance in the year it was received. Therefore, for purposes of these investigations, we are capturing only assistance provided in the period for which we are measuring subsidies (generally 1981). In 1981, member state contributions accounted for 20.05% of the ECSC budget. Therefore, for the reasons discussed above, 20.05% of the assistance under Article 56 provided to steel companies for programs benefitting steel production in 1981 constitutes a subsidy on the manufacture or production of steel.

b. *ECSC Interest Rebates*

(1) Certain Article 54 industrial investment loans qualify for further interest reductions depending on whether they are for environmental projects, removal of industrial bottlenecks, promotion of steel industry competitiveness, or stabilization of coal production. The rebates generally reduce the interest expense for the first five years of the loan repayment schedule by three percentage points. The interest rebates are paid out of the ECSC budget. Therefore, we preliminarily determined that this program does not confer countervailable benefits.

(2) Certain Article 56 industrial reconversion loans qualify for further interest reductions. Like the interest rebates on Article 54 industrial investment loans, these rebates are paid out of the ECSC budget. In a few instances the underlying loans made under Article 56 benefit the products under investigation. (Most Article 56 loans were given to non-steel ventures).

For the reasons discussed above, we have now determined that both these programs described under (1) and (2) above confer countervailable benefits to the extent that the ECSC budget in the year concerned is financed by member state contributions. In view of the relatively small amounts concerned, we are expensing this assistance in the year it was received. Therefore, for purposes of these investigations, we are capturing only assistance provided in the period for which we are measuring subsidies (generally 1981). In 1981 member state contributions accounted for 20.05% of the ECSC budget. Therefore, for the reasons discussed above, 20.05% of the assistance provided in 1981 constitutes a subsidy on the manufacture and production of steel.

c. *ECSC Coal and Coke Aids*

Petitioners have alleged that ECSC assistance to coal producers in EC countries constitutes an indirect benefit to steel producers purchasing that coal. In our preliminary determinations, we did not consider this program to confer countervailable benefits on steel. The basis for this conclusion was our understanding at that time that the ECSC coal aids are bestowed on all types of coal, used widely throughout many industries. Therefore, we reasoned, the ECSC aids on coal cannot be intended to benefit, and do not benefit, the steel industry in particular; consequently, under section 771(5)(B) of the Act, there is no subsidy to steel in these circumstances, even though steel producers in ECSC countries purchase some ECSC coal.

However, we have verified that, in fact, certain ECSC coal aids are bestowed exclusively on coking coal, which is used primarily by the iron and steel industry. Nonetheless, we continue to believe, for other reasons, that the ECSC coking coal aids do not confer a countervailable benefit on the manufacture or production of steel. We have no evidence that ECSC-assisted coking coal is sold to ECSC steel companies at prices less than the prices for other freely available coking coal produced in ECSC member countries but not assisted by the ECSC, or for freely available coking coal produced outside ECSC member countries. To the contrary, we have verified information that some coking coal is sold in Europe at prices below the prices of ECSC-assisted coking coal. This indicates that the coking coal subsidies to coal producers are not being passed along, in whole or in part, to steel producers purchasing that coal in arm's length transactions.

Where a subsidized coal producer and a steel producer are related companies, it is reasonable to question whether, in fact, the transfer price for coking coal is established on an arm's length basis. In general, our tests for whether the prices for coking coal charged to a related company were established on an arm's length basis include: (1) Whether the coal producer sold to its related steel producer at the prevailing price, and/or (2) whether the coal [producer] sold to its related steel producers and all other purchasers of coking coal at the same price.

B. ECSC Programs Determined Not to Confer Subsidies

1. ECSC HOUSING LOANS FOR WORKERS

Article 54(2) of the Treaty of Paris authorizes the ECSC to provide loans for residential housing for steel workers. In some cases these loan funds are provided directly to steel companies which relend them to their workers. In other cases, they are administered through financial institutions or housing authorities. These loans for the construction or purchase of homes are at highly concessionary one percent interest rates.

The preferential ECSC housing loans provide substantial benefits directly to steel workers. In our preliminary determinations, we assumed that they also indirectly benefit the employer steel companies by relieving them of certain labor wage costs. However, we have been unable to substantiate and verify this assumption. To the contrary, in many of the countries concerned there is a high rate of unemployment, which reduces upward pressure on wages. Moreover, we found no instance in which wage rates varied—depending upon the presence or absence of these mortgage loans to steel workers—either within a steel company or between steel companies. Since we have no firm basis for determining that the wage demands of steel workers would be responsive to the (non)availability of this mortgage subsidy, we conclude that the hypothetical benefits to their employer steel companies are too remote to be considered subsidies to these companies.

2. ECSC R&D GRANTS AND LOANS

a. Article 55 of the Treaty of Paris provides funding in the form of grants for up to 60 percent of an R&D project's cost. The projects must be for improvements in the production and use of coal and steel. On the ground that these grants are funded exclusively from the ECSC budget, we preliminarily determined that this program does not confer countervailable benefits.

For the reason discussed above, we have decided to consider ECSC budget-funded programs as countervailable to the extent that the ECSC budget for the year concerned is financed by member state contributions. Nevertheless, because we have evidence that the results of the R&D are made publicly available, we have determined that this program does not confer countervailable benefits.

b. With respect to ECSC R&D loans—also made under Article 55 of the Treaty of Paris—we preliminarily determined that additional information was necessary: *i.e.*, information as to how widely available the results of research are, and from which source the funds derive. Upon verification, we learned that the results of the research are made publicly available. Therefore, we determine that ECSC R&D loans do not confer countervailable benefits.

II. The European Investment Bank

The European Investment Bank ("EIB") was created by the Treaty of Rome establishing the EEC to fund projects that serve regional needs in Europe. Article 130 of the Treaty of Rome authorizes the EIB to make loans and guarantee financial projects in all sectors of the economy. These projects include the provision of funds to further the development of low income regions. Funds are drawn from debt instruments floated on world capital markets and from investment earnings. Because EIB loans are designed by charter to serve regional needs, we find them to be countervailable where the interest rate is less than the rate which would have been available commercially from a private lender without government intervention.

The EIB also provides loan guarantees to companies in EC member countries. Again, because this guarantee was available in some but not all regions, it is regarded as a countervailable benefit. These determinations remain unchanged from our treatment of this issue in our preliminary determinations.

III. European Regional Development Fund

The European Regional Development Fund was established by the EEC to provide funding in the form of low-interest loans for industrial projects designed to correct regional imbalances within the EEC. The fund also awards interest subsidies on EIB loans.

We preliminarily determined that this program is not used by any of the manufacturers, producers or exporters for any of the products from countries under investigation. We confirmed this determination through our verification, so it remains unchanged.

Comments Received from Parties to the Proceeding

COMMENT 1

Petitioners argue that persistent ECSC subsidization of its coal industry has resulted in severe trade distortions.

DOC POSITION

Perhaps ECSC subsidization of coal has distorted trade in coal. However, we do not believe that it has distorted trade in steel.

COMMENT 2

Petitioners argue that subsidization of European coal industries, both by the ECSC and member governments, prolongs the operation of uneconomic European coal producers. They maintain that if the subsidies were discounted, the coal industries would collapse, and that coal prices would rise around the world unevenly depending upon which industries had captive sources of coking coal.

DOC POSITION

Even assuming *arguendo* that subsidization of the European coal industry by the ECSC and member states does significantly depress world market prices, we can only speculate that cessation of this subsidization would have similar price effects in that the price of *all* coal would rise. We are not sure whether and to what extent these price effects would differ depending upon which industries had captive sources of coking coal. We note that in addition to the existence of captive sources, another key factor would be the potential entrance into world commerce of alternate suppliers of coal and their effect on market prices.

COMMENT 3

Petitioners argue that the Department did not correctly interpret the term "subsidy" and did not countervail ECSC assistance programs to the extent that funds for these programs were derived from the ECSC budget.

DOC POSITION

As explained in detail *supra*, the Department has determined that ECSC budget-funded assistance is potentially countervailable to the extent that the ECSC budget for the year concerned is financed by Member State contributions.

Whether or not we found particular ECSC budget-funded assistance to confer a subsidy on the products subject to these investigations depended on other factors as well. For example, we found that the results of ECSC funded research and development projects were made publicly available, and therefore did not confer subsidies.

COMMENT 4

Petitioners argue that ECSC budget-funded assistance programs confer subsidies on ECSC steel producers despite levy financing of the budget, because the ECSC must borrow massively to supplement the levies.

DOC POSITION

As indicated in detail *supra,* to the extent that the ECSC budget in a given year is funded by Member State contributions, we consider any assistance funded generally from the budget in that year to be partially countervailable. Also as explained *supra,* to the extent that ECSC loans financed by ECSC borrowings on world capital markets are made to steel companies at preferential interest rates, we believe that they are countervailable.

COMMENT 5

Petitioners maintain that ECSC budget-funded programs confer subsidies even when financed through levy funding; that the ECSC borrows to finance its programs; and there is no delineation between the programs funded by the levy and the programs funded by debt.

DOC POSITION

As explained in detail *supra,* we agree that many (though not all ECSC) budget-funded programs confer some countervailable benefit if the assistance was provided in a year in which the ECSC budget was derived partially from Member State contributions. Where it can be shown that ECSC budget-funded assistance derives exclusively from levies and levy-generated funds ultimately derived from steel producers, no countervailable benefit is conferred upon steel producers by the return to them of their own funds. However, for the period of investigation we did not find that any program's funding derived [or] could be shown to derive exclusively from levy financing.

COMMENT 6

Petitioners argue that all ECSC readaptation and retraining assistance to steel producers confers a subsidy. They argue that the steel companies did not supply sufficient information regarding their obligations to employees who received this assistance, and that the Department preliminarily allowed an offset not permitted by law.

DOC POSITION

With respect to ECSC assistance for readaptation and retraining of workers provided under Article 56, we have verified whether (and the extent to which) this assistance relieved recipient steel companies of expenses that they would otherwise have been obliged to incur, and whether the retraining was for jobs related to steel production. Based upon verified information, we have concluded that most ECSC assistance provided under Article

56 does not confer countervailable benefits in these investigations. In the [few] instances where it does (either because assistance was provided for retraining for jobs related to steel production or because the companies were relieved thereby of an obligation they otherwise would have been required to fulfill), we have found subsidies.

COMMENT 7

Respondents argued that the ECSC's credit rating is based not upon its quasi-governmental nature, but on an ECSC reserve fund financed by levies and levy-generated funds, and by the fact that the ECSC represents the financial resources of the steel industry in ECSC Member States. Since the ECSC credit rating is based upon the levy, ECSC loans to steel companies at rates below those which an individual firm could obtain represent solely a partial return to the company of its levies.

DOC POSITION

For the reasons indicated *supra,* we agree that a program benefitting the steel industry which is financed exclusively by ECSC levies and levy-generated funds does not confer a countervailable benefit on steel production since it merely returns to companies funds which they originally paid in. However, based upon our examination and analysis of the ECSC budget, we are unable to conclude that the reserve fund is composed exclusively of levies and levy-generated funds. In any event, we do not agree that the ECSC's credit rating is based solely upon its reserve fund, or upon the implied backing of European steel industries. We think its credit rating necessarily reflects, at least in part, its quasi-governmental nature. Therefore, we disagree with the arguments tendered by respondents on this issue.

COMMENT 8

Respondents claim that ECSC worker rehabilitation programs, such as retraining or early retirement payments, do not confer a subsidy on steel because the benefits go to workers no longer employed in steel production. Even if those benefits are funnelled through a steel company, that company simply serves as a conduit of funds and receives no benefits from them.

DOC POSITION

For the reasons indicated *supra,* we agree that retraining assistance does not confer a benefit on a steel company so long as the job for which a worker is being retrained is a non-steel job. Likewise the payment of early retirement benefits does not confer a subsidy on a steel company unless it is thereby relieved of a cost that it would otherwise be required to assume. As indicated *supra,* the facts in these cases in some instances require, in applying the above principle, that a subsidy be found to exist.

COMMENT 9

Respondents claim that the ECSC and Member State production and marketing aids for the coal industry do not subsidize steel because the prices for European coal paid by the steel industry are not below world market prices. Thus, these aids do not affect steel trade and do not distort normal conditions of competition.

DOC POSITION

[DOC position missing in original Federal Register text.]

COMMENT 10

Respondents claim that ECSC aid to coal under Articles 54 and 56 does not confer subsidies on steel because the aid is given through ECSC loans made on commercial terms or grants financed from levy-generated funds.

DOC POSITION

We agree that ECSC assistance to coal companies in Member States does not subsidize steel companies in Member States, but for other reasons set forth *supra*. In general, we note that where ECSC assistance can be satisfactorily shown to be exclusively financed by levy-generated funds, the Department would agree that it is not countervailable. Likewise, any ECSC loans which were made on truly commercial terms would not include a preferential interest rate, and therefore not confer a subsidy.

COMMENT 11

Respondents argued that ECSC budget-funded programs are financed exclusively from producer levies and levy-generated funds, and not from Member State contributions which allegedly are used exclusively for non-steel purposes.

DOC POSITION

In our preliminary determinations, we did not consider ECSC budget-funded assistance to confer subsidies on steel production in view of our conclusions that total ECSC levies and levy-generated funds historically have exceeded all ECSC assistance provided to steel companies. However, in these final determinations, based upon verification and more thorough understanding of the ECSC budget, we have determined that it cannot be shown that ECSC budget-funded assistance derives exclusively from levies or levy-generated funds. Although such funding accounts for the vast majority of ECSC budget-funded assistance (79.95% in 1981), a portion of this assistance (20.05% in 1981) derives from Member State contributions. As explained *supra*, where it can be shown that Member State contributions are clearly earmarked for particular programs and that Member State contributions are fully expended in such programs, then we agree that the other programs are fully funded by levies on steel production and thus not countervailable. For example, we noted that beginning with 1982, all Member State contributions appear earmarked for one particular ECSC program, industrial investment assistance. Provided that verification during the annual review process confirms this, then for 1982 we could not consider ECSC budget-funded assistance—other than this one program—to confer subsidies on steel.

COMMENT 12

Respondents claim that certain rehabilitation measures by the European Communities and Member States do not subsidize steel because the aid is used to promote sectors other than steel.

To the extent that assistance is provided to sectors other than steel, we agree. For example, with respect to ECSC industrial reconversion loans, we have found that for the most part, they do not provide subsidies for steel production. Likewise with respect to certain ECSC labor assistance programs, for the most part we found that this assistance benefitted industrial sectors other than steel; *e.g.*, a grant bestowed and used to train former steel workers to assume new jobs unrelated to the steel sector, even if the training program is administered by a steel company.

COMMENT 13

Respondents claim that measures adopted by the European Communities and Member States under the Community Steel Policy to restructure the steel industry within Europe do not subsidize steel because they are bestowed for the purpose of reducing the manu-facture, production and export of steel in Europe.

DOC POSITION

Where a restructuring program involves subsidies to steel products and the US industry is injured by the import of such products, we are required by our domestic law, and authorized by the Subsidies Code, to impose appropriate countervailing duties. All subsidies are indisputedly subject to countervailing duties under Part I of the Subsidies Code, provided only that injury is determined and that procedural requirements are satisfied. The provisions of Article 11 of Part II of the Code—stating that the Code "does not intend to restrict the right of any signatory to use (domestic) subsidies to achieve. . .policy objectives (including) to facilitate the restructuring, under socially accepted conditions, of certain sectors"—do not preclude the United States from imposing countervailing duties in appropriate cases. Part II of the Code, including Article 11, merely establishes that domestic subsidies for restructuring are not precluded by the Code. A code member retains the right under Part I to impose countervailing duties on imports, injurious to its industry, which benefit from domestic subsidies aimed at restructuring. Further, while restructuring aids may be devoted in part to reducing production capacity, such aids, by making the recipient steel companies more efficient and relieving them of significant financial burden, are of unquestioned benefit to the continuing production of steel aid [sic] and, as such, confer subsidies.

COMMENT 14

Respondents argued that the Department's preliminary determinations to countervail ECSC housing loans were based on supposition rather than on evidence in the record.

DOC POSITION

We agree. For the reasons set forth in detail *supra*, we were not able to find sufficient evidence that the provision of ECSC housing loans to steel workers had any measurable effect upon the steel companies by whom such workers were employed. Therefore, in these final determinations, we have decided not to consider ECSC housing loans as conferring a countervailable benefit on steel companies.

Some petitioners have claimed that ECSC assistance funded by producer levies confers subsidies wherever an individual producer receives assistance in excess of levies paid by that producer.

DOC POSITION

As explained elsewhere in this Appendix and in Appendix 4, we do not consider ECSC budget-funded programs to confer subsidies on steel producers to the extent such programs are funded by producer levies. Our view is not affected by the degree to which individual producers which have contributed levies do not participate in or receive benefits from these programs. The producers probably should be viewed as pooling their resources, for their mutual benefit, to create and maintain certain programs which are available to all the producers. Over the relatively short period for which we were measuring subsidies, certain producers have more frequent occasion to use certain programs than other producers. In principle, this is not different from other types of cooperative behavior, such as jointly funded risk insurance, under which not all participants will have identical claims although all contribute equal premiums. Accordingly, insofar as producer levies are directly funding the programs, no subsidies can be said to arise from any apparent short-term disparity of benefits received.

COMMENT 16

Some petitioners have challenged our preliminary determinations that benefits received under certain ECSC programs funded by ECSC coal and steel producers levies were not subsidies. They assert that, in reaching such a determination, we have allowed offsets from subsidies in a manner contrary to law.

DOC POSITION

We disagree with petitioners' characterization of the determination on this issue. To the extent that we have viewed benefits received under ECSC programs as attributable or allocable to producer levies, we find that no gross subsidy exists. No "offset" or reduction in subsidy amount is made, because the recipients of the program benefits are directly funding those benefits themselves and thus the ECSC is not creating a subsidy. This is not analogous to governmental benefits funded by general tax revenues, for the levies in question are—and since the inception of the levy system have been—strictly earmarked for the ECSC budget-funded programs for which they are, in fact, used. In reality, the ECSC acts as no more than the administrator and distributor of levies collected, and does so under such tight restrictions as to preclude the conclusion that the return of levy funds to the producers gives rise to a gross subsidy.

COMMENT 17

Petitioners reject the Department's view that a party receiving a benefit on the production of its merchandise is not assumed to share that benefit with an unrelated purchaser. They maintain that a party may market its products at a lower price than it would be able to charge absent the subsidy in order to secure or hold on to a larger share of the market, and thus to increase its profitability by realizing lower unit costs and increased unit sales.

We agree that there is more than one way to seek to achieve maximum profitability. In these investigations, in fact, assistance to coal has been provided to enable some coal companies to sell below their cost of production. However, the German coal companies do not sell below the prices of coal as sold in Europe and elsewhere. In fact, German steel producers are required to pay a slight but significant premium for German coal. Under these circumstances, we disagree with petitioners' argument that German steel companies are indirectly subsidized through German coal subsidies.

COMMENT 18

Petitioners argue that the ECSC and the FRG government, through an "intense program of coordinated subsidy financing," have assisted the German coal and steel industries in order to sustain production at cost efficient levels, in significant part by producing for export.

DOC POSITION

Although the arguments seem ambiguous, we believe that petitioners mean to imply that the German and ECSC coal assistance programs constitute an export subsidy for steel. If so then we disagree, since in both cases coal assistance is provided without the establishment of any condition concerning the exportation of steel produced using that coal.

COMMENT 19

Respondents argue that even if Germany entered the world market for coal and world coal prices were driven up, they would be the same to all purchasers.

DOC POSITION

We have no firm basis upon which to predict possible effects on world coal prices by cessation of German subsidization of its coal industry.

COMMENT 20

Petitioners object to the Department's alleged requirement that a subsidy on an input be demonstrated to confer an unfair competitive advantage. Petitioners imply that in so doing, the Department is usurping the jurisdiction of the International Trade Commission which is authorized to determine injury.

DOC POSITION

Under the Act, the Department is required to determine whether respondents have received subsidies within the meaning of the Act. To do so, the Department seeks to determine whether or not respondents have received directly or indirectly an economic benefit. Whereas this is relatively easy in the case of the direct bestowal of a grant, it is quite difficult with regard to indirect subsidies allegedly conferred through the subsidization of inputs used in a final product. In this more complex area, we believe it is required for the Department to consider whether there is an economic benefit to foreign manufacturers of the final product of subsidies bestowed on manufacturers of an individual input. This is quite distinct from the ITC's determination whether imports of the final product into the United States injure a US industry. The Department therefore disagrees with petitioners on this issue.

Appendix 4   General and GATT-Related Issues

General Issues

COMMENT 1

Some of the petitioners contend that many of the conclusions in our preliminary determinations were erroneous insofar as they found that particular programs of general applicability and availability within a country do not give rise to domestic subsidies. They assert that subsidies must be found to exist from any governmental programs providing benefits, regardless whether those programs are generally available.

DOC POSITION

Section 771(5) of the Act, in describing governmental benefits which should be viewed as domestic subsidies under the law, clearly limits such subsidies to those provided "to a specific enterprise or industry, or group of enterprises or industries." We have followed this statutory standard consistently, finding countervailable only the benefits from those programs which are applicable and available only to one company or industry, a limited group of companies or industries, or companies or industries located within a limited region or regions within a country. This standard for domestic subsidies is clearly distinguishable from that for export subsidies, which are countervailable regardless of their availability within the country of exportation. We view the word "specific" in the statutory definition as necessarily modifying both "enterprise or industry" and "group of enterprises or industries." If Congress had intended programs of general applicability to be countervailable, this language would be superfluous and different language easily could and would have been used. All governments operate programs of benefit to all industries, such as internal transportation facilities or generally applicable tax rules. We do not believe that the Congress intended us to countervail such programs. Further, our conclusion is supported by the clear Congressional intent that "subsidy" be given the same meaning as "bounty or grant" under section 303 of the Act. Never in the history of the administration of this law or section 303 of the Act has a generally available program providing benefits to all production of a product, regardless whether it is exported, been considered to give rise to a subsidy or a bounty or grant. In enacting the Trade Agreements Act of 1979, Congress specifically endorsed that interpretation of section 303. Finally, the fact that the list of subsidies in section 771(5) is not an exclusive one in no way compels the conclusion that domestic benefits of general availability must or can be considered subsidies. Indeed, in view of the statute and its legislative and administrative history, we doubt that we are free to treat such generally available benefits of domestic programs as subsidies; certainly we are not compelled to do so.

Petitioners contend that our preliminary negative determinations regarding critical circumstances were erroneous. They allege that, in determining whether imports were "massive" within the meaning of section 703(e) of the Act, we acted inconsistently with the law and past practice by examining imports in the period subsequent, rather than prior, to initiation of these cases, thereby denying petitioners the ability to provide adequate documentation to support their allegations. They also disagree with our characterization of the import levels as not being massive.

DOC POSITION

This issue is moot. Under section 703(e) of the Act, in order to determine that critical circumstances exist, we must determine that "(A) the alleged subsidy is inconsistent with the Agreement, and (B) there have been massive imports of the class or kind of merchandise which is the subject of the investigation over a relatively short period." Section 355.29(e) of the Commerce Regulations (19 C.F.R. 355.29(e)) on critical circumstances provides, *inter alia,* that we will determine "whether the alleged subsidy is an *export* subsidy inconsistent with the Agreement" (emphasis added). For purposes of this law, then, under existing regulations, a subsidy may be viewed as inconsistent with the Agreement only if it is an export subsidy. Since all of the subsidies determined to exist in the cases in which we are issuing final determinations in these notices are domestic, rather than export, subsidies, we are precluded from determining that critical circumstances exist in any of these cases.

COMMENT 3

Some respondents claim that our adoption in the preliminary determinations of a number of new methodologies for the ascertainment and calculation of subsidies was procedurally deficient as a matter of law. They assert that these new methodologies conflict with past practice and, therefore, cannot be implemented in any case before rulemaking procedures have been completed, which procedures would have to provide published notice of proposed changes and opportunity to comment.

DOC POSITION

We do not agree that the methodologies employed in these cases have to be the subject of rulemaking procedures or that such methodologies could not be employed until such procedures have been completed. The adoption of these methodologies is neither rulemaking nor adjudication within the meaning of the Administrative Procedure Act. Some of the methodologies employed cannot be said to be in conflict with any past practice under sections 701 or 303 of the act, for they address issues and factual situations which, to the best of our knowledge, have not previously been encountered. Others, such as the present value methodology of valuing money over time, do represent a departure from past methods for determining the existence or size of subsidies. However, the prior practice, with which the methodology used in these cases has been alleged to be inconsistent has never been prescribed in the Commerce Regulations or, before that, the Customs Regulations.

Decisions as to the use of such methodologies are not matters requiring rulemaking procedures, but are questions of policy left to the judgment and discretion of the Department and decided on a case-by-case basis, applying the law, as we understand its requirements and intent, to the facts of each case. While the Department could prescribe such methodologies in its regulations, we have not chosen to do so. Unless and until that occurs, no rulemaking procedures can be considered necessary before changing methodologies. At the outset of these investigations, respondents may have anticipated that certain prior methodologies would be employed in place of ones actually used, but they have no legal right to the maintenance of such prior practices.

Further, our preliminary determinations and subsequent disclosures to all interested parties fully explained these methodologies and each respondent took advantage of its opportunity to comment upon them, both orally and in writing. We took all of these comments fully into account in reaching our final determinations. As such, each respondent fully participated in the decision-making process to the extent of its legal rights, and cannot properly be viewed as having been denied any such rights. Moreover, there is no substantial evidence in the record in any of these cases which would support a conclusion that the respondent governments, when establishing or administering the programs investigated, relied to their detriment on prior methodologies. Indeed, it would be difficult to conclude that these governments in any way considered the possible consequences under the US countervailing duty law before taking the actions which resulted in countervailable benefits to the products under investigation.

COMMENT 4

Some respondents contend that many of the benefits received by the steel companies investigated, such as aids for restructuring, are directly analogous to procedures and benefits common to bankruptcy proceedings. As such, they are consistent with normal commercial considerations and should not be considered subsidies.

DOC POSITION

No respondent has furnished us any evidence that it has been subject to formal bankruptcy proceedings, or that its restructuring or other procedures actually employed remotely resemble normal bankruptcy procedure in its country. In the absence of any such evidence the contention of respondents is entirely too speculative a basis upon which to base a determination in these cases.

COMMENT 5

Respondents allege that the use of the present value methodology is inconsistent with US law.

DOC POSITION

The use of the present value methodology is fully consistent with the countervailing duty law. Section 701(a) states that where the Department determines there to be subsidization and, where appropriate, the ITC determines there to be injury, ". . .then there shall be imposed upon such merchandise a countervailing duty. . .equal to the amount of the net subsidy." So long as the present value (in the year of grant receipt) of the amounts allocated over time does not exceed the face value of the grant, the amount countervailed will not exceed the total net subsidy.

COMMENT 6

The European Communities (EC) assert that in order for a countervailable subsidy to exist under the GATT, there must be a charge on the public account. In support of this contention, the EC cites in particular item (l) of the Illustrative List of Export Subsidies (the List), included as an annex to the Agreement on Interpretation and Application of Articles VI, XVI and XXIII of the General Agreement on Tariffs and Trade (the Code). Item (l) of the List defines as an export subsidy, "Any other charge on the public account constituting an export subsidy in the sense of Article XVI of the General Agreement."

DOC POSITION

Item (l) does not limit the definition of subsidy to a charge on the public account, but rather makes clear that such a charge is included in the universe of subsidies which constitute on their face prohibited export subsidies. Items (c) and (d) of the List show that preferential treatment for exports, without regard to a charge on the public account, can also constitute a subsidy on its face. These items define as subsidies:

(c) Internal transport and freight charges on export shipments, provided or mandated by governments, on terms more favorable than for domestic shipments.

(d) the delivery by governments or their agencies of imported or domestic products or services for use in the production of exported goods, on terms or conditions more favorable than for delivery of like or directly competitive products or services for use in the production of goods for domestic consumption, if (in the case of products) such terms or conditions are more favorable than those commercially available on world markets to their exporters.

Item (l), cited by the EC, derives from the original illustrative list of subsidies of 1960, which represented an agreed interpretation of Article XVI:4 of the GATT. However, the Department notes that this list also includes items (c) and (d) of the current List. Since the negotiation of Article XVI:4 in the 1950's, there has never been a consensus on an interpretation such as that advanced by the EC. Rather, it has been generally accepted that the range of activities covered by the term subsidy as used in the GATT is quite broad, including charges on the public account as well as certain activities which do not necessarily involve such a charge.

COMMENT 7

The EC argues that subsidies other than export subsidies cannot be considered counter-vailable under the Code unless such subsidies "[a]dversely affect the conditions of normal competition. In the absence of any such distortion, subsidies, other than export subsidies, are recognized as important instruments for the promotion of social and economic policy objectives against which no action is envisaged by the Code." The EC further argues that the Department considered regional aids countervailable "[w]ithout taking into consid-eration any disadvantages incurred by companies having to operate in economically retarded and remote areas . . . . This approach does not take into account, that under GATT and the Code countervailable subsidies are only those, which adversely affect the conditions of normal competition." In support of this contention the EC cites Article 11 of the Code, "Subsidies other than export subsidies."

The language of Article 11 does not prejudice the right of any signatory to the [C]ode to countervail against non-export subsidies. The language of the Article is the result of compromise between the United States and the EC at the time of the negotiation of the Code; the United States proposed to include an illustrative list of domestic subsidies, while the EC position was that such subsidies should not be considered countervailable. The Department notes that, while no list of domestic subsidies was incorporated *per se* in the Code, examples of such subsidies are included in Article 11. In contrast, the position of the EC was not adopted, as no such prohibition regarding the countervailability of domestic subsidies appears in the Code. The fact that certain subsidies are not prohibited by the Code is not relevant to a determination as to whether such subsidies confer a countervailable benefit in a specific case.

In addition, the Department notes that Article 11:3 of the Code states, "[t]he above form of [non-export] subsidies are normally granted either regionally or by sector." Article 11:2 states:

> Signatories recognize, however, that subsidies other than export subsidies. . . may cause or threaten to cause injury to a domestic industry of another signatory or serious prejudice to the interests of another signatory or may nullify or impair benefits accruing to another signatory under the General Agreement, in particular where such subsidies would adversely affect the conditions of normal competition. Signatories shall therefore seek to avoid causing such effects through the use of subsidies. In particular, signatories when drawing up their policies and practices in this field in addition to evaluating the essential internal objectives to be achieved, shall also weigh, as far as practicable, possible adverse effects on trade. They shall also consider the conditions of world trade, production (e.g. price, capacity utilization etc.) and supply in the product concerned.

While there is no agreed definition of the term "normal competition" in the context of the GATT, the term can reasonably by construed to include comparative advantage, a concept about which little, if any, serious dispute exists among economists. The argument of the EC flows against the logic of comparative advantage. Subsidies used to alter the comparative advantage of certain regions with respect to the production of a certain product or products are by definition distortive of trade and the allocation of resources, and, therefore, must affect normal competition, including competition with producers in the market of the importing country. There is no evidence that the governments of the countries in question, with regard to most of the programs and benefits under consideration, specifically sought to avoid causing injury to the domestic industries of other Code signatories, or even considered possible adverse effects on trade, as required by Article 11:2.

Finally the Department notes that Article 4 of the Code, "Imposition of countervailing duties," makes no distinction between domestic and export subsidies.

COMMENT 8

In objecting to the methodology used by the Department to calculate the subsidies found to exist by virtue [of] grants, preferential loans and loan guarantees (*See* Appendix 2, Methodology), the EC argues that "Article VI of the GATT provides that a countervailing duty may not exceed the amount of subsidy 'determined to have been *granted*'. The use of the word 'granted' rather than 'received' and the absence of any reference to 'value' or 'benefit' indicates clearly that the countervailable amount is the financial contribution of the government rather than the much more nebulous benefit to the recipient." (Emphasis in the EC brief.)

DOC POSITION

The position of the Department with respect to the need for a specific financial contribution of the government is discussed above. With respect to the calculations of the amount of the subsidy, the Department believes that the use of the word "granted" in Article VI:3 does not control the question of calculation of the amount of a subsidy, but merely refers to the existence of the subsidy. In fact, as the EC itself notes, Footnote 15 to the Code states, "An understanding among signatories should be developed setting out the criteria for the calculation of the amount of subsidy." Were the amount of subsidy always equal to a charge on the public account, such an understanding would be unnecessary.

Article 4:2 of the Code states, "No countervailing duty shall be levied on any imported product in excess of the amount of the subsidy found to exist. . . ." The position of the Department is that the subsidy is the benefit received by the producer or exporter. In no way does the language of Article 4 of the Code or Article VI of the GATT mandate a methodology to be used by signatories in the calculation of a subsidy as long as no consensus to the contrary exists (as referred to in Footnote 15). As a matter of general interpretation of the Code and the GATT, the omission of language dealing with a specific issue must be seen as a purposeful decision on the part of the signatories to leave the question open. (*See* Comment 9 and DOC Position, below.)

COMMENT 9

The EC has criticized the Department for making unilateral interpretations of various provisions of the Code, in particular with respect to determinations as to whether certain specific practices are subsidies and with respect to the methodologies employed in calculating the value of a subsidy.

DOC POSITION

The Department will follow, as far as US law permits, the mandatory provisions of the Code, as well as any interpretations on which a consensus exists among all Code signatories including the United States. However, the Code does *not* require inaction by signatories with regard to areas not clearly covered by the Code or by agreed interpretations of the Code. Such a requirement would be inconsistent with practice under the GATT as it has developed since its inception in 1947. The fact that the Code is silent with respect to whether a specific practice constitutes a subsidy does not mean that no signatory may make a determination with respect to that practice in the course of a proceeding. The fact that the signatories have not agreed on a methodology for the calculation of the amount of a subsidy does not mean that no signatory may adopt a methodology in the absence of such agreements, since the inability to calculate the amount of the subsidy found to exist would clearly frustrate the intent of the Code and the GATT.

COMMENT 10

The EC objects to the Department's use of average return on investment as a measure of the commercial reasonableness of a government infusion of equity in the absence of a market price for shares. The EC argues that "It follows from the GATT that the decisive criterion is the cost to the Government and therefore the investment should be treated as a long-term loan by the Government and the long-term return should be measured against the rate at which the Government borrowed money to make the investment."

DOC POSITION

The Code notes in Article 11:3 that possible forms of non-export subsidies include "[g]overnment subscription to, or provision of, equity capital." However, the Code and the GATT are silent on the question of precisely when such activity does constitute a subsidy and, where found, how such a subsidy should be calculated. The position of the EC with respect to this issue turns on defining a subsidy as the cost to the government. As discussed above in the response to Comment 6, the Department rejects this position. In any event, the equity infusions in question were not long-term and had no provisions for repayment. Accordingly, it is not possible to conclude that the decision of the Department is inconsistent with the GATT or the Code. (*See* Appendix 2 for a discussion of the methodology employed by the Department with respect to equity infusions.)

COMMENT 11

The EC avers that "This distinction (between creditworthy and uncreditworthy companies) is a complete innovation and is not provided for anywhere in the GATT. Since the GATT criterion for the determination of a subsidy is the financial contribution of the government, the creditworthiness of the companies is irrelevant."

DOC POSITION

The fact that the GATT does not address this issue specifically does not preclude consideration of the issue where it arises in the course of a proceeding. As discussed above, the Department does not agree that the only criterion for the determination of the existence of a subsidy under the GATT is the financial contribution of the government. Therefore, the question of the creditworthiness of a borrower is relevant because a loan to a company unable otherwise to obtain credit is a greater benefit to that company than a comparable loan to a company which is able to obtain financing on its own.

[Comment 12 missing in original Federal Register text.]

COMMENT 13

The EC argues that the Code must be interpreted in its entirety, and that the various provisions must be considered in relation to each other. In particular, the EC emphasizes that the List prescribes by implication the manner in which subsidies must be determined to exist and must be calculated.

DOC POSITION

The Department agrees that the Code must be interpreted as a whole. This includes the Code's distinction between subsidies which are prohibited *per se* and subsidies which are prohibited only under certain circumstances. The subsidies which are enumerated in the List are prohibited *per se* under Article 9, and, hence, actionable under "Track II," as provided for under Articles 12, 13, 17 and 18. As its title implies, the List is *illustrative* of the types of practices which constitute grounds for the invocation of Track II dispute settlement procedures. The list is thus descriptive of *prohibited* practices, not dispositive of the calculation of the value of any subsidy conferred under any particular practice. Thus there is no inconsistency between the Department's calculation of benefits conferred under domestic programs, since the Department employs uniform methodologies without regard to any distinction between the two types of subsidies.

COMMENT 14

The EC states that "Appendix B (of the Preliminary Determinations) contains a disturbing assertion: 'In the absence of special circumstances, a party receiving a benefit on the production of its merchandise *is not assumed to share a benefit with an unrelated purchaser.'* (47 FR 26307, 26309 (1982) emphasis supplied) The implication is that the existence of a countervailable subsidy, i.e., 'benefit' can be assumed in certain circumstances. . . ." The EC asserts that the Code requires that the elements necessary for the imposition of countervailing duties be established by positive factual evidence. Further, the EC adds that, "The only instance in which Title VII permits a presumption is under section 771(7) (E)(i). . . ."

DOC POSITION

The Department agrees that determinations as to the existence of a subsidy should be based on verified facts. However, this is possible only insofar as the facts are made available to the Department during the course of a proceeding. As a matter of normal procedure, the Department requires information from all interested parties, including the foreign government involved, in order to establish the facts upon which its determinations may be based. The Department followed this procedure in the instant cases. In those instances where the Department has been forced to make a determination on the basis of incomplete information, the responsibility rests with the interested parties who, despite the requests of the Department, failed to provide such information to the Department in a timely manner.

Where incomplete information has formed the basis of decisions of the Department in particular cases, there is no contravention of the obligations of the Department with respect to the Code or the statute. Article 2:9 of the Code provides:

In cases in which any interested party or signatory refuses access to, or otherwise does not provide, necessary information within a reasonable period or significantly impedes the investigation, preliminary and final findings, affirmative or negative, may be made on the basis of the facts available.

Furthermore, Section 776(b) of the Act provides:

In making their determinations under this title, the administering authority and the Commission shall, whenever a party or any other person refuses or is unable to produce information requested in a timely manner and in the form required, or otherwise significantly impedes an investigation, use the best information otherwise available.

References

Anderson, Kym, and Rodney Tyers. September 1983. "International Effects of the European Community's Grain and Meat Policies." Research School of the Pacific Studies. Canberra, Australia: Australian National University.

Balassa, Bela. 1978. "The 'New Protectionism' and the International Economy." 12 *Journal of World Trade Law* 409–36.

Baldwin, Robert E. 1970. *Nontariff Distortions of International Trade*. Washington: Brookings Institution.

———. 1980. "The Economics of the GATT." In *Issues in International Economics*, ed. Peter Oppenheimer. London: Oriel Press.

Banerjee, Sumitra. 1981. "The Antidumping and Subsidy Codes and the Trade Agreements Act of 1979." Unpublished manuscript. Washington: Georgetown University Law Center.

Baranson, Jack, and Harald B. Malmgren. October 1981. *Technology and Trade Policy: Issues and an Agenda for Action*. Report prepared for the US Department of Labor and US Trade Representative. Washington.

Barber, Edwin, III. 1982. "The Investment-Trade Nexus." In *US International Economic Policy 1981: A Draft Report*, ed. Gary Clyde Hufbauer. Washington: International Law Institute.

Barcelo, John J., III. 1977. "Subsidies and Countervailing Duties—Analysis and A Proposal." 9 *Law and Policy in International Business* 779–853.

———. Summer 1980. "Subsidies and Countervailing Duties and Antidumping after the Tokyo Round." 13 *Cornell International Law Journal* 257–88.

———. 1984. "An 'Injury-Only' Regime (for Imports) and Actionable Subsidies." In *Interface III*, ed. Don Wallace, Jr., Frank J. Loftus, and Van Z. Kirkorian. Washington: International Law Institute.

Barshefsky, Charlene, Alice L. Mattice, and William L. Martin, II. 1983. "Government Equity Participation in State-Owned Enterprises: An Analysis of the Carbon Steel Countervailing Duty Cases." 14 *Law and Policy in International Business* 1101–58.

Bergsten, C. Fred. 1980. *The International Economic Policy of the United States: Selected Papers of C. Fred Bergsten, 1977–1979*. Lexington, Mass.: Lexington Books, DC Heath and Co.

———. 1981. *The World Economy in the 1980s: Selected Papers of C. Fred Bergsten, 1980*. Lexington, Mass.: Lexington Books, DC Heath and Co.

Brown, Craig M. 1977. "'Bounty or Grant': A Call for Redefinition in Light of the Zenith Decision." 9 *Law and Policy in International Business* 1229–57.

Bryan, Greyson. 1980. *Taxing Unfair International Trade Practices*. Lexington, Mass.: Lexington Books, DC Heath and Co.

Bureau of National Affairs. 30 August 1983. "State Efforts to Establish Export Financing Facilities Meet with Local Opposition, Administration Ambivalence." *US Export Weekly*, Special Supplement.

Butler, E. Bruce. 1969. "Countervailing Duties and Export Subsidization: A Re-emerging Issue in International Trade." 9 *Virginia Journal of International Law* 82–152.

Carlson, George N. October 1980. "Value-Added Tax: European Experience and Lessons for the United States." Washington: Office of Tax Analysis, US Department of the Treasury.

Carlson, George N., Gary Clyde Hufbauer, and Melvin B. Krauss. 1976. "Destination Principle Border Tax Adjustments for the Corporate Income and Social Security Taxes: An Analysis of Sectoral Effects." *Proceedings of the 69th Annual Conference*. National Tax Association–Tax Institute of America.

Note: This is a general list of current references; not all are cited in the text.

Carlsson, Bo. April 1982. "Industrial Subsidies in Sweden: Macroeconomic Effects and an International Comparison." Working Paper 58. Stockholm: Industrial Institute for Economic and Social Research.

Clements, William. May 1983. "US High-Technology Trade: A Policy in Search of a Beginning." Unpublished manuscript. Washington: Georgetown University Law Center.

Cline, William R. February 1982. "Exports of Manufactures from Developing Countries: Performance and Prospects for Market Access." Unpublished manuscript. Washington: Brookings Institution.

Cline, William R., Noboru Kawanabe, T.O.M. Kronsjo, and Thomas Williams. 1978. *Trade Negotiations in the Tokyo Round: A Quantitative Assessment*. Washington: Brookings Institution.

Coffield, Shirley A. Summer 1981. "Using Section 301 of the Trade Act of 1974 as a Response to Foreign Government Trade Actions: When, Why, and How." 6 *North Carolina Journal of International Law and Commercial Regulation* 381–405.

Cohen, Edwin S., and Michael D. Hawkin. Spring 1982. "A Decade of DISC: Genesis and Analysis." 2 *Virginia Tax Review* 7–58.

Cohen, Richard A. 1980. "The Trade Agreements Act of 1979: Executive Agreements, Subsidies, and Countervailing Duties." 15 *Texas International Law Journal* 96–115.

Cole and Corette. July 1982. "Foreign Tax Practices Affecting Exports." Study prepared for the Dow Chemical Company. Washington.

Collado Associates. November 1982. "Update on DISC." *Collado Report*. Washington.

Cooper, Richard N. 1978. "U.S. Policies and Practices on Subsidies in International Trade." In *International Trade and Industrial Policies*, ed. Steven J. Warnecke. New York: Holmes & Meier Publishers.

Corrigan, Richard. 26 February 1983. "Choosing Winners and Losers." 15 *National Journal* 416–43.

———. 2 April 1983. "The Latest Target of the Japanese–US Preeminence in Supercomputers." 15 *National Journal* 688–92.

Cunnane, Joseph, and Clive Stanbrook. 1983. *Dumping and Subsidies*. Brussels: Business Publications.

Czinkota, Michael. 1982. "The Export-Import Bank." In *U.S. International Economic Policy 1981: A Draft Report*, ed. Gary Clyde Hufbauer. Washington: International Law Institute.

Dally, Lester. November 1981. "The Impact of Export Subsidies on International Trade." *New Zealand Law Journal* 490–94.

Dam, Kenneth W. 1970. *The GATT: Law and International Economic Organization*. Chicago: University of Chicago Press.

Deardorff, Alan V. November 18, 1983. "Some Theoretical Thoughts on Investment Performance Requirements." Seminar Discussion Paper 122. Ann Arbor, Mich.: Department of Economics, University of Michigan.

Denman, Sir Roy. 18 May 1982. "Trade Relations between Industrialized Countries in Times of Crisis." *European Community News*, 11/1982.

———. 15 September 1982. "European Community-United States Relations: Twisting the Dragon's Tail." *European Community News*, 24/1982.

Diamond, Walter H., and Dorothy B. Diamond. 1977. *Tax-Free Trade Zones of the World*. New York: M. Bender.

Dixit, Avinash. May 1983. "International Trade Policy for Oligopolistic Industries." Discussion Paper 48. Princeton, NJ: Princeton University, Woodrow Wilson School.

Echols, Marsha A. 1982. "Managing Trade Relations in the 1980s: Issues Involved in the GATT Ministerial Meeting-1982." American Society of International Law, Washington.

Emery, James J., and Michael C. Oppenheimer. November 1982. "The US Export-Import Bank: Criteria in the Direct Loan Program." Glastonbury, Conn.: The Futures Group.

Ethier, Wilfred J. 1982. "Dumping." 90 *Journal of Political Economy* 487–506.

European Community Green Europe Newsletter. December 1980. "A New Start for the Common Agricultural Policy." Brussels.

European Communities. 1979. "The Agricultural Policy of the European Community." Brussels.

Evans, John W. Fall 1977. "Subsidies and Countervailing Duties in the GATT: Present Law and Future Prospects." 3 *International Trade Law Journal* 211–45.

Feenstra, Robert C. May 1983. "The Case for Export Subsidies: Market Linkages." Unpublished manuscript. New York: Columbia University, Department of Economics.

Feinberg, Richard E. 1982. *Subsidizing Success: The Export-Import Bank in the US Economy.* Cambridge, England: Cambridge University Press.

Feller, Peter Buck. 1969. "Mutiny Against the Bounty: An Examination of Subsidies, Border Tax Adjustments, and the Resurgence of the Countervailing Duty Law." 1 *Law and Policy in International Business* 17–76.

Finger, J.M. June 1975. "Tariff Provisions for Offshore Assembly and the Exports of Developing Countries." 85 *Economic Journal* 365–71.

———. September 1976. "Trade and Domestic Effects of the Offshore Assembly Provisions in the United States Tariff." 66 *American Economic Review* 598–611.

———. 1977. "Offshore Assembly Provisions of the West German and Netherlands Tariffs: Trade and Domestic Effects." 113 *Weltwirtschaftliches Archiv* 237–49.

———. December 1982. "Incorporating the Gains from Trade into Policy." 5 *The World Economy* 367–78.

Fontheim, Claude G.B., and R. Michael Gadbaw. 1982. "Trade Related Performance Requirements under the GATT–MTN System and U.S. Law." 14 *Law and Policy in International Business* 129–80.

Frenkel, Orit, and Claude G.B. Fontheim. 1981. "Export Credits: An International and Domestic Legal Analysis." 13 *Law and Policy in International Business* 1069–88.

Galvin, Robert W. March 16, 1983. "Improving US Trade Remedy Laws." Statement before the Subcommittee on Trade of the House Ways and Means Committee. 98th Cong., 1st sess. Washington.

GATT Secretariat. 1961. Ninth Supp. *Basic Instruments and Selected Documents* 186–87. "Declaration Giving Effect to the Provisions of Article XVI(4) of the GATT." Geneva, 19 September 1960.

———. 1979. *Agreement on Interpretation and Application of Articles VI, XVI, and XXIII of the General Agreement on Tariffs and Trade.* Geneva.

Givens, William L. 22 November 1982. "The US Can No Longer Afford Free Trade." *Business Week.*

Graham, Edward M. July 1983. "World Trade Law and Government Subsidies to Industrial Innovation." Unpublished manuscript. Geneva: Institute of Advanced International Studies.

Gray, H. Peter, and Ingo Walter. 1983. "Investment-Related Trade Distortions in Petrochemicals." 17 *Journal of World Trade Law* 283–307.

Greenwald, John D. January 1982. "Material Injury." 29 *Federal Bar News and Journal* 38–40.

Grey, Rodney de C. 1983. "A Note on US Trade Practices." In *Trade Policy in the 1980s*, ed. William R. Cline. Washington: Institute for International Economics.

———. 1984. "Some Notes on Subsidies and the International Rules." In *Interface Three*, ed. Don Wallace, Jr., Frank J. Loftus, and Van Z. Krikorian. Washington: International Law Institute.

Grunwald, Joseph, and Kenneth Flamm. Forthcoming 1984. *The Internationalization of Industry.* Washington: Brookings Institution.

Guido, Robert V., and Michael F. Morrone. 1974. "The Michelin Decision: A Possible New Direction for US Countervailing Duty Law." 6 *Law and Policy in International Business* 237–66.

Harris, Kevin M. Summer 1983. "The Post-Tokyo Round GATT Role in International Trade Dispute Settlement." 1 *International Tax and Business Lawyer* 142–76.

Hartland-Thunberg, Penelope, and Morris H. Crawford. 1982. *Government Support for Exports.* Lexington, Mass.: Lexington Books, DC Heath and Co.

Horst, Thomas. September 1981. *An Economic Analysis of the Foreign International Sales Corporation Proposal.* Washington: Taxecon Associates.

Horst, Thomas, and Gary Clyde Hufbauer. 1983. "International Aspects of Basic Income Tax Reform." In *New Directions in Federal Tax Policy for the 1980's,* ed. Charls E. Walker and Mark A. Bloomfield. Cambridge, Mass.: Ballinger Publishing Company.

Houdaille Industries. May 3, 1982. Petition filed with US Trade Representative. *Also see* Japan Machine Tool Builders' Association, et al. July 29, 1982. Comments in Opposition to the Petition.

Hudec, Robert E. 1984. "Regulation of Domestic Subsidies Under the MTN Subsidies Code." In *Interface Three,* ed. Don Wallace, Jr., Frank J. Loftus, and Van Z. Krikorian. Washington: International Law Institute.

Hufbauer, Gary Clyde. March 1975. "The Taxation of Export Profits." 28 *National Tax Journal* 43–60.

———. October 3–4, 1980. "Analyzing the Effects of United States Policy." In *International Economic Policy Research.* Papers and Proceedings of a Colloquium, National Science Foundation, Washington.

———. September 28, 1981. "The US Response to Foreign Performance Requirements." Statement before the Subcommittee on International Economic Policy of the Senate Foreign Relations Committee. 97th Cong., 1st sess. Washington.

———, ed. 1982. *US International Economic Policy 1981: A Draft Report.* Washington: International Law Institute.

Hufbauer, Gary Clyde; Joanna Shelton Erb; and H.P. Starr. 1980. "The GATT Codes and the Unconditional Most-Favored-Nation Principle." 12 *Law and Policy in International Business* 59–93.

Jacobsen, Mark P. 1983. "Mexico's Computer Decree: The Problem of Performance Requirements and a US Response." 14 *Law and Policy in International Business* 1159–95.

Jackson, John H. 1969. *World Trade and the Law of the GATT.* New York: Bobbs Merrill.

———. 1978. "The Jurisprudence of International Trade: the DISC Case in GATT." 72 *American Journal of International Law* 747–81.

Jackson, John H., Jean-Victor Louis, and Mitsuo Matsushita. December 1982. "Implementing the Tokyo Round: Legal Aspects of Changing Economic Rules." 81 *Michigan Law Review* 267–397.

Japan Economic Institute. February 1983. "Agricultural Protectionism: Japan, United States, and the European Community." Interview with Dr. Fred Sanderson of the Brookings Institution. Washington.

Journal of Commerce. 8 November 1982. "Free Trade Zones Worldwide." Sec. C.

Journal of World Trade Law. Vol. 11 note, 564–80. November-December 1977. "GATT: DISC and Other Discriminatory Income Taxes."

Kelkar, Vijay Laxman. 7 June 1980. "Export Subsidy: Theory and Practice." 15 *Economic and Political Weekly* 1010–21.

———. July-August 1980. "GATT, Export Subsidies and Developing Countries." 14 *Journal of World Trade Law* 368–73.

Krauss, Melvin B. 1979. *The New Protectionism: The Welfare State and International Trade.* New York: International Center for Economic Policy Studies.

Kwako, Thomas. 1980. "Tax Incentives for Exports, Permissible and Proscribed: An Analysis of the Corporate Income Tax Implications of the MTA Subsidies Code." 12 *Law and Policy in International Business* 677–725.

Labor–Industry Coalition for International Trade. 1981. *Performance Requirements*. Washington.

Macdonald, David R. 11 March 1976. "Annual Report on International Unfair Trade Practices." Address to the International Trade Club of Chicago, US Treasury Department, Washington.

Malmgren, Harald B. 1977. *International Order for Public Subsidies*. London: Trade Policy Research Centre.

Malmgren, Golt, Kingston & Co. 1983. "Government Actions, Subsidies, and the Costs of Firms." Report prepared for private clients, London.

Marcuss, Stanley J. 1984. "Understanding Direct and Indirect Subsidies: Are the Problems Negotiable or Incurable?" In *Interface Three*, ed. Don Wallace, Jr., Frank J. Loftus, and Van Z. Krikorian. Washington: International Law Institute.

Marks, Matthew J., and Harald B. Malmgren. 1975. "Negotiating Nontariff Distortions to Trade." 7 *Law and Policy in International Business* 327–411.

McGovern, Edmond. 1982. *International Trade Regulations: GATT, the United States and the European Community*. Exeter, England: Globefield Press.

Metzger, Stanley D. 1967. "The US–Canada Automotive Products Agreement of 1965." 1 *Journal of World Trade Law* 103–8.

———. 1973. *Lowering Nontariff Barriers*. Washington: Brookings Institution.

Moore, John L., Jr. Forthcoming 1984. "Export Credit Arrangements: Background and Rationale." In *Emerging Standards of International Trade and Investment: Multinational Codes and Corporate Conduct*, ed. Seymour J. Rubin and Gary Clyde Hufbauer. Totowa, NJ: Littlefield, Adams & Co.

Muchow, Dan. Spring 1981. "Export Incentives: United States DISC Legislation as Invalid Subsidy Under the GATT Provisions." 20 *Washburn Law Journal* 535–56.

Mundheim, Robert H., and Peter D. Ehrenhaft. 1984. "What is a 'Subsidy'?" In *Interface Three*, ed. Don Wallace, Jr., Frank J. Loftus, and Van Z. Krikorian. Washington: International Law Institute.

Mutti, John. January 1982. *Taxes, Subsidies and Competitiveness Internationally*. Washington: NPA Committee on Changing International Realities.

Mutti, John, and Harry Grubert. December 3–4, 1982. "D.I.S.C. and its Effects." Conference on the Structure and Evolution of Recent U.S. Trade Policy, National Bureau of Economic Research, Cambridge, Mass.

Nelson, Douglas R. July 1981. "The Political Structure of the New Protectionism." *World Bank Staff Working Paper*, no. 471. Washington: World Bank.

Organization for Economic Cooperation and Development, Working Party of the Trade Committee on North–South Trade. February 1984. "Current Trends and Issues Relating to Anti-Dumping and Countervailing Measures." TC/WP(84)12 Paris.

Organization of American States. September 12, 1977. "GATT Rules and U.S. Law Regarding Export Subsidies and Countervailing Duties." Report prepared by Tracy Murray, OEA/Ser. H/XIII. Washington.

Ortwine, Bruce A. Summer 1981. "Injury Determinations Under United States Antidumping Laws Before and After the Trade Agreements Act of 1979." 33 *Rutgers Law Review* 1076–1107.

Pestieau, Caroline. 1976. *Subsidies and Countervailing Duties: The Negotiating Issues*. Quebec: Canadian Economic Policy Committee, C.D. Howe Research Institute.

Price, Victoria Curzon. 1981. *Industrial Policies in the European Community*. London: Trade Policy Research Centre.

Rivers, Richard R. April 19, 1983. "Summary of Testimony on the Need to Amend U.S. Trade Remedies Relating to State-Owned Enterprises in Nonmarket and Mixed Economies." Statement before the Subcommittee on Trade of the House Committee on Ways and Means. 98th Cong., 1st sess. Washington.

Rivers, Richard R., and John D. Greenwald. 1979. "The Negotiation of a Code on Subsidies and Countervailing Measures: Bridging Fundamental Policy Differences." 11 *Law and Policy in International Business* 1447–95.

Safarian, A.E. 1983. *Governments and Multinationals: Policies in the Developed Countries.* Washington: British–North American Committee.

Saxonhouse, Gary R. June 15, 1983. "Tampering with Comparative Advantage in Japan." Statement before the US International Trade Commission. Washington.

Schott, Jeffrey J. March-April 1982. "Can World Trade Be Governed?" 25 *Challenge* 43–49.

———. May-June 1983. "The GATT Ministerial: A Postmortem." 26 *Challenge* 40–45.

Schwartz, Warren F., and Eugene W. Harper, Jr. April 1972. "The Regulation of Subsidies Affecting International Trade." 70 *Michigan Law Review* 831–58.

Semiconductor Industry Association. 1983. "The Effect of Government Targeting on World Semiconductor Competition." Washington.

Shuman, Shannon Stock, and Charles Owen Verrill, Jr. 1984. "Recent Developments in Countervailing Duty Law and Policy." In *Recent Issues and Initiatives in U.S. Trade Policy,* ed. Robert E. Baldwin. Cambridge, Mass.: National Bureau of Economic Research.

Snape, Richard H. February 1984. "Subsidies of International Concern." Paper prepared for the World Bank. Washington.

Staple, Peter D. July 1980. "Implementing 'Tokyo Round' Commitments: The New Injury Standard in Antidumping and Countervailing Duty Laws." 32 *Stanford Law Review* 1183–1209.

Tarullo, Daniel K. Forthcoming 1984. "The MTN Subsidies Code: Agreement Without Consensus." In *Emerging Standards of International Trade and Investment: Multinational Codes and Corporate Conduct,* ed. Seymour J. Rubin and Gary Clyde Hufbauer. Totowa, NJ: Littlefield, Adams & Co.

Trozzo, Charles. 1982. "Steel Trade." In *US International Economic Policy 1981: A Draft Report,* ed. Gary Clyde Hufbauer. Washington: International Law Institute.

US Chamber of Commerce. October 1983. "Recommendations of the Trade Laws and Agreements Task Force to the International Policy Committee on the Trade Remedies Reform Act of 1983." Proposed by Representative Sam M. Gibbons (D-Fla.). Washington.

US Congress. House Subcommittee on Trade, Committee on Ways and Means. 1983. *Options to Improve the Trade Remedy Laws.* Hearing. 98th Cong., 1st sess. Washington.

———. Joint Economic Committee. 1965. *Subsidies and Subsidy-Effect Programs of the US Government.* 89th Cong., 1st sess. Washington.

———. Senate Committee on the Budget. 1975. *DISC: An Evaluation of the Cost and Benefits.* 94th Cong., 1st sess. Washington.

———. Senate Subcommittee on International Finance and Monetary Policy, Committee on Banking. July 7, 1983. *Foreign Industrial Targeting.* Hearings. 98th Cong., 1st sess. Washington.

US General Accounting Office. August 15, 1983. *Benefits of International Agreement on Trade-Distorting Subsidies Not Yet Realized.* GAO/NSIAD 83–10. Washington.

US International Trade Commission. January 1983. *Economic Impact of Foreign Export Credit Subsidies on Certain U.S. Industries.* Washington.

———. September 1983. *Competitive Assessment of U.S. Metal Working Machine Tool Industry.* Publication 1428. Washington.

————. October 1983. *Foreign Industrial Targeting and its Effects on US Industries. Phase 1: Japan.* Publication 1437. Washington.

US Treasury Department. September 16, 1982. *International Export Credit Negotiations (1981– 1982).* Washington.

————. 1972–83. *The Operation and Effect of the Domestic International Sales Corporation Legislation.* Annual reports for tax year 1972 and succeeding years. (The 1981 annual report was released June 9, 1983.) Washington.

Verrill, Charles O., Jr. 1984. "State-Owned Enterprises and the Countervailing Duty Law: Where, Oh Where to Draw the Line." In *Interface Three*, ed. Don Wallace, Jr., Frank J. Loftus, and Van Z. Kirkorian. Washington: International Law Institute.

Viner, Jacob. 1923, 1966. *Dumping: A Problem in International Trade.* New York: Augustus M. Kelley.

Wall, David. September-October 1976. "Export Processing Zones." 10 *Journal of World Trade Law* 478–99.

Wallace, Don, Jr.; Frank J. Loftus; and Van Z. Krikorian, eds. *Interface Three: Legal Treatment of Domestic Subsidies.* Washington: International Law Institute.

Wallen, Axel, and John M. Duff, Jr. 1981. "The Outlook for Official Export Credits." In *The International Framework for Money and Banking in the 1980s*, ed. Gary Clyde Hufbauer. Washington: International Law Institute. Also published, with minor changes, in 13 *Law and Policy in International Business* 891–960 (1981).

Walsh, John. 17 June 1983. "MCC Moves Out of the Idea Stage." *Science*, pp. 1256–57.

Walters, Kenneth D., and R. Joseph Monsen. March-April 1979. "State-Owned Business Abroad: New Competitive Threat." 57 *Harvard Business Review* 160–70.

Warnecke, Stephen J., ed. 1978. *International Trade and Industrial Policies.* New York: Holmes & Meier Publishers.

Weaver, Kathleen T. Summer 1980. "Subsidies and Countervailing Duties Under the Trade Act of 1979." 5 *North Carolina Journal of International Law and Commercial Regulations* 533–45.

Wolff, Alan Wm. March 23, 1983. "A Trade Strategy for America." Paper presented at the Donald S. MacNaughton Symposium, Syracuse University, Syracuse, NY.

World Bank. 24 July 1978. "Export Processing Zones." Sec. M 78–612. Washington.

Other Publications from the Institute

POLICY ANALYSES IN INTERNATIONAL ECONOMICS

BOOKS

SPECIAL REPORTS

Subsidies are no longer an arcane issue discussed only by trade technicians in periodic bargaining sessions at mountaintop resorts. To the contrary, subsidies have captured the attention of senior government officials in the United States, Canada, European Community, Japan, and key developing countries. The reason is simple: markets. Nearly all countries have a stake in the increasingly acrimonious skirmishes—in steel and agriculture, to name just two—arising from the fundamental question of what governments may and may not do to help their industries and farmers in good times and bad.

While many governments express opinions as to which foreign practices amount to "unfair trade," most governments resist international surveillance over the workings of their own economies. Even after decades of international debate and negotiation, sharp differences remain over the legitimacy of various subsidy practices.

Subsidies in International Trade analyzes the economic problems caused by various subsidy practices and summarizes international efforts, spanning many years, both to limit each country's use of subsidies and to regulate countermeasures aimed at another country's subsidies. The historical discipline of subsidies and countermeasures is largely a story of US initiatives, taken both unilaterally and in the context of the General Agreement on Tariffs and Trade (GATT). In recent years, other major trading countries—particularly the European Community and large developing nations, such as Brazil—have played an increasingly active role in designing the emerging system of international rules.

This volume first analyzes the trade-impact thresholds that must be crossed before a subsidy practice is deemed to create an offense to other trading nations. *Subsidies in International Trade* next summarizes and evaluates the complex rules that define and discipline "export subsidies," namely subsidies that differentiate between goods sold on the home market and goods sold for export. The growing question of "domestic subsidies," namely subsidies that make no overt distinction between goods sold at home and abroad but nevertheless may affect the conditions of international trade, is then explored. The volume proceeds to outline the remedies presently available to countries faced with subsidized trade, ranging from countervailing duties to matching subsidy for subsidy. Finally, the authors summarize their